Lincoln's
Jewish Spy

ALSO BY E. LAWRENCE ABEL
AND FROM MCFARLAND

*Intoxication in Mythology:
A Worldwide Dictionary of Gods, Rites,
Intoxicants and Places* (2006)

Confederate Sheet Music
(2011 paperback; 2004)

*Arab Genetic Disorders:
A Layman's Guide* (2003)

*Jewish Genetic Disorders:
A Layman's Guide* (2008 paperback; 2001)

Lincoln's Jewish Spy

*The Life and Times
of Issachar Zacharie*

E. LAWRENCE ABEL

McFarland & Company, Inc., Publishers
Jefferson, North Carolina

LIBRARY OF CONGRESS CATALOGUING-IN-PUBLICATION DATA

Names: Abel, E. Lawrence, 1943– author.
Title: Lincoln's Jewish spy : the life and times of Issachar Zacharie /
E. Lawrence Abel.
Other titles: Life and times of Issachar Zacharie
Description: Jefferson, North Carolina : McFarland & Company, Inc.,
Publishers, 2020 | Includes bibliographical references and index.
Identifiers: LCCN 2020030105 | ISBN 9781476680460 (paperback : acid free paper) ∞
ISBN 9781476639833 (ebook)
Subjects: LCSH: Zacharie, I. (Isachar) | Lincoln, Abraham,
1809–1865—Friends and associates. | Podiatrists—United
States—Biography. | Jews—United States—Biography. | Spies—United
States—Biography. | United States—History—Civil War,
1861–1865—Secret service. | British Americans—Biography. | Eccentrics
and eccentricities—United States—Biography.
Classification: LCC E415.9.Z33 A24 2020 | DDC 973.7/85092 [B]—dc23
LC record available at https://lccn.loc.gov/2020030105

BRITISH LIBRARY CATALOGUING DATA ARE AVAILABLE

ISBN (print) 978-1-4766-8046-0
ISBN (ebook) 978-1-4766-3983-3

© 2020 E. Lawrence Abel. All rights reserved

*No part of this book may be reproduced or transmitted in any form
or by any means, electronic or mechanical, including photocopying
or recording, or by any information storage and retrieval system,
without permission in writing from the publisher.*

Front cover image of Zacharie in later years
(photograph courtesy American Jewish Historical Society)

Printed in the United States of America

*McFarland & Company, Inc., Publishers
Box 611, Jefferson, North Carolina 28640
www.mcfarlandpub.com*

To Barbara,
My soulmate, wife, editor, and conscience,
With much love.
You are the best of me.

Table of Contents

Acknowledgments	ix
Author's Note	xi
Introduction	1

Part One. The Past Is Prologue

1. "Sucking the egg"	4
2. "Act according to the custom of that place"	11

Part Two. I. Zachariah, Jr., Cheroperdist

3. "No Cure No Pay"	18
4. "Where more money could be made faster"	24
5. "We the undersigned"	28
6. "A humble individual"	30
7. California	36
8. "Prince of chiropodists"	43
9. The Mystic Cords of Memory	53
10. "A chiropodist of marvelous skill"	58
11. "Dr. Zacharie has operated on my feet"	66
12. "Ode to Dr. Zacharie"	70
13. "My own chiropodist is a Jew"	76

Part Three. Spy and Diplomat

14. The General Prohibition	80
15. "Spare no expense"	89
16. Spymaster	96

Table of Contents

17. "Monomaniacs"	111
18. A Service He Alone Was Capable Of	118
19. He Lacks Stability	126
20. "Done things for me that would astonish you"	136
21. "Can't go Lincoln"	142
22. "I promised I would elect you"	149
23. "My family are crazy with joy"	156

Part Four. Later Years

24. "Surely you don't intend to go for Grant"	164
25. "Republics are unquestionably ungrateful"	174
26. Return to England	179
27. Death of an Eccentric Man	184
28. Aftermath	188
Appendix: Zacharie's Accounts	199
Chapter Notes	201
Bibliography	231
Index	245

Acknowledgments

Every historian is indebted to librarians and archivists. As always, I want to thank the interlibrary staff at Wayne State University for their efforts in locating and making available materials from other libraries across the country. A very special word of appreciation goes to Jeffrey Flannery and the archivists at the Library of Congress for their help with the Banks correspondence, and the archivists at the National Archives for lifting the hernia-heavy four volume Smith-Brady Commission onto the cart, along with the Zacharie correspondence.

I also want to give special thanks to Melinda Wallington, Rush Rhees Library, University of Rochester, for sending me copies of Zacharie's correspondence with Seward; to Elisa Ho at the Jacob Rader Marcus Center of the American Jewish Archives for sending the Bertram Korn correspondence and materials; and to Rabbi/historian Gary P. Zola at the American Jewish Archives for sending me the correspondence between Zacharie and Judah Benjamin.

Thanks to Professor Jonathan Sarna for comments and help with locating materials at the Shapell Museum, and to William Binzel for material on Stanton and Yulee. Thanks also to Alison Bundy, John Hay Library, Brown University; Anne Rollins and Wendy Truman, Historical Society of Washington, D.C.; and Heather Green, Williams Research Center, Historic New Orleans Collection, who likewise provided advice and relevant materials. Thanks also to Marcia Ely at the Brooklyn Historical Society; Megan Lewis, reference librarian at the National Institute for Holocaust Documentation; Steven Greenberg, National Library of Medicine; Boni J. Koeliker, American Jewish Historical Society; Patricia D. Klinkenstein, New York Historical Society; and Catherine Robertson, Peabody Essex Museum, Rowley, Massachusetts, for efforts in searching for and/or providing relevant materials.

Special thanks to Timothy Reid, Senior Archivist, Westminster Archives in London, UK, for information on Zacharie's home in London; and to the interdisciplinary librarians at Wayne State University for research assistance. A special note of thanks to Robert Marcus for providing the very rare photo of Zacharie.

Acknowledgments

I wish also to express my appreciation (in alphabetical order) to the scholars who critiqued various chapters of this book: Barbara Abel, William Binzel, Kathryn Canavan, John Fazio, Roberta Russ, Dr. Jonathan Sarna, Richard Willing, Rabbi Herbert Yoskowitz, and Dr. Gary P. Zola.

Author's Note

Most of the information about Issachar Zacharie comes from letters to and from him. These letters contain so many misspellings that to note them all with the usual "sic" would have been tiresome for the reader. Accordingly, I have not noted or corrected the misspellings in these letters. Misspellings from other sources are duly noted. I have also, in some instances, taken the liberty of transforming comments in letters into spoken comments. The wording, however, is still as it appeared in the original.

Introduction

John Hay, President Abraham Lincoln's personal secretary, knocked on Lincoln's office door at the White House and entered. Turning to the dapper, bearded man behind him, Hay introduced Dr. Issachar Zacharie. Lincoln and Zacharie shook hands. Chatting briefly, each man took the measure of the other. Then Lincoln sat down, peeled off his slippers and stuck out his bare foot.

Issachar sat down on a chair opposite the President, opened his bag, and took out a sharp knife. Holding the President's foot in his left hand, he offered a few brief words of assurance that he would feel little pain and began to scrape away his corns. Afterwards, a grateful President wrote a public testimonial to the chiropodist: "Dr. Zacharie has operated on my feet with good success and considerable addition to my comfort."

What they talked about while the foot doctor scraped away is not known. The two men were opposites in almost every imaginable way. Lincoln was a towering six foot four inches in height, one of the tallest men in the country. Issachar Zacharie was no more than five foot seven inches. Lincoln's face was craggy; Issachar had a round, cherubic face. Lincoln dressed casually; Issachar dressed to the nines. Lincoln was President of the United States. Issachar was a foot doctor, born in England and still a British citizen. Lincoln's parents were Baptists; Issachar's parents were Jewish.

Despite their differences, a camaraderie developed between the two men. In future letters to the President, Issachar headed his correspondence, "My Dear Friend," and regularly sent baskets of pineapples, bananas, and oranges to Lincoln along with "kind regards" to Mrs. Lincoln. Issachar was one of the few people on friendly terms with the President's mercurial wife, Mary Todd Lincoln, a woman John Hay called a "Hell-Cat" and "Her Satanic Majesty."

Lincoln was on cordial terms with many Jews, but his relationship with Issachar was by far the most intimate. The President, the *New York World* told its readers, "has often left his business apartment to spend an evening in the parlor of his favored bunionist." When a visitor came to the White House to discuss an early Zionist idea of reestablishing a Jewish homeland in Palestine, Lincoln told him he was not at all opposed to the idea. "I myself have regard for the Jews," he said, "my chiropodist is a Jew, and he has so many times 'put me on my feet' that I would have no objection to giving his countrymen 'a leg up.'"

Issachar was far from a paragon of virtue. He claimed to have been tutored in chiropody by the most famous physicians of his day, which was a lie. He was largely self-taught. He claimed to have earned a medical degree from a medical school in, of all places, Cuba. This also was not true. All the more unbelievable because Issachar didn't know a word of Spanish. He claimed to have authored a text on chiropody. Not true. He plagiarized the book and substituted his own name for the author's.

Lincoln sensed the corn-cutter was duplicitous, but Lincoln had a peculiar fondness for flawed characters. Lincoln was himself not above a certain amount of duplicity. A slightly damaged, overly ambitious man like Issachar Zacharie, he thought to himself, would make a good spy. Lincoln sent him to New Orleans, telling General Nathaniel P. Banks, head of the Department of the Gulf, that Dr. Zacharie could be of help. He could keep him abreast of citizens' attitudes about the Union occupation and Confederate activities in and around the city. Unbeknownst to Banks, Issachar was a double agent. Lincoln was also sending him to New Orleans to keep him informed about Banks' performance. Lincoln had such confidence in the man that he later entrusted him to be his unofficial envoy to confer with Judah P. Benjamin, the Jewish Secretary of State, and other Confederate leaders in Richmond about a peaceful end to the war.

Issachar Zacharie is not known today, although during the Civil War, his name regularly appeared in the newspapers throughout the North. A smattering of historians, Jewish and gentile, are aware of his friendship with Lincoln and his role as Lincoln's spy and unofficial envoy, but other than a paragraph or two, most rarely go beyond mentioning it. Even fewer have been curious about what happened to him after the war, mistakenly assuming he just faded into oblivion.

My aim in this book is to tell the hitherto unknown story of an eccentric man whom the war-time *New York World* newspaper characterized as "the most favored family visitor at the White House." I started this project anticipating something akin to hero-worship for a man who came from nothing, to be on speaking terms with the President of the United States and the Secretary of State of the Confederacy. I finished uncertain of whether he was a well-meaning entrepreneur or a self-serving opportunist. But uncomplicated men or women rarely make history. Or hold the interest of a biographer or a reader.

Part One

The Past Is Prologue

1

"Sucking the egg"

Issachar Zacharie was born in 1825 in Chatham, England. It was the year composer Johann Strauss II, biologist Thomas Henry Huxley, and neurologist Jean-Martin Charcot were born, and the year inventor Eli Whitney, composer Antonio Salieri, architect Pierre Charles L'Enfant, and astronomer Edmond Halley died. The most significant inventions that year were the electromagnet and cement. In America, John Quincy Adams took the oath as the sixth president of the United States, and the Erie Canal opened. On the Indiana frontier, a tall, lanky 17-year-old Abraham Lincoln was splitting rails for 25 cents a day.

Lodged along the banks of the River Medway about 30 miles southeast of London, Chatham was an industrial naval dockyard and mercantile port dating back to the time of Queen Elizabeth I, "notorious for its poor health and living conditions."[1] The streets were muddy and filthy with manure and rotting garbage. The air reeked from its stench, from hot tar oakum and oak chips wafting from the dockyard, and from a fetid stream coursing through the back part of the town to the river.

Off-duty seamen and dockworkers with nowhere to go spent their time in public houses and brothels. An undermanned police force contended with drunks, vagrants, pickpockets, thieves, pimps, and prostitutes who wandered the streets in search of prey. Royal marines armed with rifles herded convicts, like animals, to hulk prison ships on the River Medway. Not for nothing was Chatham called "the wickedest place in the world."[2]

Issachar's family lived above a wooden dry goods shop on High Street, Chatham's business district. The offal-saturated street was Issachar's front garden and playground. He fell asleep to the din of drunken men singing, shouting, and pummeling one another in midnight brawls. Unlike Charles Dickens, who lived in a house on a hill in Chatham far above the streets and dockyards during his early childhood and fondly remembered those days, Issachar never spoke about his early years in Chatham.

* * * * * * * *

1. "Sucking the egg"

Issachar's father, Jan Zachariah, was born in 1797, and emigrated to England sometime around 1820, from eastern Prussia. Many years later, when a census taker in the United States asked him about his homeland, Jan proudly said Poland,[3] although that country no longer existed at the time of his birth. It had been partitioned and annexed in the late 1700s by Prussia, Russia, and Austria.

Like many of the Jews who emigrated to England and America in the late 1700s and early 1800s, Jan left because he saw no future for himself if he stayed. Most of those who emigrated were single men between the ages of 20 and 26; some were as young as 16.[4]

Jewish emigrants making their way to England mainly settled in the East End of London. Others headed for the naval dockyard towns of Chatham, Portsmouth, Plymouth, Exeter, and Bristol. Dockyard towns and their surroundings were home to thousands of men and their families. A man could earn a modest living as a merchant or peddler in those places.[5]

Jan may have made his way to Chatham because other Jews from his community had gone there before him. Emigrating to places where family or friends of family were already living meant there would be someone there to help a newcomer get settled. In 1780, there were enough Jews in the village and nearby Rochester to build a synagogue called the Chatham Cottage Jews' Tabernacle.[6] It was a small wooden building with Hebrew lettering on its face and a clock visible from several streets away.

Chatham's Jews were third on Charles Dickens' list of what was "principally remarkable" about that seaport town. First and second were its soldiers and sailors.[7] Dickens was exaggerating about Chatham's Jews. When Dickens lived in Chatham between 1817 and 1822, there were only about 60 Jewish families in the town and surroundings among the city's estimated 15,000 dock workers, seamen, and marines.

Most of Chatham's Jews are "the humbler sort," a visitor commented. Their main means of earning a living was dealing in "civil habiliments shed by the recruits when they assume the military or naval uniform."[8]

The "richer sort" of Jews in Chatham and the nation's other seaport towns were the butchers, apothecaries, tobacconists, dentists, chiropodists, silversmiths, watchmakers, pawnbrokers, and shopkeepers who bankrolled itinerant peddlers.

With no known skills, Jan eked out a living as a peddler. If he had some money, he would have bought wares from a local businessman to sell on the street or in the countryside. If he didn't have enough to get started, he would have asked a Jewish merchant for start-up funds or merchandise. In many instances, merchants in smaller Jewish communities who had unmarried daughters loaned peddlers money or goods interest free. Those loans often resulted in marriages through which the peddler became a salesman or partner in the family business.

In 1818, when he was 21, Jan, now calling himself Jonathan, married a local girl, Amelia Cohen. Amelia was the only daughter of Eliezer Cohen, the *Hazzan* (cantor) for Chatham's Jewish community.[9] A year later, in 1819, Amelia gave birth to their first child, a daughter they named Martha. A second daughter, Francesca, "Fanny," was born in 1820. Two years later, in 1822, Rebecca was born. Jonathan and Amelia's eldest son, the boy who would later become Lincoln's Jewish doctor, was born in 1825, and named Issachar Zachariah, Jr. They named their next two children, both daughters, Amelia Lavinia and Jane.

Seemingly inconsequential, Jonathan's and Amelia's naming their son Issachar, Jr., and one of their daughters Amelia, the same name as her mother, implies that either Jan, Amelia, or both may have been of Sephardic heritage. Sephardic Jews are the descendants of Jews banished from Spain and Portugal in 1492 and 1495, respectively. Sephardic Jews consider it a great honor to have a baby named after a father, mother, or other family member.

Until recently, Ashkenazi Jews, who hailed from Russia, and Central and Western Europe, rarely named a child after a living relative. This is because a longstanding superstition among the Ashkenazi is that if a child has the same name as a living relative, the Angel of Death might get confused. When the time came for him to take the older relative, he might mistakenly take the life of the baby with the same name. It is customary, on the other hand, to name a child after a recently deceased relative as a way of keeping his or her memory alive.[10]

Eight days after Issachar was born, he was circumcised in accordance with an age-old Jewish practice and given his name, Issachar, Jr. In Sephardic tradition, it is customary to name sons after grandparents in a prescribed order. Firstborn sons are named after a paternal grandfather (Jonathan's father); second sons are named after a maternal grandfather. Jonathan and Amelia named their second son, born later in America, Eleazar after Amelia's father. Issachar used the "Jr." and "Jun." suffix in his name until 1843, when he dropped it and changed his surname from Zachariah to Zacharie.[11]

Coming from Poland, Jonathan should have been Ashkenazi. But not all Polish Jews were Ashkenazi. During the 16th century, a small enclave of Sephardic Jews came to Poland from Italy, where they had relocated after being banished from Spain and Portugal in the late 15th century. A small remnant of these Sephardic Jews, known only by their surnames,[12] continued to live in and around Lublin for many generations[13] The best known of these Sephardic descendants is the Yiddish novelist Isaac Leib Peretz (1852–1915) (originally "Perez"). Issachar's mother's maiden name, Cohen, is both Ashkenazi and Sephardic.[14]

By the time Issachar was born, his father was doing well enough to afford becoming one of the lessees for Chatham's Cottage Jews' Tabernacle.[15]

1. "Sucking the egg"

Jonathan's name on the lease was "Jonathan Zacharia of Chatham, salesman."[16] A "salesman," in mid–19th century England, was a storeowner, not a clerk.[17] Attaching the name of a town to his name was a sign Jonathan Zachariah was a respectable member of his community.[18] The other leasees were two other "salesmen," five shopkeepers, five "slop sellers," three stockbrokers, a tobacconist, an apothecary, and a butcher.[19]

* * * * * * * *

In June or July 1832, Jonathan and Amelia Zachariah and their six children, Martha, 13, Fanny, 12, Rebecca, 10, Issachar, 7, Amelia Lavinia, 4, and one-year-old Jane, boarded a coach to London, where they boarded a ship headed to the United States.[20]

The Zachariahs were just another family, among the thousands of immigrants from Britain, Ireland, Germany, and other areas of Central Europe, who left their homes for America in the 1830s and 1840s, to escape an economic depression that had the Continent and England in a tight-fisted grip.[21] Chatham had been especially hard hit. Budget tightening forced the Navy Board to reduce dockyard expenditures. Shipbuilding was put on hold. Dock workers were laid off. By the early 1830s, Chatham's workforce was half what it had been before the Napoleonic wars.[22] The Zachariahs may also have left to escape a cholera outbreak that Chatham experienced, along with much of England. "We have witnessed in our days the birth of a new pestilence," a contemporary magazine agonized, "which in the short space of fourteen years has desolated the fairest portions of the globe, and swept off at least fifty million of our race."[23]

* * * * * * * *

Issachar's father had known how heart-rendering it was to leave his home. It took a lot of courage to say goodbye to family, friends, and a country he had grown up in. No matter how dismal a future it might have been at home, England was a country of strangers. He had had to learn a new language, find a place to live, and make a living. Now he once again was starting over. This time he had a family to provide for.

Had Issachar's father not had the money to pay for his family, he would have left on his own and sent for Amelia and his children when he could pay for their passage. It was not unusual for a family to be separated for several years until a father or brother saved enough to bring them to America. The possibility of his going it alone must have been discussed. Perhaps Amelia did not want to wait and have to live with and burden her parents, despite the possibility they might succumb to cholera on the ship.

Jonathan had an inkling of what to expect in emigrating to a new country. For Amelia, it was the first time she was leaving home and family. Like many of those sailing to America, she undoubtedly was fearful, not just of what awaited her across the Atlantic, but of the long dangerous voyage across the sea. Issachar and his sisters were probably excited about the new adventure, but they must have been apprehensive as well about going to a foreign country where they had no friends. When it came time to leave, there were the final tearful goodbyes with family and friends.

There were practical things to consider once Jonathan and Amelia decided to leave. Jonathan had to sell his business. It was a buyer's market. He had to take whatever offer came his way. Amelia had to decide what belongings to take. Space aboard ship was limited. Besides clothes, bedding, and utensils for cooking on board, they had to decide what items reminded the family of home. Immigrants were advised to mark all their luggage clearly with their names. It was not unusual for sailors or passengers to "mistake" another passenger's belongings for their own. One guide to prospective immigrants advised packing as little as possible. "Hard cash is the only substance worth bringing."[24]

Immigrant guides and government pamphlets all recommended making the Atlantic crossing in early spring. Crossing in late fall or winter was treacherous. Arriving in spring or summer gave immigrants time to get settled without having to make hasty decisions. The most reliable crossing was by packet ships because they departed from port on a regular schedule, an innovation at that time. The *Hendrick Hudson*, the ship the Zachariahs sailed on,[25] left London for America three times a year.[26]

Packet ships were tubby-looking. They averaged about 170 feet in length and about 35 feet in width and displaced about 750 tons. The ships were called "packets" because when ships in the 16th century first began carrying mail, it was called "packettes."

The Atlantic crossing was not cheap. The *Hudson*'s first-class cabins, located under the upper deck were the most comfortable of the accommodations, came with a mattress, linens, wash basin, and some drawers. They were also the most expensive at £12 to £20 (about $1700 to $2850 in 2020 dollars) per person.[27] Even so, first-class cabins were not sole accommodations. In some cabins, four to 12 passengers shared the room, two to a bunk. Second-class cabins, situated on the same level but behind the first, were lightly furnished. Steerage passengers in the decks below made do as best they could with little more than cots.

Steerage passage (so-called because ships were once steered from that part of a ship), also called "emigrant class," cost £4 to £5 for adults (the modern equivalent of about $700) and half that for children under 14.[28] (Steerage aboard the *Titanic*, 80 years later, was about $700 for adults and $300 for children.) For the Zachariah family of seven, the cost of steerage on the *Hudson* would have been the equivalent today of more than $3,000.

1. "Sucking the egg"

Like everyone else, within hours of leaving England, the Zachariahs were seasick. Huddled on the lower decks, many passengers couldn't hold their stomachs and retched on the floor before they could reach slop buckets. Some managed to get to the upper deck to vomit over the side of the ship. Some passengers became so weak they couldn't walk without help. In violent gales, typically occurring at least once during a transatlantic crossing, hatches were fastened down to prevent the interior from flooding. The heat and lack of air made seasickness even worse. After a while, the Zachariahs and other passengers no longer cared about the nauseating odor. By the end of the 40-day plus voyage, the stench was overwhelming. A standing joke was that immigrant ships could be recognized by their smell.[29] Until the mid–1800s, as many as 20 percent of the passengers died on board the "coffin ships" from typhus and cholera. Sometimes, entire families were wiped out and their bodies were summarily cast overboard.

When the *Hendrick Hudson* docked in New York on August 24, 1832, the captain handed his passenger list to the port authorities to comply with the American immigration act of 1819. The law required ship captains to record and submit passengers' names, ages, occupations, country of last residence, name of ship, port of embarkation, and date of arrival.[30] Jonathan listed his occupation on the manifest list as "mechanic."[31] In the 19th century, a "mechanic" was a tradesman or general workman.[32] Issachar's birth year on the manifest was 1825.[33] He was seven years old.

* * * * * * * *

So many people immigrated from England to New York during the 1830s that enterprising authors wrote manuals for them to find their way once they landed. When a man is determined to leave England for the United States, Charles Knight wrote in the preface to his manual, *The British Mechanic's and Labourer's Handbook, and True Guide to the United States*, "he does so in most cases from a wish to better his circumstances…. He fancies he possesses, to use a familiar phrase, a new and improved mode of 'sucking the egg.'" "It would not be all 'beer and skittles,'" Knight cautioned, using another familiar English phrase that meant a good time. "If he should happen to be a little too sanguine in this respect," the newcomer stood "a very fair chance of being most egregiously disappointed."[34]

Knight advised passengers not to be in a hurry to remove their baggage from the docking area once they cleared customs. Under no circumstances, he cautioned, should they "accept the aid of those who swarm about and press their services" upon new arrivals. "Too frequently here, as in the steamboats of the interior, this class of persons are much more ready to help themselves than the stranger."[35]

The Zachariahs had no relatives in New York to meet or help them among its quarter of a million inhabitants. If New York had been their destination, they didn't stay long. Shortly after landing, the Zachariahs boarded a train to Philadelphia. The 90-mile trip cost $3.00 for each family member.[36]

2

"Act according to the custom of that place"

New York, Philadelphia, Newport, Baltimore, Charleston, and Savannah, the earliest North American cities where Jews mainly settled, were port cities. They were also cosmopolitan communities. Unlike Boston, colonial America's most homogenous city, cosmopolitan cities offered greater economic and social opportunities for immigrants.[1] New Orleans would have been a destination, except that until the 1800s, the authorities discouraged Jews from settling there.[2]

Philadelphia in the 1830s was America's cultural center, the "Athens of America." Its port bustled with cargo ships from Europe and South America and with packet liners bringing immigrants from Liverpool and Continental Europe and from other parts of America. Immigrants headed there for a good reason: jobs. Pennsylvania was in the midst of a building frenzy. Hundreds of miles of canal beds and railway lines were created connecting Philadelphia with Pittsburgh, Harrisburg, and other parts of the state and with other eastern cities. There was work for unskilled laborers, and they came in droves. The frontier was constantly spreading westward. It was a perfect place to start an itinerant peddling business or a more permanent shop.

There was another reason Jonathan and Amelia headed for Philadelphia—the Dessaus. Jonathan and the Dessaus were either distantly related or had known each other beforehand. The Dessaus (the surname is variously spelled "Dessan" and "Dessaue" in street directories) were originally from Dessau, a town in Saxony-Anhalt, Germany, the birthplace of Moses Mendelssohn. Jacob H. Dessau and his brother, M. H. Dessau, had emigrated to America in the late 1820s. Jacob owned a dry goods store at 108 Sassafras Street in Philadelphia. The Zachariahs would have a place to stay with the Dessaus until they found a place of their own. Four years later, in 1836, Jonathan and Amelia's second daughter, Fanny, married Abraham Dessau,[3] a "trader."[4] Several years later, Jacob Dessau married Issachar's sister, Amelia Lavinia, the "third daughter of Jonathan Zakeriah Esq."[5]

* * * * * * * *

After moving in with the Dessaus, Jonathan lost no time "starting a business." Slinging a pack filled with household goods, sponges, tools, ribbons, combs, pins and needles, inexpensive jewelry, and sundry other wares over his shoulder, he trudged the countryside, leaning on a long stick that he also used to beat off dogs that barked and bit "whenever a Jewish peddler comes."[6]

Jewish peddlers became known far and wide in farming communities, where they were regarded less as itinerant merchants than as friends bringing things they needed. Usually welcomed by a lonely housewife whose husband and older sons were away in the field, he would show her his wares, and she would invariably buy some trifling "notion" so he would return the next time he was in the area.[7]

Jewish peddlers still clinging to their religion made it a point to reach a Jewish home before the Sabbath. Simon Wolf, a future president of B'nai B'rith, recalled how 20 to 30 Jewish peddlers would start out with packs weighing more than 80 pounds on their backs. After walking 60 to 80 miles, they would return a week later, with a much lighter load "and an adequate return in their pockets."[8] When the money the peddler earned was "adequate" enough, he bought a horse and wagon so that he could carry many more items, including ready-made clothes and heavier items.

By 1850, there were 10,669 peddlers in America. By 1860, they numbered 16,594.[9] The actual numbers were likely much higher since itinerant peddlers were often not counted by census takers. Less than one percent of the peddlers in mid–1800s America were Christian. "Eleven times out of ten the peddler is a Jew," a German writer chuckled.[10]

Shortly after coming to Philadelphia, Jonathan became a member of Mikveh Israel (Hope of Israel). Founded in 1782 by Sephardic Jews, Mikveh Israel was Philadelphia's first Jewish congregation and included some of Philadelphia's most influential Jews, among them the Gratz family. Five of the Gratzes were members of the Philadelphia Club, the oldest and most exclusive men's club in Philadelphia.[11] German-born Isaac Leeser was Mikveh Israel's hazan-minister. Leeser became one of the best known and most influential Jewish leaders during the American Civil War.[12] Several years after Mikveh Israel was founded, in 1795, a group of primarily German and Dutch Ashkenazim founded a second synagogue they called *Rodeph Shalom* (Pursuit of Peace), making Philadelphia the first city in America with two Jewish congregations and the first to follow the prayers, customs, and rituals of Ashkenazi tradition.[13]

When Jonathan's and Amelia's second son, Eleazar, was born in Philadelphia in March 1834, there was one more mouth to feed. Jonathan had joined Mikveh Israel when he first came to Philadelphia, but its dues were beyond what he could afford. Jonathan resigned from Mikveh Israel and joined

2. "Act according to the custom of that place"

Rodeph Shalom, which assessed minimal annual dues of $4. In cases of hardship, it exempted them.[14] Jonathon became a founder of its charitable Hebrew Society that provided relief for the poor and the sick. Although a founder, Jonathan could not afford the $50 joining membership that exempted members from all further contributions and all fines "except fines for improper conduct at a meeting." Founding member Jonathan Zachariah wasn't able to come up with enough for the exemption.[15] He was bankrupt.[16]

The Zachariahs would have been in dire straits had it not been for the Dessaus. With money she borrowed from them, Amelia opened a millinery store on Cedar Street (now South Street), the downtown avenue of Philadelphia's retail trade, selling straw bonnets, ribbons, and caps.[17] Amelia had a head for business. A year later, she relocated to Sassafras,[18] the same street Jacob Dessau's shop was on.[19]

* * * * * * * *

Nothing is known about Issachar's childhood in Philadelphia, except by inference. At 13, Jewish boys were accepted as adults in their religious community. They were expected to be able to read or at least pronounce Hebrew words. In a rite of passage, they were called to the synagogue bema on their birthday or the Sabbath closest to it and read a portion of the Torah before the congregation. After that, they were obliged to obey all the commandments of Jewish law and could be counted as one of the 10 adult men required for a *minyan* necessary for communal prayers. There was no equivalent of the modern-day *bar mitzvah*, the Jewish rite of passage. Issachar never mentioned having participated in this rite of passage or his ever being able to read Hebrew.

Many years later, Issachar married Mary Ann Lawson, a Christian girl from Philadelphia. How his and Mary Ann's romance began isn't known. Since they lived in the same neighborhood—Issachar's mother's clothing goods shop was on Cedar Street, which intersected with Green Street, where the Lawsons lived[20]—they may have met at one of Philadelphia's "free schools." Other than Mary Ann, there is no record of Issachar's involvement with any other woman before or after they were married.

In 1840, for some unknown reason, the Zachariahs were on the move again. They packed their belongings, 15-year-old Issachar said goodbye to 12-year-old Mary Ann and his other friends and neighbors, and he boarded a train with his family for the 680-mile trip to Charleston, South Carolina.

* * * * * * * *

By the mid–1700s, Charles Towne was the busiest seaport on the Atlantic and the largest and wealthiest city in the South. Ships from all parts of Europe docked at its harbor, unloaded their goods, and loaded their cargoes of indigo dye for England's navy uniforms, along with rice, deerskins, and tobacco for all parts of the world. Although the South had been growing cotton since colonial days, relatively small amounts were exported in the mid–1700s.

That arguably changed after France's Queen, Marie Antoinette, posed for her portrait in a provincial cotton dress. Women of her stature normally wore lavish silk gowns at court. Like the millions of men and women who adopt the fashions worn by movie stars today, fashionable women of her day wanted to dress like the exotic French Queen. Demand for cotton soared throughout Europe. Voracity for cotton increased even more after the French Revolution, when economies across Europe plunged and the zeal for more costly silk collapsed. By the end of the century, cotton and muslin had nearly completely replaced silk as the fashionable fabric of choice.[21]

Up until then, most of Europe's cotton had come from India, but when India could not keep up with demand, Europeans began looking elsewhere. Eli Whitney's invention of the cotton gin in 1794 made it possible to keep up with demand. The Industrial Revolution alchemized it into textiles on a massive scale. In 1790, the American South exported 3,000 bales a year. By 1810, exports amounted to 178,000 bales.

Following the American Revolution, most Northern states outlawed slavery (Delaware was a notable exception). It seemed the South would follow. When cotton became an important cash crop, the insatiable demand for it created a surge in demand for slave labor in the South. In 1790, the slave population numbered about 654,000. By 1810, it was 1.1 million. Marie Antoinette's dress had launched an unimaginable "butterfly effect."[22]

After cotton became "king," it took over as South Carolina's main staple. Fortunes were made almost overnight. For $5,000 to $6,000, which included wages for an overseer and food and clothing for slaves, a cotton crop could fetch more than $40,000.[23] Jewish merchants who catered to rich plantation owners or were owners themselves likewise became wealthy.

Relatively few manual laborers went south to work. Because of the South's large slave force, wages in the south for mechanics, carpenters, blacksmiths, construction workers, and other manual laborers were lower than in other parts of the country. Where others saw unemployment, Jewish merchants saw opportunity. Some remained in Charleston, some went up country and opened stores in surrounding districts, and some ventured further into the backcountry. Eventually, there was at least one Jewish shop in every town in South Carolina that sold clothing, hardware, groceries, notions, trinkets, cigars, and any other marketable goods.

Jonathan's profession is not known. Possibly he peddled clothes and trinkets in the country side while Amelia operated a woman's clothing store at 147 King Street between Queen and Clifford streets.[24] King Street today is a long, pedestrian-clogged hodge-podge of bars, restaurants, souvenir

2. "Act according to the custom of that place" 15

shops, jewelers, antique dealers, a library, and Charleston's preservation society. Original store fronts from the 1840s and 1850s have been torn down or renovated. Across the street from the bygone Zachariah store is a three-story building, one of the few buildings from that time that is still standing. The salesgirl selling jewelry inside did not know how old it was, but it looked very much like it could have been built in Issachar's time.

Amelia was an astute businesswoman. An advertisement in the 1849 *Charleston Courier* informed the city's women that Mrs. Zachariah was adding a second branch to her business at 147 King, succeeding Mrs. Rayne: "She hopes by strict attention and economy in her charges, to deserve the patronage of the friends of her predecessor." In addition to "French corsets, shoulder braces, girdles or Zohans," Amelia advertised "cleaning, dying and altering straw hats."[25]

Like Amelia, many of the store owners on King Street were women. Miss Ellen M. Cambridge had a millinery next door to Amelia at 146 King, where she exhibited "a select and most fashionable display" of straw bonnets and accessories, "all of which have been purchased with cash, from extensive importers of the latest and most fashionable style of goods in N. York." Madame Figeroux sold silk and spring bonnets and some of the finest "Artificial French Flowers" at 188 King. Further down the street at 253 and 304 King were Mrs. F. Day's and W. Hancock's dry goods stores. A Miss Babcock sold bonnets of "Chameleon and Drab Velvets and silks" at 322 King Street.[26]

Rebecca De Mendes Benjamin, whose son Judah became one of only two Jews to be elected to Congress before the war and who later become Secretary of State for the Confederacy, owned a fruit store on King Street near the docks.[27] Judah was no longer living in Charleston when Issachar was growing up there. Although they would not have known one another then, fate brought them together many years later. Their parents, on the other hand, were probably acquainted.

The Benjamins drew the ire of Charleston's traditionalist Jewish community because Rebecca kept her store open on Shabbos, the Jewish Sabbath on Saturdays. Traditionalists expected the Sabbath should be strictly observed. Since storekeepers were not allowed to operate on Sundays, the Christian Sabbath, closing her store on Saturdays would have meant two days without income, a financial burden for a family struggling to make ends meet. In 1845, Judah's brother Solomon was charged with violating Charleston's 1801 ordinance by selling a pair of gloves on Sunday. He was fined $20.[28]

Women like Amelia and Rebecca Benjamin were often the family's main income earners or took over the family business from their husbands when it fell on hard times. Amelia's daughters probably helped out in her stores, but young Issachar was out of place in a business catering to women and was more likely to have been on his own, wandering about Charleston's streets. It was a vibrant city, with craftsmen going about their work and markets bustling with wagons filled with oranges from Florida, pineapples from Cuba, and vegetables from local farms.

Charleston was also a major center for the slave trade. By the 1850s, there were 32 active slave brokerages in the city.[29] Wandering through the streets, Issachar probably saw black men, women, and children in chains being sold at auction houses throughout the city. But Issachar didn't have to wander the streets to become familiar with slavery. His family owned two house slaves, Harriet Segars, age 60, and Charlotte Bright, age 40.[30]

Except for their religion, Jews were no different from non-Jews in the South in nearly every respect. Charleston's Jews did not question the Talmudic principle that "the law of the land is the law."[31] The principle was inherent in the Sephardic precept, "Every place you go, act according to the custom of that place."[32]

Acceptance and assimilation meant conformity to the South's "peculiar institution." If Jews needed to own slaves and could afford them, they bought them.[33] Since most Jews lived in cities and towns, most of the slaves they owned were domestic servants. Judah Benjamin's parents owned several house slaves. As a successful Louisiana lawyer and plantation owner, he himself owned 140 slaves.[34]

By 1830, 83 percent of the Jewish households in Charleston owned at least one slave, slightly less than the percentage owned by gentile households[35]; by mid-century, there were 5.5 slaves per Jewish household.[36] Charleston's free African Americans, by comparison, owned three times more slaves than Charleston's Jews.[37]

In 1850, Amelia and Jonathan were living in St. Michael's and St. Philip's parish, around Broad and Meeting streets.[38] All of Issachar's sisters were married by then and had left home.[39] Issachar's niece, his sister Rebecca's 12-year-old daughter, also named Rebecca, was living with Jonathan and Amelia instead of her own parents for some unknown reason. Besides Issachar's family and Harriet Segars and Charlotte Bright, and their two household slaves, there were seven others in their home: Lewis and Anne Loyal and their two children, ages 1 and 3, and Frances Martin and his two sons, Jacob, 21, and James, 20.[40] Nothing is known as to whether the Loyals and the Martins were distant relatives or boarders. Lewis Loyal was born in France; his wife, Anne, was born in South Carolina. The Martins were all born in South Carolina.[41]

Part Two

I. Zachariah, Jr., Cheroperdist

3

"No Cure No Pay"

In April 1843, 16-year-old Issachar Zachariah, Jr., placed an advertisement in the *Charleston Southern Patriot*, "respectfully" informing "the Ladies and Gentlemen of Charleston" that he "will EXTRACT CORNS at his office at No. 154 King St., in five minutes without giving any pain whatever and guarantees the Corns will never return." The ad stated he was only charging a "'moderate' fee," for his services, and guaranteed "NO CURE NO PAY." It was signed I. Zachariah, Jr. Cheroperdist.[1] Besides cutting corns, he was also selling patent medicines and perfumes at his King Street store.[2]

Issachar's advertising himself as a chiropodist, or as he termed it, a "cheroperdist," came out of nowhere. There is nothing to indicate how he learned how to treat corns and bunions or why he even went into that line of work instead of the family dry goods business.

* * * * * * * *

Corns, bunions, and ingrown toenails seem rather trivial problems compared with our present-day anxieties and dread about cancer, heart disease, and other ailments. But in mid-nineteenth-century America, people rarely talked about those diseases. Instead, they were much more concerned about annoyances that made everyday life painful in one way or another. High up on the list of distressing irritations were corns and bunions. Newspapers were full of commentaries about the effects of these "excrescences." Many people would have agreed with the *New London* Connecticut *Daily Chronicle*'s comment, "Corns have produced more bad tempers and caused more swearing than any other grievance that flesh is heir to."[3]

Corns and bunions made it painful to walk. For women, it was not just painful, it was embarrassing if their corns and bunions became public. Chiropodists, as podiatrists were then known,[4] advertised their willingness to treat women in their homes to avoid public embarrassment. Some chiropodists provided separate entrances at their offices for women desiring privacy.[5] It was not an idle whim.

In Paris, a ladies' shoemaker blackmailed his female patients by threat-

3. "No Cure No Pay"

> **Corns, Corns, Corns!!!**
> **NO CURE NO PAY**
> I. ZACHARIAH, Jr. respectfully informs the La-
> dies and Gentlemen of Charleston, that he will
> EXTRACT CORNS, in five minutes without giv-
> ing any pain whatever, and guarantee that the Corns
> will never return—(charge moderate.) Ladies and
> Gentlemen waited on at their residence if required.
> I. ZACHARIAH, Jr., Cheroperdist,
> Office, No. 134 King-st., Charleston, S. C.
> Ap 25 tuf

One of Zacharie's early advertisements, using his birth name (*Charleston Southern Patriot*, 1843).

ening to reveal details about their feet. He sent them a proof copy of a memoir he was writing about his patients. For 15 francs, he promised to leave their names out of it. One of the entries described a "Madame A___lives Rue___, No___first floor; married in 1844; three children, pays badly; feet very difficult to fit, instep too flat, two corns and three bunions; walks awkwardly, and wears her shoes out in the inside very fast."

The blackmailer characterized a "Madame B___Rue___, No.___" as "still an old maid … pays her bills, but makes a hard bargain; feet spreading, toes crowding one over the other; two corns and a bunion." Madame C "gives her children nothing, and never pays until served with a writ; feet flat, large, and very apt to burst the leathers; a great many corns and bunions, all mixed up together."

When several of the women he was blackmailing complained to the police about the "literary shoemaker," he was arrested and sent to jail for a month.[6]

* * * * * * * *

People have been hacking corns and calluses from their feet with coarse tools or sharpened instruments on their own or enlisting the help of someone else for the task from the time such tools were invented. As far back as the ancient Egyptians, specially trained professionals took care of foot problems. Hippocrates, the "father" of medicine, mentions removing hardened skin on the feet and invented a scraping tool for just that purpose.[7]

After a 12th-century Papal decree, forbidding clerics from treating foot problems that might cause bleeding, barber surgeons and others took over the trade. An early 17th-century play has one of the characters at a fairground, selling herrings, oysters, pies, and tarts and offering to sharpen knives to "very nicely cut your corns."[8] Corns became much more of a problem during the 17th century, when people began wearing closed-toed leather boots and shoes. Kings and queens who luxuriated in the palaces of Europe experienced the same discomfort as farmers who toiled behind a plough.

The term "chiropody" came into existence in 1785, when a London corn cutter, David Low, wrote a textbook on foot care. Low plagiarized much of his book from an earlier French text, *L'Art de Soigner les Pieds*, written in 1781 by King Louis XVI's corn cutter. To create the impression of originality, Low changed the title to *Chiropodologia*, combing the Greek word *chiro*, meaning hand, and the Latin word *pod*, for foot. *Chiropodologia* eventually became chiropody.[9]

Most medically trained doctors in the 18th and 19th centuries considered treating foot problems literally and figuratively beneath them. Medicine's snobbery left it to barber surgeons and corn cutters to take care of corns, bunions, and related foot problems. Heyman Lion was awarded a doctor of medicine degree from the University of Edinburgh in 1796, and passed his exams with high honors, but the College of Physicians and Surgeons in London denied his application for a diploma. Lion said he intended to specialize in treating foot ailments. The college stated its denial was to maintain the dignity and high standard of the profession. A doctor of medicine, the college said, should not be involved in a degrading business like "corn-cutting."[10]

Despite physicians' low opinion of foot healers, people suffering from painful corns were more than willing to pay to have their annoying foot growths removed. By the 18th century, cutting corns or "corn operating," as practitioners preferred to call what they did, had become a burgeoning profession. Some chiropodists even became very respectable and influential. In 1774, a Mr. March, a prominent London corn cutter, was appointed nail cutter to His Royal Highness, the Prince of Wales, at an annual salary of 50 guineas (about $6,000).[11] After word got out that the Prince of Wales had his own personal "corn operator," aristocrats and anyone else with money had no qualms about employing chiropodists to remove their corns.

By the mid–18th century, corn cutters were such a common fixture in English society that they were featured in popular illustrations. One such picture shows an elegantly dressed corn operator wearing a wig and spectacles and standing before an array of surgical instruments. The fact that he was worth depicting indicates the profession had gained respectable traction.[12] Napoleon Bonaparte's constant companion and confidant, Monsieur Sagrada, was the emperor's personal "corn operator."[13] Napoleon's nemesis, the Duke of Wellington, had no liking for corn cutters. The Duke sued a London corn cutter for claiming in the press that he had cut Wellington's corns.[14]

Since foot care, and especially removing corns, was not a recognized profession, there was no formal apprenticeship for that line of work. In most cases, individuals learned whatever there was to know from someone in their family who trained them. Fathers taught their sons, who in turn taught their sons. Every city had at least one corn cutter.

Prevented from attending Europe's medical schools, many Jews became proficient at treating foot problems, a skill credentialed physicians regarded as undignified. By the 18th century, Jewish barber surgeons and bloodletters in Europe and England were considered specialists in the profession.[15] "Surgeon-chiropodist" Lewis Durlacher (1792–1864), the most famous chiropodist of his day, treated the foot ailments of three British monarchs, George IV, William IV, and Queen Victoria.

Durlacher was taught chiropody by his father, Solomon Durlacher, "Dr., Surgeon, Dentist and Corn Operator." Solomon took his last name from the town of Durlach in Germany when Jews were made to take surnames. He came to England in the 1780s, settled in Birmingham, and married Betsy Harris. The couple later relocated to Bath, where he taught the skill to both his son and his wife Betsy, corn cutter "for the ladies."[16] Jewish "Surgeon-chiropodist" John Eisenberg, an Austrian émigré to England, claimed he had pared the corns from the feet of European nobility, including French Emperor Napoleon III.[17]

* * * * * * * *

Issachar may have decided to become a "cheropedist" after watching itinerant corn cutters who travelled along the Atlantic coast treating patients. Eighteen-year-old Nehemiah Kenison (1824–1891) left home in New Hampshire in 1842 trying to find some kind of work that interested him and found "the very business that I had been hunting and praying for ever since I first left my native town." Kenison started out as peddler in the rural South. This is how Kenison described his epiphany:

> "What do you suppose I saw upon entering the hotel (in Greenville)? Well, I thought, I have found it at last, and it's mine.
> A man by the name of James McMellon was operating on a gentleman's foot, for the relief of a corn, as I entered the hotel. That would be nothing uncommon now. But it was new to me; and it made a very strong and favorable impression upon me when I saw the doctor receive $5.00 for his fee for only a few minutes' work. I watched the operation and made up my mind that was the business for me."

Kenison persuaded McMellon to take him on as an apprentice. In the early part of the century, many of the corn cutters treated corns by digging them out with a scalpel as far down as they dared, until the person being treated howled in pain. McMellon taught Kenison how to remove corns painlessly by first softening them with acid and then carefully shelling them out with a dull bone blade.

A few months later, he returned home to New Hampshire, married his sweetheart, and in 1846, opened an office in Boston where "I soon began to operate, and was a success from the first. I soon bought me a horse and travelled in a number of different Southern States for twenty-two months."[18]

Issachar's "James McMellon" was Dr. E. Barinds, a German chiropodist who set up a corn-removing office in Charleston in 1840, at 97 King Street, several stores down from Issachar's parents' dry goods store at 147 King St.[19] Barinds' advertisement assured Charlestonians he "effectually extracts corns" without pain, cures bunions and defective nails "with treatment entirely his own," and "particularly attended diseases of the teeth." A curious 15-year-old boy, Issachar watched Barinds extracting corns. Like Kenison, he realized, "there is money in it."

Many itinerant corn cutters like Barinds also advertised their skills as dentists (until the mid–19th century, both professions were often practiced by the same individual). Barinds offered to "scale teeth to a pearly whiteness, and arrest carious Teeth from further decay." If a client suffered from rheumatism, Barinds sold a "European Linament which has never been known to fail."[20] When Barinds wasn't cutting corns or pulling teeth, he sold homemade remedies to treat conditions that for "ages baffled the skill of the profession." With Barinds as his role model, Issachar decided corn cutting had a future for him.

* * * * * * * *

At age 16, I. Zachariah, Jr., went into business for himself as a chiropodist (undoubtedly with the support of his parents) at 154 King Street. Taking a page from Barinds and other chiropodists, he promised, "NO CURE NO PAY." Clients were also offered "nostrums, salves, lineaments, balms, soaps, plasters, lotions, perfumery" and "a large number of other articles too numerous to mention" at "Thirty Per Cent Cheaper Than Can Be Bought Elsewhere." In addition to those remedies, he sold his own "Zachariah's celebrated patent Labor saving preparation for cleaning brass." Issachar offered potential customers who were used to bartering or buying on credit "a large discount for cash."[21]

Issachar got the idea to hawk nostrums he claimed to have invented himself from other local businesses in Charleston that were selling eponymously named potions. At 19 Hayne Street, a P. M. Cohen, was doing a thriving business selling "Peter's Pill," the "wonderful cures" of which were "the all-engrossing subjects of the day" because of its power to "procrastinate death for years."[22] Further up the street from Issachar's shop, Haviland, Harral & Allen at 286 King Street sold a wide variety of nostrums, including "Sand's Sarsaparilla," "for the removal and permanent cure of all diseases arising from an impure state of the blood" at $1 per bottle, six for $5. If Sands' Sarsaparilla

3. "No Cure No Pay"

didn't do the job, customers suffering from scrofula, or King's Evil, incipient cancers, syphilitic and mercurial diseases, and a host of other disorders could also try "the Indian Panacea."[23]

Issachar's dual ads ran continuously from April through July. Two months after embarking on his new-found career as a corn cutter, and a month after inventing his patented labor-saving device, he placed a new ad in the *Charleston Southern Patriot*. In those two months, Issachar had acquired the self-proclaimed medical title "doctor" (in the early 19th century, there was no licensing for practicing medicine—anyone could practice medicine) and invented a new medicine to purify the blood and remove "bilious diseases":

> THE SUMMER HAS COME! and every person that wants to purify their BLOOD now is their chance!—for Dr. I. Zachariah Jr. Has just invented a new preparation for purifying the Blood and removing all Bilious diseases, called Zachariah's Compound Alternative Prepared and sold by the INVENTOR & SOLE PROPRIETOR.[24]

4

"Where more money could be made faster"

In August 1843, just four months after opening his store in Charleston, Issachar received a letter from his mentor, Dr. Barinds, advising him to come to New Orleans, "where more money could be made faster than any other place on the continent."[1] Issachar was never to return to Charleston. Packing his tool kit and clothes, he said goodbye to his parents and siblings and boarded a stagecoach to New Orleans.

Stagecoaches were so-called from their changing relays of horses at regular stages, stopping every 10 to 15 miles to change to a fresh four-horse team at relay stations along the way.[2] A stagecoach journey like Issachar's was nothing to take lightly. For one thing, it was expensive. At about 10 cents a mile, the 510-mile trip from Charleston to Montgomery, Alabama, where he could board a ferry to Mobile, would cost the equivalent of about $1 per mile today. Added to that was the costs of lodging and food along the way.[3]

The stagecoach part of the journey was over bone-rattling rutted roads that continuously bounced Issachar against the passenger sitting next to him. Each coach carried up to nine passengers seated on three benches, three to a bench. The front and back seats faced inward and had back rests. The middle bench, the most uncomfortable, had a broad strap for a back support. Front and back seats were given to women. If they were with their husbands, they sat beside them. Issachar's other passengers, few if any, recently washed and tidy, in their "little ark of humanity"[4] could have been gamblers, prostitutes, merchants, or young or old fortune-hunters like himself.

After 12 or more hours, the coach stopped overnight at an inn, where Issachar slept, his shirt on and trousers off, with two or three other men on greasy pillows in the same soiled bed.[5] Three or four days after leaving Charleston, he arrived in Montgomery, Alabama. From there, he boarded a steamboat for another two-day trip to Mobile, then boarded a train to New Orleans.[6]

* * * * * * * *

4. "Where more money could be made faster"

Located between Lake Pontchartrain and the Mississippi River, "The Crescent City" (so-called because of the large crescent bend the Mississippi makes near the French Quarter) was the gateway into and from the country's heartland. New Orleans was much larger, much more cosmopolitan, and much more raucous than Charleston. Peddlers, merchants, planters, factors, sailors, gamblers, pimps, prostitutes, and con men were everywhere. About 40 percent of the population were foreign born, mainly French, German, and Irish.[7] Free blacks made up more than 40 percent of its African American population.

In 1724, the French governor of Louisiana had issued the Code Noir, which expelled Jews from the colony. In 1803, New Orleans became an American city as part of the Louisiana Purchase, and the ban was no longer enforced. Although most of the Jews coming to Louisiana, settled in New Orleans, a sizable number ventured farther inland to Baton Rouge, the second largest town in the state, or Shreveport and Donadlsonville.[8] Judah Benjamin came to New Orleans in 1828. The year before, the Sephardic community, with the help of local merchants like Judah Touro and Jews in other parts of the country, built the city's first synagogue, the Gates of Mercy.[9]

Most of New Orleans' Jews were small businessmen selling clothing or textiles at the wholesale or retail level or jewelry, tobacco, and fancy import goods at fixed store locations on Chartres Street. Others sold wares at temporary stalls and pushcarts along the river in the French Quarter or at auction or by peddling. A few operated taverns.[10]

Canal Street, with its small, specialized, expensive stores, had carriage tracks and rows of sycamores in the center of the street extending its whole length. Judah Touro, the richest man in the city, lived on Canal Street.[11] Issachar took in all the wealth and allure as he strolled down Canal to St. Charles Street. Dr. Barinds had his office and living quarters at No. 3 St. Charles, at the corner of Canal.[12]

No. 3. St. Charles Street was a large rooming house where "a few young gentlemen [could] be accommodated with board and lodging, or board only, on reasonable terms."[13] Within days of moving in, Issachar placed an ad in the New Orleans *Times-Picayune* that was not much different from his ads in Charleston. Starting off with the same bold "CORNS!" heading and the same guarantee of "No Cure No Pay," "Dr. Z" assured the ladies and gentlemen of New Orleans that if their corns returned after he removed them at his office or their homes, their money would be refunded.[14]

There was money to be made in New Orleans, but corn-sufferers preferred seeing the older Dr. Barinds. Issachar left after only two months.[15] He did not return for another three years.

After he packed his tool bag and left New Orleans, Issachar headed for Richmond, Virginia, where he briefly leased an office in May 1844, at the

Columbian Hotel at 26 Cary Street.[16] He didn't stay long. An ad he placed in the *Richmond Whig* only ran for one day. Issachar's whereabouts for the next few months are not known. In September, he was back in Philadelphia to marry his childhood sweetheart.

* * * * * * * *

Issachar and Mary Ann Lawson met in Philadelphia when they were teenagers, before his family moved to Charleston. They probably met in school or when Issachar's family lived on Cedar Street near Green Street, where the Lawsons lived. Mary Ann was the oldest of Jacob's and Elizabeth Lawson's five children (four girls and one son). The Lawsons were a middle-class Christian family. Mary Ann's parents were both born in Philadelphia. Jacob was a saddler, and Mary Ann was a dressmaker at the family's new home at 44 Coates.[17] None of the letters Issachar and Mary Ann sent to each other has survived, but they must have written often enough for Issachar to ask her to marry him.

They married in Philadelphia on September 11, 1844.[18] They were both 17. It was a Christian ceremony. Issachar's parents did not attend.

Although Issachar was the grandson of the leader of a Jewish community in England and his father had been an active synagogue member in Philadelphia's and Charleston's Jewish communities, Issachar didn't feel he was turning his back on his ancestral religion when he married Mary Ann. Many Jews who married Christians continued to regard themselves as Jews,[19] although the children of mixed marriages were nearly always raised as Christians by their Christian mothers. Issachar was not a practicing Jew. For him, being Jewish was an ethnicity, not a religion.[20]

* * * * * * * *

Shortly after marrying, Issachar left Mary Ann with her parents while he continued moving from city to city practicing his profession. In April 1846, he was back in New Orleans clipping corns at a "fancy store" at the St. Charles Hotel, when he was arrested.[21]

The charge was forgery, a crime the newspapers called swindling. A New Orleans lawyer, acting on behalf of his brother, a man named Glenn, alleged that when Issachar was in Philadelphia, he had cashed a draft for $217.50 with Glenn, on Issachar's father-in-law Jacob Lawson's account, "under false pretenses."[22] Glenn hadn't pressed charges because Issachar had left Philadelphia, and he did not know where he had gone. By chance, he learned through his brother in New Orleans that Issachar was in that city. Glenn's brother swore out a warrant for Issachar's arrest on his behalf. Issachar was arrested, released on bail, and scheduled to appear in court two days later.

The case drew such wide interest in the newspapers that the New Orleans *Daily Delta* informed its readers it had been requested to ask them not to prejudge the case until Dr. Zacharie had his day in court.[23] At the hearing, Glenn's lawyer said he had no personal knowledge of the facts other than what his brother had told him. Issachar's lawyers strongly objected to his request for a delay and moved for dismissal. They contended Issachar had been charged based on an affidavit from his accuser who was not in court, and there was no evidence corroborating the alleged fraud. The judge agreed, and Issachar was released.[24] Although the case had been dismissed, many people in New Orleans believed he was guilty and stopped coming to his "fancy store." Issachar closed his business and returned to Philadelphia.

After a brief stay there, he and Mary Ann moved to Baltimore, where Issachar leased a home and set up a new practice. In June 1846, "Dr. I. Zachariah, Jr. Surgeon Chiropedist" placed an ad in the *Baltimore American and Commercial Daily Advertiser* stating he was now "permanently located" in Baltimore and "would be treating patients, either at his home at 111 Lexington Street or at their residence if required."[25] Shortly after moving to Baltimore, Mary Ann became pregnant. Months later, she moved back to Philadelphia so her mother could help her during and after her pregnancy. Issachar's and Mary Ann's first-born son, Charles Lawson Zacharie, was born in 1847.[26]

5

"We the undersigned"

Baltimore was a city on the make, a city whose mantra was "Death or Go-Ahead." In the 1840s, it was the third largest city in America, outranking Boston and Charleston. With a population increasing by 20,000 every decade, Baltimore was challenging New York and Philadelphia for number one.[1]

Issachar's first office at 111 Lexington[2] was in the heart of the Jewish district. To give himself credibility, he claimed he had been treating foot problems in Baltimore for the last three years. It was the beginning of a long series of lies he told about himself.[3]

Although he was the only chiropodist in Baltimore, Issachar was too ambitious to be content with merely cutting corns. Six months later, he moved to a new office at 24 Gay Street, inviting prospective patients to visit him at his "new operating rooms," where he added dentistry to the services he offered.

His work "inserting, plugging, cleaning, extracting, filing, &c" teeth was "equal to any in the city," he said.[4] He used "the latest improvements in the science" to maintain the beauty and preservation of teeth "at one third less than usual rates." He cleansed and filled "carious teeth with gold, thereby arresting the progress of decay, and rendering them useful for life." He also inserted "mineral teeth of a superior quality, with or without colored Gums." Those inserts "so nearly resemble natural Teeth, both in appearance and usefulness," that patients who favored him with their patronage would be entirely satisfied.[5]

Issachar assured "his friends and the public in general" he wasn't giving up his chiropody practice. He would still be extracting "hard and soft corns, bunions [and] club nails penetrating the flesh, in five minutes." No one need worry about the pain. He promised to remove a patient's corns "without the least pain or blood." Their corns, he assured them, "will never return."[6]

Issachar's "new operating rooms" sounded professional and dignified. Patients would not be treated in an ordinary room where shelf after shelf harbored patent medicines and various sundries. Patients would have their ailments attended to in a separate "operating room"—not just one, but "operating rooms," one for their lower extremities and another for their topmost.

Issachar also came up with what would become his most convincing self-promoting logo: "references ... and certificates from the first Surgeons and Physicians in the world" that could be seen at his office. It was a bold assertion for the teenage chiropodist.

In January 1847, Issachar went "on a professional tour" to Washington, where he was "happy to operate upon all" who could benefit from his experience and skill at his room at the posh Coleman's Hotel on Pennsylvania Avenue. (President-elect James Polk had stayed there with his wife two years earlier.) The advertisement for his new venture contained the first of the many testimonials he was beginning to cite from prominent physicians:

> We the undersigned, having examined Dr. I. Zachariah, Jr.'s, method of curing corns, bunions, &c. we do not hesitated to recommend him to the public, and say that his method is a most rational one as well as effectual.[7]

It's possible these physicians gave Issachar their endorsement, but there's a nagging suspicion that, like his claiming he had been practicing in Baltimore for three years, he made them up. It stretches probability that the 19-year-old was able to corral these eminent physicians not only into meeting as a group with him, but also into watching him perform corn cutting procedures that as physicians, they had no interest in and in fact looked down upon as degrading.

Issachar's citing endorsements from eminent physicians without their knowledge was nothing new. Drs. W. H. Handy, Charles Bell Gibson, and Nathan R. Smith, three of Issachar's endorsers, are cited in an advertisement for Reinhardt's Patent Glass Pad Double and Single Lever Truss.[8] Issachar sold that same truss in his office above Parker's Fancy Store between 4th and 6th on Pennsylvania Avenue a year later when he was back in Washington treating foot problems and pulling teeth.[9] Drs. Pierre Chatard's, Gibson's, and Smith's names were also cited as endorsing Baltimore dentist Thomas Badaraque.[10]

Issachar got the idea of fake celebrity endorsements from chiropodist John Eisenberg's *Surgical and Practical Observations on the Diseases of the Human Foot*.[11] Among Eisenberg's made-up testimonies were those from France's Prince Louis Napoleon Bonaparte, Prussia's Ambassador to England, Lord Dufferin, "Lord in Waiting to her Majesty," the Duke of Wellington, and many others of Europe's eminent nobility. Eisenberg's fake endorsement marketing ploy was obvious. Issachar saw no reason he shouldn't do the same.

Eisenberg and other corn cutters claiming to have treated Europe's "A-list" elite weren't publicly challenged because those worthies couldn't be bothered—with one exception. When the Duke of Wellington was informed his name had been so used, he sued the corn cutter for his fraudulent endorsement.[12]

6

"A humble individual"

Issachar was emboldened when the testimonials he cited from Baltimore's eminent physicians went unchallenged. Why not claim an endorsement from one of the world's most famous physicians, especially since he was dead. Who was there to refute him?

A month after he cited the Baltimore endorsements, Issachar quoted an endorsement from Dr. Astley Paston Cooper that he dated June 27, 1837:

> This is to certify, that I. Zacharie studied the profession of Chiropodist under me, and from this day I consider him fully competent to perform the duty of a Chiropodist upon all who may favor him with their patronage.
>
> Given in the city of London, under my hand and seal, this twenty-seventh day of June, in the year of our Lord, one thousand eight hundred and thirty-seven.[1]

Sir Astley Paston Cooper had been England's preeminent surgeon and anatomist, famous for breakthrough procedures in vascular and hernia surgeries. Born in Norfolk to a prominent family, his father sent him to London when he was 16 to study medicine under London's best surgeons. A gifted student, he was appointed demonstrator, and a few years later, lecturer of anatomy at St. Thomas' Hospital. Cooper was said to have mastered anatomy first by dissecting pets he stole from neighbors and then on the stolen corpses of those same neighbors. As his surgical practice grew, he organized a network of body snatchers to steal corpses to dissect.

Cooper was so highly regarded that he was the physician called upon to remove a tumor from the head of King George IV. The operation was a success. In return, the King made him a baron. He was subsequently appointed sergeant-surgeon to the King and later to Queen Victoria.[2] Cooper's fame was such that several streets in British cities were named after him, e.g., Astley Cooper Place in Norfolk; Astley Road and Paston Road in Hempstead, as were newly described diseases (e.g., Cooper's testis [neuralgia of the testicles] and Cooper's neuralgia [neuralgia of the breast]).

An endorsement from Sir Astley Paston Cooper stating Zacharie had been one of his pupils would have given him serious gravitas in the medical community. But Cooper's endorsement was fiction. Had Cooper been

Issachar's mentor, Issachar would have been no more than 12 when Cooper wrote the testimonial Issachar attributed to him. In the early 1800s, some children from working families did go to work when they were five or six,[3] but those children were employed as servants, factory workers, miners, and street sweepers. After Charles Dickens' father was imprisoned for failing to pay a debt, Dickens was sent to work, but not as an apprentice to a posh physician. Dickens worked in a rat-infested shoe-polish factory blacking boots.[4]

Apprentices spent several years with their mentors, not several weeks or months, and surgeons did not take on apprentices for free. Some charged hundreds of British pounds to take on an apprentice. Only the sons of men with money could afford to have their sons apprenticed to a prominent surgeon like Cooper. And no medically trained surgeon would ever have tutored anyone in what the medical profession considered as unworthy of their time as the treatment of corns and bunions. None of that is really relevant. In 1837, when Issachar was 10, he was living in Philadelphia. In 1846, when he boasted of Cooper's personal endorsement, Cooper had been dead for five years. Who was going to take the time or had the interest to challenge him?

Dr. Zacharie wasn't the only chiropodist citing impressive testimonials in his advertisements to enhance his credibility. "It is a remarkable fact," the editor of the *Spectator* magazine bemoaned, "that every corn-cutter of any eminence who appears above the horizon can display testimonials from a number of Peers and other persons of distinction." Nearly all of them, it chafed, were fraudulent.[5]

How did Issachar Zacharie, who had little formal schooling and no medical training, come up with Dr. Cooper's name? He found it in advertisements for *Sir Astley Cooper's Corn Salve* that was sold in America's major cities, including Charleston, when Issachar first began his career. Like all such nostrums, it came with alleged testimonials from "distinguished physicians.... No one acquainted with the character of the distinguished Surgeon whose name it bears, can for a moment doubt the efficacy of SIR ASTLEY COOPER'S CORN SALVE [which] meets with the most favorable reception wherever its genuine virtues are known. In New York this salve is regarded by hundreds and hundreds and even by distinguished Physicians, as the only specific for corns; while in Boston, ample proof is already given by our citizens of its real value."[6] Those who preferred a poultice with an even more prestigious genealogy, one offering "miraculous cures" discovered in the Holy Land, had *Jew David's Plaster* for its "genuine virtues."[7] For skeptics who had no faith in salves, there was always the "positive cure for corns" used by Lowell, a Maryland man afflicted with painful corns on two of his toes. Determined to put an end to his affliction, he "went into a joiner's shop, took a mallet and chisel, and deliberately severed the two toes from the foot."[8]

Dr. Cooper never invented, sold, or knowingly lent his name to any corn salve. Issachar had no fear of contradiction for claiming to have been personally taught by Cooper or selling a salve with his name. The first advertisements for his eponymous salve did not appear until 1842, a year after Cooper died.

* * * * * * * *

If Issachar didn't learn his skills from Dr. Cooper, from whom did he learn them? Other historians trying to salvage Issachar's credibility speculate he was tutored by Dr. Valentine Mott or Dr. William Gibson, two American physicians who were actually mentored by Cooper.

Valentine Mott (1785–1865) worked under Dr. Cooper at his clinic from 1835 to 1841. He subsequently returned to the United States as a professor of surgery at the New York University Medical College from 1841 to 1850. Like his mentor, Dr. Mott pioneered many new procedures in vascular surgery, including successfully tying the carotid artery in one patient and cutting two inches from the deep jugular vein and reconnecting them, using a tincture of opium as his only anesthetic.[9] Cooper once said of Mott, "he has performed more of the great operations than any man living, or that ever did live."[10] Mott also pioneered the treatment of what today men using Viagra or Cialis are warned not to ignore—an erection lasting four hours or more. The medical emergency stems from the same ailment humorously called in Mott's day and still today "a fractured penis." Mott said when "the newly made bride" was "informed of the nature of the fracture, plaintively and innocently remarked, 'it never would have happened, if he had been at home.'"[11] The four-hour plus erection and the "fractured penis" both result from engorgement of the corpus cavernosum, the spongy erectile tissue in the penis. (Fracture is a misnomer since no bone or cartilage is ruptured.) These two areas become engorged with blood during sexual arousal, causing an erection. Viagra and Cialis work by inhibiting the enzymes that normally keep the blood from draining from the corpus callosum. If the blood does not drain, it can cause serious damage to the penis. The treatment for both the drug-induced erection and the "fractured penis" is draining the blood. Now it is done with a needle drainage. In Mott's day, cold "discutient lotions" (lotions that drained internal fluids) were applied to the penis to cause drainage.

The reason some historians credit Zacharie as one of Mott's students is a testimonial, dated New York, August 1858, that Mott allegedly wrote on Zacharie's behalf:

> Dr. Zacharie was a pupil of Sir Astley Cooper of London, he has been regularly educated as a Surgeon.
> For the last twenty years he had given particular attention to the troubles and diseases of the feet, such as Corns, Bunions, and inverted nails
> "His treatment is founded on the strictest rules of science, such as all Surgeons will

approve. I can recommend him to those who may be suffering from those maladies as the most expert and delicate operator I have ever seen."[12]

In appreciation for that testimonial, Issachar dedicated both editions of his book, *Surgical and Practical Observations on the Diseases of the Human Foot*, to Mott:

> I am indeed rejoiced that this tribute of my respect and admiration has been accepted by you, and that you consider the labours of a humble individual, upon a neglected branch of knowledge, not unworthy of your kind protection and consideration.[13]

Mott's endorsement, backdated to 1844, appears in two editions of Issachar's *Surgical and Practical Observations*. He plagiarized the first edition, published in 1860, almost verbatim from John Eisenberg's 1845 text. By dating Mott's endorsement a year earlier, Issachar claimed Eisenberg had copied him instead of the other way around. In Issachar's *Corns, Operations on the Feet* certificate book, Mott's testimonial is dated 1858. In 1844, Issachar was still living in the South. He published a second text with the same title in 1876. This time, he stole the entire text from an American, C. H. Cleaveland, whose text, *Causes and Cures of Diseases of the Feet*, was published in 1862.[14] Valentine Mott was never Issachar's mentor.

Zacharie wasn't even creative enough to write the dedication himself. Instead, he cribbed it verbatim from Eisenberg's dedication to Dr. Marshall Hall, even to the point of the signature: "I am, sir, Your obliged and humble servant." The only difference was that Zacharie erased Eisenberg's name and replaced it with his own.

Zacharie learned about Mott the same way he learned about Cooper—from advertisements using his name on countless products and service without Mott's awareness or approval. *Gold Medal Cognac Brandy* carried a fake endorsement: "highly recommended by Dr. Valentine Mott, the acknowledged head of the medical profession."[15] *Charles' London Cordial Gin* falsely quoted Dr. Valentine Mott of New York as it being "far preferable to even Pure Holland Gin, and is the best article of its kind I have ever seen."[16] Another ad for *Charles' London Cordial* had an endorsement from both Cooper and Mott: "Recommended By the Late Sir Astley Cooper, Of London, And Dr. Valentine Mott, Of New York, The acknowledged Heads of the Profession in Either Hemisphere."[17] *Ayer's Cherry Pectoral*, a patent medicine, stated "Dr. Valentine Mott, the widely celebrated Professor of Surgery in the Medical College, New York City," said it gave him "pleasure to certify the value and efficacy of Ayer's Cherry Pectoral, which I consider peculiarly adapted to cure diseases of the throat and lungs."[18]

The irony of these endorsements for gin and cordials is that Mott was an avowed teetotaler: "It is my full conviction that the pernicious practice of even temperate drinking," he declared, "cannot be too severely reprobated."[19]

Mott's name was even used to sell cleaning products like *Lyon's Magnetic Powder and Magnetic Pills*, "guaranteed to clear a dwelling of bed bugs, cockroaches, rats and mice."[20]

Dr. William Gibson (1788–1868), the other of Cooper's American pupils Issachar cited, was considered the best lecturer in America in his day and was renowned for his prodigious memory.[21] Gibson's testimonial was similarly a fake.

With all the suspicions about Zacharie's testimonials from Astley Paston Cooper, Valentine Mott, and the other physicians he cited, how much faith can we have that any of his testimonials are authentic? Are the testimonies he recorded in *Corns*, his certificate book, from some of the most famous politicians and other luminaries in America any more truthful? It turns out they are, which is why the man is such an anomaly. He was as skilled as the false medical endorsements he cited said he was.

* * * * * * * *

In a letter Zacharie wrote to President Lincoln in 1863, he said it had been his "good fortune to have secured the friendship of many of our most distinguished statesmen, commencing in my boyhood with the great Henry Clay...."[22] Mentioning his having "secured" Clay's friendship would have more than impressed Lincoln. Senator, congressman, speaker of the House, secretary of state (1825–1829), and three-time presidential candidate (in 1824, 1832, and 1844), Clay was Lincoln's "ideal of a great man."[23]

Clay wrote two endorsements for Issachar. The first, dated January 29, 1848, took "great pleasure in saying Dr. Zacharie operated on me for Corns in Washington with perfect comfort, and to my entire satisfaction, and I derived great and immediate benefit from the exercise of his skill and judgement." The second, dated May 22, 1849, and written from Ashland, Clay's Lexington, Kentucky, plantation, stated, "Since January, 1848, when Dr. Zacharie operated on my feet, there has been no return of my Corns, and I have been completely exempt from them, and my feet always comfortable."[24]

"That commendation naturally opened many doors to the young chiropodist," writes Jonathan Sarna in his and Benjamin Shapell's landmark *Lincoln and the Jews*.[25] Within the year, Zacharie had additional testimonies from Alabama Senator Dixon H. Lewis ("Dr. Zacharie has surprised me by extracting two Corns and one nail from my smallest toe without a particle of pain," February 29, 1848),[26] Michigan Senator Lewis Cass ("Dr. Zacharie has operated upon my feet with great skill, affording immediate relief without causing the slightest pain," September 12, 1848),[27] Missouri Senator Thomas Hart Benton ("Dr. Zacharie has operated on several Corns on my feet with the most perfect comfort to myself," September 24, 1848),[28] Supreme Court Justice R. C. Grier ("I take pleasure in testifying to the skill of Dr. Zacharie,

6. "A humble individual"

having experienced great relief from his opeations,"September 1848)[29] and John C. Calhoun, former vice president, secretary of state, and South Carolina senator ("I take pleasure in saying Dr. Zacharie extracted my Corns without the slightest pain, and to my entire satisfaction," November 1848).[30]

Professor Hugh Holmes Maguire's testimony ("I have had two Corns removed by Dr. Zacharie … the method is new and I believe will provide a radical cure"), however, is implausible. Maguire's statement is dated November 1, 1848. The professor would have been 13 years old at the time![31] Another testimony from Judge J. Harlan, dated May 17, 1849, is equally fishy. His honor would have been a 16-year-old boy when he "derived much benefit from his [Issachar's] labors."[32]

Advertisements in the *Washington Daily Whig* and the *Daily National Intelligencer* corroborate that Zacharie was living in Washington when those testimonials were dated.[33] Either they were backdated or dated incorrectly, or Zacharie made some of them up. Historian Charles M. Segal was certain they were all authentic. His reasoning was that many of the people whose testimonials appear in Issachar's *Certificate Book* were still alive when they allegedly wrote them and they would have denied making those statements if they knew of them.[34] That presumes the people whose testimonials were in the book knew they were in it or cared. Valentine Mott would certainly have known his name was being used to sell nostrums, but unlike the Duke of Wellington, he did not take legal action to have his fake endorsements removed.

The only way to be really sure any of Issachar's endorsement were authentic is to compare the handwriting and signatures in his book with the handwriting and signatures of those cited from other sources. I was able to do this for Henry Clay and Samuel D. Lecompten.[35] I did not have access to the handwritten version of Issachar's original certificate book, now in the Shapell Collection, but samples are reproduced in Sarna and Shapell's *Lincoln and the Jews*. Based on those handwriting samples and signatures, those endorsements are without question authentic.

This leads to at least two intriguing questions. How did Zacharie approach Henry Clay and the other prominent politicians in the first place? They did not travel in the same social circles. Did Zacharie just walk up to them in Washington, introduce himself, and say he would be more than happy to relieve them of any corns or other foot ailments free of charge? And why did Clay write him a second testimonial? Did someone question Clay's endorsement and Zacharie wrote to him for a second to prove its authenticity? It's improbable Clay wrote them without prompting from Zacharie. But even with endorsements from Washington's elite, there still weren't enough patients for Zacharie to remain in Washington.

7

California

Issachar was living with his family at 402 N. Street in Baltimore, cutting corns and marketing "Dr. Zacharia's Celebrated Corn Elixir," when his second son, Samuel Purdy, was born in 1848.

With so many testimonials from so many eminent personages, Issachar should have had a thriving practice, but it was not thriving enough for his ambition. There were stories of men making fortunes overnight on the other side of the continent. He wanted his share of the pie.

In January 1848, two years after California became part of the United States, gold was discovered at Sutter's Mill in northern California. The discovery ignited gold-rush fever across much of the world. Thousands came from England, France, Holland, Eastern Europe, and as far away as Australia to make their fortunes. San Francisco's harbor wasn't large enough to accommodate the schooners, ships, brigs, and other vessels bringing passengers and cargoes from abroad. Shipments had to remain aboard for days because there were not enough places on shore for storage.

"A most singular state of things prevails here … without precedent in the history of the world," wrote a newly arrived "intelligent merchant." "All we heard in the States about the gold mines is fully confirmed here. There is gold in abundance. All who go to the mines do well—some return with fortunes; new discoveries are made every day. The millennium, so far as plenty of gold is concerned, cannot be far off. That this mining region, so extensive and so rich, and traveled over by Indians for hundreds of years, should have remained a secret is certainly astonishing."[1]

Although many Jews came to dig in the gold fields, most, including Issachar, had no intention of moiling for gold in the muck. They were not besotted with what lay under the earth. They came to do what they knew best—to get gold by selling the axes, shovels, pans, crockery, shirts, pants, hats, shoes, and other essentials miners needed in their quest for riches.

Some like the "intelligent merchant" loaded their wagons and headed for the mine fields. "Everything is selling very high at retail," the "intelligent merchant" beamed. Flour was $4 a pound, $800 a barrel. Shoes could be had for $50 a pair; pants for $40. "A paltry launch of a few tons of flour or other items earns $1200 or $1500 in a few days." Anything with a steam engine capable of transporting goods inland was a fortune in itself. One merchant offered $8,000 for a leaky launch that might sell for $100 or $150 in the East and had buyers begging him to take their money.[2] Other entrepreneurs went into business as hoteliers, livery stablers, saloon keepers, pharmacists, bathhouse owners, booksellers, jewelers, watchmakers, theater owners, or any other kind of business that catered to miners who came back from the fields with and without their pouches and nuggets of gold.

Most of the newly arriving Jews settled in San Francisco, the Gold Rush's commercial center. A newspaper described them as a "distinct class of dealers in boots and clothing" who had "almost a monopoly of the business."[3] Others set up shops in Sacramento, the gateway to the northern mines, or Stockton, the starting point for the southern diggings. Most of the newcomers, Jewish or otherwise, were unmarried men or men who left their families behind until they could get financially settled. Once they got themselves habituated, they sent for or returned to their homes to bring their wives and children, siblings, and parents.

* * * * * * * *

In a room above Lew Franklin's wood-framed store on Jackson Street near Kearny, where just hours before Franklin had been weighing and paying for gold dust, 50 Jewish men and 18-year-old Mrs. Hanna Solomon Keesing held an impromptu Yom Kippur service on September 26, 1849. It was the first Jewish service on the Pacific coast.[4] A few days later, a steamer arrived with news that the "49 Service," the holiest day in the Jewish calendar, had been observed on the wrong day.[5]

Soon after arriving in San Francisco in 1850, August Helbing, a single-minded, energetic German-Jewish immigrant, founded the Eureka Benevolent Society, the first of many Jewish self-help organizations. Within a few years, so many Jews had headed west that there were Jewish benevolent societies in Nevada and Montana, before there was even one in Delaware.[6] Helbing's purpose in starting a benevolent society was to provide San Francisco's Jews with a

> suitable ways of spending our evenings. Gambling resorts and theatres, the only refuge then existing in 'Frisco to spend an evening, had no attraction for us. We passed the time back of our stores and often times were disgusted and sick from the loneliness of our surroundings. Besides, our services were in active demand; every steamer brought a number of co-religionists, and they did not always come provided with means. In fact, some came penniless, having invested their all in a passage to the Coast.[7]

The Eureka Benevolent Society and America's other Jewish benevolent societies were committed to helping indigent Jews. They were not overly religious. The one thing they insisted upon was Jewish burial. In a very real sense, writes historian Jacob Marcus, "it was often the cemetery that motivated Jews settling in new communities to bond together and kept Judaism alive. Once a congregation was formed, one of their members became the *shochet* (ritual slaughterer), *mohel* (ritual circumciser) and *malamed* (teacher). The next step was to buy an old church building and convert it into a synagogue."[8]

Helbing's own story is worth telling for no other reason than to show that while they were mainly shopkeepers, California's enterprising Jews were no pushovers. "When I was young," Helbing recalled. I was "as strong as a lion. I had taken two prizes as an athlete in Munich, and had gone to America in spirit of adventure."

Helbing and a friend had made their way across Panama, bought passage for California, and then waited in their stateroom for their steamer to head up to San Francisco. While they were waiting, another passenger who had bought a ticket at the head office in New York for the same room as Helbing claimed the room was his. Helbing refused to leave. The man sought out the purser. The purser told Helbing he had to vacate immediately. Helbing still refused. The purser summoned the captain. The captain tried to persuade Helbing to leave. When Helbing still refused, the captain threatened to have him bodily removed. Helbing wasn't intimidated. He drew a pistol from his belt, stuck it in the captain's face, and vowed he would kill the first man who tried to enter his room. "I had paid for it and had a right to its possession. But right or no right, I would keep this room or die." The captain backed down. Not eager for bloodshed, his own or his crew's, he found accommodation for the other passenger.

Later that night, despite a drizzling rain, Helbing went out on deck for some air. Cuddled up in a corner, shivering with cold and wet, a man and his wife were holding their little child, keeping him as warm as they could. The family were Jews from Australia who had paid for their passage but couldn't get a room on board. Helbing brought them back to his room. He and his friend gave them their beds and went back on deck where they slept rolled in blankets.[9] The woman was Mrs. Hugh Simon, the first Jewish woman in California from Australia.

Issachar and his brother Eleazar docked in San Francisco in late 1849 or early 1850.[10] Like Helbing, they came by way of Panama. Long before there was a canal across the isthmus, steamers leaving East Coast ports docked at Colon, Panama's port city on the Atlantic. From there, Issachar and Eleazar trekked to the Pacific by flatboat and pack mules, through tropical jungles and mosquito-infested swamps, risking yellow fever and malaria, all the while on the lookout for local bandits. At Gorgona, where they rested, they spent a sleepless night nervously watching natives honing their machetes.

7. California

From Gorgona, they slogged their way to Panama City on the Pacific coast, where they boarded a steamer to San Francisco.[11]

* * * * * * * *

On June 14, 1850, less than a year after the first Yom Kippur service, the *Daily Alta California* reported "that one of the most solemn and impressive ceremonies of the Hebrew faith was performed yesterday at the Albion House."[12] The solemn and impressive ceremony was the first *bris* (ritual circumcision) on the Pacific coast.

In Judaism, circumcisions are a symbol of the Biblical covenant Abraham made with God. By tradition, all Jewish ritual circumcisions take place on the eighth day of life. The *mohel* (the person performing the ritual circumcision) was the only Jew in San Francisco with any skill with a knife—Dr. Issachar Zachariah.[13]

The baby was the eight-day-old son of Barnett and Hannah Keesing, the couple who had taken part in the first Yom Kippur service.[14] The Keesings were originally from New Zealand. Whereas most of the gold seekers from around the world came alone, most of the Australian and New Zealander men came with their wives.[15] The Keesings owned a combined boarding house and saloon at the corner of Jackson and Dupont Streets,[16] where they "respectfully invited (the public) to call and taste a glass. A reduction in price will be made when taken by the battle." This was down the street from where the first Yom Kippur service had been held. Downstairs, they sold malt, spirituous liquors, and beer, "drawn from a beer engine, the only one is San Francisco." The bris took place in a room upstairs. Keesing later became a wealthy real estate investor, selling prefabricated wood homes he imported from Australia.

* * * * * * * *

Issachar and Eleazar did not stay in San Francisco for long. There was too much competition. They decided to head 80 miles away to Stockton, which was also booming from the gold trade. In early 1849, Stockton was an outpost with one or two log cabins. A few months later, its harbor was packed with brigs, baroques, and schooners.[17]

In 1850, Issachar and Eleazar opened a small six by 10-foot clothing store on El Dorado Street.[18] They chose it because of its low rent and their willingness to endure whatever inconveniences it entailed to keep down overhead. They dispensed with fancy fixtures. They didn't hire clerks, working long, tiring hours themselves. They bought stock and sold it off as quickly as they could, with little profit. But their reputation for bargain prices brought customers to their door, and the profit from their "cheap store" accumulated. Once their business took off, they stocked more costly items.

Stockton was no bucolic hamlet. It was a rough and violent mining town. Home invasions and burglaries were commonplace.[19] A clothing dealer on Center Street near Issachar's store was robbed of $500 in cash and $200 in clothing. A servant boy walking across a bridge was choked by "two hombres, for the two dollars in his pocket."[20] The *Daily Alta California* groaned that Stockton had become "the rendezvous of a gang of desperate men who fear neither God nor the law."[21] "In defiance of weak, and badly administered civil laws," Stockton turned to "the more sure and just code of Lynch law."[22] Twelve minutes after a man shot another in a bowling alley, Stockton's vigilante committee tried, convicted, and hanged him.

* * * * * * * *

In a relatively short time after settling in Stockton, Issachar was one of its leading Jewish citizens and the community's *mohel*. He continued performing circumcisions in Stockton until early 1852, when Abraham Abrahmsohn, "peddler, tailor, miner and matza baker" took over the job.[23] Abrahamson had been a *mohel* in Germany. "Through this religious profession," he writes, he "had access to the richest and most prominent families" who didn't balk at his charging $50 (the equivalent of $1,600 today) for a circumcision. "I had much to do and in about half a year had laid by a profit of 800 dollars [equivalent to $26,000 today]."[24]

Issachar's and Eleazar's clothing store proved to be its own gold mine. From an initial investment of $50, Issachar realized a profit of $21,500 (equivalent to $700,000 today) in less than six months. Now wealthy, he bought a home at the corner of Grant and Park Streets and planted a flower garden and orchard.[25] Flush with financial success, he left his brother Eleazar in charge of their store and brought his wife and children from Philadelphia and sent for his parents in Charleston.

In the fall of 1851, Issachar became the founding president of Stockton's Hebrew Benevolent Society.[26] Weeks later, he headed a committee to ask Captain Charles Weber, Stockton's founder, to donate an area to bury their dead. Weber generously gave them a 100-square-foot block on what was then the edge of the city. The committee built a fence around the perimeter and planted cypress trees on the grounds. In 1854, Weber formally deeded the cemetery to I. Zacharie and the other trustees of Stockton's Hebrew Benevolent Society.[27] "The Jews have stolen a march on the Christians," the *Daily Alta California* told its readers. "They have provided a cemetery for their dead, which is enclosed with a strong, solid fence, and is in every way a credit and an honor to them. It is situated near the Calaverns. We are told that our cemetery is unenclosed and the swine root up the interred bodies."[28]

Issachar's and Mary Ann's first daughter was born in 1852.[29] They named her Amelia, after Issachar's mother. Grandmother Amelia stayed with the family only one more year. In failing health, she and Issachar's father went back east to live with their daughter Jane and her husband, Abraham Backer, in Savannah, Georgia.[30] Leaving his brother Elly,[31] as the family affectionately called Eleazar, to look after their store and his family, Issachar accompanied his parents back to Savannah, remaining long enough for his name, along with his father's, to be listed among the new members of Congregation Mikveh Israel in Savannah.[32]

Issachar's mother died in December 1856. Despite having left Stockton three years earlier, Issachar's family had become such a fixture in the city that Julius Eckman's newly launched *The Weekly Gleaner as a Voice to Israel* (1858), California's first Jewish-based magazine, printed two obituaries about her.

The longer and first notice informed readers that it had "a sad duty to perform in announcing the death of Mrs. Amelia Zachariah wife [who] departed this life at Savannah, Ga., surrounded by her family, with whom but a short stay was allowed her after her return from California. Mrs. Zachariah," it continued, "was the only daughter of the Rev. Eliezer Cohen, who for thirty years was cantor at the Hebrew congregation of Chatham England. The early religious impressions received in youth, were the faithful companions and supporters of our deceased friend in her age." The obituary went on to say she was a devoted wife who refrained from work on the Sabbath and holy days and was very frail in her last days before she left for Savannah. The second, briefer obituary stated that Amelia, a former Stockton resident, died in Savannah on December 26, 1856.[33]

Back in California, in August 1853, Issachar was elected grand marshal of the newly formed Masonic Grand Lodge in San Francisco. *The Ark*, the Masonic newspaper reporting the installation, informed its fellow Masons that it had "no knowledge of any of the officers except the Grand Master [who] is known as a most energetic, accomplished and efficient Brother, and under his administration the Order must prosper."[34] By then, Issachar was a pillar of the community, sending flowers from his garden, reputed to be the most beautiful garden in the Stockton area, to the city's various social gatherings. School children were allowed to have their picnics on Issachar's grounds, and Stockton's residents were generously invited to visit the garden. Those who cared to could buy peaches at $3 each from the orchard he had planted four years before.[35] Issachar's and Mary Ann's second daughter, Clara Louise, was born in 1854.[36]

Merchandizing had made Issachar a rich man, but he began to miss the kind of social life of a bigger city than Stockton. After a fire destroyed his and many of the other stores on El Dorado Street,[37] Issachar moved his family to San Francisco, where he resumed his chiropody practice and became more involved in the Masons. After he was elected the first "grand Master of Masons in California," he became one of the principal founders of the "Order of the Secret Monitor," an appendant order of Freemasonry, one of the many Masonic orders that didn't involve elaborate ceremonies.[38]

Issachar's chiropody office in San Francisco was located at 148 Montgomery Street. Had he thought of it, he could have advertised himself as not just the only chiropodist in all of San Francisco, but the only chiropodist west of the Mississippi.[39] His advertisements were little changed from his earlier pitches offering to show his certificate book, "containing certificates from many of the most eminent men in the United Sates" to "all who may think proper to examine the same…. His success for the last fifteen years has been such as to warrant him in promising to all who may confide to his expertise…. His charges are quite moderate—trifling, indeed, compared with the relief and satisfaction he affords the sufferer."[40]

Eventually even San Francisco lost its allure, or perhaps an incident left Issachar so humiliated that he felt he had to leave. In November 1856, thieves burgled his apartment while he was asleep and stole all his clothes. With no clothes of his own, he wore one of Mary Ann's dresses to shop for a shirt, trousers and boots. Hoping to avoid being noticed by leaving as soon as the stores opened, he was seen in a clothing store dressed "in the latest style of female attire." He could forgive the man who stole his clothes, he was overheard telling the salesman, but if he found him, he would "lick the rascal that carried off his boots."[41]

8

"Prince of chiropodists"

Back in New York in 1857, Issachar waited a year to set up shop as a chiropodist and instead opened a grocery at 129 Eighth Ave., while Elly went into business as a perfumer at 278½ Hudson.[1] A grocery store was not what we think of today. Issachar did not sell fruits and vegetables. A grocery store in mid–19th century was a general merchandise store. Issachar sold the same items that had made him rich in Stockton—cloth, pins and needles, ribbons, buttons, shoes, and other dry goods, patent medicines, and liquor.[2] A year later, he bought a three-story brick house at 760 Broadway between Eighth and Ninth streets (the site is now a Loft department store) and resumed his profession, "curing bunions and enlargements of the great toe" from his office and upstairs home.[3] His next door neighbors were Hegeman, Clark & Co. Druggists, whose Cod Liver Oil was "recommended by the most eminent physicians," and a tailor shop.[4]

Broadway was New York City's main artery, a bustling, hustling thoroughfare lined with wholesale and retail businesses. "There is no street in London that can be declared superior, or even equal, all things considered to Broadway," wrote Charles Mackay, an English writer who visited the city in 1858. "It is a street *sui generis*." In his mind, it was truly American. There was no "uniformity in the design of its long lines of buildings ... each man builds exactly as he pleases ... the total absence of plan and method ... seems to be inevitable in a country where every man is a portion of the government and of the sovereignty, and considers himself bound to consult nobody's taste but his own."[5]

Early in the morning, horse-drawn carts and wagons brought food and other goods from the country to those hotels and markets along Broadway while the street was still navigable before the shops opened. Once the dawn hours faded and day took hold, the sidewalks swarmed with peddlers, financiers, and beggars. Newsboys and newsgirls, most of them Irish, peddled their papers on every corner and at the entrance of the main hotels. French, German, and Jewish dry goods jobbers, merchants, tobacconists, and other businessmen huddled together on six-cent horse-drawn omnibuses on their way to work. By the early 1850s, those horse-drawn omnibuses were carrying over a hundred thousand passengers a day,[6] leaving tons of manure in their wake that had to be removed, stored, and disposed of. Around 9 a.m., professional men, lawyers, doctors, theatrical managers, and clergymen made their way to their offices and places of business. On an average weekday, fifteen thousand omnibuses and personal horse-drawn carriages rumbled across the Broadway and Fulton intersection.[7]

Further into the day, women in bustling crinolines clogged the streets. "As regards the mere volume and circumference of hoop or crinoline," Charles Mackay chuckled, "the ladies of London and Paris are, to those of New York, but as butterflies compared with canary birds."[8] The *New York Tribune* was less sanguine about the fashion. "There is not only a craze for crinoline here, but crinoline itself is crazy—huge, unwieldly, preposterous, and offensive,"[9] forcing gallant men in a hurry to zigzag around them, carefully stepping off the sidewalk onto the manure-laden road to pass.

Visiting the city from Cincinnati for the first time, Rabbi Isaac Wise mused, "the great characteristic of New York … is business. People, it appears, care less for wealth, or the enjoyment thereof, than they do for a position in the commercial world. Everybody aspires to the high position of being one of the greatest merchants, bankers, manufactures or shippers. The highest compliment you can bestow on a gentleman is to tell him you never saw an establishment so extensive and well managed as his own."[10] A hundred and fifty years later, listening to Jewish stand-up comic Jackie Mason, you'd think he was cribbing his routine from Rabbi Wise.

The city's great industry was making and selling clothes. Tens of thousands of New York's Jews worked as tailors, milliners, shirt makers, collar makers, embroiderers, and seamstresses. By 1860, New York was producing 40 percent of all the garments in America,[11] many of which were sent to Southern plantations to clothe slaves.

Broadway's "business palaces" were its magnificent hotels. When the rich and famous came to New York, they stayed at John Jacob Astor's 309 room six-story Astor House at 223 Broadway, the "wonder of strangers" when it opened in 1836.[12] Henry Clay, Daniel Webster, and John Calhoun were regular guests. Webster said, "he would stay at no other hotel." William Seward lived there for 30 years. Lincoln was a guest there in February 1860, when he came to New York to give his Cooper Union speech, and again a year later, in February 1861, on his way to Washington for his inauguration.[13]

Although still in the Bowery district, the swanky hotels in the "sunshine" part of the city were far above the "shadow" of Lower "Mannahatta," as Walt Whitman called the lower Bowery section. The lower Bowery was where New York's worst overcrowded slums were located. It was where drunks, derelicts, prostitutes, and German and Irish working-class immigrants eked out existence.[14] It was also where native-born and immigrant gangs battled for turf. In 1857, the Dead Rabbits gang from neighboring Five Points and the "Bowery B'hoys" mixed it up and splattered blood at the corner of Bayard and Bowery streets in what came to be called the "Dead Rabbit Riot," one of the Bowery's more vicious street fights.[15]

During the day, the Bowery was alive with the sights and sounds and smells of shoppers prowling for bargains on Chatham Street, the center for the city's second-hand goods trade. "Asked to name the street in New York where the greatest number of dirty shirts were bought and sold, chances are ten to one you would name Chatham," said a New Yorker.[16] With an underlying antipathy, later turned into self-deprecation by Jewish comedians, the same New Yorker described Chatham's typical Jewish shopkeeper. He is "a great artist, especially in coats. Step into the nearest clothing-store in Chatham street and slip on a coat—any coat—and we'll wager our wedding-suit it is a 'splendid fit.' There is no such thing as an ill-fitting coat in Chatham Street. Every coat there fits everybody."[17]

Jewish merchants selling or buying used clothing for resale had street stalls cheek by jowl next to fruit peddlers and food sellers and merchants hawking trinkets, tools, and every portable item that could possibly be sold or traded. A reporter for the *Christian Register* who praised Broadway's Jewish merchants for closing their shops on their Sabbath was dismayed at the "poorer and less educated portion of the race" who "avenge this ecclesiastically enforced reticence by keeping open their places of business on Sunday as we walk through Chatham street (in the Bowery)."[18]

At sundown, the stalls all closed. The lower Bowery was a dangerous place after dark. Men who had to travel downtown at night always carried guns.

* * * * * * * *

Unlike in San Francisco, Issachar wasn't the only chiropodist in New York, and not the only chiropodist on Broadway, for that matter. Further down the street at 516 Broadway, directly opposite the St. Nicholas Hotel, chiropodists Littlefield and Westervelt offered the same services and "provided a separate entrance and rooms for ladies." Further up the street at 821 Broadway near 12th, "Madame Berhard, Chiropodist" offered to remove corns, bunions, and nails "at a moderate charge."[19] At fashionable 74 Fifth Avenue, Issachar faced competition from "Dr. Schlosser," "chiropodist to his Majesty the King of Bavaria and many of the principal sovereigns and dignitaries of Europe."[20]

Issachar was no slouch when it came to crafting for himself what *New York Times* columnist David Brooks calls "résumé virtues," the skills one brings to the marketplace.[21] Issachar's fabrications had started with fake testimonials from Drs. Astley Paston Cooper and Valentine Mott and likely the

Baltimore physicians he named in his earlier testimonials. He had lied about those associations. Why not about attaching the M.D. medical degree to his name? Anyone could call himself "Dr." There was no licensing requirement at the time for using that title. An M.D. after a name, on the other hand, was a title with prestige, backed by a university education.

Ironically, warning potential clients to be wary of "imposters who have from time to time, deceived the public," Issachar did just that. He tacked M.D. after his name and claimed he'd been awarded the degree from the Academy of Medicine in Havana, Cuba.[22] Making up bogus degrees from a foreign university is nothing new today. It is so common that the Federal Trade Commission has a booklet to help identify such fake degrees.[23] In Issachar's day, there was no Federal Trade Commission.

Issachar's claiming to have earned a degree from a Cuban university was ludicrous, but no one called him out on it. A degree from a foreign university has some plausibility if the person speaks the language of the country where that university is located. Issachar didn't speak or understand Spanish. He had never been to Cuba. Had he applied, he would not have been accepted. Havana's only medical school at San Jeronimo University, founded in 1842, only offered medical training and a medical degree after a preliminary four years of study in math, physics, chemistry, and other subjects.[24] By his own admission, Issachar said he had had very little formal education.[25] Issachar claimed he graduated in 1847 from the Cuban Academy of Medicine,[26] but the academy did not exist in 1847. It wasn't founded until 1861.[27]

No one could ever accuse Issachar of modesty. Once settled in his new office, he boasted how for the last 15 years as a "corn operator," he had earned the trust of everyone who had relied on his skill. Patients were welcomed at his office. If they preferred, he treated them in the privacy of their homes. His fee, he stated in his advertisements, was "quite moderate—trifling in deed, compared with the relief and satisfaction he affords the sufferer." He was also "happy" to look after their feet on a yearly contract.[28]

Despite these fabrications, Issachar's chiropodist skills were undeniable. The *New York Atlas* editorialized that New York's "professors of chiropody" were society's patrons and the best of these "Benefactors of the Human Race" was Dr. Zacharie of 760 Broadway, "the most successful [corn] operator of his class" the city had ever known. "We have tried him to our satisfaction and relief, [and]we would say to the army of sufferers from corns and bunions—go do likewise."[29] The *New York Atlas* was a Sunday-only newspaper with a circulation of 3,500, second only to the 9,000-copy Sunday edition of the *New York Herald*. Issachar beamed at the accolade and reprinted it in his certificate book.[30]

William Cullen Bryant, poet and editor of the *New York Evening Post*, was especially effusive in praising Issachar. "An indefatigable walker," Bryant "tramped" three miles every morning along the Hudson River from his home to his office in downtown Manhattan and three miles back at night. He kept up that journey for 50 years, not to mention his afternoon strolls. Walt Whitman recalled munching on bread and sausage with Bryant as they strolled through Flatbush. On one particularly long outing, Bryant walked 40 miles.[31]

Bryant had mixed feelings about Jews. Jews were "noble" and spiritual, had strong family ties, and a "disposition to triumph by intellect rather than violence," he said, but they also had an "unquenchable lust for lucre" and were like snakes "in search of prey."[32] But when it came to his feet, Bryant wasn't aware or didn't care that Issachar was Jewish. All he cared about was Issachar's guarantee he could relieve his troublesome corns, bunions, and ingrown toenails "in five minutes, without pain, so that the boot can be worn immediately without the least inconvenience to the patient."

Bryant was so satisfied and impressed with Issachar's skill that he wrote several articles on chiropody and became one of the Jewish chiropodist's most ardent boosters. "Treatment of diseases of the feet," Bryant editorialized, demanded "as delicate a hand, as nice a judgment, and as much anatomical knowledge, as that of diseases of the eye,"[33] Dr. Zacharie at 760 Broadway was "one of the best practitioners of the profession" he had ever seen. "He has no secrets or nostrums, depending entirely for success upon his knowledge of the structure of the human foot and the consummate dexterity of his operations. He coaxes out a corn by solicitations so gentle you feel absolutely refreshed while the operation is going on.... If you have a diseased nail, he will peel it from the toe with as much expedition as he might peel an orange and without drawing blood or giving pain."[34] Dr. Zacharie should be seen by everyone suffering from "all that torture and annoyance which those afflicted with corns are condemned to suffer." Dr. Zacharie is "the prince of chiropodists."[35]

A journalist for the Washington *Constitution* brought a friend to see Issachar about a toenail that was causing him pain and was similarly impressed. The toenail wasn't the problem. It was a corn growing under it. The only way to relieve the pain, Issachar explained, was to remove the nail to get at the corn underneath.

The patient blanched at the anticipated pain. The only way the corn could be removed from beneath the nail, he thought, was if Dr. Zacharie ripped the nail out with forceps. When Issachar assured him he could remove the nail without pulling it out, the corn-sufferer still hesitated, but held out his foot.

Issachar was as good as his promise. As the trembling patient looked away, he dissected the nail from the toe and removed the corn in less than five minutes. Minutes later, the patient walked out of Issachar's office, thanking him profusely for taking care of his corn so painlessly.[36]

* * * * * * * *

48 Part Two—I. Zachariah, Jr., Cheroperdist

Issachar could have been satisfied with the praise he had earned by his adroit skill, but he had a deep longing for public recognition beyond kudos from Bryant and other appreciative patients. He longed to be respected by men he respected. Fudging (a euphemism for lying) about one's background was no different in Issachar's day than it is today. According to "HireRight.com," about a third of job applicants lie on their résumés. The most common lies concern education and job titles.

Not being challenged about his fake medical testimonials and medical degree emboldened Issachar even more. He felt he had no reason to fear being held to account for his next elaborate fabrication, a full-length book about problems affecting the feet and how chiropodists such as himself treated them. The long-winded title of his 96-page opus was *Surgical and Practical Observations on the Diseases of the Human Foot, With Instructions for Their Treatment. To Which Is Added Advice on the Management of the Hand. Illustrations with Six Colored Plates,* By I. Zacharie, Surgeon Chiropodist.[37]

Zacharie in middle age, "A prince of chiropodists" (courtesy the collection of Robert Marcus).

When the book came out in 1860, Issachar was so well-known in New York that notices for the book simply advertised it as "Zacharie on the Foot." The *New York Tribune* told its readers, "among the books upon our table we find a small, neatly bound volume entitled *Zacharie on the Foot,* which contains a surgical and practical treatise on the diseases of the human foot and the proper remedies for their cure."[38]

William Bryant captioned his review of Issachar's book "The Poetry of the Foot." One would scarcely look into a book bearing this prosaic title for anything like poetry or entertaining reading material:

8. "Prince of chiropodists" 49

"Yet Mr. Zacharie manages to combine both with his 'surgical and practical observations. Of course, it is to the latter that the little volume, with its handsomely colored illustrations, is chiefly devoted.

"Mr. Zacharie gives a lucid account of the diseases to which the foot is subject, and maintains that the chiropodist is as necessary and important a member of the great body of men who have devoted their lives to the healing art, as the dentist. Fortunately, diseases of the foot are not as common as disease of the teeth, and thus there will fewer interested in the book than would otherwise be the case; but all those who haves suffered from their feet will be anxious to see what an experienced and successful chiropodist like Dr. Zacharie has to say on the matter. For others we extract the following chapter on THE POETRY OF THE FEET."

The excerpts included several passages from Shakespeare's plays.[39]

What would Bryant's reaction have been had he known Issachar had copied, almost word for word, Lewis Durlacher's 1845 book, *A Treatise on Corns, Bunions, the Diseases of Nails, and the General Management of the Feet*?[40] Even his title and dedication were copied from John Eisenberg's book, *Surgical and Practical Observations on the Diseases of the Human Foot*, also published in 1845.[41] Many years later, when Issachar published a second edition of his book in 1876, his title page read "New York, 1844—revised London 1876." Issachar deliberately misdated the first edition to leave the impression Durlacher and Eisenberg had copied him, rather than the opposite.[42] Issachar also backdated the fake testimonial from Dr. Valentine Mott dated 1858 in the 1860 version to 1844, but he made a careless mistake. The second edition, with the altered 1844 date, was dedicated to "Valentine Mott.... Emeritus Professor of Operatic Surgery." Mott didn't become "emeritus" until 1849.

* * * * * * * *

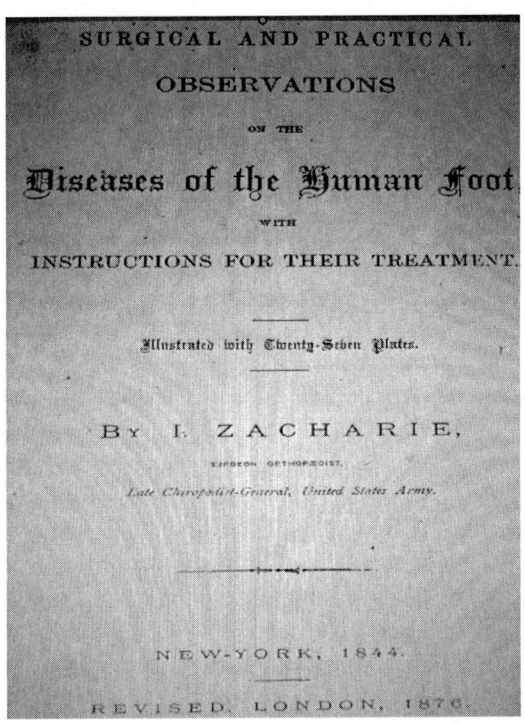

Title page of Zacharie's book. Note the back-dated 1844 notation.

Issachar's early goal in life had been to accumulate wealth. Now that he had it, he set his sights on climbing New York's social ladder. Social advancement was not easy. "American society rigidly observed the principle that it took at least three generations to produce a gentleman, the minimum prerequisite for acceptance into higher society."[43] One of his first efforts in social advancement was changing his surname from Zachariah to Zacharie[44] and jettisoning his "Jr." suffix.

A name is a person's identity. When Issachar changed his from Zachariah to Zacharie, it was not a minor change. For Issachar, it meant a new identity, a way of reinventing himself. His new name reflected the person he wanted other people to be thinking about when they spoke about him. It may also have been a business decision. By the 1850s, more than a million Germans, Jews, and gentiles had immigrated to the United States. Zachariah was a Jewish surname; Zacharie was German.[45] The image of the German-Jew in the 1850s was success. By then, there was a widespread conviction in America that someone with a German-Jewish name "would not disappoint."[46] Jewish community life in America derived much of its vibrance from the streets. Although Jews sold to gentiles more often than they sold to Jews, Jews preferred to buy and sell to other Jews. Networking, to use a modern term, was inherently a way of sustaining in-group connectedness and cohesion.[47] Changing his name from the Sephardic Zachariah to the Ashkenazi Zacharie was a way to encourage the now-predominantly German Jewish immigrants to patronize his business.

Dropping the "jr." suffix was similarly psychological and pragmatic. A "jr." implies much more than simple descent. It implies certain attributes. A "jr." is not just someone younger than the person he is named after. It implies someone lacking experience, someone in a father's shadow. Author Henry James hated being a "junior." He felt the name robbed him of his own identity; it made him feel diminished.[48]

Albert Arnold Gore, Jr., the 45th vice president of the United States, held onto his "junior" suffix when he ran for the House of Representatives and the Senate, but when he first campaigned for president, Gore dropped the "Jr." from his name because it called attention to his youthfulness. Despite jettisoning his own suffix, Gore juniored his first-born son. "Chatterbox" journalist Timothy Noah found Gore's naming his son "jr." "hard to understand, since Gore must have personally experienced the diminishment that comes from being a Junior."[49] Issachar Zacharie was not someone to let himself feel diminished in his own eyes or anyone else's.

Holding on to his "jr." would also have identified him as Sephardic. Ashkenazis do not name their children after living relatives. A name like Dr. Zacharie, Jr., would have labeled him Sephardic. Dr. Zacharie without "the jr." was Ashkenazi. Despite abandoning his public Sephardic name, privately,

8. "Prince of chiropodists"

Issachar held on to the Sephardic naming custom of not giving children traditional Ashkenazi Jewish names. When Issachar's and Mary Ann's fifth daughter was born in New York in 1858, they gave her the very un-Jewish name of Victoria Mariposa. Mariposa was the name of a gold mine on the river near Stockton where a lump of gold weighting a 130 pounds had been found.[50]

Acceptance into New York society also required conspicuous consumption. Issachar had to demonstrate his wealth. He had to be known as a somebody, someone who lived in luxury, gave lavish parties, and dressed extravagantly for his new social status to be visible. Issachar began dressing ostentatiously, wearing a "dazzling diamond breast pin."[51]

Mary Ann was no longer expected to be a housewife, cleaning the house, cooking and serving meals, and washing and ironing clothes. To be taken seriously by upper class society, the Zacharies had to have servants to do the household work. Mary Ann had to be a woman of domestic leisure. Soon after moving into his new home, Issachar placed a series of advertisements beginning with a "servant girl of all work." When he could not find someone "for all work," his next advertisements were for waiters, waitresses and cooks, "for a private family," and a nursemaid, "who understands the care of children," and a woman who could wash, iron and sew the family's clothes at her own residence. Applicants had to be "nice" and "clean,"[52] with a "kind and obliging disposition." None need apply unless they "understand their business." Those hired would be paid "the best of wages."[53]

When Issachar began hosting parties for New York's prominent elite, none of the cooks he'd hired satisfied him. Supposing foreign born cooks would be more up to the job, his next advertisement for a cook stipulated she should be "an English or German woman." When none of the women who applied seemed suitable, Issachar dropped the nationality requirement, although someone English or German was preferable. The most important qualifications were that she be "a good cook," "well recommended,"[54] someone "who understands cooking in all its branches, such as meats (and) pastry."[55]

Issachar was very demanding and not easily satisfied. Even if the food were cooked to perfection, Issachar's reputation as a gracious, elegant host would be slighted if the food he offered his guests was not served with aplomb. None of the waiters, "colored," "English" or "German" who applied seemed competent. Frustrated at their inexperience, Issachar's next advertisements clearly stipulated the prospective candidate had to "understand his business." He had to be able take full charge of parlors and dining room," including "how to make fires." Issachar was taking no chances. The applicant had to be "well recommended."[56]

Young boys hired to do odd jobs were just as hard to keep. In February 1859, Issachar was looking to hire "a smart, active colored boy from 13 to 18 to attend door and make himself generally useful." "Generally useful" meant "nice," "tidy," and willing to pick up around his office, as well as watching who came through the front door.[57]

* * * * * * * *

Hiring a "Colored Woman; one who is a good cook" meant he did not keep kosher. Issachar was not a practicing Jew. He was married to a Christian, and his children were presumably raised as Christians (with one exception, they would all marry Christians). He ignored the constraints and rituals of Jewish belief, but not its identity or solidarity. Whatever else, he considered himself a Jew. As such, he maintained an abiding interest in what was happening in the Jewish world. In the days before television and radio, when transportation between cities was measured in days, not hours, when news from Europe could take weeks to come to America, newspapers and periodicals were the only way people could learn what was happening in their communities across the country and the world. In 1858, an incident far off in Italy horrified the Jewish world.

Acting on Catholic canon law, Italian police had forcibly removed Edgardo Mortara, a six-year-old Jewish boy, from his parents in the Italian city of Bologna and placed him in a convent to be raised as a Catholic. The abduction was based on his nursemaid's testimony that she had secretly baptized the boy when he was one year old and sick, and in the nursemaid's belief, he was about to die.

The kidnapping galvanized Jews across America. A mass meeting of over three thousand Jews was held at Mozart Hall in New York to protest the outrage. An appeal was sent to President James Buchanan to intervene. The do-nothing president declined, saying he had no authority to intervene in the affairs of another country. In 1859, a Jewish delegation headed by Sir Moses Montefiore unsuccessfully met with Pope Pius IX to arrange the return of the boy to his family. Years later, Mortara became a missionary. Despite his Catholic identity, he still remembered his mother and attended her funeral in 1895.[58]

Issachar could read about what was happening in the United States and Europe in New York's 13 daily English language newspapers[59] and its various weekly and monthly periodicals. But the best way to keep abreast of momentous events like the Mortara case was through New York's Jewish newspaper, *The Jewish Messenger*. In 1858, the secular Dr. Zacharie took out a subscription.[60]

9

The Mystic Cords of Memory

Washington was enjoying a balmy spring during the first days of April 1861. Temperatures were in the 60s and 70s. The magnolia trees were just about to blossom. It should have been another pleasant season in the nation's capital, but instead, it was in turmoil. Reacting to the election of the "Black Republican" Abraham Lincoln in November 1860, seven Southern states[1] had declared themselves separated from the United States and had formed a new nation, the Confederate States of America.

President-elect Abraham Lincoln declared no state had the right to secede. No government, he said, provided for its own demise. During his inauguration speech, he had stated that as president, he had an obligation to "hold, occupy, and possess (the) property, and places belonging to the government, and to collect the duties and imposts, but beyond what may been necessary for these objects ... there will be no invasion of any state—no use of force against, or among the people anywhere."[2]

Speaking directly to the South, Lincoln said, "in your hands, my dissatisfied fellow countrymen, and not in mine, is the momentous issue of civil war." Lincoln closed his address with memorable words: "We are not enemies, but friends. We must not be enemies. Though passion may have strained, it must not break our bonds of affection. The mystic chords of memory, stretching from every battle-field, and patriot grave, to every living heart and hearthstone, all over this broad land, will yet swell the chorus of the Union, when again touched, as surely they will be, by the better angels of our nature."[3]

When Issachar woke on the morning of April 12, 1861, the better angels had taken flight. America was at war with itself. The new Confederacy had demanded the surrender of Fort Sumter, in Charleston Harbor. When that demand was refused, at 4:30 a.m., the "friends" became "enemies." General Pierre Gustave Toutant Beauregard, commanding the Confederate battery at Charleston, gave the signal to open fire. Moments later, a ten-inch mortar exploded above Fort Sumter. Confederate batteries then began pounding the fort into rubble. Major Robert Anderson, commanding officer at Fort Sumter, ordered his men to return fire, but the fort's guns did little damage to the opposing batteries. After 33 hours of back-and-forth Union and Confederate cannonade, with more than 4,000 shells being fired, Anderson surrendered the fort on April 14, 1861.

The following day, Lincoln called on each loyal state's militias to provide 75,000 volunteers to suppress the insurrection. "The insurgents [had] committed the flagrant act of civil war" by firing on the fort, said Lincoln, severing "hope of immediate conciliation."[4] Each state was given a quota of men to militarize. New York was charged with providing 17 regiments (approximately 13,000 men). Enlistments were to last for only three months, long enough, Lincoln believed, to restore the Union. That in turn resulted in four more Southern states declaring their independence from the Union and throwing in with the Confederacy.[5]

* * * * * * * *

At the start of the war, and for its duration, Issachar's father, his brother Eleazar, his sisters and their families were all living in the South and were as Southern in their views as their gentile neighbors. Southern Jews had made comfortable lives for themselves. Most had some kind of small business, but there were also Jews who were politicians and civic leaders, delegates to state conventions, chairmen of local political parties, active members of local Chambers of Commerce and various social and civic organizations, and members of Congress. Despite an undercurrent of anti–Semitism prevalent wherever they lived, the South's Jews regarded themselves as Southerners who were Jewish, not just Jews who lived in the South.

Speaking to a crowd of Jews and Christians at the dedication for Beth Elohim in 1841, Charleston's Rabbi Gustavus Poznanski had expressed a widely held sentiment among Charleston's Jews. "This synagogue is our temple," he told the crowd, "this city (is) our Jerusalem, this happy land our Palestine. And as our fathers defended with their lives that temple, that city and that land, so will our sons defend this temple, this city and this land."[6] Those sentiments were as true in 1861 as they were in 1841.

In late 1860, Issachar's father and his brother Eleazar had moved from Savannah back to Charleston. In January 1861, they both enlisted in the Charleston Home Guard in anticipation of imminent civil war.[7] Jonathan was almost 70 years old at the time. Enlisting in the guard was a pure act of Southern patriotism. As a British or Polish citizen, and at an age "not liable to ordinary militia duty," he was exempt from service. But like many Jews who had spent much of their lives in the South, Jonathan felt the same patriotic devotion as those who were born there.

The Home Guard was a mainly Jewish voluntary police force of 30

9. The Mystic Cords of Memory

mostly elderly men, several with white hair and whiskers, uniformed in long overcoats of homespun gray. It was captained by Myer Jacobs. M. Erlich was the guard's sergeant. Other members included J. Cohen, S. Cohen, C. Hyman, L. Rich, M. Rich, J. Triest, J. Volaski, J Wetherhahn, M. Wetherhahn, and E(leazar) and J(onathan) Zachariah. Jacobs was subsequently raised to the rank of colonel, but he died a few months later in November 1861.[8]

Some members of the Home Guard were Charleston's "oldest and wealthiest citizens, merchants, physicians, clergymen, lawyers, down to the humblest individuals in our community." All were "animated by the single motive of patriotism." When the war erupted, they all pledged to remain in the guard until the "young men on active duty shall return to their homes, and no further call shall be made upon them for service out of the city." One of General Beauregard's batteries pounding Fort Sumter into submission was commanded by Jewish Lieutenant Isaac Valentine.[9] After the fort surrendered, Anderson's garrison was ferried aboard the *Isabel* to a federal fleet outside the harbor. The *Isabel* was owned by one-time immigrant German peddler and now Charleston's shipping tycoon Moses Cohen Mordecai, who named it after his mother.[10] In December 1861, after the Charleston Home Guard was merged into the Regiment of Reserves,[11] Jonathan returned to Savannah to live with his daughters and their families. As a 30-year-old, Eleazar was subject to the draft but never seems to have served in the regular Confederate army.

Jews, it has been said, are like everyone else, only more so.[12] Jews in the South sincerely believed in the South's deeply held principle of states' rights. They did not question whether slavery was right or wrong; they simply accepted it as part of the Southern way of life. Southern Jews fought to preserve the South's customs and institutions, including its caste system, with the same patriotic fervor as gentile Southerners. They wore the same uniforms. They served as privates and officers. They dug latrines, drove wagons, did picket duty, killed and died for their commitment to the South in the same percentages as gentiles.[13] Rabbi Max Michelbacher of Beth Ahabah Synagogue in Richmond, the Confederacy's capital, published a prayer for the Confederacy's soldiers that began with the *Sh'ma*, the watchword of the Jewish faith and the oldest prayer in Judaism. It is the only prayer specifically commanded in the Bible (*Deuteronomy* 6:4–9) to be recited in the morning after one gets up and at night before one goes to sleep.[14]

Southern women as a whole, Jewish and gentile, were just as resolute and vocal in backing the Confederate cause. Phoebe Yates Levy Pember, a member of an elite Jewish family in Charleston, recalled how the "women of the South had been openly and violently rebellious from the moment they thought their states' rights touched.... They were the first to rebel—the last to succumb."[15] In Richmond, Catherine Moses told her son Ezekiel "she would not own a son who would not fight for his home and country."[16] Before the war, Southern women would never have imagined themselves doing tasks they readily committed themselves to in support of the war effort. Throughout the South, they rolled up their ruffled sleeves and roughened their hands making cartridges, rolling bandages, sewing uniforms, knitting socks and gloves, and assembling sandbag fortifications. They formed their own women's auxiliaries and organized clothing collections, solicited donations for families of soldiers, cared for wounded soldiers in their homes, and did whatever else they could for the cause. Some Northern generals believed their efforts in support of the Confederacy prolonged the war.[17] In New Orleans, teenager Clara Solomon railed at how Northerners were "raging an unholy and unrighteous war against us." In November 1861, just after leaving services at the Sephardic Dispersed of Judah, Clara and her friends and families and thousands of others cheered as the "grand review" of local soldiers marched down Canal Street. Clara beamed with pride at seeing her cousin, Samuel Myers, F Company, 4th Louisiana, at the head of his company imagining them pitching into the Yankees and giving them "a sound thrashing."[18]

Northern Jews were not under the same pressures to conform. Like other Northerners, they held different views of slavery. Three of the North's best-known Orthodox rabbis, Morris Raphall in New York, Isaac Leeser in Philadelphia, and Reform Rabbi Isaac Meyer Wise in Cincinnati, the editor of *The Israelite,* preached slavery was not a sin.[19] Rabbis David Einhorn and Abraham B. Arnold in Baltimore, Sabato Morais in Philadelphia, and Liebman Adler in Chicago preached against slavery. Prominent Jews who did not openly condemn slavery were singled out as Christ killers by fire-breathing abolitionists. The abolitionist editor of the *Liberator,* William Lloyd Garrison, viciously attacked Mordecai Manuel Noah (1785–1851), calling him a "miscreant Jew," a "Shylock," an "enemy of Christ and Liberty," and "the lineal descendant of the monsters who nailed Jesus to the cross."[20] Isaac Meyer Wise in turn vilified abolitionists, calling them warmongers. It wasn't Lincoln's election, he said, that threatened the destruction of the Union—it was Lincoln's and his supporters' "irrepressible conflict doctrine."[21]

As the editor of the *Jewish Messenger*, Myers Samuel Isaacs had the largest forum. Isaacs was against slavery but refrained from publishing letters for or against the institution. Isaacs insisted America's religious leaders should keep religion out of politics. His *Jewish Messenger* largely avoided political commentary not involving Jewish issues, but after Fort Sumter was shelled, on April 26, 1861, Isaacs wrote an editorial urging all Jews to "stand by the flag." Shreveport Louisiana's Jewish congregation responded to Isaac's editorial with a resolution rejecting Isaac's exhortation and wrote Isaacs that it was discontinuing its subscription to the *Jewish Messenger* and all Northern papers opposed to "our holy cause." Isaacs chuckled when he read the rebuke.

9. The Mystic Cords of Memory

Only one of Shreveport's Jews subscribed to the *Messenger*, and he hadn't paid his bill for two years.[22] Later on in the war, Isaac Meyer Wise did a complete 180 degree turn in his admiration for Lincoln, even to the point of maintaining Lincoln was a Jew. In a eulogy he delivered after the assassination, Wise told his congregants, "Abraham Lincoln believed himself to be bone from our bone and flesh from our flesh. Wise said Lincoln supposed himself to be of Hebrew parentage. He said so in my presence. And, indeed, he preserved numerous features of the Hebrew race, both in countenance and character."[23] When asked about Lincoln's Judaism, his son Robert answered it was the first he had heard about it.[24]

10

"A chiropodist of marvelous skill"

On Monday, April 15, 1861, the same day Lincoln called for volunteers, New York City's wealthiest businessmen and most influential citizens met on Pine Street to organize a huge mass meeting in support of the Union, to take place the following Saturday "We are either for the country or for its enemies," the Chamber of Commerce's president declared.[1]

A day later, after New York State's Legislature voted to call out its state militias, Colonel Marshall Lefferts, the commanding officer of the 7th militia, one of the city's oldest and best-known militia units, sent word to his men to prepare to leave for Washington. The 7th militia was known as the "Silk Stocking Regiment" and the "Blue Bloods" because it was made up of so many of the city's social elite, men whose surnames were Vanderbilt, Tiffany, Van Buren, Fish, and Hamilton. On Friday, April 19, the 1,050-man militia gathered at the armory in Tompkins Market and mustered into federal service as the 7th New York Militia Regiment.

At 4 p.m., Issachar Zacharie looked on as the "Blue Bloods" marched past his office at 760 Broadway toward the ferry that would take them across the Hudson River to the train depot and on to Washington. Perhaps he recognized several of the men marching by. The day before they left, he had advertised "he was willing to give the country the benefit of his professional services," offering to "relieve" all the men in the 7th Regiment and all men enlisting in every other New York volunteer regiment of their corns and bunions "gratis" if they visited his office between 4 and 9 p.m.[2]

The same day the "Blue Bloods" were mustered, the first blood of the Civil War was shed. The 6th Massachusetts Volunteer Militia had been the first state militia to answer Lincoln's call for volunteers. The unit was changing trains in Baltimore on its way to Washington when it was attacked by a jeering mob of secessionists. At first, the mob threw bricks. Then someone fired at the soldiers. The soldiers fired back. When the mêlée ended, four militia men and nine of their assailants were dead, and many more were wounded.

10. "A chiropodist of marvelous skill"

Word of the mêlée quickly spread across the nation. Tempers flared as both sides accused the other of provoking the riot.[3] In New York City, all businesses closed at 2 p.m. Many of the merchants gathered for a scheduled meeting or had at least one representative there. The organizers of the rally had intended it to show that "the chief representatives of [the city's] wealth and influence" supported the war effort.[4]

New York City and its boroughs would eventually send 22 infantry regiments of about one thousand men each to war. The most colorful regiments were the Zouaves, known for their distinctive dark blue jackets with red trim, red sashes with blue trim, baggy red pantaloons, and yellow tasseled red fezs. The 11th New York Infantry, composed of firemen from around the city, was organized by Colonel Elmer Ellsworth, a personal friend of President Lincoln, and was popularly called "Ellsworth's Zouaves" and the "Fire Zou Zous." Another Zouave unit, the 6th New York Volunteers, popularly known as "Billy Wilson's Zouaves," was manned by gang members and criminals from the Bowery.

* * * * * * * *

By the second year of the Civil War, the North was reeling from setback after setback. Everyone had envisioned a short war. Both sides had believed it would be over by Christmas. Northerners had been confident their superior manpower and industrial strength would bring the South to its knees and the country would be reunited in short order. The North had four times the population as the South. It had an overwhelming advantage in money. It had more industrial muscle. Its factories turned out more guns and heavy weaponry, more boots and shoes, more cloth for uniforms and tents. It had more trains and more ships. It could move more troops and supplies and transport them faster to wherever they were needed. It had a navy that hemmed in the South's major ports. The South believed it had the upper hand. It had the better military leaders. It had men who had grown up with guns and riding horses. It had shorter supply lines. For the South, it would be a defensive war.

In the first two years of the war, the South was not only holding out, but it was also beating the North. The war was turning into a bloodbath. Thousands of husbands and sons had been killed or maimed. There was no end in sight. Despite all its advantages, the North was losing. As more and more dispiriting news about the war sapped Northern morale, Issachar left New York for Washington, confident he could help the war effort.

Issachar believed the Army of the Potomac had what Lincoln called the "slows" because its soldiers were plagued by corns and bunions. Dr. Zacharie, said the *Indiana State Sentinel*, had "patriotically determined to dedicate his services to the Army of the Union."[5] If he could persuade the government to create a chiropody corps, with Issachar as its commander, he would not only be helping the war effort, but it would also be the opportunity for him to gain a recognition he craved apart from his reputation as a chiropodist.

Issachar knew he faced an uphill battle. A chiropody corps was completely new to the army. To make it happen, he would have to convince President Lincoln, Secretary of War Edwin Stanton, Surgeon General William Hammond, and the generals in the field of its desirability and effectiveness. Issachar was not naïve. He couldn't just walk into the offices of those leaders. He had to have letters of introduction and endorsements from influential people, people who were well known and highly respected. And Issachar knew who to approach first to give him that entrée.

Bryant was not just one of Issachar's appreciative patients who had written a glowing editorial about him, but he was also a personal acquaintance of Lincoln's. Bryant had introduced Lincoln at his February 27, 1860, speech at Cooper Union in New York, the speech that had launched his bid for the presidency. Since then, he and Lincoln had frequently written to one another, and Bryant was a frequent visitor at the Lincoln White House.[6]

On August 21, 1862, Issachar met with Bryant and told him of his idea to help the war effort by creating a chiropody corps "to inspect the feet of the men and keep them in order for marching." The "indefatigable walker" didn't need any convincing. He was more than willing to endorse Issachar's plan. He knew firsthand (in his case, first foot) how proficient Issachar was at removing corns and bunions and other foot ailments. An army was said to march on its stomach. Bryant knew that before that army sat down to eat, its feet brought it to the campfire. Bryant concurred when Issachar outlined his idea for a "Corps of Chiropodists" with himself as its "Chief." He wrote two letters of introduction on Issachar's behalf, one to Lincoln and another to Secretary of War Edwin Stanton.

Bryant's letter "To Mr. Lincoln" was brief and to the point: "The bearer of this note, Dr. I. Zacharie, a chiropodist of marvelous skill, as I have had occasion to experience, has desired I would say to you what I know of him. He is a regularly educated surgeon, whose operations on the feet are performed with a nicety and delicacy, which is truly surprising. If you or any of your family are incommoded with any disease whatever of the feet, he will be happy to give proof of his skill."[7]

Bryant's letter to Secretary Stanton introduced Issachar and urged him to consider his idea of a corps of chiropodists, headed by Dr. Zacharie, "to inspect the feet of soldiers and keep them in order for marching." "A soldier who cannot march," he said, "is a useless incumbrance." Bryant assured Stanton that Dr. Zacharie's skill in this branch "is truly astonishing."[8]

After handing Issachar those letters, Bryant also wrote a long editorial, "Chiropody in the Army," outlining the reasons the army ought to establish a chiropody corps. It was hardly a new idea in the history of war, Bryant

10. "A chiropodist of marvelous skill"

explained. Prussia's Frederick the Great had made a chiropody corps part of his army, and in no small way, it had led to its effectiveness. A reliable source, he said, had informed him that some Rebel commanders had chiropodists on staff to keep their men in marching order (this was not true). "The remarkable rapidity of some of the manoeuvres by which they have effected so much," he speculated, "is in a degree owing to this cause."[9]

Citing Napoleon's maxim "a general whose forces are inferior in number to the enemy, should do his best to make up for the difference in numbers by being able to march swiftly," Bryant protested "men should not hobble on corns nor limp with bunions, club nails and distorted joints, nor drag themselves along on swelled feet." In a not-so-subtle word of support for Issachar in his upcoming meetings with Lincoln and Stanton, Bryant commented how "only the professional chiropodist" (meaning Issachar) was competent to treat diseases of the feet. "Performed rudely and imperfectly," he warned, possibly from experience with other chiropodists, "the operation often does more mischief than it prevents."[10]

Bryant's article caught the attention of other newspapers across the North, which assumed the proposed chiropody corps had already been approved. The *Buffalo New York Commercial* informed its readers, "the Government is about to introduce chiropody in the army, and to have the feet of the men regularly inspected, and, if necessary, operated upon. This practice is adopted in some of the European armies."[11]

Four days after the *Post*'s article, the *New York Herald* waded in with the same headline and support. "We understand several gentlemen, medical and surgical, of the highest eminence, have united in recommending to the government the organization of a corps of chiropodists, to inspect the feet of the men and keep them in order for marching."[12] The *Boston Daily Advertiser* noted, "during the recent movements in Virginia many of our troops were injured in the feet by severe marching over rough roads—the shoes of many of them being of poor quality."[13]

"It has occurred to us," James Gordon Bennett, the New York *Herald*'s influential editor/owner editorialized, "this branch of surgery might be introduced into the army with very positive utility, not only with an eye to the comfort of the soldier, but the efficiency of the service. There can be no greater hindrance to rapid marching, or to celerity of movements of every sort," he said, "than the pain, irritation and halting propensities arising from afflictions incident to the feet, and almost inseparable from army life and exposure." Also citing Frederick, the Great and Napoleon, the *Herald* commented, "careful attention to the condition of the feet of their soldiery was what made their armies formidable. Humane considerations, not less than the efficiency of the service recommend the introduction of this branch of surgery; and under an able and skillful head an organization of operators throughout the army might be perfected of the highest practical value and importance."[14] It was unusual praise from the normally acerbic newsman, better known for his mocking sarcasm than for genuine tribute.

Issachar could not have been more pleased. He clipped the article from the *Herald*, attached it to a piece of his letterhead, and sent it to Secretary Stanton.[15] He sent another copy to Surgeon General Hammond, asking Hammond to give his idea of a chiropody corps his "favourable consideration."[16]

A week later, Issachar arranged meetings with George Opdyke, New York's Republican Mayor, and General Rufus F. Andrews, head of the New York Customs Office, to ask for their endorsements. Despite his view that slavery robbed "its victims of their dearest rights, and [sunk] them almost to a level with the brute creation," Opdyke had become wealthy manufacturing cheap slave clothing for plantation owners.[17] Had Issachar known Lincoln had no love for Opdyke (Opdyke had backed Salmon Chase, Lincoln's rival for nomination as president at the Republican National Convention in Chicago), he might have thought differently about asking for his endorsement.[18]

Unlike Opdyke, Andrews was a personal friend of Lincoln's and had supported his nomination at the 1860 Republican convention. Lincoln had rewarded him by appointing him Surveyor of the Port Office. After Lincoln's death, when Mary was distributing mementoes to Lincoln's personal friends, she gave Andrews the pen Lincoln had used to sign the Emancipation Proclamation.[19]

Both men agreed to support Issachar. Writing on mayoral letterhead, Opdyke recommended Dr. Zacharie "for your favorable consideration as the Chief of a Corps of Chiropodists, which, I learn, and I hope truly, is to be organized for the benefit of the country, by keeping in good marching condition, the feet of those who go forth to fight our battles." It was "unquestionably very important," he added, "all our soldiers, should be able at all times to command the use of their feet."[20]

Andrews' letter, dated a day after Opdyke's, was more personal. Addressing Lincoln as "His Excellency Abraham Lincoln, President," Andrews took "great pleasure in introducing to you my friend Dr. Zacharie." Dr. Zacharie, he went on, was coming to Washington "on a highly patriotic mission, which he will explain to you. If you can give him a hearing & examine his testimonials, I feel you will put him in the way of doing the country a good service in providing for the comfort of the soldier."[21]

Several days later, the *New York Times* also editorialized about the idea of "attaching a corps of chiropodists to the army" that had recently been broached in Washington. Issachar had not left the proverbial stone unturned. The *Times* could only have known about the idea from Issachar. Up until then, the only broaching in Washington was Issachar privately lobbying Secretary Stanton and Surgeon General Hammond. A chiropody corps, said the

Times, would be "decidedly utilitarian" by relieving soldiers of much of the fatigue and suffering imposed on them from "military locomotion." The *Times* urged Washington to "let the idea receive prompt and strenuous attention."[22]

* * * * * * * *

Armed with his letters of introduction and Bennett's and Bryant's "Chiropody in the Army" editorials that he had already sent to Stanton and Hammond for their "favorable consideration," Issachar left for Washington in September to personally lobby for his cause.

Wartime Washington was nothing like the Washington of Issachar's early career. The city was as squalid as ever. Most of its streets were still unpaved, and none of them was lighted except Pennsylvania Avenue. Clouds of dust covered everything. There were still no streetcars and no sewage system. Animals still roamed the sewers rooting for garbage. The air still swarmed with mosquitoes. The stench and squalor were not unlike his early years in Chatham. The main difference was Washington was under strict military rule. Mounted sentries were posted at every street corner. The city's hotels and boarding houses were full. Restaurants had long queues waiting for a table. Where Issachar managed to find a room isn't known.

Issachar's first visit was to Secretary of War Stanton. Edwin Masters Stanton, a short, stocky, full bearded man, did not suffer fools gladly. Initially, he had been no admirer of Lincoln. After the Battle of Bull Run (July 1861), he blamed the "imbecility of this administration … for the national disgrace."[23] As a private citizen, Masters' annual income had been about $50,000.[24] His sense of duty made him reluctantly agree to take over as Lincoln's Secretary of War in January 1862, at $8,000 a year, after his predecessor, Simon Cameron, was forced to resign because of corruption. Pennsylvania Congressman Thaddeus Stevens had joked there were limits to Cameron's honesty, saying he didn't think Cameron would steal a hot stove. When Cameron was told what Stevens had said about him, he demanded Stevens apologize. Stevens did. He said Cameron was not above stealing a red-hot stove.[25] Lincoln, no slouch when it came to a political jab, appreciated the wit.

Stanton was a workaholic, totally dedicated to his job. Within days of taking office, he wrote to the *New York Herald*'s assistant editor, Charles Dana, who had supported his appointment, "as soon as I can get the machinery of the office working, the rats cleared out, and the rat holes stopped we shall move."[26] Dana, he said, was "right in supposing my acceptance of the War office means 'thoroughness, earnestness, & no compromise.'" He would "not do the Lord's work deceitfully."[27]

Stanton was at the War Office promptly at 9 o'clock and left late at night. Fifteen-hour days were not unusual. Sometimes he didn't come home until early morning on the next day. When Stanton's carriage came into sight, the doorkeeper at the War Office leaned inside and said two words: "The Secretary." Nothing more had to be said. "Stragglers and loungers scurried to their desks." As he got out of his carriage, Stanton was beset with favor-seekers on the sidewalk. Sometimes he stopped and briefly chatted with a soldier or a needy-looking woman. Others were curtly told to wait in the reception room upstairs until called upon.[28]

Issachar waited with the rest of the visitors in the corner of Stanton's office on the second floor of the War Department until it was his turn. The room was stark. There were no carpets and no furniture other than the high, long desk that Stanton customarily stood behind facing the door. When Stanton came to work, it was to work, not entertain. Stanton gave no thought to privacy. Visitors bided their time until it was their turn and stepped up to his desk. Stanton did not like long-winded appeals. Visitors were told to state their business as briefly as possible and within the hearing of everyone in the room. When they finished, they received a prompt and final answer.

When it was finally his turn, Issachar handed him the letter Bryant had written on his behalf and reminded him about the clippings he had sent him. Stanton looked up at him through his thick eyeglasses. Issachar outlined his idea of creating an army corps of chiropodists to look after the feet of battlefield soldiers. Stanton heard him out but was non-committal. He saw some merit in the idea, but before giving Issachar a yes or no, Stanton sent him to confer with the country's foremost generals. Issachar would need their approval to move freely within Union lines.

Issachar wasted no time. Possibly with an introductory note from Stanton, a day or two later, on September 5, 1862, he met with "Little Napoleon," Major General George B. McClellan, the imperious commander of the Army of the Potomac. McClellan had a few foot problems of his own and was more than happy to let Issachar take care of them when Issachar assured him it would hardly hurt at all. Clipping McClellan's corns, Issachar outlined his idea for a chiropody corps. The operation went well. Before leaving, he asked McClellan to write him a testimonial for his certificate book. McClellan saw no reason not to. Dr. Zacharie, he wrote, had relieved him of "all trouble with my feet" without the slightest pain and "I am sure that the exercise of similar skill would be productive of great benefit to our troops, and save them from much necessary pain."[29]

A day later, Issachar treated Major Generals Ambrose Burnside ("I take great pleasure in acknowledging a kind service of Dr. Zacharie, by relieving my feet from Corns … much suffering in the army would be avoided could a proper attention be given to this subject; besides, it would add to the efficiency of our soldiers"), Nathaniel Banks ("I acknowledge with infinite pleasure, the services which Dr. Zacharie has rendered … to my feet … attention to the feet of the solider is as important as other medical assistance which is furnished

10. *"A chiropodist of marvelous skill"*

them"), and George Cadwallader ("Dr. Zacharie … has operated on my foot with much satisfaction … the efficiency of the army would be promoted by more attention to keeping the feet of the soldiers in good condition").[30]

Hearing about Issachar's visits to McClellan and the other generals, the *Boston Advertiser* jumped to the conclusion that a New York chiropodist had received authority from the War Department to cross the Potomac to Alexandria to inspect the feet of the troops. These men had just returned from continuous severe marching for two weeks over rough roads in Virginia. Because of the poor quality of their shoes, they had injured their feet and needed treatment.[31]

Other papers began building the story. The *Newport* (Rhode Island) *Mercury* told its readers, "Dr. Zacharia the Chiropodist, had been summoned to Washington to discuss the subject of Chiropody as applied to military pedestrianism," implying Stanton had been the one to ask Issachar about his proposal and not the other way around. The proposed chiropody corps, it opined, was "on a fair way to be accomplished."[32]

The *New York World* incorrectly reported Surgeon General Hammond fully supported the planned chiropody corps. It was obvious to Dr. Hammond, the *World* editorialized, one surgeon was not enough to take care of the army's foot soldiers. "If it is necessary to attend to the wounds of the soldiers after a battle, it is … even more necessary to attend to his marching capabilities anterior to the engagement. A chiropody corps of assistants specially educated to the care of the feet, in conjunction with or under the orders of Dr. Zacharie [would] be a direct benefit to the army, and will cause his name to come pleasantly into their memories when they contrast the subsequent with the anterior condition of their feet."[33]

Frank Leslie's Illustrated Newspaper reported Secretary of War Stanton had sent Dr. Zacharie to Surgeon General Hammond to discuss "military pedestrianism," and they were now meeting on a daily basis. "No fitter man could be made available than this gentleman (Dr. Zacharie), should the matter [of a chiropody corps] be seriously entertained."[34]

11

"Dr. Zacharie has operated on my feet"

Issachar shook hands with Lincoln on September 20, 1862. The two men could not have been more different. At 53, Lincoln was more than 20 years older than Issachar and looked it. Lincoln was sinewy, rawboned, and 6 feet 4 inches in height. He had long pendulous arms that tapered to long bony hands, big even for his large frame. His size 14 feet were even proportionately larger than his hands. Issachar was about 5 feet 7 inches in height, portly, and normally proportioned for his size.

The only facial features they had in common was a relatively large nose. Both men had beards, but they were nothing alike. Lincoln's beard was scraggly. Issachar's mutton-chopped beard was neatly trimmed. "Fashionable whiskers" was how the *New York Herald* described Issachar's facial hair.[1]

Lincoln had large floppy ears to go with his prominent nose. His eyes were deeply set; his eyebrows were bushy. He had high, prominent cheekbones. There was a large mole on the right side of his sallow, deeply furrowed face. An overly large Adam's apple bulged from his throat. During one of his debates with Stephen Douglas years before, Douglas had accused Lincoln of being two-faced. Lincoln shot back that if he had another face, "would I be wearing this one?"[2] Issachar had a full round face, smooth skin, and the energetic look of youth. His ears weren't overly large or small for his head. He had no moles or other distinguishing facial features, and his hair had begun to recede.[3]

They were also opposites when it came to what they wore. Lincoln dressed casually. He wasn't slovenly, but he was careless about his clothes. Issachar was fastidious. He dressed nattily and sported a "dazzling diamond stick pin in his vest."[4]

Entering Lincoln's office, Issachar wasn't impressed. The floor was covered with oil cloth. A large walnut table, laden with maps and books, occupied much of the room. There were two horsehair sofas, several wooden chairs, and a fireplace. When he came in, Lincoln was sitting at a dilapidated

11. "Dr. Zacharie has operated on my feet"

desk. As the tall lanky President rose from his chair and walked over to greet him, the chiropodist could not help noticing Lincoln walked with a loose, almost unsteady gait.[5]

After shaking hands and a few pleasantries, Issachar handed Lincoln the letter of introduction Bryant had written on his behalf and showed him the testimonials McClellan and the other generals had just written for him. Issachar said he had been informed Lincoln was having problems with his feet and was more than happy to relieve him of his discomfort.[6] Issachar didn't broach his idea of a chiropody corps just yet. What better way to convince Lincoln of its potential value and his own skill than by a firsthand demonstration?

Lincoln didn't pay much attention to his own appearance or his clothes, but he was very much mindful of his oversized feet. His bootmaker, Dr. Kahler, had a card Lincoln gave him to show John Hay, Lincoln's secretary. "When this man comes," the card read, "show him right in." On one occasion, Dr. Kahler arrived in the middle of Lincoln's cabinet meeting. After showing Hay the card, Hay led him into the room. Lincoln looked up and without pausing slipped off his boots and stepped on to a piece of paper Kahler had placed on the floor to trace the outlines of his feet. At another cabinet meeting, Lincoln told his cabinet the "state of their minds indicated they need to be measured for new shoes."[7] Lincoln's corns were so bothersome that when he wasn't walking or riding or was at the Soldier's Home, his summer retreat, he wore soft goatskin slippers.[8]

* * * * * * * *

Assured by the testimonials Issachar had just handed him that he was not a charlatan, at least when treating foot problems were concerned, Lincoln sat down in his chair, removed his slippers, and stuck out a bare foot.[9] Issachar removed his jacket, seated himself in a chair opposite the president, took hold of the bony foot, and carefully examined it. Spreading Lincoln's toes apart, Issachar felt the thickened corns on the top of his toes and the bunion bump where Lincoln's big toe joined his foot. Then he opened his instrument bag, laid out his rasps and fine-grained sandpaper, dabbed Lincoln's corns with silver nitrate to harden them, and carefully scraped away the dead skin.

As Issachar packed up his equipment, he made his usual request for a testimonial. Lincoln saw no reason not to comply and wrote out a few words:

> Dr. Zacharie, has with great dexterity, taken some troublesome corns from my toes— He is now treating me, and I believe with success, for what plain people call backache. We shall see how it will end.
> Sep. 20, 1862   A. Lincoln[10]

It ended well. On September 22, 1862, five days after Lincoln announced his preliminary Emancipation Proclamation declaring slaves would officially be emancipated as of January 1, 1863,[11] Issachar was back at the White House treating Lincoln's back and wrist, along with his corns.[12] Before Issachar left, Lincoln wrote him another testimonial:

> Dr. Zacharie has operated on my feet with great success, and considerable addition to my comfort.
>
> Sept. 22, 1862   A. Lincoln[13]

After handing him the testimonial, Lincoln told him to come back the next day, and he would write him a letter endorsing his chiropody corps. The following day, September 23, 1863, Issachar had the promised testimonial. Lincoln had asked him to come back so Secretary of State William Seward could cosign it. Seward had no hesitation in lending his name to the proposal; Issachar had previously scraped away Seward's corns as well:

Abraham Lincoln: "Dr. Zacharie has operated on my feet with great success, and considerable comfort." 1864 (courtesy Library of Congress).

> Executive Mansion
> Washington, D.C. Sept. 23, 1862
>
> From numerous testimonials of the highest character, and from personal experience,[14] we approve the very great success of Dr. I. Zacharie in operating upon corns, bunions, and other troubles of the feet, by which instantaneous relief is afforded, and we desire the soldiers of our brave army may have the benefit of his surprising skill.
>
> Lincoln
> William H. Seward[15]

The next day, Issachar showed Lincoln's and Seward's endorsements to Secretary Stanton at the War Office. Stanton had more pressing issues on his mind than questioning something he considered trivial. He had questioned Lincoln's policies on other matters relating to the war, but he did not foresee any risk of allowing this foot doctor to travel within Union lines. Still, Stanton was not a man to act on impulse. He told Issachar to come back the next day. On September 24, 1862, Stanton issued Issachar an official pass.

11. "Dr. Zacharie has operated on my feet"

<pre>
                                War Department
                                Washington, D.C., Sept.24, 1862
</pre>

Dr. I. Zacharie has permission to pass within the lines of the United States forces around Washington and on the Potomac for the purpose of operating upon the feet of the soldiers for corns, bunions, & this pass to continue for thirty days.[16]

In November, General John Tucker, Assistant Secretary of War, extended the pass for another 60 days.[17]

September 25, 1862, the day after he received Stanton's pass, was the first day of Rosh Hashanah, the Jewish New Year. Zacharie's whereabouts during the Jewish holidays of Rosh Hashanah in September or Yom Kippur, a week later, are not known. In mid–October he left Washington for Fortress Monroe."

Secretary of War Edwin M. Stanton: "Dr. I. Zacharie has permission to pass within the lines of the Unites States forces around Washington and on the Potomac for the purpose of operating upon the feet of the soldiers for corns, bunions, & this pass to continue for thirty days." Ca. 1865 (courtesy Library of Congress).

12

"Ode to Dr. Zacharie"

James Gordon Bennett, the *New York Herald*'s editor, was a staunch supporter of the Union. But like many New Yorkers, he rejected abolition and supported slavery, which he deemed the "natural position of the Southern colored races."[1] Abolitionist William Goodell called the *Herald* a "pestilent sheet" and denounced its editor as a traitorous secession sympathizer.[2]

Bennett was a pioneering newspaperman. He had emigrated to the United States from Scotland and still spoke with a broad Scottish accent. He had a long narrow head, a firm jaw, a prominent aquiline nose, a perpetual squint, and a giant-sized ego. He founded the *Herald* in 1835 and turned it into the most widely read and influential newspaper in America. Bennett's *Herald* pioneered many of the features that are now the stock-in-trade of modern-day news media, including a sports section, interviews, photos, banner headlines, weather reports, gossip, and paid ads. The *New York Times*' motto, "All the News Fit to Print," writes *Times* columnist Ted Widmer, was almost certainly a riposte for the *Herald's* willingness to print anything.[3] New York diarist George Templeton Strong wasn't a fan of Bennett's gossipy and often vitriolic editorials. Strong opined that Bennett had "done more than any living man to debase American journalism."[4]

Bennett was no fan of Lincoln. Prior to Lincoln's 1860 election, Bennett called him an "illiterate Western boor" "without education and refinement," in short, a "vulgar village politician."[5] On April 14, 1861, after a mob almost destroyed his paper's offices, Bennett clipped his talons for the time being. As a gesture of goodwill, he assured Lincoln that hereafter the *Herald* would be "unconditionally for the radical suppression of the Rebellion by force of arms." Never one to back down completely, Bennett held out a wilted olive branch. As a further gesture of goodwill, he offered his playboy son's yacht for government service.[6]

Lincoln was more than aware of Bennett's influence on public opinion and courted his amity. On those occasions when Bennett's editorials had been favorable, Lincoln wrote him personal notes thanking him for his "able support."[7] Lincoln had never seen a yacht, let alone known anyone who owned one. But he was astute enough to accept the olive branch, wilted or not. In return, he arranged a desirable commission in the navy for Bennett's son. Lincoln also quashed a congressional investigation into the *Herald*'s leaking of his annual message to Congress. (Lincoln's wife had been charmed by one of Bennett's employees and had let him make an advance copy.)

Bennett may not have been a "secession sympathizer," but he was less than a staunch Lincoln supporter. When he could, he gleefully stepped on Lincoln's toes with a sharp pun. In October 1862, Bennett ragged that Lincoln's proposed Emancipation Proclamation had had something to do with the corns on his feet that Dr. Zacharie was treating. Learning of Issachar's testimonials from Lincoln and Seward, Bennett wrote a long editorial he titled, "The Head and Feet of the Nation."[8]

> It is a true but trite maxim great events are determined by insignificant causes. It is no less trite and true that the most important decisions of the mind are often controlled by small but aggravating ailments of the body. Tight boots have been the origin of many a family quarrel which has unhappily resulted in divorce. From evidence before us, "we are inclined to believe that many of the haps and mishaps of the nation, during this war, maybe traced to a matter no greater than the corns and bunions which have afflicted the feet of our leaders.[9]

The President, for one, hadn't been able to resist abolitionists' badgering for emancipation, said Bennet, because of his aching feet. "How could the President put his foot down firmly," Bennet mocked, "when he was troubled with corns?" Had Dr. Zacharie doctored him earlier, Lincoln might never have thought of it.[10]

Bennett mused that foot ailments were also responsible for the "personal animosities and ill-timed bickerings among the members of Lincoln's Cabinet." Undoubtedly their animosities and bickerings were caused "by the honorable Secretaries inadvertently treading upon each other's bunions under the council board."[11]

The reason some of the country's generals hadn't moved their men more quickly into battle was also because of the army's corns, a sarcastic swipe at Issachar's chiropody corps. "It would seem, therefore, that all our past troubles have originated not so much with the head as with the feet of the nation. Dr. Zacharie has shown us precisely where the shoe pinches and he now proposes [referring to Issachar's chiropody corps], to remove the difficulty."[12]

Bennett ended his lampoon by saying now that the nation's leading statesmen and generals had certified they had been completely cured of their corns and bunions, the war should be over before January 1, 1863. "If this expectation be disappointed, we shall certainly suggest someone be found to operate upon the heads of our rulers, and to remove the corns, bunions and proud flesh from their brains, as Dr. Zacharie has from their feet."[13]

Lincoln was not at all offended by Bennett's jabs. Just the opposite.

Lincoln liked a good joke, even at his own expense. Visitors could always tell when he was about to regale them with a humorous anecdote. Just before a jest, a half-suppressed smile appeared on his face in anticipation of the pleasure his visitors would have upon hearing it.[14] One newspaper claimed some of Lincoln's off-color stories were smutty jokes Issachar had told him.[15]

The same month as Bennett's "Head and Feet" editorial appeared, *Vanity Fair* magazine paid tribute to Issachar in a humorous, although a less biting, take on his newly acquired notoriety, calling upon the "U.S.A. Chiropodist, to keep the toe-joints of our gallant boys in good repair."

ODE TO DR. ZACHARIE

King of Chiropodists, salaam!
Thy skill provides a sovereign bin
   For every toe cornuted,
Boots shone bright when thou was born
To bless a shoe-pinched world forlorn,
And tenderly of toughest horn
   Believe the tender-footed.

Our soldiers for the South en route
Are cursed with corns that sharply shoot
   As SHARP'S sharp-shoot rifle;
And, as their way they slowly pick,
Too often, goaded to the quick,
Find words suggested by old Nick
   Quite difficult to stifle…

When first thou didst arrive in town,
The gracious Abe his foot put down,
   A foot of full ten inches,
And in his roman manner said:
"Zacharie, old fellow, go ahead!
Let soldiers' corns be re-mo-ved
   Whenever the shoe pinches.

And now, O man of dexterous fist!
Thou're U.S.A. Chiropodist,
   And drawest pay and ration:
Millions of toe-joints are they care,
Oh! keep them all in good repair,
That they our galltant boys may bear
   To Treason's castigation."[16]

The poem was unsigned but is believed to have been written by William Cullen Bryant. A month before, a shorter poem appeared in *Vanity Fair* calling Zacharie the "MOTHER GOOSE OF MILITARY CORNS: Zacharie, Zacharie dock/The knobs our soldiers that balk;/Dispose of their bunyons/ That crop out like onions,/Obstructing their freedom of walk."[17]

* * * * * * * *

12. "Ode to Dr. Zacharie"

While *Vanity Fair* was calling upon the "U.S.A. Chiropodist" to keep "the toe-joints of our gallant boys in good repair," Issachar had already left Washington for just that purpose. With Secretary of War Stanton's pass in hand, Issachar was on his way to Fortress Monroe, on the tip of the Virginia Peninsula, 80 miles from Richmond. The fort guarded the lower Chesapeake Bay and was a major base for launching Union operations.

Issachar's mission did not go unnoticed and was widely reported, even by Southern papers.[18] The *Philadelphia Public Ledger* informed its readers Dr. Zacharie had gone to Fortress Monroe "to examine the feet of the soldiers, and remove any corns, bunions, etc. He brings testimonials from a large number of the commanding officers in our army, President Lincoln heading the list."[19] The *Ledger* knew about Issachar's mission to Fort Monroe because Issachar had had a broadside printed informing the rank and file at the fortress he had been authorized by the Secretary of War to treat their foot problems:

> "All Soldiers Having CORNS BUNIONS OR BAD NAILS Upon their feet, can have them CURED without pain, by the undersigned, who is with you, UNDER THE AUTHORITY OF THE SECTARY OF WAR. You will therefore have your feet EXAMINED, So as to keep them in good working order and FREE FROM PAIN. I. ZACHARIE, M.D., Surgeon Chiropodist."[20]

Fortress Monroe's commanding officer was 63-year-old "shoot him on the spot" General John Adams Dix.[21] Before the war, he had been President Buchanan's Secretary of the Treasury. At the beginning of the war, he had sent a telegram to treasury agents in New Orleans telling them, "if any one attempts to haul down the American flag, shoot him on the spot." The telegram was intercepted by a Confederate telegraph operator who forwarded it to Confederate authorities in Louisiana. They in turn leaked it to the press.

Within days, Dix's order appeared in newspapers throughout the North and the South, making Dix one of the North's first heroes and the South's first villains. From then on, he was "shoot him on the spot" General Dix in the Northern news media.[22] Dix was one of the 5,000 men whose feet Issachar treated at the fort, "to the entire satisfaction of all," said Dix.[23]

As with all things involving Issachar, his motives for heading a chiropody corps with himself as its commanding officer were never solely altruistic. As a commissioned officer, his expenses would have been paid for by the government and he would have received a salary. As a volunteer, he was not entitled to either a military uniform or salary.

Issachar had Stanton's permission to pass through Union lines, but he was still only a civilian with no official commission. Years later, relying on the same duplicity he'd used to give himself a medical education and degree, Issachar would claim Stanton had in fact commissioned him before he went to Fortress Monroe and petitioned Congress' Committee on War to pay him retroactively for his work. In 1862, he could not make that claim because Stanton was still alive and certainly would have been outraged had he done so. In any case, he could not have been commissioned as a military surgeon because such appointments were under the purview of the Surgeon General, Dr. William Hammond.[24] Issachar had written to Hammond before going to Fortress Monroe, asking him to authorize that commission. Hammond refused.[25]

Thirty-four-year-old William Alexander Hammond was a large man with a brusque and authoritative voice that expressed an underlying "arrogant and pompous" demeanor. He is best known for organizing the Army Medical Museum (now the National Museum of Health and Medicine. originally located in Washington and relocated to Silver Springs, Maryland). Hammond also initiated what would become the *Medical and Surgical History of the War of the Rebellion*, a compendium of reports by physicians treating the war wounded.

Before being appointed Surgeon General in April 1862, he had shown an aptitude for organizing hospitals and sanitary stations. His peers respected his ability, but he was not well liked. Officers more senior in rank resented that he was appointed instead of them.[26] Hammond's banning of calomel and tartar emetic, two mercurial medicines many army surgeons had long relied on as part of their drug treatments, made him even more unpopular with many of his colleagues.

Like many physicians, Hammond had a low opinion of nonmedically trained "corn cutters."[27] Issachar had previously sent Hammond the newspaper clippings endorsing his chiropody corps, but Hammond was not impressed. Even had he seriously considered the idea, Hammond may also have read a *New York Times* report that Dr. Zacharie was organizing his own department of a corps of chiropodists for the army with 25 assistants. Organizing a separate department without his approval, if true, was undermining Hammond's authority, and Hammond resented Issachar's going over his head to Stanton for a pass to treat the men at Fortress Monroe.

Hammond had not been Stanton's choice for Surgeon General. After his appointment, Hammond attempted to make the medical department independent of the War Department in constructing hospitals and transporting supplies. Other efforts to free his department from Stanton's oversight strained his relationship with Stanton even more. Hammond was not about to sanction a commission for Dr. Zacharie, knowing as he did that Stanton had allowed Issachar to go to Fortress Monroe without consulting him.

Two years later, in August 1864, facing court martial for taking bribes to buy inferior blankets for the army,[28] Hammond claimed he was the victim of a Jewish conspiracy. One of the reasons he'd been charged, he said, was because he had refused to sanction the commission of "the Jew corn doctor,

12. "Ode to Dr. Zacharie"

Zacharie."[29] The *Medical Times and Gazette* accused Issachar of forging the letters about Hammond's mismanagement that had led to his dismissal.[30]

Hammond's blaming a Jew for his troubles was nothing new. As often happened in times of national crisis, Jews were dogged by accusations of corruption and illegal profiteering in the war effort. Jewish manufacturers were accused of providing inferior clothing, tents, hats, blankets, and whatever else that could be attributed at their factories and businesses. Animosities barely dormant before the crisis rose to the surface. "The tribe of gold speculators" who "create distrust of the government" are "'exclusively hooked-nosed wretches,' speculating on disasters. A battle lost to our army is chuckled over by them, as it puts money in their purse."[31] Horace Greeley, editor of the *New York Tribune*, labeled Jews, "the most persistent and cunning contrabandits."[32]

13

"My own chiropodist is a Jew"

In the ancient city of Jerusalem, between Keren Hayesod and King David streets, writes historian Jonathan Sarna, professor of American Jewish history at Brandeis University, is a crooked street called Abraham Lincoln Street. Most Jerusalemites have no idea of why a street in their city is named after the American President. If asked, Sarna said, they simply shake their heads or shrug.[1]

Sarna is not the first scholar to unveil Lincoln's unusual relationship with America's (and Israel's) Jews, one that had all been but forgotten until his and Benjamin Shapell's groundbreaking book *Lincoln and the Jews* and Gary Zola's *We Called Him Rabbi* made us once again aware of Lincoln's unique relationship with this country's Jews.

Unlike many Americans at the time, Lincoln considered Jews as equals and advocated for them on numerous occasions. Three months after issuing his Emancipation Proclamation, Lincoln met with Henry Wentworh Monk, a Zionistic Protestant from Canada. Monk had come to Washington in March 1863 to lobby Lincoln to emancipate persecuted Jews in Russia, Turkey, and Prussia and to help restore them to their homeland in Palestine. Monk was Zionistic only in the sense that he believed that Christ's second coming would only occur after the Jews were back in Palestine, with Jerusalem as the capital "of a reunited Christendom."[2]

It is a "noble dream ... one shared by many Americans," said Lincoln. "I myself have a high regard for the Jews. My own chiropodist is a Jew." He "has so many times 'put me upon my feet,'" he quipped, "that I would have no objection to giving his countrymen 'a leg up.'"[3]

Lincoln's passing comment about his chiropodist is the only known instance in which he described Issachar as Jewish. Lincoln's attitude toward Jews in general had begun forming over the course of his earlier years in Illinois. Before he met Issachar, Lincoln called Abraham Jonas, an Illinois lawyer and state legislator, as "one of my most valued friends."[4]

Abraham Jonas was a slender man with black eyes and hair and a dark complexion. He'd immigrated to the United States from England in 1819

13. "My own chiropodist is a Jew"

after his brother, who had previously settled in Cincinnati, wrote there were great opportunities in what was then the western frontier. After his wife, the daughter of Rabbi Gerson Seixas (the first rabbi born in America), died in 1825, Jonas left Cincinnati. Sometime later, he opened a carriage business in Williamstown, Kentucky, and remarried. After he joined the Masons, he became active in Whig politics and moved once again, this time to Quincy, Illinois, where he studied law and served in the Illinois state legislature.

Lincoln met Jonas in 1843, when they were serving in the Illinois state legislature. Despite their different backgrounds, the two men found they had the same humor and wit in common, in addition to their similar Whig political views. When Lincoln debated Stephen Douglas in Quincy, Illinois, in the fall of 1858, for the U.S. Senate, Jonas was the local chairman of Lincoln's supporters.

Lincoln was seriously thinking about quitting politics for good after he lost that election and would have, had Jonas not strongly encouraged him to go after the nomination for president of the newly formed Republican Party. Once Lincoln made up his mind to make a bid for the nomination, Jonas worked tirelessly to garner support for him at the party's convention in May 1860 in Chicago.[5] Lincoln was grateful for Jonas' support before and during the 1860 election. In 1861, he appointed Jonas postmaster in Quincy. Jonas worked as postmaster until his death in 1864. Despite Jonas' steadfast loyalty to Lincoln and the Union, four of his sons sympathized with the South and served in the Confederate army. When Jonas' health began to fail, Lincoln secured a parole for Jonas' son Charles from his prisoner-of-war camp on Johnson's Island, Lake Erie. Charles reached Quincy just in time to be with his father when he died.[6] Several years later, Lincoln's Jewish foot doctor was not only another of his "most valued friends," but he was also "the most favored family visitor at the White House."[7] Quite possibly, Lincoln had come to regard Jonas and Issachar as American Jewry personified.[8]

Lincoln's close friendships with Jonas and Issachar were unusual in an age when Jews were considered outsiders at best and were frequently maligned by politicians and the press. In no small measure, Lincoln's efforts to overturn an exclusionary clause in the early years of the Civil War stipulating a military chaplain had to be "a regular ordained minister of some Christian denomination" was due to his earlier friendship with Jonas and the Jews of Springfield.[9]

Part Three

Spy and Diplomat

14

The General Prohibition

On the eve of the war, New Orleans was one of the world's major port cities and the South's main hub for exporting cotton from the upper Mississippi and surrounding areas. Over 30 different steamship lines docked in its harbor at one time. Cotton and other exports leaving the port were valued at over $108 million; imports came in at over $21 million. Such was its financial muscle that several foreign countries had embassies and banks in the city.[1]

Because of its strategic and economic importance, New Orleans was one of the first port cities to be blockaded as part of the Union's "Anaconda Plan," aimed at strangling trade in and out of the Confederacy's port cities. The blockade succeeded in ending virtually all foreign trade with the Confederacy. Business in the city collapsed. Stores and offices closed. Commercial banks shipped their gold and silver farther into the Confederacy's interior as a precautionary measure against possible invasion. Warehouses bursting with cotton and sugar that hadn't made it out of the city before the blockade were set on fire rather than allowing the products to be confiscated if the city fell. Thousands of unemployed workmen wandered listlessly through the streets. Many of the poor died of starvation.[2]

Confederate military strategists had believed any Union attack against the city would come from further up the Mississippi and not from the mouth of the Mississippi. Two masonry gun batteries, Fort Jackson with its 74 heavy guns and Fort St. Phillip with its 52 canons, guarded the entrance to the city 70 miles downriver, along with gunboats in the river itself. Eight hulks, joined by a heavy chain, obstructed naval passage further up the river.

On April 18, 1862, 43 Union ships commanded by Admiral David G. Farragut's Gulf Expeditionary Force began pounding Forts Jackson and St. Phillip day and night with mortar, while crew men in smaller boats braved shells raining down on them from the fortress to cut a gap in the chain spanning the river. By April 24, Farragut's 17 warships had broken through New Orleans' defenses. After brief resistance from within the city, New Orleans surrendered.

* * * * * * * *

14. The General Prohibition

On May 1, 1862, a 2,500-man occupying force headed by Major General Benjamin Butler took military command of the Confederacy's largest city. Butler was one of Lincoln's many "political generals," men given high rank not because of any military training, but because of their political connections. Lincoln disliked him intensely. Butler is "as full of poison gas as a dead dog,"[3] he said. But Lincoln needed support from the men who supported Butler.

A portly 5-feet 4-inches in height, Butler was both cross-eyed and burdened with a drooping left eyelid, a defect he had from birth. Mark Twain described him as "dismally and drearily homely ... the forward part of his skull looks raised like a water-blister."[4]

Determined not to brook any resistance from longtime residents who were overwhelmingly still loyal to the Confederacy and considered traitors, Butler reacted swiftly and mercilessly to quell any public support for the Confederacy. Within days of his taking command of New Orleans, he executed William B. Mumford on June 7, 1862, for hauling down the Stars and Stripes at the New Orleans mint. It was not officially a hanging offense, but Butler was mindful of General Dix's "shoot him on the spot" comment about anyone taking down the flag. The sentence was carried out on the grounds where Mumford had committed the offense.[5]

New Orleans' socially prominent women, however, remained defiant. Confident their "armor of gender would protect them,"[6] they openly showed their disdain for Butler and his occupying army. They crossed to the other side when passing federal soldiers on the street, they got off streetcars when soldiers got on, they left services when officers came to church, and on occasion, spat in the faces of federal officers.[7] When one of them emptied a slop jar on Admiral David Farragut as he was passing below a window, Butler said enough was enough. On May 15, 1862, he issued his infamous "woman's order": "Hereafter when any female shall, by word, gesture, or movement, insult to show contempt for any Union officer or soldier of the United States, she shall be regarded and held liable to be treated as a woman of the town plying her avocation (prostitution)."[8]

Butler's order outraged the South. Southern newspapers began calling him "Beast Butler," and teenager Clara Solomon wished "he could only have as many ropes around his neck as there are ladies in the city & each have a pull."[9] But his order put an end to the insults women publicly made against Union soldiers.[10] No Southern woman would remotely allow herself to be considered "a woman of the town."

Having prohibited public displays of disloyalty on the part of New Orleans' women, Butler was determined to root out disloyalty within his department. Boasting that "in six months New Orleans should be a Union City or—a home of the Alligator," in June, he ordered all public officials in occupied

Louisiana to take an oath of loyalty to the Union or resign. If any citizens or foreigners wanted to use the courts, they also had to take the oath.

Next to New Orleans' uppity women on Butler's enemies list were the city's Jews. Butler had a "special penchant for attacking Jews," writes historian Eli Evans.[11] While he and his brother were lining their pockets, Butler accused "army contractors, principally Jews," of making "fortunes by the war." Jews, he said, were the Confederacy's most effective supporters. An Associated Press journalist in New Orleans shared Butler's venom for Jews, calling for all of them in the South to be "exterminated."[12] Butler was especially outraged by Eugenia Levy Phillips. She was so truculent that Butler sent her off to Ship Island in the Gulf of Mexico.

"I do not call you a common woman of the town," he said as she was being taken away, "but an uncommon vulgar one."

Eugenia shot back that Ship Island had "one advantage over the city ... you will not be there."[13] Eugenia spent three months in the summer of 1862 in the mosquito-infested prison. For some unknown reason, Butler pardoned her. Possibly it was through the influence of a family friend with important political connections.[14] Given the option of remaining in New Orleans if she took the oath of allegiance to the United States, Eugenia and her husband refused and left by boat for Mobile, Alabama, along with other Southern loyalists who refused to swear allegiance to the United States.[15]

Butler's animosity toward Eugenia was due to her intransigence, but it was also a reflection of Butler's animus toward Jews.[16] The "most active agents and most efficient supporters" of the foreign merchants speculating in cotton, he said, were "mostly Jews."[17] New Orleans' "army contractors, principally Jews," were making "fortunes by the war."[18] If it were up to him, he would "suck the blood of every Jew, and detain every Jew" as long as he could.[19]

Meanwhile, Butler was creating havoc in Seward's State Department. In July 1862, Congress passed the Second Confiscation Act providing for the confiscation of property of those "aiding, countenancing or abetting" the Rebellion. In one incident, Butler seized $800,000 from the Dutch Consulate in New Orleans, claiming the money was intended for the Confederacy (the money was later returned). Butler was also involved in numerous disputes with the consuls of Britain, Belgium, France, and other countries. Butler made no secret of his disdain for the foreign "whipper-snappers" whose offices, he contended, were "asylums" for aiding the Confederacy.[20]

Lincoln said his ultimate goal throughout the war was "the speedy restoration of our Union." Secession had not been as popular in Louisiana as it had been in other parts of the lower South. The state had strong economic trading ties to the North. Although its cotton oligarchy resented the tariffs imposed by the North on imports, Louisiana's sugar planters had supported

14. The General Prohibition

tariffs to make them competitive with sugar producers in Cuba and Brazil. Because of its economic interests, Lincoln believed Louisiana was the most susceptible of the seceded states to being coaxed back into the Union. From the moment New Orleans was captured in April 1862, he was optimistic Louisiana could be lured back into the Union if New Orleans' military and civil leaders now in charge were able to organize a loyal state government. If that could be accomplished, it would set the pattern for the return of the seceded states to the Union.

Based on Congress' Confiscation Act passed in July 1862, in September 1862, Butler required all citizens in New Orleans and lower Louisiana who had not renewed their allegiance, or had any allegiance or sympathy to the "so-called Confederate States" to take the oath by October 1. Those who refused to take the oath were ordered to report to the Provost Marshall and list all their property. The Provost Marshall would record their assets and give them a certificate of registration identifying them as "an enemy of the United States." Those not registering were subject to a fine and/or imprisonment at hard labor and confiscation of all their property. "Oath offices" were swamped by thousands of secessionists who took the oath, which they considered mainly words, so as not to lose their property. About 4,000 came to the oath office to record their property, but refused to take the oath and were branded "registered enemies."

In early October 1862, Lincoln urged Butler to arrange elections in Louisiana's two congressional districts under Union control.[21] Lincoln was annoyed to learn nothing had been done about the elections he demanded and handed the job to General Shepley, the military governor of Louisiana's occupied parishes.[22] The election was held on December 2, 1862. Although the election was highly controversial, the elected representatives, Michael Hahn and Benjamin Flanders, eventually took their seat in the House of Representatives in February.

On December 5, 1862, Butler ordered all "registered enemies" to report on or before December 10 to the Provost Marshal, who would arrange for their exile across enemy lines. Those leaving were only allowed to take their personal clothing and not more than $50.[23]

By then, Lincoln was attentive to Seward's warning him that Butler's treatment of New Orleans' foreign community threatened European neutrality, and he was annoyed at constant complaints from its residents over Butler's hard-fisted administration. In November, he decided Butler had to go and chose General Nathaniel P. Banks as his replacement. Butler was relieved on December 17 before the order expelling "registered enemies" could be fully implemented, but Banks later enforced it.

* * * * * * * *

Issachar had been disappointed his treatment of men at Fortress Monroe had not received the recognition he so earnestly sought. Ever the opportunist, when he heard Lincoln was about to replace Butler with General Nathaniel P. Banks as military commander of the Department of the Gulf, Issachar believed he could gain that recognition if he could persuade Banks to take him with him to New Orleans in some official capacity.

On November 16, 1862, a week after Banks' announced appointment, Issachar wrote Banks a hasty letter from Philadelphia. "I can be of more service to you than I first imagined," he said. He would like to meet him in private in New York at his headquarters at the Astor Hotel or at Banks' home to explain.[24]

When Banks received Issachar's letter, he was curious. Dr. Zacharie had to have had something in mind besides tending to the military's feet, something of considerable personal benefit to Banks. Banks was aware Issachar had Lincoln's ear and was savvy enough to listen to what Issachar had to say. What Issachar told him isn't known, but possibly he said if Banks would allow him to accompany him to New Orleans, he would be an asset in softening the city's Jewish population's attitude toward the incoming military commander. If nothing else, Issachar said he would be at hand to treat the feet of federal soldiers stationed in the area. Banks was not opposed to what Issachar was offering, but Issachar was a civilian and a British citizen as well. He would need official approval to go to New Orleans from someone higher up.

That was not going to be a problem. Issachar wasted no time. He left New York for Washington and met with Lincoln. From his previous time in New Orleans, Issachar was aware of New Orleans' relatively large Jewish population (about 8,000 at the start of the war) and its Southern loyalties. Lincoln was also well aware of New Orleans' sizable Jewish population. A year earlier, Abraham Jonas, his "trusted friend," had written him he had "a very large family connection in the south," including six children in New Orleans, and "a host of other near relatives."[25] If Louisiana were to be lured back into the Union, New Orleans would be key to readmission. Lincoln would need all the support he could muster. Issachar likely promised he could make that happen. At the very least, he could be his eyes and ears in the city. Lincoln told Issachar he had no hesitation about sending him to New Orleans, but like Banks, given Issachar's British citizenship, Lincoln said such permission should come from Secretary of State Seward.

Issachar immediately sent a note to Seward. "I have just seen the President," he said. I "am satisfied that if you will speak a Kinde word for Me to Day, that I will obtain what I desire that is to accan pay [accompany] Gnl. Banks, in Some Capacity So as to Render Some Service to the Geverment."[26]

Seward sent a note with "a Kinde word" about Dr. Zacharie back to Lincoln, saying he had no objection to Zacharie going to New Orleans with

14. The General Prohibition

Banks. The next day, November 25, 1862, Lincoln wrote Banks: "Dr. Zacharie, whom you know as well as I do, wishes to go with you on your expedition. I think he might be of service to you, first, in his peculiar profession, and secondly, as a means of access to his countrymen who are quite numerous."[27] He was ordering Banks to take Issachar. It was not even a request. It was merely a *permission* "excepting his case from a general prohibition which I understand to exist."[28]

* * * * * * * *

The "general prohibition" Lincoln was referring to was General Ulysses S. Grant's orders restricting the movements of Jews south from any point under his command in the Department of the Tennessee.[29]

One of the reasons the South had felt confident about going to war was its cotton. Secessionists anticipated New England's textile mills and its dependent industries would be ruined without Southern cotton. On May 21, 1861, the Confederate Congress prohibited cotton sales to the North. Secessionists were confident Britain and France would support Southern independence militarily because their economies were dependent on Southern cotton. Were it not for slave-produced cotton, the South would not have had the wealth and confidence to go to war.

Confidence was inspiring, but it could not arm men, clothe them, keep them warm in winter, or treat their wounds and diseases. The Confederacy never had enough of any war materiel. What it did have was thousands and thousands of bales of cotton stored in southern warehouses. Cotton itself was of no practical use to the Confederacy since it had no industry to turn it into clothes or blankets, but "white-gold" cotton could be traded for real gold and silver. With gold and silver, blockade runners could buy guns and ammunition from Britain, and quinine, surgical supplies, and other war materiel could be obtained from northern traders passing across the lines.

While the South could not have waged war for long without trading for cotton, the federal government was torn between totally restricting and allowing the South to export some of its cotton. At the start of the war, the government allowed merchants in the border states like Kentucky, which had remained in the Union, to continue to trade for cotton to discourage them from joining the secessionists. As cotton shortages in the North became dire, pressure from mill owners grew, and with the possibility of foreign intervention ever present, Lincoln loosened restrictions for trading for cotton in occupied parts of the Confederacy. Treasury Secretary Salmon Chase instructed generals to "let commerce follow the flag" and permit "all possible facilities" for shipping cotton.[30]

After New Orleans and Memphis were captured in early 1862, trading for and shipping large amounts of cotton became feasible. Profits were enormous. "So gigantic has grown this species of transaction of late, and so profitable, that many persons heretofore, not overly wealthy, have been enabled to purchase steamboats and carry on a trade entirely upon their own responsibility."[31]

Generals Grant and William Tecumseh Sherman took a grim view of the government's allowing trading with the enemy. They did not perceive or care about the grand strategy of keeping Europe out of the war. Grant, Sherman, and other generals fumed that cotton buyers were providing gold to the rebels to buy guns and other supplies from England and medicine and other contraband in return for cotton. For Grant, unprincipled cotton traders were undermining the war effort.

By "unprincipled" traders, Grant and many others meant Jewish traders. For men like Grant, who was born and raised in rural America and whose only familiarity with Jews was through the Bible or Jewish peddlers, the predisposition to believe the stereotype of the unscrupulous Jew was pervasive. Grant was "captive to old attitudes" about Jews.[32] Reflexive anti–Semitism that had always been lurking below the surface in America became more overt. Judah Benjamin, Confederate President Jefferson Davis' Secretary of State, was the poster boy for barbs about Jewish corruption and betrayal.[33]

The prejudice against Jews ran so deeply that "Jew" was used indiscriminately to refer to anyone engaged in the cotton trade.[34] "Jews," Grant bristled, "seem to be a privileged class that can travel anywhere. They will land at any wood yard or landing on the river and make their way through the country."[35] General Sherman, Grant's second-in-command, shared his dire views about unscrupulous ubiquitous Jews. Sherman groused to General John Rawlins, Grant's adjutant general, that "swarms of Jews" were in Memphis trading with secessionists for cotton with gold. The "commercial enterprise of the Jews," he wrote Treasury Secretary Chase, was buying "a pound of Cotton behind our Army" and turning it into an enormous profit in Boston. Sherman had a sullied view of Jews even before the war. When he was stationed in San Francisco in 1858, he wrote his wife Ellen, "the Christ killing Jews" were still "without pity, soul, heart or bowels of compassion."[36]

In December 1861, a naval officer patrolling the Ohio River warned that smuggling on the river was being carried out "as usual chiefly by Jews." By July 1862, Grant was convinced that smuggling was seriously undermining the war effort, and the main culprits were Jews, whom he said were "sharks, feeding upon the soldiers." They were a "nuisance" he planned to "abate."[37] On July 26, he telegraphed General J. T. Quimby to examine the baggage of all speculators coming South. Jews, he said, "*should receive special attention*" (italics mine).[38] Although Grant would later protest he wasn't anti–Semitic, calling Jews "sharks" and a "nuisance" was clearly so.

In November, Grant ordered train conductors to remove all Jews from

14. The General Prohibition

their trains travelling south in his department because they were such "*an intolerable nuisance the department must be purged [of] them*" (italics mine).[39]

Issachar had been ready to travel south to New Orleans, but Grant's order effectively prevented him from doing so by rail. Lincoln would later deny knowing anything about Grant's restricting Jews from rail transport, but when he wrote Banks that Issachar would have been able to get to New Orleans in late November, except for "a general prohibition which I understand to exist,"[40] he was clearly aware of it.

Two weeks later, Grant again telegraphed orders "*the Israelites especially should be kept out*" [of his department][41] (italics mine). Two weeks later, in early December, he wrote to General Sherman, "my policy is to exclude them so far as practicable from the Dept."[42]

On December 17, 1862, he did just that. "General Orders No. 11" expelled all Jews from his jurisdiction:

> The Jews as a class, violating every regulation of trade ... are hereby expelled from the department (of Tennessee which included Tennessee, Mississippi, Kentucky, and parts of southern Illinois) within twenty-four hours from the receipt of this order.

Anyone returning would be arrested and held in confinement until an opportunity occurs of sending them out as prisoners.[43]

Historians have offered diverse explanations for Grant's sweeping order banishing all Jews from his department. Excuses vary from pressure from Washington to capture Vicksburg quickly because the administration needed an important victory to offset defeats in the east to outrage he felt at his father, Jesse Grant, who had appeared at his headquarters, asking for a permit on behalf of the Mack brothers, Jewish clothing manufacturers, to buy cotton confiscated in occupied Union territory. The Mack brothers were major suppliers of uniforms for the Union Army.[44]

Grant's General Orders No. 11 touched off a firestorm. Lincoln and congressmen were besieged with telegrams, letters, and delegations from individuals and their congressmen protesting the inhuman order, a gross violation of the constitution. Cesar Kaskel, one of the Paducah Kentucky Jews who was forced to leave his home, wrote to Lincoln that he and the other Jews were "good and loyal citizens of the United States and residents of this town, for many years engaged in legitimate business as merchants." If the fiat were not retracted, it would brand Jews "as outlaws before the whole world."[45]

Paducah's Jewish delegation arrived in Washington on January 3, 1863. Issachar was undoubtedly aware, as were most of Washington's Jews, of Grant's sweeping order and the reason Paducah's Jews were coming to see Lincoln. While Issachar was waiting in Washington for the pass that would allow him to travel through Grant's jurisdiction, like Jews everywhere in America, he was stunned by Grant's anti–Jewish expulsion order. Issachar was aware Grant had prohibited Jews from boarding trains passing through his department, effectively keeping him from going to New Orleans. He had heard rumors that a delegation of Jews had come to Washington to protest and had read about Grant's banishment order in the *Jewish Messenger*, to which Issachar subscribed. But if Issachar brought it up with Lincoln, there is no record of any such correspondence or conversation.

Carrying letters of introduction from several of Cincinnati's Jewish leaders, and with ex-Ohio Republican Congressman John Addison Gurley, who was still vice president of Paducah's pro–Lincoln Union League Club, at his side, Kaskel apprised Lincoln of the dire plight of Paducah's Jews as a consequence of Grant's order.

Lincoln assured Kaskel the neither he nor General Henry Halleck, Grant's superior, were aware that Grant has issued such an absurd order. He vowed he would not allow "a citizen in any wise be wronged on account of his place of birth or religious confession."[46]

An apocryphal exchange is said to have occurred during that meeting, with Lincoln asking Kaskel and the others with him, "And so the children of Israel were driven from the happy land of Canaan?"

"Yes," replied Kaskel, "and that is why we have come unto Father Abraham's bosom, asking protection."

"And this protection they shall have at once," Lincoln allegedly replied.[47]

That same day General Halleck sent Grant a telegram: "General Orders, No. 11, issued by you December 17, [which] it expels all Jews from your department ... will be immediately revoked."[48]

The following day, Halleck's adjutant, Col. John C. Kelton, on his own wrote Grant, that in his own opinion, Lincoln had no objection to his expelling traders and Jew peddlers. Had "peddler" been inserted after Jew, "I do not suppose any exception would have been taken to the order."[49] Several days later, Halleck wrote Grant stating that had the order been enforced, Grant would have had to expel all Jewish soldiers and officers in his department as well.[50]

Three days after receiving Halleck's order to rescind and two days after receiving Kelton's wire, Grant issued a new directive revoking General Orders No. 11.[51] Issachar was now free to travel south in Union occupied territories.

Grant's expelling Jews from his lines remained a sore spot among them for many years and was used as an argument against electing him President. Grant did his best to make amends towards America's Jews, and he was filled with remorse over what even his wife called his "obnoxious order"[52] to his death, so much so he omitted any reference to it in his memoirs.[53] In 1907, journalist Isaac Markens wrote Grant's son, Frederick, about the omission. Frederick wrote back that when his father was writing his memoirs, he asked him if he were going to refer to Orders No. 11. Grant replied that it "was a matter long past and best not referred to."[54]

15

"Spare no expense"

General Banks arrived in New Orleans on December 14, 1862. The next day, he met with Butler and showed him his orders. The meeting was cordial. Butler had heard rumors he was to be replaced, and now the rumors had turned out to be true. They shook hands, chatted, and took leave of one another. On December 16, 1862, Banks formally took over as head of the Department of the Gulf.

Banks was immediately overwhelmed by civil administrative duties. Assessing taxes, fines, and punishments and managing charities, trade, regulation of churches, and confiscation of disloyal estates required his immediate attention. In addition to oversight of the ordinary affairs of a military department, he had inherited a political minefield from Butler's administrations. One of his first tasks was to mollify the British, Dutch, and French consuls in New Orleans, whom Butler had suspected were acting on behalf of the Confederate government. Butler had nearly precipitated their foreign intervention in the war by denying them diplomatic immunity.

"Broken eggs cannot be mended," said Lincoln about affairs in Louisiana.[1] But not all the eggs were broken. Lincoln was still hopeful Louisiana could be coaxed back into the Union. To that end, he had selected Banks to clean up Butler's mess. In addition to wresting control of the Mississippi River from the secessionists, Lincoln was relying on Banks to make that happen. It was a daunting challenge. Banks would not only have to restore Unionist sentiment in the state, but he would also have to reconcile secessionists to the prospect of abandoning slavery. This was all the more difficult because much of the state was still controlled by slave-owning secessionists.

Just as daunting was the prospect of a Confederate counteroffensive to retake New Orleans. The city's dismal defenses alarmed him. He had only a small force of "raw men." Most were poorly armed and had never even handled a musket. He had no artillery. He didn't have enough cavalry to reconnoiter Confederate-held territory surrounding the city, making it "impossible to obtain timely information of the movements of the enemy." "I am depressed," he wrote his wife Mary.[2]

Banks was more than aware of the resentment toward the government on the part of New Orleans' upper-class white populace, whom Butler had stripped of their pride and property. "The dainty damsel carefully gathers up her skirts as she goes by a Union soldier, or wears a breast pin on which is gaudily painted the rebel flag; the strong man, standing on the corner of the street, mutters something about the damned Yankees; the mob, at dead of night, hurrah for Jeff Davis," said one of those damned Yankees.[3]

"Assuming command here," Banks wrote General Halleck in Washington, "I had but one of two courses before me, either to continue abuses" or "to reform its character." I chose "the latter course." "No government could stand the weight of abuses that existed here … no military operations could be successfully carried on with such a disturbed and excited community in the rear as that which I found here." "A wise and conciliatory policy" might coax them back to the Union.[4] In place of Butler's iron-fisted occupation, Banks offered an olive branch. He rescinded Butler's infamous "woman's order" branding insolent Confederate women as prostitutes. He released more than a hundred political prisoners. He reopened churches Butler had closed because their pastors had refused to pray for the President of the United States. and he curtailed confiscating property of Confederate sympathizers. "Butler had stroked the cat from tail to head, and found her full of yawl and scratch." Banks was "determined to stroke her from head to tail, and see if she would not hide her claws, and commence to purr."[5] At the same time, he let it be known that he would not brook disorder. Those disturbing the peace would be "punished with the sharpest severity known to military law." The *New York Herald*'s correspondent in New Orleans told his readers that General Banks received visitors with courtesy, but if they "imagined that the General would give these secessionists their own way they have discovered their mistake. He treats them all in a gentlemanly manner, but is as firm as a rock."[6]

If Banks believed his conciliatory policies would soften loyalist sentiment for the Confederacy, he was mistaken. On January 4, while riding through the city. he passed a number of women whose grimacing faces openly indicated their antipathy. One of them was the same woman who had spat on Admiral Farragut.[7]

Banks also had to contend with a department rampant with corruption. Butler had condoned, participated, or been bribed to turn a blind eye to speculators openly trading with the enemy. All it took to bring cotton to New Orleans and ship it to Europe was "a little greasing," said a Confederate agent engaged in the illegal trade.[8] Within days of taking over from Butler, Butler's brother Andrew offered Banks $10,000 to look the other way: "Dear Sir: If you will allow our commercial program to be carried out as projected previously to your arrival in this Department, giving the same support and facilities as your predecessor (Butler), I am authorized on obtaining your assent to place at your disposal one hundred thousand dollars."[9] Andrew is believed to have made $1–2 million from illegal cotton trading. When Butler came to New Orleans, his personal worth amounted to about $150,000. When he died in 1893, his estate was valued at more than $7,000,000, most of it derived while he was in New Orleans.[10]

"I never despaired of our country until I came here," Banks wrote his wife about the bribe. "Thank God, I have no desire for dishonest gains."[11] Banks' ambitions were for power, not money. He may not have taken anything for himself from a "secret services fund," but expenses paid from that fund that are suspicious.[12]

* * * * * * * *

Nathaniel Prentice Banks had an overriding ambition to make something of himself. He did not have a happy childhood. His family was poor. When his father wasn't drinking, he was a foreman at a cotton mill in Lowell, Massachusetts. One of Banks' early jobs was replacing empty bobbins with full ones at his father's factory. His lingering moniker from those boyhood days was "Bobbin-boy." Banks' mother was emotionally detached.[13]

While still working in the mills, Banks attended school and later found time to edit several local newspapers, including one for mill workers. He also courted another factory worker, Mary Theodosia Palmer. Besides where they worked, they had another thing in common. Mary had also had a miserable childhood.[14]

Banks wrote her love letters. What he liked about her, he said, was her "sweet disposition," her ambition "for improving herself," her "taste for dress," her "eyes!" and her "legs."[15] After the mill closed, they both went to night school. Banks eventually obtained a law degree. After a lengthy courtship, Banks and Mary married in 1847. It had been, as Fred Astaire complained to Ginger Rogers in the movie *Swing Time*, a "fine romance with no kisses" because Mary disliked kissing.[16] Still, theirs was a happy marriage. The couple had four children, three of whom made it into adulthood.

At 5-feet 8-inches in height (average for that era), Banks was a handsome man with gray eyes, generous hair, a walrus mustache, and a pleasant commanding voice. He had an infectious smile. His wife said she liked to see him smile because he did it so well.[17] He was very conscious of his appearance and liked to dress well, perhaps compensating for what was likely shabby childhood clothing. "Being long in body and short in legs, like (Stephen) Douglas and Napoleon, I need a dark coat and vest and light pants. I am to wear a mulberry or dahlia colored coat with velvet collar and pants of a certain color but light. I shall be pleased."[18]

Banks rarely lost his temper. Like many children of alcoholics, he tried to avoid confrontation. He maintained equanimity even under stress, but it took a toll on him at night and kept him awake with insomnia. He was courteous and affable, but distant, another characteristic of children of alcoholics. "He is not very communicative even to those men in his command," said his second-in-command in 1861. "Although always pleasant and courteous, he cannot be said to be a companionable person."[19]

After obtaining his law degree, he appeared in one or two cases. William Robinson, a contemporary, said he had no talent as a lawyer. His talent, said Robinson, was "histrionic." He decided he would be better off pursuing a political career. Banks, said Robinson, had "a genius for being looked at." What better talent could a rising politician have than that? He "was born for a talker.... Few men appear better on the political platform."[20]

After serving in the Massachusetts legislature, he was elected to the U.S. House of Representatives, where he was catapulted into national prominence when he was elected speaker in 1856. Flush with success, he considered running for president in the Republican party's first bid for the Presidency, but decided the time was not right. Instead, he backed John C. Frémont, who lost to Democrat James Buchanan. When the Democrats also won control of the House of Representatives, Banks lost his job as speaker. He returned to Massachusetts and the next year campaigned for governor and was elected.

Three years later, Banks began seriously planning a bid for the Presidency. An article in the *Boston Journal* in March 1859, that was picked up by the *New York Times* said it had been reviewing the probabilities of all prominent candidates for a presidential nomination and had concluded "Governor Banks occupies a very strong position." New York Senator William Seward would probably garner most votes at the Republican convention on the first ballot, but it would not be enough to give him the nomination, leaving the way open for Banks.[21] In the months leading up to the 1860 Republican convention, the three names most often mentioned as frontrunners were Ohio Governor Salmon P. Chase, New York Senator William Seward, and Massachusetts Governor Nathaniel P. Banks.[22] By April 1860, however, support for Banks collapsed. After Lincoln clinched the nomination, Banks was touted as vice president, but the vote went to Maine Senator Hannibal Hamlin.

When the war broke out, Banks let Lincoln know he was immediately ready to serve. Banks, an influential New Englander, expected Lincoln would give him a cabinet post, but Lincoln let Vice President Hamlin pick the New England member. Hamlin chose Gideon Welles as secretary of the navy. Banks' name was then floated for a prominent military appointment. Treasury Secretary Salmon Chase felt that while Banks lacked military experience, "in my opinion [he would] make a very fine general."[23] Lincoln was amenable. Banks had reorganized Massachusetts' militia when he was governor, and that militia had been first to answer Lincoln's call for volunteers and had battled its way through Baltimore to protect the capital.

15. "Spare no expense"

Banks himself had no military training. He had never served a single day in the military. But he was an influential politico who could attract volunteers and money for the Union cause. In May 1861, Lincoln appointed him Major General of Volunteers. He was then the fourth highest ranking general in the Union army, even outranking General Ulysses Grant, until 1864.

Banks' lack of military training was apparent from the beginning. He blundered his way through battle after battle. He was totally outmaneuvered by the Confederacy's generals. Banks lost so many wagons, rifles, and other military supplies to General "Stonewall" Jackson's army that he literally became the Confederates' supply depot. Jackson's men nicknamed him "Commissary Banks." Despite embarrassing defeats on the battlefield, Banks had a well-deserved reputation as an organizer and a coalition builder. Lincoln decided the best place for someone with that ability would be the Gulf Department, replacing the divisive General Butler.

* * * * * * * *

As military commander of the Gulf Department, Banks needed to know if and when the Confederates might be planning an attack. New Orleans was still "hostile," despite the seeming calm. Southern loyalists could be a fifth column should Confederate forces launch an attack on the city. Banks could try to obtain such information from rumors in the city, but no one would willingly talk about what they knew to just anyone. Lincoln had sent him to the Gulf Department to wrest control of the Mississippi River from the Confederates. He also wanted to lure Louisiana back into the Union. To do that, Banks needed to know where the people stood in terms of their continued loyalty to the Confederacy and their opposition to the federal government. If Louisiana could be coaxed back into the Union, other Southern states might follow. Banks had been sent to New Orleans on assignment. But if he could engineer Louisiana's return, he believed he would gain the recognition he craved. Such recognition would pave the way to another bid for the Presidency. For that to happen, he needed information about opposition to reconciliation in New Orleans from someone he could rely on. Lincoln had assured him that Dr. Zacharie would be a valuable asset in that regard, especially among the city's influential Jewish population.

By 1860, New Orleans had the seventh largest Jewish population in the United States and the largest Jewish population in the South. About 8,000 of Issachar's "countrymen" lived in the city (out of a total population of about 169,000), and roughly the same number of Jews lived in towns and villages in rural Louisiana.[24] After the federal occupation, the Jewish population increased even more as many moved from the countryside to New Orleans to avoid being caught in the middle of the war, making New Orleans an even larger and more concentrated Jewish community.[25]

As a Jew, Zacharie would be able ingratiate himself with New Orleans' influential Jews and learn about any subversive activities they were aware of. In sending him to New Orleans, Lincoln assured Banks, Dr. Zacharie would be a valuable asset in that regard. Increasingly apprehensive about possible subversive activities in New Orleans, Banks was impatient for Issachar's arrival.

"Spare no expense" getting to New Orleans, Banks urged him. "Lose no time. Mingle freely with everyone, especially with your own countrymen." The letter, marked "confidential," contained his instructions. He was to "report public sentiment about present and probable future reactions to the Government" in the city, and "as far as possible, people in Mississippi, and the adjacent country." Banks wanted to know "What [do they] wish. How far [can] the Government comply with their desires? ... Ascertain ... as far as you can the plans of the public Enemy." Zacharie was to pay special attention to any information about the location and number of troops in the surrounding area and "the extent of their supplies and ammunition, and the different organizations of which their army may be composed." Banks cautioned him about the credibility of the information he uncovered. "Report fully the character of your informants, the relations which they hold to the Government of the United States, and its people" he cautioned, "so that a fair estimate may be placed upon the reliability and value" of their information. Banks ended his tall order by expressing his "entire confidence in your fidelity and success."[26]

Issachar had planned to leave for New Orleans shortly after Banks' departure, but he could not have foreseen Grant's prohibiting Jews from travelling anywhere in his department. Lincoln could have issued him a pass, but he hadn't. Grant was mounting his offensive against Vicksburg, and Lincoln did not want to make him resentful and lose focus.

While still in Washington, Issachar wasted no time in preparing for his assignment. Writing to Union loyalist William Kursheedt, one of the founders and president of New Orleans' Sephardic *Dispersed of Judah* congregation, Issachar asked him to send him a list of names along with "particulars as to parties" willing to "go beyond the lines as peddlers to gather information."[27]

Issachar got the idea of sending peddlers as spies from General Dix when Issachar was at Fortress Monroe. Dix had "an arrangement" with a man who had a pass from Confederate officials to peddle in and around Richmond. Dix didn't have a "secret-service fund" to pay him but was allowing him to "carry some articles for peddling" and to "bring back tobacco" to compensate him. The spy had crossed the lines in his wagon four times without arousing suspicion and brought back information about troop deployments and intended general troop movements.[28]

* * * * * * * *

15. *"Spare no expense"*

Issachar arrived in New Orleans during the second week of January. A week earlier, he received Kursheedt's list of "all the particulars as to the parties for whom I aske permission to go beyond the lines." As soon as he had settled in at the St. Charles Hotel, New Orleans' poshest hotel, he began interviewing people on Kursheedt's list. Most of them, he felt, were unsuitable. One of them was a woman "expecting to be confined in a very short time." In other words, she was pregnant. "I find it very difficult to obtain the right kind of men to cross the lines for information," he told Banks. It would be foolhardy to send "wild reckless persons of doubtful character." Their reports would not be reliable.[29]

General Nathaniel P. Banks: "Mingle freely with everyone, especially your own countrymen." Ca. 1861 (courtesy Library of Congress).

At the end of the month, Issachar sent General Banks a bill for his first two weeks. General Banks had told Issachar to "spare no expense." Issachar understood Banks was authorizing him not just to pay for information, but also his own expenses. The bill came to $700 (almost $14,000 in today's money). A $117 item was for Issachar's hotel bill at the St. Charles. Another $150 was for his personal secretary, Charles Johnson. A $100 went to someone named Lewis Bach. Another $300 was for "services of self to date." The remaining $90 was for unnamed "expenses" and "information."[30]

16

Spymaster

Almost as soon as he was settled at the St. Charles Hotel, Issachar began chatting with local merchants, attending meetings, concerts, auctions, and public gatherings, and listening for tidbits about Confederate activities in the area and possible sympathizers in the city. His reports to Banks were peppered with observations.

> A person in town from the Lafourche (a parish southwest of New Orleans), says....
> 'Tis reported that...
> In conversation this evening...
> Having passed most of the day among the retailers, they state...
> Among mechanics and others...
> On visiting the different auction houses this morning...
> Last evening had an interview with a person who left Jackson (Mississippi) on Saturday the 10th.
> Having passed most of the day visiting different establishments.
> Had a long conversation with two merchants recently arrived here.
> Passed the morning with a Rebel recently from Vicksburg...[1]

Whenever he could, Issachar tried to verify what he had heard. When he overheard rumors about Union troop movements, he tried to track down the leaks. On one occasion, he'd heard that several federal regiments, batteries, and a cavalry company had left to confront the Confederates at Franklin, Louisiana. Issachar was able to trace the source of that information to clerks in the Quartermaster Office.

Within weeks of coming to New Orleans Issachar wrote Banks, "I now know the whole 'ring' [of secessionists] with its ramifications."[2] Levy and Dietes, a firm in New Orleans, was sending two wagons of goods to Baton Rouge that they intended to take into enemy lines. He advised Banks to "have a watch kept on them."[3] A day later, Issachar's spies informed him that Levy and Dietes' wagons were headed for Confederate lines. If Banks could immediately contact the commanding officer in Baton Rouge, "he'll [be able to] overhaul them."[4] Boats leaving upriver "should be well watched." A Mr. Ziegler of Messer. Otta. and Co. was sending 50 sacks of salt and 50 barrels of

16. Spymaster

flour to Baton Rouge. "Messrs. McKinzie and Williams, supposedly sutlers," are shipping 200 cases of shoes to Baton Rouge. "There is something wrong about these shipments and should be looked into."[5] "They are at this time throwing dust in the eyes of the commission and no person but a thorough businessman (meaning himself) can detect them."[6]

Issachar eventually found several men he believed were competent and trustworthy to send into Confederate territory as spies. "They know the State well," he told Banks. They had families and had been in business in New Orleans, but they had fallen on hard times because of the war. "I have known two of these men from my infancy." They "will not deceive me," he assured Banks. "They are under obligations to me for past favors."[7]

"Knowing them from infancy" implies the two men grew up with him in England. But if Issachar were using the term loosely, it was much more likely he knew them from his early days in Philadelphia or Charleston. What favors they owed him is anyone's guess. Issachar assured Banks "these are intelligent men." Their information "may be relied on with confidence." One whom he was sending to Mobile was "a very reliable educated man." "He is well acquainted there," he said. "If any person can obtain reliable information, he is the person."[8]

He and the other spies he was sending out had to have a cover, he told Banks. They had to "have some good excuse for [crossing enemy lines]." They had to be able to gather information "without the least shadow of suspicion."[9] A good cover would be to send them out as peddlers and traders. "Give them fifty to two and fifty dollars in merchandise for them to sell to cloak to their real object. The risk which these men run is very great."[10] If they were arrested as spies, they could be hanged.

Issachar was confident the information these spies would garner would be of immense value. It would also "inaugurate a system of usefulness which up to this time has been greatly disregarded by us, but which has been used with much success by our enemies."[11]

"And so," writes historian Bertram Korn, "instead of organizing a 'corps of corn doctors,' as he had originally intended as his effort to aid the war effort, Issachar had become the head of a network of secret agents."[12]

* * * * * * * *

At the end of his first two weeks in New Orleans, Issachar sent Banks a summary of his "observations about the city." Issachar peppered his report with accolades about Banks. His appointment here "is regarded with much favor." He was "spoken of by all, with all due respect. A very violent secessionist" told Issachar "he was d__d glad" Banks hadn't been sent here first. If he had, New Orleans "would have been a Union city."[13]

Issachar was not done stroking Banks' ego. New Orleans' Jewish population, he said, was also happy with the way he was governing the city. "Among Israelites, you are looked upon with a great deal of favor." Many of the things "you have already done" have been "a benefit to them all as a class." After the harsh treatment at the hands of General Butler, Banks' "kind actions" in time would encourage them to "embrace once again the Union cause."[14] Banks could not have been more pleased.

Everyone in high places seemed to have their own personal spies. A little more than a week after New Orleans fell into federal hands, Treasury Secretary Salmon Chase appointed George Denison the customs collector in New Orleans. As Chase's cousin and personal watchdog, Denison sent Chase weekly reports, "fully and without reserve, all that relates to persons and things not proper for the subject of official communcations."[15]

Two weeks after Issachar began interviewing potential spies, Denison duly reported that "a person here of the Jewish persuasion, an Israelite indeed named Dr. Zacharie who is said lately to have been a healer of corns and bunions, in New York," was in New Orleans as a "Confidential Agent, or Correspondent, of the President."[16] He wears a "flowered velvet" vest. His hair is "beautifully oiled." He perfumes himself with a distillate "sweeter than the winds that blow from Araby." The "vulgar little scoundrel takes bribes." An inveterate anti-Semite, Denison mistook Issachar's spy ring as just a way "to make money."[17]

Denison's accusations that Issachar was corrupt were the proverbial "pot calling the kettle black." Denison used his post as customs collector to liberally line his own pockets. Denison, said Thomas Durant, a contemporary was "a corrupt Treasury agent … pandering to Secretary Salmon Portland Chase via a flood of letters purporting to tell all from the Department of the Gulf, while he calmly gathered to himself numberless casks of fine cognac and palmed envelopes stuffed with promiscuous cash, flirting in the meantime with his patron's most virulent political foes."[18]

A month after Banks took over from Butler, Denison wrote to Butler, "the happiest day of my life will be the day when a steamer arrives with you on board." Were he to return, Denison was certain everything would change for the better, including "a very disagreeable condition of things here." By "disagreeable condition," Denison meant "a host of speculators, Jews and camp followers" pouring into New Orleans. "I regard them as natural enemies. The whole crowd, and Dr. Zachary [sic] among them, with eager expectancy [are] like wolves about to seize their prey."[19]

The anti-Semitic tax collector didn't believe Issachar was sending spies into Confederate territory as disguised peddlers. Denison called Issachar a "humbug." When the "Israelite" asked him to issue a permit for a man named Simon, another of his "friends," to take $20,000 worth of goods to Baton Rouge for sale, Denison fumed, "Jews take to trade, as ducks to water."

16. Spymaster

Denison was willing to take "the risk of impairing the Doctor's efficiency as [a] government agent." He wouldn't issue Simon a trading permit without a written order from General Banks. Issachar explained the man had to look like a peddler "to conceal the real reason for being in Baton Rouge." Denison wouldn't budge. After Issachar came back with Banks' authorization, Denison reluctantly issued the permit, convinced that like himself, Issachar was going to personally profit from it.[20]

General George Foster Shepley, another of Butler's anti–Semitic loyalists, was equally contemptuous of Issachar. The "retired corn-doctor, Jew, is here as a spy." Dr. Zacharie, he griped, "is said to be directly under the appointment of the President, but [is] the intimate associate and confidential advisor of Banks." Shepley was Louisiana's military governor. No less corrupt than Denison, when he wasn't occupied with his military duties, he found time to engage in illicit trading for Southern cotton. Shepley was embittered that Issachar's agents were looking for information "that would tell" against his former boss. "The Christ killers," he said, "have it all their own way."[21]

Denison and Shepley weren't Issachar's only detractors. Based on a letter a clerk in Banks' office sent him, a Boston merchant, Joseph H. Hill, wrote Banks that "to prevent your reputation from being injured by one, in whom I think you place confidence," he was alerting him to "a person who spends considerable time in your office, Zachery [sic], I think is the name."

"This Mr. Z." was overheard offering an agent for a company that owned a steamer that had been seized by the government to get it released "for the sum of one thousand dollars, two hundred to be paid down—the balance when the job should be consummated." The agent had rejected Issachar's attempted bribe, although he would gladly have paid that amount, Hill said, had the fine been officially levied. A day or so later, when the agent was in General Banks' office waiting to talk to him about the seizures, Stephen Hunter, the clerk in Banks' office, wrote Hill he had overheard Issachar repeating his bribe.[22] A month later, Hill sent a more detailed letter to Banks elaborating the details of alleged bribe, adding he would prefer his name not be used in any follow-up unless it was strictly necessary.[23]

Issachar's most ambitious efforts as a spymaster was a deception involving William G. Betterton, a New Orleans grocer, commission agent, and suspected Confederate agent. Issachar had heard rumors that Betterton was sending supplies across government lines. After gaining Banks' approval for what amounted to a sting operation, Issachar approached Betterton with a proposition.

For a payment of $4,000 and a 25 percent share of the profits, plus his expenses, Issachar promised to go to Washington and "use my influence" with "government authorities" to get their "permission to ship one or more loads of goods through the Federal lines into the Confederacy" and bring back cotton and naval stores.

Betterton would be responsible and would keep an account of all the goods they would send and receive. Betterton's "friend who has permission or a contract with the Confederate authorities to export cotton and naval stores" would make all the arrangements inside Confederate lines. Betterton would provide protection for him and any others who went with him. Betterton and his "friend" would divide "the remaining seventy-five percent interest in profits." If it becomes necessary for the parties interested on the Confederate side to visit New Orleans, "they shall have every facility so far as is my power and influence for safe and unmolested return."[24]

Betterton was well aware of Issachar's reputation as Banks' agent. Even Confederate newspapers were regularly reporting on his public life and activities: The "spy department" in New Orleans was headquartered at the St. Charles Hotel. "The chief spy is from Washington City. He was formerly Lincoln's corn-doctor. It is currently reported that he has succeeded in converting many of the Hebrew persuasion to his views, and makes good use of them in executing his plans. The authorities (Confederate) cannot be too careful of such persons."[25]

Betterton had also heard rumors that Issachar was bribing officials. Government officials were notorious for taking bribes. Still, Betterton was leery of duplicity. To remove any doubt of Issachar's sincerity, Betterton told Issachar he wanted their agreement in writing. The agreement, dated March 7, 1863, described each of their roles and compensation in the smuggling operation.

Betterton had good reason not to trust any verbal agreements with government agents. In May 1861, he and his then-partner, a J.E. Challard, had met with Colonel Theodore Lewis, "Confidential Agent of Confederate States of America," in Montgomery, Alabama. They showed him samples of military weapons they said they could purchase in Havana and said they could deliver them to the Confederacy from Vera Cruz, Mexico.

If Lewis agreed, they wanted to know, "where you will make a deposit of the amount of freight which will have to be paid?" Betterton and Challard weren't willing to make any deal, "except on this basis." They also wanted to know if he would pay for bribes that had to be given "to fee any official to let the vessel or vessels depart in peace." If they didn't hear from him by July 19, they would be leaving for Richmond.

Lewis agreed to pay $17 for rifles but declined to pay $8 each for sabers. He also refused to give Betterton a deposit in advance. Betterton and Challard accused Lewis of trashing their mission and asked President Davis to compensate them for their time and efforts.

"Having done everything in our power to execute our mission and having failed only through stupidity (if not worse) of your agent, we think we have justly earned our commissions, and respectfully ask the same for our trouble and expense."[26]

16. Spymaster

Betterton's calling Lewis stupid and incompetent was a mistake. Lewis' brother had heard "rumors derogatory to the honor and integrity of my brother" (who was now a prisoner of war) circulating in New Orleans and other communities. "I traced their origin to a certain W. G. Betterton," he told the *New Orleans Crescent*, "and confronted him to prove his 'foul aspersions'" by "this Betterton's agency."[27]

Betterton had no written proof of his arrangement with Lewis and apologized. Insulting a Confederate government agent was bad for business. Betterton's apology appeared in the *Crescent* below Lewis' brother's accusation. "I hereby retract all I may have said derogatory to his character," said Betterton. He was cheerfully making this correction to restore "myself in a proper position before the community and the Government."

Once bitten, Betterton was now more careful to get Issachar's agreement in writing.

To further convince Betterton he could deliver his side of their deal, Issachar showed him letters Banks had written him proving he had personal contact with Lincoln and Secretaries Seward and Chase. Several months later, Betterton told Banks there was another part of his arrangement that Issachar had left out of their written contract.

According to Betterton, to get Banks' cooperation, Issachar said he would give Banks' wife $50,000 from the money he expected to make. Dr. Zacharie "gave me to distinctly understand that from this speculation, fifty thousand dollars were to be taken and given to Mrs. Banks your wife. The reason why the money was to be given to her, was that it could not be said that you had received any thing, for any such enterprises or operations."

Believing Banks could be bought was assuring. It was the way Betterton did business. "From the manner in which the whole subject was broached, and the free use made by Dr. Zacharie of Banks' name and his wife as the one receiving the bribe," Betterton "gave credence to it."[28]

Even with Issachar's assurances and the written agreement, Betterton still had lingering doubts Issachar had the connections to make the deal happen. To satisfy Betterton he was not bamboozling him, the day before he left for Washington, on March 7, 1863, the same date as he signed the agreement with Betterton, Issachar wrote a letter of introduction for Betterton to give to Banks. Calling Betterton "our mutual friend," Issachar said Betterton "would be most happy to have you visit his family. Any favor conferred upon him will be fully appreciated."[29]

Issachar was nothing if not self-confident and grandiose. His deal with Betterton was not just to shut down Betterton's smuggling operation. By March 1863, Issachar envisioned himself as a peacemaker. To initiate a peace negotiation with the Confederacy, he had to meet in person with someone high up in the Confederate command who could arrange for him to talk to influential Confederate leaders. The nearest Confederate of that stature was General John Pemberton, commanding officer at Vicksburg. Issachar hoped that if he gained Betterton's trust, Betterton would use his influence to arrange a pass for Issachar to meet with Pemberton, and through him, to arrange a meeting with Confederate leaders in Richmond.

The $4,000 bribe to Betterton and Issachar to outfit his spies as peddlers came from the sale of confiscated cotton. "We all know," the secretary of the treasury reported to Congress, "officers in various places were in the habit to taking property wherever they could find it … and using it, as they said, for the purposes of the government, and in many instances probably for their own purposes." Banks used some of that money to buy and sell cotton to pay for provisions. In late December 1863, Banks' quartermaster warned Banks if he didn't sell more cotton, his department would be bankrupt. Banks also used his fund to pay for his wife to come from New York to host lavish parties as a way of winning the support of New Orleans' civic and business leaders.[30]

Issachar's February's invoice for $740 was not very different from January's. There was a charge for a $100 paid to a Mr. Collins, the spy Issachar had recruited to go to Mobile,[31] and an additional $10 charge for "information." The remaining $630 was for Issachar's routine expenses for that month: $121 for his hotel bill at the St. Charles Hotel, $150 for his secretary, and another $360 for "services of self to date."[32] Banks did not question the expenditures.

Issachar was aware "some enemies" were accusing him of profiteering from illegal cotton trading.[33] Issachar "most earnestly" protested any wrongdoing to Lincoln. Knowing Lincoln's well-known fondness for humorous anecdotes to make a point, Issachar said he was like "the Irish Biddy who remarked to the lady of the house, 'shurr Mistress darlent a poor gal that works hard like to know if she gives satisfaction to youz.'"[34]

"Never since I have been here," Issachar groused to Lincoln, "have I bought sold or bartered, or been interested in any speculation." His profession, he said, had earned him money enough that he had no need to speculate.[35] Despite his absence in New Orleans, Issachar claimed his New York office cleared $10,000 over expenses.[36] It was either an exaggeration, or he lied to the Internal Revenue Service.[37]

Despite complaints, the law did not provide any means for enforcement. Issachar listed his earnings with the IRS at $1,000 in New York and $800 at his Philadelphia office.[38] He claimed he was exempt from federal tax because of the $800 personal exemption (equivalent of $30,000–$40,000 in today's money). He wasn't exempt from New York State retail tax and had a $10 tax bill.[39]

Issachar passed on every snippet of information to Banks and also sent periodic flattering reports about Banks to Lincoln and Seward. He had gone to New Orleans, he said, "to use my best efforts, humble though they be, in aiding to unite our country. Should I in any way be instrumental in consummating so great a result, my ambition will be satisfied. For I shall know full well my name will not be forgotten either by the United States government or the people of Louisiana."[40]

* * * * * * * *

Issachar's relationship with Banks was odd. Issachar felt a special camaraderie toward Banks. Did Banks feel the same? Banks was an introvert who didn't socialize much. Banks' wife repeatedly said he had no intimates. Vice president Hannibal Hamlin called him "cold and selfish."[41] William S. Robinson, who knew him personally, said Banks was "not a warm-hearted person." He "was never known to go out of his way an inch to confer a favor on a friend or supporter, unless another was expected at a future period."[42] What did he expect from his relationship with Issachar? Banks was uncomfortable in groups, but when Issachar invited him to a party at his hotel, Banks accepted. Issachar was outgoing and ebullient. If he read anything, it was the newspapers and his own testimonial book. Two things they did have in common: both were ambitious, and both dressed meticulously.

Soon after Banks was transferred to New Orleans, his wife began hosting parties in New York, charming the rich and powerful. Among those she entertained were New York's political boss, Thurlow Weed, influential newspaper editors, and Horace Greeley's and James Gordon Bennett's wives. The Astors, Roosevelts, Vanderbilts, Bancrofts, Goulds, and Blodgetts were all guests. Banks told her not to worry about the cost. "'You deserve to be an empress,' he said. Behind all Mary's activities in 1863," writes Banks' biographer, "was a deliberate effort to make friends with the people who counted." Mary's activities were "redolent of a political campaign, rather than a socialite's party schedule."[43]

Issachar rarely missed an opportunity to pass on compliments he'd heard about the general. "A very influential gentleman of this city, who is a registered enemy" had nothing but praise for the general. "The nervous excitability of the population under Genl. Butler's infamous rule, has given way to a hopeful feeling" now that Banks was in charge. The "registered enemy" was full of praise for him. "I can and must respect an officer who while fulfilling his duties acts with generosity & does not forget that he is a gentleman."[44] Banks basked in the praise. He was no longer depressed. "All the people seem to think well of me—even the thieves take off their hats."[45]

Banks wanted to believe what Issachar was telling him. He wanted to believe that his policies were winning public sentiment. He was mistaken, and Issachar no less so. Thieves may have tipped their hats to the General, but New Orleans was still very much a secessionist city. In February 1863, a crowd of about 10,000 people, most of them women, gathered at the levee. Waving little Rebel flags, singing Confederate songs, they cheered and waved their handkerchiefs to say goodbye to captured rebels as they boarded their ship. The Union officer in charge ordered them to move back. None moved. Instead, they began hurling insults at the Union men. Fed up with their refusal to move, the provost marshal ordered his men to advance on the crowd with fixed bayonets. Several of the women were arrested. Many in New Orleans considered Banks no better than Butler.[46]

Issachar also sent Lincoln flattering reports about Banks: "You cannot imagine the vast amount of business he (Banks) gets through with each day, never losing his self possession, listening patiently to all, I sometimes wonder that his health stands it as well as it does." Then came what would become a typical self-serving, self-congratulatory note. "For my own part I have endeavoured to assist him all in my power, my great desire is that *our* efforts (italics mine) may prove of benefit to your administration."[47]

Once he started congratulating himself, Issachar couldn't hold back. He began to imagine he was more than just Banks' and Lincoln's ears on the ground. He was their ambassador.

"My profession and my habits of life [have] thrown me among all classes of people." He had "secured the friendship of many of our most distinguished statesmen, commencing in my boyhood with the great Henry Clay." Issachar felt "flattered at the success I have met with, not only among my own people but among the most wealthy and influential citizens." Disingenuously, he continued, "do not think it egotism on my part [when I relate these things]." The day before, "one of the most prominent gentlemen had told him, 'Doctor, had the President sent six missionaries amongst us like you it would have more effect upon us than hundreds of Canon.'"[48] Issachar's ego did not think it was too much of an exaggeration.

* * * * * * * *

The night before Issachar left for Washington, the *New York Herald* reported General Banks had been the guest of honor at a "small, but very select, dinner party" at Issachar's suite at the St. Charles Hotel.[49] Issachar's departure for Washington was duly reported by the *Times-Picayune*. Dr. Zacharie, it informed its readers, was leaving at the request of the President. "The doctor has, we understand, (has) discharged to the entire satisfaction of His Government the important trusts confided to him." Although his "duties here are not yet closed, he expects to return after the elapse of a few weeks."[50]

Lincoln had not summoned Issachar to Washington. He was going on his own and with Banks' approval. Issachar was about to broach his plan to negotiate a peaceful settlement to the war. He himself was the source for the *Times-Picayune*'s comment about Lincoln's summoning him to Washington.

After exchanging pleasantries with Lincoln, Issachar handed him a letter

16. Spymaster

from Banks dated March 6, 1863, a day before Issachar signed the agreement with Betterton. The dating of Banks' letter implies that Issachar had worked out the deal with Betterton and had Banks' approval, some time before it was written out and signed.

Banks began his letter by praising Issachar's efforts in New Orleans: "He has during his stay here been very active and among the People. Especially among his own countrymen, who are numerous and powerful, he has exercised a beneficial influence." Banks was aware Issachar had been accused of speculating. "Some of my own officers have entertained this idea, but, he has constantly assured me that it was not the fact, and I have fully credited his statement. I mention this because I am informed that such representations have been made to you."

Having praised and defended Issachar, Banks broached the subject of "suggestions" Issachar would be making to him. Banks did not elaborate on what those suggestions might be, leaving it to Issachar to explain.

> Dr. Zacharie from his earliest life here and his extended acquaintance with his own People through the South has had very important opportunities of obtaining information as to the condition and feeling of the southern People. The suggestions he can make to you I believe to be practicable, and worthy of consideration. In a word, I believe, making due allowance for a somewhat sanguine temperament, that you can receive his report of the condition of affairs here and in the South generally with full confidence.[51]

Banks' comment about Issachar's "sanguine temperament" acknowledged Issachar's exuberance. But he was optimistic his plan was worth paying attention to.

Both sides were war weary. In public, Lincoln was steadfast in his pursuit of the war. In private, he was willing to be generous. The Emancipation Proclamation had added a moral element to the war, but as long as the South remained undefeated, it was an empty gesture. The war might drag on for years. Lincoln believed that despite Confederate President Davis' intransigence, most Southerners, especially the South's wealthy planters, were disenchanted with secession and could be induced to return their allegiance to the Union, including giving up their slaves if it were in their material interest.[52]

In 1862, Lincoln had first floated the idea of buying the freedom of slaves in the border states and the District of Columbia. At $400 per person, the price tag would have been about $1.6 billion. Since the value of the slaves was estimated at $4 to $6 billion, slave owners turned it down.[53] Despite the rebuff, Lincoln clung to his lifelong belief in the power of economic forces.[54]

In 1863, with the tide turning in the North's favor, Lincoln believed compensating the South for liberating it slaves was now more viable. When Issachar first offered himself as a peace negotiator, Lincoln saw an opportunity to put his economic overtures back in play. Issachar outlined his agreement with Betterton and the ultimate mission of going to Richmond, "of obtaining information as to the condition and feeling of the southern people."[55]

Banks had said that Issachar would be bringing him "suggestions," but had left it up to Issachar to elaborate. One of those suggestions was to allow Issachar to go to Richmond. Another likely "suggestion" Banks said Issachar would be bringing him was Banks' own idea for using economic incentives to entice planters west of the Mississippi who were still loyal to the Confederacy to switch their loyalties.

Ever since coming to New Orleans, Banks had been aware of the rampant corruption in his department involving illicit cotton trading. Banks proposed a win-win situation to curtail it. Northern manufacturers would still get the cotton they needed, planters would get more money for their staples, and corruption involving speculators would be curtailed.

Issachar had one more suggestion. He proposed the government assume "payment of their (Confederate) debt, which more or less influences every individual in Rebeldom."[56] Taking on all or some of the South's wartime debt, in addition to compensating them for their lost property of slaves, would be a major expense. But the cost of one, two, or more years of war would be an even greater economic burden. If there were a possibility some in the Confederate leadership might be amenable to economic incentives as a way of saving face to a negotiated peace, Lincoln wanted to know their conditions. Lincoln could not officially back Issachar's mission to Richmond. But if Issachar were to go as a private citizen, Lincoln could not be accused of capitulating to the South. Lincoln told Issachar he would get back to him after conferring with Secretary Seward.

After meeting with Lincoln, Issachar left for New York to visit his family. On March 17, he telegraphed Lincoln from New York. "Arrived here last night. Am quite unwell. Will have the honor of seeing you in day or two."[57]

Three days later, Issachar's secretary, Charles Johnson, wrote Betterton from New York that Issachar had been ill for three days in bed. They were now en route for Washington. "Having all the influence we could possibly desire, we have no reason to doubt our success."[58]

On March 25, 1863, Issachar sent Lincoln his visiting card, letting him know he was back in Washington. Lincoln returned the card with an enigmatic note on the back of it: "I am running your matter down as fast as I can. It would not advance it for you to see me tonight."[59] The "matter" was the letter from Banks that Lincoln had intended to forward to Seward, which had been mislaid.

The next day, it was located. Lincoln sent it to Seward with a note: "Instruct Banks to furnish Zacharie with funds from secret service and in Bank's [sic] discretion—spend up to $5,000. Say to Banks that he can draw up to five millions." The note included a pass for "I Zacharie MD. & his secretary."[60]

16. Spymaster

Issachar returned to New York on March 27, without knowing whether Lincoln had approved his mission. Before leaving, he wrote Lincoln a note greatly regretting that "policy" had prevented him from personally saying goodbye.

"My mind is much agitated on account of the great responsibility resting on me. I trust everything will be consummated to realize your best wishes. If it does not the fault shall not be mine. I hope you will aid my efforts by giving such orders as will tend to carry out suggestions contained in my memorandum."[61] Issachar's note didn't indicate what was in the memorandum. It likely mentioned his agreement with Betterton to gain his trust to arrange a meeting with General John Pemberton. Issachar and Lincoln had obviously discussed something Lincoln considered feasible.

Issachar ended his note by thanking Lincoln "for the prompt and kind manner you have acted towards me"[62] and the wrote a jubilant note to Banks telling him "everything that I could do here has been done."[63]

The same day Seward received Lincoln's note approving funds for Issachar's mission, Seward dispatched his own note to Banks: "If you think the doctor can be useful to the public service in the prosecution of his plans for obtaining information," he was authorized "to provide transportation and funds for expenses, not to exceed five thousand dollars."[64] In the same dispatch, Seward said he was authorizing a $5 million dollar line of credit from a "secret service fund" that Banks could draw on if needed.

Seward stressed the need for secrecy. "I need hardly say that it is important that it should be guarded against any accidental disclosure."[65] That same day, Seward sent his son, Colonel William H. Seward, to deliver the secret dispatch to Banks.

A $5 million disbursement from Lincoln's "secret service fund" was "remarkable," writes Banks' biographer, Raymond Banks. Lincoln had already secretly authorized a secret payment of up to $5,000 in December 1862, for spies when he appointed Banks military commander of the Department of the Gulf.[66]

As commander of the Continental Army, General Washington had relied on intelligence to track the movements of British forces during the Revolution and had created a spy ring to analyze their reports. In his first State of the Union address as President, he asked Congress for funds to finance continued espionage operations. In 1790, in response to his request, Congress created the "Contingent Fund of Foreign Intercourse," also known as the "Secret Service Fund." The original authorization was for $40,000. Three years later, the fund had ballooned to $1 million, amounting to 12 percent of the government's budget. Although Congress required certification of disbursements, it also allowed the President to conceal the purposes and recipients of the funds. In 1846, Congress questioned the secrecy provision. Citing national security and protection of sources, President Polk refused to comply.[67] The secrecy provision was not challenged again, but a report of the amount of funds dispersed was sent to Congress. In 1863, when Lincoln authorized Banks the $50,000 from the fund, expenditures amounted to almost 20 percent of the total $227,000 sent by the dispersing clerk at the War Department to Banks and other recipients.[68]

The Secret Service Fund was just that, a fund. It was not an intelligence agency, and the funds were often used for payments for purposes besides espionage. Banks' biographer noted several payments Banks issued from the fund for Michael Hahn's election bid for Louisiana governor in 1864, including a preelection parade with six military bands. Other payments included $1,500 to Hahn's law partner and $300 to a local dentist who endorsed Banks' policies.[69]

Back in New York, Issachar paid an unexpected visit to Banks' wife, Mary. "I should judge from his conversation," she wrote her husband afterward, "his great wish is to make money. And for you to make some also. I told him I thought he could not persuade you to do that."[70]

Was Issachar following through with the part of the deal Betterton claimed Issachar had made with Banks to funnel $50,000 in bribe money to him through his wife? Was his deal with Betterton in fact a scheme to make money for himself? Had Banks in fact taken a bribe?

Issachar's motives may not have been entirely aboveboard. As much as he believed he was doing his patriotic duty, he may not have been able to resist temptation. The lure of enormous profits from trading in cotton had seduced generals, politicians, and even men closely tied to Lincoln, although Lincoln himself never sought to gain from the trade. Lincoln's long-time friend Orville Browning discussed a "scheme" with Lincoln for him and several "prominent men" to send James Singleton to Richmond with the government's approval and official permission to negotiate contracts for cotton, tobacco, and other staples. Browning said they hoped to "make some money and do the country some service."[71] Sending greenbacks into the destitute Confederacy, he rationalized, would induce secessionists back into the Union.[72] Browning eagerly predicted the scheme "will make us rich if we can only get it out."[73]

If Issachar told Betterton he had bribed Banks only to convince Betterton that Banks was in on the deal, why did Mary write Banks after Issachar left that his "great wish was to make money" and for him "to make some also?" Betterton could not have known about Issachar's visiting Mary. Was Issachar in fact corrupt? Did Banks succumb to a bribe? Or did Mary misinterpret Issachar's intentions about Banks making some money too?

Dr. Zacharie had talked "large," said Mary. He had spoken very kindly of Banks, but she felt that Banks was being "too free and intimate with him."

16. Spymaster

Judging from what Issachar said during his visit, Mary sensed some chicanery was involved. "I do not want, my dear husband, to do wrong," she said.[74]

Issachar visited her again a few days later, adding to Mary's misgivings. "I felt a little afraid of him," she said. Issachar had invited her to come to dinner at his house, but she had made some excuse not to go. From the way Issachar talked about him, someone might think Banks and Dr. Zacharie were intimate friends. That was not likely, said Mary. "You have no intimates."[75]

It was because Banks had "no intimates" that she believed him susceptible to Issachar's flattery. Her concern would have been greater had she known Banks had been a guest at Issachar's "very elegant dinner" two weeks before he left for Washington.

When Issachar gave a party, he went all out. "Nothing was lacking that might be desired by the epicure or bon vivant!" the *Times-Picayune* told its readers. "The dishes were as many (and) as varied" as before the war, "as were also the wines, which surely came from cellars stocked for years ere the terms 'blockade' and 'contraband' became familiar to our ears." Some of the guests, "travelled gentlemen," were overheard saying "not even in the most celebrated of the Paris restaurants or hotels, had they ever sat down to a more elegant dinner."[76]

Mary continued to brood about Issachar's influence on her husband. Several weeks later, she wrote Banks, mentioning she had treated Dr. Zacharie well, "but did not allow him to make any arrangements for me," implying he should do the same. Mary reiterated he had no "intimates." "I want your life pure, and correct, faultless," said his dutiful wife. "We all know that you are a good man. I know that you are good"[77]

Banks' $6,600 a year salary as a major general plus the $125–150 a year he received from rental property should have been enough to live on. But he seemed always to be living just above his income. He continued to pay his bills on installments. He continued to carry a mortgage on his home in Massachusetts. His clothes were in poor condition. Mary was living in a boarding house on East 14th Street with their three children. She was paying rent by the week. As a general's wife, she told Banks she was "obliged to spend money pretty freely." She was hosting parties for the Astors, Vanderbilts, and other wives of New York's elite to win their support should Banks make a bid for the Republican nomination in 1864. "You know I like to look well and to appear well."[78] "Both partners," writes Banks' biographer, Fred Harrington, "were fond of show."[79] "Grand entertainments staged by Mrs. Banks" required money. Banks' expenditure "hinted at large peculation or bribes at New Orleans"[80]

There were also irregularities in charges Banks made to his secret services fund. Banks paid his barely literate clerk, William Palmer, $150 a month, much more than a clerk's usual salary. Palmer was Mary's brother. He paid his servant $102, although his salary was already paid for out of government allowances. Banks' also footed General Grant's hotel bill when he briefly visited New Orleans. Although the room and food bill normally came to $1, Banks deducted $800 from his "secret fund. Banks also used his secret services fund to pay for Mary to come to New Orleans to host his parties. Banks was not extravagant. During the war, he only spent half his secret services fund."[81]

17

"Monomaniacs"

On April 17, Seward's son, Colonel William H. Seward, personally delivered the authorizations to Banks at his headquarters near Port Hudson.[1] When he left, Banks immediately dashed off a letter to Secretary Seward. He assured him he had destroyed the secret dispatches in his son's presence and would not do anything inconsistent with government interests.[2]

Back in New Orleans on April 17, 1863, Issachar telegraphed Banks who was "in the field," informing him of his return.[3] When Banks didn't reply, Issachar sent him a note the next day. "You cannot imagine how anxious I am to see you," he said, "in fact I'm boiling over."[4]

Issachar was "boiling over" with worry that either Seward had reconsidered, or the authorization letters he had promised to send Banks had been lost. He had to speak with him. "Should I remain here and wait your return or should I join you." Issachar closed his letter saying his "heart leaped with joy when I heard of your success. many congratulations."[5] Banks' initial mission had been to bypass the Confederate stronghold at Port Hudson and strengthen Grant's attack against Vicksburg. But instead of joining up with Grant, Banks decided to attack Port Hudson on his own. When that effort sputtered, he led a large part of his forces further to the south up the Red River, where he "annihilated" Confederate forces and captured Opelousas, the rebel capital of Louisiana.

Still "boiling over," Issachar dashed off another letter to Seward that same day. Using the same congratulatory words he had sent Banks, Issachar repeated how his heart had leaped with joy when he heard about Banks' success and praised him as "truly a man of action." Issachar ended his note saying "parties" had been "anxiously waiting my return" to carry "out my suggestions."[6] The "parties" anxiously waiting for his return was "Betterton," who Issachar had visited that day and assured him he had accomplished everything he had set out to do in Washington.[7]

Banks was in high spirits after his military victory. He told Issachar he had received Seward's letters authorizing his mission. Stroking Banks' vanity, Issachar wrote back he had taken the liberty of relaying news of Banks' victory to Lincoln and Seward, sure they would be proud of his "brilliant achievement."[8] Issachar was also feeling so secure he ventured to give Banks military advice. "Pardon a suggestion I make, you know 'tis a fault or mine.... I urged the President to send you reinforcements."[9]

Although Banks believed he had won a major military objective, he was soon to learn he was in the doghouse. Instead of being praised for dislodging the Confederates at Opelousas, General-in-Chief Henry Halleck reprimanded him. By not linking up with Grant, he had weakened Grant's attack on Vicksburg. "Operations up the Red River [or] toward Texas," he scolded Banks, were "only of secondary importance, to be undertaken *after* we get possession of the river (Mississippi)."[10]

Meanwhile, New Orleans "was in a state of intense excitement." Banks had believed his conciliatory policies would soften attitudes toward his administration. Business was improving, and even thieves were tipping their hats to him. But despite token signs of compliance, New Orleans was still at heart a Rebel city. Newspapers remained openly pro-Southern. Fed up with their intransigence, prior to leaving for Port Hudson, Banks issued a renewal of Butler's "registered enemies" order. Every citizen in New Orleans who had not already done so had to take the oath of allegiance to the Union. Those refusing would be transported into the Confederacy by May 15, 1863.[11] Unwilling to leave their homes, belongings, businesses, and friends, many took the oath, although their loyalties were still with the Confederacy. The more steadfast were allowed to take enough food to last them 10 days, some clothing, beds and bedding, and as much Confederate money as they had, but no gold or silver.

New Orleans' Jewish community was lax in its Judaism[12] but not in its loyalty to the Confederacy. The city's Jewish women were especially patriotic. The whole male population would have taken the loyalty oath, Issachar told Lincoln, were it not for the "female portion of their families who ... have become perfect monomaniacs" in their refusal to do so.[13]

The *Cincinnati Enquirer* wisecracked that the result of extradition was that younger refugees would voluntarily enter the Confederate army while the middle aged would be conscripted. "And thus does New Orleans, by the generosity of the Federal Government, add at least two good regiments to the Confederate army."[14]

With no one else to turn to, other New Orleans' Jews who refused to take the oath but did not want to leave sought Issachar's help. Issachar did what he could. "Dr. Zacharie, the chiropodist ... has of late been exceedingly active in assisting the Jewish portion of the registered enemies, of which class there are, or were, a great many, in their flight to Dixie," the *New York Herald* told its readers. "The Doctor appears to have taken them under his wing; for he has been beset with them morning, noon and night, and his elegant apartments

17. "Monomaniacs"

at the St. Charles Hotel have sometimes been crowded with Israelites, waiting his leisure, in order to obtain his advice as to what they should do."[15] What could he have told them? If they wanted to stay, they had to take the oath.

Rabbi James K. Gutheim was one of the most prominent Jews refusing to take the loyalty oath. Born in 1817 in Westphalia, Germany, Gutheim was largely self-taught. He came to America in 1843 and worked as a merchant and taught Hebrew school until he took a job in Cincinnati as congregational leader at B'Nai Jeshurun (Children of Righteousness). In 1850, he moved to New Orleans as head of New Orleans' Sephardic congregation, the "Dispersed of Judah," Eight years later, he married Emilie Jones, the daughter of a wealthy merchant in La Grange, Georgia.[16]

Emelie was one of the "monomaniacs" who refused to take the loyalty oath. Issachar mistakenly imagined Gutheim was deep down a Union loyalist who held Lincoln in high esteem.[17] Issachar had convinced himself that Gutheim would not take the oath because of his wife.[18]

But Gutheim's heart was not for the Union. He did not hold the Union or Lincoln in high esteem. The day before Gutheim was deported to Mobile, he wrote his friend Rabbi Isaac Lesser in Philadelphia that the "Dictator in Washington" had ordered him and nearly all of his congregation who refused to take the oath of allegiance to leave with nothing but what they could wear and provisions for 10 days. He was more fortunate than the others, he told Leeser, he had somewhere to go because his wife's father was a wealthy merchant in Georgia and a leader in that city's Jewish community.[19] Soon after leaving New Orleans, congregations in Montgomery, Alabama, and Columbus, Georgia, both offered him the pulpit in their synagogues. Gutheim moved to Montgomery with his wife. He spent the rest of the war shuffling between the two congregations.[20]

Days after taking the position in Montgomery, Gutheim held a prayer dedication for the synagogue, asking God to lend his "abundant favor and benevolence (on) our beloved country, the Confederate States of America" and to "judge between us and our enemies, who have forced upon us this unholy and unnatural war." It was his hope, he said, that the Union would recognize its transgression and "relinquish their cruel designs of subjugation, their lust of gain and dominion." The South, he said, was defending

> our liberties and rights and independence, under unjust and equitable laws ... bless and protect the armed hosts that now stand forth in the defense of our sacred cause. May the breaches lately made in our lines soon be repaired, a series of glorious victories blot out our recent reverses, and the unrighteous invaders be repulsed on every side, abashed, confounded and discomfited ... and our independence be recognized by all families of the earth.[21]

After the war, Gutheim was an active member in the Southern Historical Society, a group intent on keeping Confederate loyalties alive. His wife was one of the founders of New Orleans' Ladies Confederate Memorial Association and was reputed to have raised more money for the erection of their Confederate monument than any other member.[22]

Before his death in 1886, Gutheim was asked whether it was acceptable for Jews to be buried in Metairie Cemetery, New Orleans' cemetery for local elite. Gutheim gave his blessing, assuming all burials would be below ground and separated from gentile interment. (Burials in New Orleans' cemeteries are above ground because of the high water table.) A few months later, he died and became the first Jew to be buried in Metairie in Temple Sinai's section of the cemetery.

* * * * * * * *

Banks was unaware of the turmoil going on in New Orleans' Jewish community. The hapless general was leading another failed mission against Port Hudson. Unmindful of Banks' preoccupation with his military undertaking, on May 5, 1863, Issachar wrote that he was impatiently waiting to hear from a "friend" (Thomas Harper, Betterton's agent) who had left New Orleans for Vicksburg.[23] Four days later, although he had still not heard from the "friend," Issachar wrote Lincoln he was waiting for "assurances" from General Pemberton regarding "a pass to travel through Confederate lines to Vicksburg."[24] The reason Issachar never heard from Harper is that all communications with Vicksburg were cut off after Grant began his siege of the Southern stronghold. Discouraged, but not undaunted, Issachar assured Seward he would continue to "press the matter."[25]

Meanwhile, Lincoln and members of his Cabinet were receiving a constant barrage of complaints from New Orleans concerning Jews and specifically about Issachar. Some were outright anti–Semitic tirades. Some were accusations of bribery and profiteering. Some of his accusers were peeved at Issachar's boasting and arrogance. Many of those pointing the finger were less than upright citizens themselves.

General Butler accused "army contractors, 'principally Jews'" of "making fortunes by the war,"[26] while he and his brother were pocketing over a million dollars from illegally trading in cotton. George Denison, a Butler loyalist, accused Issachar of taking bribes, all the while doing exactly that himself.[27] General George Shepley, the military governor of occupied Louisiana and another Butler loyalist who was likewise involved in illicit cotton trading, denounced Issachar.[28] A Jewish merchant returning to Cincinnati from New Orleans wrote Isaac Wise that "local editors and correspondents of northern papers, residing temporarily [in New Orleans], frequently ventilate their stupid prejudice against our race in revolting newspaper hoaxes and downright lies."[29]

Louisiana Congressman George Michael Decker Hahn also accused Issachar of soliciting bribes.[30] A Jew turned Christian, Hahn distanced himself

17. "Monomaniacs"

from New Orleans' Jews to ally himself with anti–Semitic Butler loyalists in case Butler might return to New Orleans or replace Lincoln as the Republican nominee in the upcoming election. Unaware of the secret arrangements Issachar had with Banks and Lincoln, Hahn wrote Lincoln, "a certain Dr. Zacharie—a Jew … is, passing himself off as a confidential or government secret agent of the government and is using his influence over many of our highest military officials" to gain commercial advantages and favors from the government officers for people bribing him. "If he is an agent of yours," he wrote Lincoln, "he should not be liable to such suspicions; and if he is not your agent, the fact should be known."[31]

New Orleans Detective John Richardson, irked that Issachar was passing himself off as "Chief of U.S. Detectives" and interfering with police business, accused Issachar of offering him a bribe. Dr. Zacharie, he said, invited him to his room at the St. Charles to talk to him about Richardson's arrest and seizure of goods belonging to an H. C. Duncan. Issachar told him he wished he hadn't made the arrest because he employed Duncan and the goods and money ($2,500) Richardson had seized were the property of the U.S. government. Issachar said he had sent this man several times into the Confederacy on government business and had allowed him to take similar amounts of goods as a "blind" to the Confederates "and to make a little for himself." Richardson said Issachar urged him to get Duncan "out of his scrape" so his cover wouldn't be blown. If he did, Issachar promised to "give me a better position." Richardson said he had refused.

Duncan was never convicted. Before his trial, he escaped, leaving his money and goods behind. Duncan himself had never claimed to be a government officer, said Richardson, and he suspected him of being a Rebel sympathizer and a speculator. "It seems proper to me," said Richardson, "that Dr. Zacharie should be called to account for such a course of conduct."[32] In Issachar's defense, Duncan may have been one of the three "right kind of men" he recruited to bring back information from behind Confederate lines.

* * * * * * * *

With Vicksburg under siege and Betterton and his "friend" no longer a conduit to Pemberton, Banks arrested Betterton. Betterton was subsequently "convicted by evidence and confession of fraudulently violating the regulations concerning trade" by shipping contraband labeled as "barrels of beef" without authority through the enemy lines. Banks fined him $25,000 and sentenced him to imprisonment for one year at hard labor at Fort Pickens in Florida.[33] Issachar's name was never mentioned in the indictment.

In a long letter he wrote to General Banks on July 22, 1863, Betterton claimed Issachar had set him up. The doctor, he insisted, had duped him.

Betterton described in detail the lengths to which Dr. Zacharie had gone to convince him his "arrangement" had been sanctioned by Banks.

In February 1863, he had become friendly with Dr. Zacharie and his secretary Charles Johnson. That acquaintance led to an "arrangement to take goods into the confederacy and bring back cotton [from the Confederacy]" through a Thomas Harper. Betterton went into detail about Issachar's approaching Banks for a permit on his side of the arrangement, Banks' advising him to go to Washington to get the government's approval, Banks' issuing him a special permit, Banks' agreeing to a $50,000 bribe, letters Issachar had sent him from Washington informing him of his progress, Banks giving him $1,000 worth of goods and a pass for Harper, Issachar's signing a receipt for the money, Banks' ordering Col. Amos Beckwith to give Issachar another

> $1,000, and many other details that had convinced him Dr. Zacharie had Banks' full approval and was not deceiving him. Had he thought otherwise, Betterton maintained he would not have cooperated with Dr. Zacharie. Betterton ended his letter asking for clemency. Betterton admitted he was in it for the money, but in light of what he had explained, he hoped "it may mitigate your sentence as I have been imprisoned already three months, by revoking the balance of the time and fine."[34]

When Banks didn't respond, Betterton appealed to Major Benjamin Rush Plumley. Plumley, Banks' staff officer and long-time acquaintance, was a man with a "limitless appetite for political intrigue" and lust for patronage.[35]

After hearing Betterton out, Plumley wrote Banks that he fully believed Betterton had acted in good faith and had been misled by Dr. Zachary [sic], who he said had "made similar proposition to me, exhibiting letters and documents from the President and from yourself." Plumley added he didn't know if Issachar was himself deceived about his authority, but he was convinced Betterton had been misled. If Betterton were guilty, Plumley said, Betterton had suffered enough. If Betterton was innocent of intentional wrong, as Plumley believed he was, common justice should see him released and his fine remitted.[36] Banks ordered Betterton's release on September 7, 1863.[37] After his release, Betterton was back in New Orleans as a shipping and commission merchant.

Despite his avowal that he had been tricked by Issachar, Betterton was on friendly terms, if not in collaboration, with both Butler and his brother Andrew. When Andrew died in April 1864, Betterton sent Butler his condolences on the death "of one whose soul when living was as noble as it was charitable." He parted with him, said Betterton, "only to remember his virtues."[38] Betterton ended his letter "hoping the administration may place you with us again." Betterton was arrested again for smuggling in late 1864.[39]

Issachar was "called to account" a year later and exonerated. Near the end of the war, Lincoln appointed a special commission in December 1864, to investigate violations of army regulations in New Orleans, choosing short, portly, shaggy-mustached 40-year-old Major General William Farrar "Baldy" Smith to head it, along with New York lawyer, James Topham Brady. The official name for the investigation was the Commission on Corrupt Practices in the South. Unofficially it was called the Smith-Brady Commission.[40]

In the course of its investigation, the commission examined issuance of cotton permits, trading activities, conduct of commanding generals, mismanagement of abandoned property and provost marshal's courts, local elections, and the activities of Dr. Zacharie. The commission discovered a broad scheme of fraud and corruption at every level of administration. Custom House officials received bribes to issue trading permits. Several of the witnesses called to testify stated they had no knowledge of Issachar's venality.

General Bowen testified he had "never granted Issachar permits without orders from headquarters."[41] Robert Montgomery, a New Orleans auctioneer, told the commission that Dr. Zacharie "led me to understand that his mission here was diplomatic more than anything else. I knew he had a great deal of intercourse with the other side. He sent people over there constantly, but as far as mercantile operations, they never amounted to anything. I never had but one operation when he sent a cargo of goods into Mobile by the consent of General Banks."[42]

Montgomery was one of the many "registered enemies" Issachar had recruited as a spy. When Montgomery was arrested for smuggling, Issachar wrote Banks to allow the provost marshal to "extend favors to registered enemies." "I may meet these people in the Confederacy," he explained.[43]

Several of the men who had accused Issachar of taking bribes were themselves found guilty of corruption, among them George Denison. A Mr. Brotts, one of the merchants summoned by the commission, said he had had difficulty obtaining permits from the Custom House until he realized the "effective way of doing business was to give presents or rewards to the officials." Brotts said on several occasions he paid Denison from $95 to $1,500 for permits. Benjamin Rush Plumley, another of Issachar's enemies, was also outed for corruption. John Richardson had taken bribes of $1,400–$1,500 to prevent delays in bringing cotton into New Orleans and shipping it down river.[44]

* * * * * * * *

The commission wound up its inquiry in late summer 1865. The four-volume report was never published. President Johnson said it was "not deemed compatible with the public interests" and refused to release it.[45]

President Grant was similarly reluctant to have it released since it documented questionable activities on the part of General Butler, Chief Justice Salmon Chase's son-in-law; U.S. Senator William Sprague, the quartermaster in his own department, and friends and relatives. A summary report was finally published in 1876.[46]

18

A Service He Alone Was Capable Of

Issachar was discouraged but not undaunted after his intended rendezvous with General Pemberton had come to naught. He was determined to "press the matter," he told Seward.[1] On June 1, 1863, Issachar wrote to Banks, who was still besieging Port Hudson, that he was "anxiously awaiting" a reply to Banks' reaction to "my heartfelt peace plan."[2] Other than payment of the Confederate war debt,[3] Issachar never spelled out any details of his "heartfelt plan" in any of his correspondence. Like Lincoln, Issachar believed in appealing to Southern self-interest. By emphasizing the immediate economic advantages of peace, Issachar believed the South might be open to considering a negotiated settlement to end the war. His overall aim, he would later claim, with characteristic immodesty, was to bring "peace with honor to the North and without humiliation to the South."[4]

When Banks did not respond, Issachar left the safety of New Orleans for Banks' headquarters.[5] He had taken the risk, he told Seward, because he had "been solicited by 'leading men of this country, connected with leaders at Richmond'" to go there to discuss peace. Issachar didn't say who those "leading men" were. They believed, he said, "I may be instrumental to inaugurate some plan which may terminate the war."[6] Uncharacteristically, Issachar wrote Seward he hadn't been willing to listen to their suggestions without first consulting General Banks. "Enough to say—he desires me to go, and as usual has promised to afford me every facility for my intended visit."[7] Issachar was optimistic that an overture from the government to pay Confederate debt would encourage peace talks.

On July 2, 1863, Issachar was back at Banks' headquarters to finalize his adventure. To pave the way for his mission, Banks sent a note to General William Emery to issue passes for Martin Gordon, Jr., and David Pretts to travel through federal lines under a flag of truce to Richmond.[8] Gordon was a cotton broker[9] with known Confederate ties, including a high-ranking brother-in-law in the Confederate army, General Richard "Dick" Taylor.[10]

18. A Service He Alone Was Capable Of

Gordon would have credibility with Confederate leaders about Issachar's proposed trip to Richmond.

Banks wrote a second letter for Issachar to give to Seward in support of this new mission to Richmond. Banks extolled Issachar's diplomatic abilities and praised him as "a zealous supporter of the Government." Dr. Zacharie's "connection with the Jewish community of New Orleans which is very large and very powerful both by its numerical strength, and the activity which distinguishes its leading members has given him great advantages." His "considerate and attentive" assistance to many of the registered enemy families ordered to leave New Orleans, had "won from leading men of the Rebel Government expressions of gratitude." Their "endorsements" would enable him to accomplish what other men of "more commanding or social political position" (a possible reference to Issachar's and Judah Benjamin's shared background) were less likely to achieve. "He has it in his power to render a service which others cannot well do."[11]

Banks sent a final note to his quartermaster, Colonel Samuel Beckley Holabird, to give Issachar $5,000 in Confederate money. The money was for expenses once Issachar passed through Confederate lines. "Get a receipt for the money," he added.[12]

Issachar was excited about his impending mission, but not so excited he didn't hand Banks a note of his own. It was a bill for $1,437 for his last two months and 13 days of "services from April 17 to date."[13]

Issachar left New Orleans on July 4, 1863. His departure did not go unnoticed. Believing he was permanently leaving, a number of people came by to say goodbye and to thank him "for the benefits I had conferred upon those of their fellow citizens who were in trouble." Knowing Banks' susceptibility to flattery, Issachar told him his well-wishers had confided to him, "among the officers of the Government [they] had but one friend here ... yourself."[14]

Banks had counted on military fame to make him a household name. Instead, he had been outmaneuvered so often that Lincoln had reassigned him to an administrative post. But Banks had not given up on his aspirations. He had regarded his assignment in New Orleans as a stepping-stone to national prominence. Reconciling competing rivalries in the city and elsewhere in Louisiana would gain him national attention as a peerless arbiter. It would catapult him, he imagined, to the cadre of leading contenders angling to replace Lincoln. Despite victories at Gettysburg and Vicksburg, Lincoln was widely regarded as not re-electable. After Port Hudson surrendered to Banks, Banks felt its capitulation would skyrocket his reputation. Instead, Grant received the credit for Port Hudson on the premise it could not have held out after Vicksburg surrendered. If Issachar's negotiated peace talks led to an end to the war, any honor he received would be shared with Banks.[15] Sponsoring a phenomenal breakthrough in the national deadlock would dramatically raise his stature as the candidate to replace Lincoln. It would be his ticket to the Presidency.

* * * * * * * *

While Issachar was preparing for his mission to Richmond, Confederate Vice President Alexander Stephens was preparing his own peace initiative. By 1863, Stephens and many other prominent Confederate office holders had become less sanguine about the South's chances for military victory.[16] Stephens had persuaded President Jefferson Davis, despite his misgivings, to allow him to open negotiations with Lincoln. He would be going under the pretext of a prisoner exchange, Stephens said. If that negotiation failed, the South would not lose face, and Southern honor would not be tarnished.[17]

Stephens' timing was not haphazard. In late June 1863, General Robert E. Lee's Confederate forces had invaded Pennsylvania. If Lee's army prevailed and made its way to Washington, Stephens would have been in position to negotiate a treaty recognizing the Confederacy. With Davis' grudging approval, Stephens headed to Union-controlled City Point, Virginia. On his arrival, he asked Admiral Samuel P. Lee to allow him to go on to Washington— he had an important letter from Davis to give to Lincoln.

After the Union victory at Gettysburg on July 3, 1863, and the capture of Vicksburg on July 4, Lincoln was inclined to meet with Stephens to hear what he had to say. The proposed meeting put members of Lincoln's cabinet at loggerheads. Historian Doris Kearns Goodwin memorably dubbed Lincoln's fractious cabinet a "Team of Rivals."[18] Secretary of War Edwin Stanton and Secretary of the Navy Gideon Welles were amenable to hearing what Stephens had to say, but they quarreled about which department should be the one to communicate with him on Lincoln's behalf. Secretary of State William Seward, Stanton, and Treasury Secretary Salmon Chase opposed any contact with Stephens. "We are in the midst of a Cabinet crisis," the *Cleveland Plain Dealer* reported.[19]

On July 6, Stephens was informed neither Lincoln nor any representative of the government would meet him. The official response from Secretary Welles was "the customary agents and channels are adequate for all needful military communications and conferences between the U.S. and the insurgents."[20]

That was the official statement. Unofficially, Lincoln had been open to contact with Confederate leaders. Lincoln's critics in both the North and the South accused his administration as being an obstacle to a serious peace settlement. "It was a difficult balancing act."[21] Lincoln couldn't appear to be interested in a compromise with the Confederate government, nor could he appear to be rejecting one outright. "It was in his interest to let peace missions go forward without his official blessing." It was also in his interest that they fail. Public awareness of his allowing such unofficial rapprochements would diffuse criticism that he was not interested in a peaceful settlement of the war.[22]

Lincoln didn't foresee any harm in allowing Issachar and other private civilian would-be peacemakers to sound out Confederate leaders, with the understanding they would be going on their own responsibility. At the very least, he might learn their thoughts about a negotiated peace.

Prior to Stephens' peace initiative, in May 1863, the Methodist Reverend James F. Jaques, a colonel in the 73rd Illinois Regiment, asked for a furlough from his commanding officer, General William Rosecrans, which Lincoln approved, to go to Richmond to discuss a peace settlement with Confederate President Davis. Jaques, a prominent minister in the Methodist Church, was in touch with the large number of Methodists in the parts of the South now under federal control. They were tired of the rebellion and ardently wanted peace, they had told him, and would happily pledge their allegiance to the Union if assured of amnesty. Davis was said to be "a praying man," Jaques explained, and "many of his people are devotedly pious ... the mission cannot fail. God's hand is in it."[23] Lincoln had refused to meet Jaques in person to avoid the perception that he was encouraging him, but gave his permission on the understanding that he was not representing the government.

Jaques eventually left for Richmond in July 1863, some time after Stephens' return. Jaques never got to Richmond. He met with General James Longstreet and several Confederate leaders behind Confederate lines, but Davis refused to see him since he lacked any authority to negotiate on Lincoln's behalf. When Jaques returned, he wrote Lincoln he had valuable information to convey to him. Lincoln never answered, and Jaques returned to his unit.

* * * * * * * *

Issachar arrived in Washington on July 15, 1863, while Jaques was still in the South. After booking a room at the Willard Hotel, he immediately sent a note to Secretary Seward. He had something important to communicate, he said. "Please let me know at what hour I may have the pleasure of seeing you."[24] When Seward didn't immediately respond, Issachar sent him a second note: "I am waiting to see you.... Will you please give me an interview?"[25]

Issachar met with Seward the next day and handed him the letter Banks had written praising Issachar as "a zealous supporter of the Government" and extolling his diplomatic virtues. His efforts on behalf of "registered enemies" required to leave New Orleans had earned him the gratitude "of people with great influence in the Confederate government." Owing to his Jewish connections, "Zacharie had potential influence with individuals in the Confederate government denied to others."

The "great influence" Banks was alluding to was with the Jewish Confederate Secretary of State, Judah Benjamin. Benjamin, the highest ranking and most trusted member of Davis' cabinet, was indebted to Issachar for easing Benjamin's "registered enemy" sister's departure from New Orleans. The "service" he alone was capable of was using his influence with Benjamin to discuss a peaceful settlement of the war.[26]

The *New York Herald* had assumed Issachar had been dismissed from his post in New Orleans because of alleged bribery and speculation. "It is very evident that Uncle Sam has suffered to a considerable extent in the department of customs." The government "has been swindled and humbugged by men who have heretofore borne the highest reputation." Now that "Doctor Zacharie has been deprived of his authority," there was nothing keeping him from returning to New York and resuming his practice.[27]

Issachar assured Seward there was no doubt in his mind Davis and Benjamin would agree to see him. If nothing else, "I will at least learn the true feelings of the people" and the Confederate leaders. If it were in his power to make a peace agreement, he said with his typical false modesty, he would feel "sanguine" about ending the war. But because he had no such power, he would "go, hear, see and say as little as possible." His great desire, he said, was to prove to them they would not regret the confidence they had bestowed on him. "What I wish to do is for the benefit of yourself & my country. I have no other aspirations."[28]

Without directly turning Issachar down, Seward did his best to dissuade him from his proposed trip to Richmond. Do you believe you would be received after Lincoln refused to see Vice President Stephens on his peace mission, he asked? Issachar would not be dissuaded that easily. He would take the risk, he said. Seward was unmoved by his bravado. If you fail to obtain a peace initiative, he replied, the whole country would blame Lincoln. Besides, after the Northern victories at Gettysburg and Vicksburg, no one was in a mood for compromise: "the people don't want it."[29]

On Friday, July 18, Lincoln and Issachar huddled at the White House for two hours. Seward had not been invited. Lincoln was still interested in learning whether Davis was willing to negotiate peace. He had no illusions that Davis would come to the table, but some of his cabinet might be willing to consider a peace deal. At the very least, he would learn something about morale in Richmond. Lincoln made it clear to Issachar any talks he had in Richmond would not be as Lincoln's ambassador. He would be going as a private individual on his own to discuss peace. Lincoln also told Issachar he would still need to convince Seward, who opposed the meeting, that he be allowed to go to Richmond.

Issachar took Lincoln's telling him to go back to Seward as a sign of approval. "From his actions & words I was led to believe that all I wished for would be granted." Calling on Seward on Saturday, the day after his meeting with Lincoln, Issachar knocked on Seward's door and handed Seward's doorkeeper a note: "I am directed by the President to report myself to you this morning and have the honor of so doing."

The doorkeeper told him to wait. The Secretary was too busy that day to see him, he said. Come back tomorrow, he said. "After church."[30]

Issachar knocked on Seward's door early Sunday afternoon. Seward was slightly shorter than Issachar. He had light hair and eyes and an especially large nose, which made him avoid having himself photographed or painted. Usually pleasant, rarely ruffled, and politically astute, after a brief bit of pleasantries, Seward asked Issachar what he wanted from the administration. "All I want for the present," Issachar answered, "is a Pass to go into the Confederacy, so that I may have the opportunity to carry out my plans."

Seward replied that he had just met with Lincoln and members of the cabinet that morning, presumably "after church." Members of the cabinet were determined not to give him a pass, he said. They wished to have nothing to do with the Confederate government. Besides, they were concerned his going there might bring complications. The Confederates might hold him as a hostage.

Issachar assured him his safety was not an issue. Gordon and Pretts, the men Banks had sent ahead to Richmond, were waiting for him with papers for his protection. He wouldn't leave without that guarantee.[31]

"Do you think they would receive you, after we refuse(d) to see Mr. Stevens?" Seward persisted.

"I will take that risk," Issachar replied with no hesitancy.

Seward was not convinced. If Zacharie failed, the country would blame Lincoln. The victories at Gettysburg and Vicksburg were still fresh in their minds. Seward told Zacharie it was not a time for compromise.

* * * * * * * *

Washington's rumor mill was little different in Lincoln's day than it is now. Within hours of Issachar's meeting with Seward, word of that meeting was leaked. In an editorial titled "Corn Cutting Extraordinary," James Gordon Bennett, the *New York World*'s editor, lambasted Seward for even listening to Issachar. "If there be one thing more remarkable than another in the career of Mr. Lincoln's Secretary of State," said Bennett, "it is his singular inaptitude to the choice of confidants, his secrets are sure to be shouted from the housetops."[32]

Casting about to find a toady, a person through whom Europe's kings negotiated their "little contracts with the Evil One," Bennett said Seward found one, "an illustrious corn cutter, Mr. Zacharie, who had distinguished himself early in the war by offering to *debunionize* the whole of the Seventh Regiment of this city." "The corn-cutter," Bennett continued, "had been speedily cajoled into forgetting his patients." He had "left Broadway to limp itself into a fever, to go to New Orleans as the 'confidential spy and agent' of the State Department and the White House."[33]

Once he arrived in New Orleans, "he rapidly made his presence and his power felt. He gave himself out as the 'representative of the federal government' and a great corn contractor, which he was." "The government paid him a salary larger than a cabinet minister's $8,000/yr." "Zacharie, the cutter of corns, had only to cut his corns discreetly in order to wax fat and prosper exceedingly. He gave fine suppers entertaining the most prominent citizens of New Orleans and the highest officers of the army and navy."[34]

Mistaking Issachar's leaving New Orleans as a sign he had been dismissed, Bennett gloated that Issachar's confrontation with General George Shepley, the military governor of Louisiana, had been his undoing. "Supper parties and contracts, salary and the sweet sense of power, all in a moment vanished like the baseless fabric of a dream. Callous as the corns he treats must be the heart which can contemplate unmoved so sudden and so steep a crash. Pared off and plastered out of sight, the hapless toady disappears, while he who made him to unmake will sorrow for him only as men sorrow for a familiar bunion gone."[35]

* * * * * * * *

The day after his meeting with Seward, a despondent Issachar wrote Lincoln that Seward had not granted his "or rather General Bank's [sic] request" for a pass to go to Richmond. "I am fearful that in my short interview, both with yourself & Mr. Seward, my intentions have been misunderstood…. I leave for home this evening. Should you wish at any time to listen to me, or if I can serve you, I am at your command."[36]

Days later, Issachar wrote Banks, "I have been so greatly disappointed, as I may say foiled in my plans." "I have no heart to do, or say anything. All my hopes & plans [have been] destroyed."[37]

Never one to accept his own failings, Issachar claimed his plan hadn't been turned down because of the merit of his plan. "They feel satisfied I would be successful." There had to be some other reason. Issachar decided it had to have been politically motivated. "I think I can see through it all," he groused. "Parties in the cabinet" didn't want Banks to get the credit for anything. If Issachar's mission were a success, Banks "would be the man of *the* people." The "masses" were behind him, and so were the "conservative men of all parties."[38] Disingenuously, Issachar told Banks, "I do not flatter when I tell you that the conservative men of all parties believe you to be the only safe man the country possess who is prominently before the people."[39] In consoling Banks, Issachar also lamented he had lost his own chance for fame. "I have some ambition & would be near the 'Rising Star' (meaning Banks)." What do you want me to do with the funds you have given me? "Like yourself I would have a clean record."[40]

19

He Lacks Stability

Issachar's ambition to be near a "Rising Star" would not let him just sit back and wait for fate to hand Banks the Republican nomination in 1864. Banks may not have been able to personally campaign for the nomination, but there was nothing to stop Issachar from campaigning on his behalf. Back at his profession and travelling back and forth between his offices in New York and Philadelphia, Issachar took every opportunity to drum up support for a Banks run at the Republican nomination. Issachar wrote him, "Permit me to say without any flattery your name is spoken with more kindness than you can imagine. Your friends are legion and those make more. Only, my dear General, continue the manner you have commenced and all will go right."[1]

According to Issachar, Titian J. Coffey, Lincoln's assistant attorney general, had told him he "would rather have your (Banks') future than that of any man in America."[2] Issachar's own secretary, Charles Johnson, was in Philadelphia forming a Banks Club. "He is a strong believer in you and says you are the only man to save the country."[3] Johnson also kept Banks informed of his popularity. He had been at several large political meetings held by both parties and had "yet to see the man, but was unwilling to trust you at the head of the Government. I don't write to flatter. I speak the words of the people who believe you can, if anyone, save our country from destruction. No man stands before you in the hearts of your countrymen."[4]

In the meantime, Lincoln had received a letter from Banks reporting what Gordon had learned from his trip to Richmond. Banks explained he had supported Gordon's mission to ascertain "the drift of public and private opinion."

Gordon reported that while Jefferson Davis was "still the soul of the Rebellion, most of the people" inside the Confederacy desired peace. "They talked at first stoutly for war, but soon allowed their desire to be known. The public men (meaning important politicians) were of the same opinion. The basis of action would be something like the terms of your proclamation—gradual emancipation of slaves, and more freedom of compensation." Confederate Secretary of State Judah Benjamin was still hoping that either

England or France would recognize and support Confederate independence, but no one else in the Confederate cabinet or other "public men" expected any intervention from Europe.[5]

Banks' letter saying the South was tired of war and would accept Lincoln's overtures of compensated emancipation in return for peace and reunification, was engrossing, but Lincoln could not authorize any formal meeting with Confederate leaders. A formal meeting could imply recognition of the Confederacy. It was an acknowledgment he refused to accept. He needed some other way of communicating with his counterparts in Richmond. Zacharie already had permission from Confederate leaders to visit. Since Issachar would be visiting Richmond as a private citizen with no authority to negotiate peace, there would be no acknowledgment of the Confederacy's legitimacy. Lincoln sent him a message to come immediately to Washington.

"Great changes has [sic] taken place in my favour," Issachar wrote Banks. Lincoln had called him back to Washington and told him "I had left Washington in too great a hurry." At the time, he hadn't been able to entertain his proposed mission. Secretary Chase and others had been vocal in opposing any peace talks. Lincoln had also received letters, presumably from Hahn and others, accusing Issachar of corruption. He had looked into the matter and was satisfied "I *was all right*." He "was now willing to afford me every facility to carry out *my plans* (italics mine)." He "felt sure I would be successful."[6]

Issachar was ecstatic. He was finally more than a spy; he was a peacemaker. "If I am successful," he gloated in anticipation, "you as well as I are made for life.... What is money, to position[?]."[7] Reading Issachar's letter, Banks must have been equally elated. He would be a national hero.

"Rest assured that you will never regret having taken me into your confidence," said Issachar. "I feel proud of having your friendship. I hope the day is not far distant when you will say well done my good & faithful friend." Issachar also crowed about how proud he felt he had outlived his enemies.[8]

* * * * * * * *

Without consulting Seward or the other members of his cabinet, Lincoln handed Issachar a letter introducing "Dr. Zacharie of New York" to give to General John Gray Foster, commanding officer at Fortress Monroe: he "has been with Genl Banks a large part of the time" and "enjoys the General's confidence in a high degree. Any kindness you may show him will be appreciated by me."[9]

Issachar arrived at Fortress Monroe on September 20, 1863, and showed Foster Lincoln's letter. Foster "received me kindly, and has offered me every facility—to do all I wish," he wrote Lincoln. "[I] leave tomorrow, for Richmond and hope to return to you in a short time, with honour to myself, and render a service to you, and my Government that will be appreciated."[10]

"The more it draws towards my departure," he wrote his secretary, Charles Johnson, "the more I feel the importance of the undertaking. But I have commenced it, & with the help of Providence will go through with it." Two days later, on September 22, Issachar left for Richmond by boat under a flag of truce.[11] Possibly he passed the time between his arrival and departure cutting General Foster's corns and treating men at the fortress for various foot ailments.

Issachar met with Benjamin, Secretary of the Navy Stephen R. Mallory, Secretary of War James A. Seddon, and Richmond's Provost Marshall General John H. Winder on September 27, 1863. The meeting took place at City Point, Virginia, instead of Richmond, so that there would be no doubt that it was not an official meeting.

Issachar was ebullient over his "success." Later that day, he met privately with Benjamin,[12] who told him he was obligated to General Banks for the kindness he had shown his "registered enemy" sister when she left New Orleans. The two men also shared some history. They were both Jews, they had both grown up in Charleston, and their parents both had stores on King Street in Charleston. Issachar took the opportunity to ask a personal favor of Benjamin—would he give him permission to travel through the Confederacy to visit his father in Savannah?

Despite Benjamin's turning him down, Issachar sent Benjamin a letter marked "confidential" the following day, thanking him for the meeting. What else they said is unknown. The next day, he sent a fulsome letter to Benjamin, outdoing himself in flattery. With no sense of vanity or hypocrisy, Issachar said he had been overcome at the pleasure of their meeting. He hoped he had made a favorable impression. "Knowing that the Confederate flag was waving over my head" my "heart was bursting with joy.... Should we meet [again]—I would gladly join the armies of the confederacy if I did not know that I could be of more service to join where I am."[13] Men had been jailed for saying far less.

Issachar suspected Benjamin had declined his request to visit his father because Issachar would be reporting back to Lincoln about conditions in the South. "Unless I can visit the confederacy without the least doubt of my sincerely towards you all," he continued, "I would rather sacrifice Father, Sister and all ... if you are satisfied of my sincerity towards you all and you can at any time grant me the permission to visit Savannah or Macon, I shall be under everlasting obligations."[14]

Issachar closed his letter saying he was going immediately to Washington to talk to Lincoln "as but few can," and would relate Benjamin's telling him "no propositions of peace may be expected from the South. I shall put matters in the right light," he assured him. "Some good must come out of our unexpected meeting." Issachar promised to inform Benjamin of "all that

19. He Lacks Stability

transpires," but he had to be "very carefull how I write." If anything important were to come after meeting with Lincoln, he would return himself.

"If I write or telegraph to you at this point, come immediately to me. You will know it is of importance. Should you know any person visiting New York in who you have implicit confidence in write to me and I will post you up on all you wish to know." Fearful his letters might be intercepted, Issachar warned Benjamin, "be careful not to sign your name. I will know who it comes from. Should I write I will sign this.... Do not think me to anxious to hear from you. I do it from pure motives." Issachar ended with the hope Benjamin would "never regret the intercourse we had last night."[15]

Back at Fortress Monroe, Issachar telegraphed Lincoln: "Just returned. Will be with you tomorrow afternoon."[16] Issachar was ebullient. He felt his mission had been more successful than he could have hoped. He had opened the door to further negotiations in which Banks would be the standard-bearer.

Lincoln welcomed him back. After they shook hands, Lincoln walked to his office door and locked it so they wouldn't be disturbed, and they talked for two hours. Lincoln, he wrote Banks, was "delighted with my success." But there was an obstacle—a "rub," Issachar called it. Lincoln had kept Seward and the rest of his cabinet in the dark about his secret mission. When he had first broached Issachar's visit to Richmond to the Cabinet, Secretary Chase, the hardest of the hard-liners, had been bitterly opposed to his going. Lincoln, he said, reminded him "of the man that won the Elephant at a Raffle, and didn't know what to do with it."[17]

Lincoln ended their meeting by saying he wanted to follow up on Issachar's initiative, but he needed time to "give it shape & life." Did Issachar have any suggestions? "This gave me an opening," he said. "Send for Genl. Banks ... you can trust him with your confidence in carrying out any negotiation." Let him go back to Benjamin and tell him General Banks would meet with him as soon as he could come from New Orleans.

It was a "happy thought," said Lincoln.[18] He would think about it. It was an idle remark. Lincoln was aware Banks had designs on the Presidency. In January 1864, Banks was listed among the five nominees to replace Lincoln.[19]

Issachar closed his letter to Banks by telling him he was surprised to read in the *Herald* that the cabinet was considering "negociations" for a "Peacefull termination of our trouble ... which leads me to believe, that revelations [of] my interview ... have been purposely made, with a view of throwing obstructions to prevent consummation of this most desirable movement."[20]

* * * * * * * *

The day before, the *New York Herald* had indeed reported the cabinet had been apprised that a secret meeting had taken place to discuss peace talks with the Confederate government. "What these propositions are we are not yet permitted to know, nor whence they came … but from this single fact, in connection with the present reduced and hopeless condition of the rebellion, we are encouraged to anticipate the happiest and most glorious results."[21]

The *Herald* was sketchy in its first account of the clandestine meeting, largely imagining Lincoln's terms for peace: the Confederacy would be abolished. "Conspirators" would be crushed or expelled from "the region of the insurrection," and loyal citizens would "resume their functions under the general government." Lincoln was "still prosecuting the war for the Union, and not as an abolition cause," the *Herald* assured its readers. Slavery was "only an incidental and secondary issue." His administration "will avail itself of the readiest means and the simplest method for the restoration of peace."[22]

Knowing nothing about what was actually said, the next day, the *Herald* concocted an illusionary Confederate invasion of Mexico based on Northern anxiety over the Confederacy's attempts, since 1861, to extend its jurisdiction to the southwest New Mexico territories and Mexico's northern territories.[23] For its part of the peace settlement, said the *Herald*, the United States would "consent and cooperate" with a Confederate invasion of Mexico. Davis and his remaining army and loyalists would invade Mexico and oust the French troops who had been occupying Mexico since late 1861. "Jeff. Davis, with a Southern army of over two hundred, or even one hundred thousand men at his back, and five hundred thousand camp followers, in order to secure a Southern confederacy south of the Rio Grande, would only have to march into the country and take possession…. Both sides will gain what they are respectively contending for—the one a restoration of the Union, and the other a magnificent Southern confederacy…. If Lincoln's Cabinet accepted such grand scheme," opined the *Herald*, "the war would be over in ninety days."[24]

Had there been any truth to the *Herald*'s story, Bennett would have put it on page one. Instead, he buried it on page six. Bennett never expected anyone to take it seriously, especially since it was an exact recycle of the harebrained scenario the *Herald* had published on July 9, 1863, before Issachar left for Richmond.[25]

* * * * * * * *

Issachar stayed in Washington waiting for Lincoln to make up his mind. Since his last letter, "nothing has been done," he wrote Banks. "Mr. Lincoln has refused to send for you but has not given me his reasons." Issachar believed he knew why he hadn't. He could "see through it[.] it will make you to popular."[26] "I am determined that no person shall have the Eclaim but you…. I know one thing that no person will be received by Benjamin, except myself, as he pledged his word to me that if any thing was to be done that I should have all the honour." Lincoln "lacks stability." "He has it in his power to stop all fighting in twenty-four hours if he would follow out *my program*" (italics mine).[27]

19. He Lacks Stability

In the meantime, Lincoln asked him to meet with Seward to brief him on his meeting with Benjamin. Lincoln had alienated Seward by sending Issachar to Richmond without informing him beforehand. Asking Issachar to meet with Seward was Lincoln's attempt to patch things up.

Issachar was not only frustrated at Lincoln's not following up on his advice about Banks, but he was also peeved at Lincoln's asking him to mollify Seward, who had never been warm to Issachar's Richmond venture. "Mr. Lincoln desired me to call upon him (Seward), but that I refused to do," he griped to Banks.[28] When Lincoln asked him a second time, Issachar relented. "You will much oblige me (by giving me) an interview," he wrote Seward. "I have matters of importance to communicate to you, which can only be done by word of mouth.... You will finde my revelations very interesting—to you it is of the utmost importance."[29]

Confederate Secretary of State Judah P. Benjamin, of whom Zacharie said: "No one will be received by Benjamin, except myself." Ca. 1856 (courtesy Library of Congress).

On Saturday, Issachar knocked on Seward's red brick three-story home facing Lafayette Park, within steps of the White House. Lincoln often strolled over to Seward's home to discuss state business and swap off-color stories. Sitting in Seward's parlor, where three years earlier Philip Barton Key bled to death after being shot by Congressman Dan Sickles for having an affair with Sickles' wife, Seward puffed on cigars while the two men talked for five hours.

Afterwards, Issachar wrote Banks that Seward "was much pleased with my revelations, and acknowledged that I had done wonders.... It was the only tangible thing that had been done since the war had commenced, but he could not inform me at present what was to be done." Seward invited him to "sup" with him the following Monday after he had a chance to consider what to do next.

Later that day, Issachar called on Lincoln. He had just met with Seward, he said. "He was verry happy that I had explained every thing." Seward had been "pleased to death" at what he had told him. "They would pull together." Seward had been optimistic. He was confident "they could fix matters when ever they wanted too."[30]

On Monday night, Issachar was back at Seward's, impatient to hear what he had to say. Seward was in no hurry; they should "sup" before getting down to business. Seward liked his "victuals." After a three-course meal and a glass or two of wine, the two men adjourned to Seward's luxuriously furnished parlor. What had he decided about his plan, Issachar asked anxiously.

Seward was not encouraging. Lighting up his customary cigar, Seward told him to go back to New York and "keep quiet." The government could not officially back any future meetings he might have with Judah Benjamin. He could communicate with Benjamin on his own, but the government could not be involved.

Secretary of State William H. Seward, ca. 1860–1865 (photograph courtesy of Library of Congress).

Issachar was downhearted. "What is the use of my goin to see Benjamin if we are not ready to do anything," he grumbled to Banks. Lincoln and Seward were duplicitous, he said. They were telling him to go home so they could take the credit for his plan. "I am affraid they wish to steal *my thunder from me, and you know that twas I that concocted the plan*" (italics mine). If they would only allow them to negotiate with Richmond, "you & I can make peace in twenty-four hours, satisfactory to the North, & without humiliation to the South."[31]

Bennett's *New York Herald*, however, was not about to "keep quiet" about Issachar's failed diplomacy. In an October 21 editorial, "More Important Negotiations for Peace," the *Herald* informed its readers the "renowned Dr. Zacharie" was the latest among the long line of "independent peace negotiators" and "amateur diplomats" who had failed to secure peace.

> We remember when the Doctor made his debut upon the national stage. Just after the war was fairly inaugurated, Dr. Zacharie went to Washington, resplendent with diamonds and surgical instruments, and cut the corns of the President, the Cabinet, General McClellan and the entire Army of the Potomac. For some time after this, the movements of the administration and the soldiers were astonishingly rapid. Now, alas! both our administration and our armies stick in the mud. The corns have evidently grown again and need cutting.[32]

19. He Lacks Stability

Despite current setbacks, the *Herald* said Dr. Zacharie had done the country a great service and Lincoln and Seward had not been ungrateful. They had "sent Dr. Zacharie to New Orleans to cut the corns of General Banks and his brave corps," quipping that the immediate capture of Port Hudson by Banks' corps was the result of his "marvelous skill."

Dr. Zacharie's value to the war effort, said the *Herald*, had contributed to the "vigorous prosecution of the war," but it had not ended there. In New Orleans, he had talked with a great many of Confederate President Jefferson Davis' friends and supporters "and learned the Southern people earnestly desired to have the war settled without further bother. But when the 'acute and diplomatic corn cutter' personally brought this information back to Washington, the goodly but ungodly city," Secretary Stanton "mistook him for some visionary fellow, like [Horace] Greel[e]y [publisher of the rival *New York Tribune*], and refused to listen to what he had to say."[33] Undeterred, Dr. Zacharie had gone directly to the President.[34]

Continuing its earlier spoof of Issachar's peace effort, Bennett said the moment Issachar entered Lincoln's private reception room, Lincoln's first thought was: here was an unexpected opportunity to have his feet taken care of. "The Chief Executive held out his foot and complained of his corns." While he was cutting away Lincoln's corns, Issachar explained what he had learned in New Orleans and his desire for a pass to go to Richmond to negotiate peace.

After describing his meeting with the Confederate government and the proposed takeover of Mexico, the *Herald* wrote Dr. Zacharie was now "only waiting for the President and the cabinet to ratify it in order to carry it into instant effect. If he succeeds, he will be the greatest man of the age.... Strange as this narrative may appear, there is a great deal more in it than most people think, and perhaps the skeptical will soon have to acknowledge the corn and the corn doctor."[35]

Issachar craved recognition and may have leaked information about his mission, although not what was actually said, to Bennett. Feigning shock over the *Herald's* continuing reports about his mission, Issachar disingenuously assured Lincoln, "I have not lisped a word respecting this matter," except to Seward and to General James Bowen, provost marshal of the Department of the Gulf, who happened to be in Washington at the time. "I beg you will not for a moment harbor any idea but that I have faithfully kept within my own breast all that has passed between us." Deflecting any breach of Lincoln's trust, Issachar ventured that the leak likely resulted from "some person in your immediate vicinity" who was following him. Issachar ended his letter asking Lincoln if he thought "it advisable for me to write the fact that you did not give me any pass to Richmond, or shall I let the paragraph die a natural death?"[36] Lincoln didn't answer.

On his own, Issachar's secretary, Charles Johnson, wrote Banks, saying that Issachar was still hopeful his plan would be implemented and was fretting that instead of Banks getting the credit, it would go elsewhere (without mentioning Lincoln). Johnson urged him to write Issachar to assure him he, Banks, had no such misgivings. "A word from you would keep him calm. I must say he has been very prudent, & kept himself as secluded as possible."[37]

Bennett believed in kicking a man when he was up or down. He simply couldn't let Issachar fade away gracefully. In November, he editorialized, "Doctor Zacharie, the chiropodist, the corn cutter, the wearer of a big diamond breastpin, and the possessor of the finest Roman nose which has ever astonished the world since the time to Caesar … has apparently failed in his mission … in spite of his magnificent nose." Dr. Zacharie had disappeared off the political map, said Bennett. "Nobody knows anything of Zacharie. Nobody has heard of him … Jeff. Davis may have slaughtered him in order to steal his diamonds, or he may be traitorously cutting the corns of the rebel army, preparatory to another invasion of the North…. In life, as in an abolition convention, extremes often meet. Who could say but that the direct road to rebel hearts and heads was through rebel toes."[38]

"We are sorry to say that the Doctor apparently failed in his mission … in spite of his magnificent nose, which is the sign that nature always hangs outside of the head when she has placed a mighty mind within. We will not admit, however, that any discredit attached to Doctor Zacharie or the president, even if our worst fears are realized and the rebels have robbed earth of his choicest corncutter."[39] In light of subsequent events, Bennett could not have been more mistaken about Issachar's disappearing "off the [political] map."

Seward had instructed him to "lay quiet." Issachar wrote Banks he suspected Seward and Lincoln, for that matter, of deceit. Pompously, Issachar said Lincoln had confessed to him, "had he the least idea that I would have been Recived that he would of never permitted me to have gone—he did not know me as well as you—he thought he had a toy to deal with and did not know that when I undertake anything. that I know no such word as fail…. You know I lack Education, but I have managed to push smoothly thus far."[40]

Despite James Bennett's making fun of him, Issachar told Banks he had had a "cozy chat" with the *New York Herald's* editor/owner about him (Banks). Bennett had told him he intended to support Banks if there was any chance of his receiving the nomination. But he wouldn't come out for Banks publicly unless he were sure to win.[41]

Issachar was confident Bennett was right about Banks' prospects, so much so that he set aside part of his new Philadelphia office as a headquarters for lobbying support for Banks.[42] He would like to visit him that winter, he said, but "there are many wires to pull, and I tell you I am watching every

19. He Lacks Stability

move." He had heard rumors Banks was being considered as Lincoln's running mate. Issachar "hope[d] to God" he wouldn't agree. "I would rather see you hold your present position than to accept any thing less than the President of the U. States."[43]

Issachar was confident he could muster the support of America's Jews for Banks' candidacy. "The Jews," Issachar said, were his "sincere friends. They publicly say you have done more for them any other public man and feel under obligations to you for your kindness towards their Brothern in New Orleans." Issachar also assured him he also held "a good position with the Catholics ... what with Catholics & Jews, it is a strong team. I would give you every Dollar I am worth, to see my predictions Realized, and I feel confident I shall live to see it."[44]

20

"Done things for me that would astonish you"

His hopes for brokering a peace dashed, Issachar returned to New York for a brief visit and then hastened to Philadelphia to set up a new practice in Philadelphia at 921 Chestnut Street with one of his students, a Dr. Barnett.[1]

But by February 1864, he was back in Washington using his influence with Lincoln to ask him to intervene in a military matter. Goodman L. Mordecai II, a Jewish Confederate from Charleston, was being held prisoner at the Old Capitol Prison in Washington. Mordecai was the son of Benjamin Mordecai, one of the wealthiest and most prominent of Charleston's citizens. His father had given $10,000 (equivalent to $250,000 in today's money) to Governor Pickens when South Carolina seceded "for such purposes as will best advance the interest and honor of our noble commonwealth."

After serving several years in the Confederate Washington Light Artillery, the 24-year-old son was honorably discharged. Owing to his family connections, a group of stockholders hired him to run the blockade to Nassau to pick up goods they had ordered from England that were docked there and then run the blockade back to Charleston. Nassau and Havana were the main foreign ports where blockade runners exchanged cotton for manufactured goods and then brought them to southern ports like Charleston, where they could unload them as exorbitant prices. Evading the federal blockade could be very profitable; blockade runners made money each way.

When Mordecai arrived in Nassau, he was officially informed that a conscription order had been issued for all able-bodied men to return to service. Instead of obeying the order, Mordecai fled North and was captured attempting to cross the Potomac. When he refused to take the oath of allegiance to the federal government, he was imprisoned in the Old Capitol Prison.[2]

Although he was a Confederate prisoner, Mordecai was able to send a message asking for help to Samuel A. Lewis, the uncle of Mordecai's fiancée, Ada Jackson. Lewis was a prominent New York businessman, vice president of Mt. Sinai Hospital in New York, and editor of the *Hebrew Leader*. Aware of Issachar's friendship with Lincoln, Lewis asked him to see if he could persuade Lincoln to release Mordecai. The next day, Issachar sent Lincoln a "Barral of Homminy." "Eat it with much enjoyment." "Perhaps I will take a run over to see you in a few days." Issachar signed it uncharacteristically, "I. Z."[3]

"Perhaps" turned into a visit during which Issachar obtained the sought-for pardon conditional on his promise not to return to the South during the war. Grateful for his release, Mordecai asked Issachar to arrange a meeting with the President to thank him personally. During their meeting, Issachar offhandedly mentioned that Mordecai's father had contributed $10,000 to the Confederate war effort. Lincoln smiled at the comment. Shaking Mordecai's hand as he left, Lincoln joked he was "happy to know that I am able to serve an enemy."[4]

Six weeks later, in March 1864, Issachar received another plea for help, this time from his nephew, Jacob G. Cohen (Cohen's father had married Issachar's sister Rebecca in Savannah in 1859). Cohen had fled the South to avoid conscription "to take up arms against the United States," but he had been taken prisoner in January 1864 when a ship he was on tried to evade the blockade. The ship was captured by the Union navy, and Cohen was detained at Port Royal.[5]

Writing to his "Dear Uncle," Cohen pleaded with Issachar to "properly represent my case to the President at Washington & get my release." Cohen also asked him to "please remember me to Aunt [Mary Ann] and the children. Tell Elly [Eleazar, Issachar's brother], I shall be pleased to see him soon and this will find all in good health."[6] On March 16, Lincoln ordered Cohen's captors to have him take the loyalty oath and then discharge him.[7]

Whatever hard feelings Issachar harbored toward Lincoln after his failed mission, they were now gone. "I do not know what to make of him [Lincoln]," Issachar wrote Banks afterwards. "He is so very kinde towards me. He has done things for me that would astonish you. In fact, it has astonished me."[8] On May 13, 1864, Issachar sent Lincoln another fruit box, this time of fine "Pine apples" with a note calling him "Dear Friend," and closed "with kind regards to Mrs. Lincoln."[9]

A week before, on May 7, some of New York's most prominent Jews gathered at Issachar's home to honor him for his endeavors on behalf of the "Israelites of America." "His influence" and his "power through the clemency of the President" had aided many "and enable them to return to the North and to freedom." "His efforts to soften the hardships and alleviate the distresses of our co-religionists [in New Orleans]" had not gone unnoticed.[10] In appreciation of his "noble and fraternal efforts" on behalf of the many Israelites who had become involuntarily involved in the rebellion and had "incurred the penalties of their unhappy position," they were proud to offer him "a silver tea service and a massive salvar."[11]

After several speeches and the reading of congratulatory letters from General Dix, Rabbi Raphall, and others unable to be present, Issachar rose to speak. He told the gathering he didn't know what to say regarding the honor bestowed on him. Then, characteristically, he went on and on. After thanking them for their appreciation, he modestly told them he had only done his duty, and then segued into a lengthy narrative of his humble beginnings.

He had been "launched out into the world a poor boy with no friend save my God, without a penny in my pocket, and deprived of that which is so essential to the elevation of man in this world, education." Despite those disadvantages, he had overcome the "rugged path" he had travelled. What had saved him was his ambition. It had given him "those inspiring tools by which man mastered men." "Ambition had carried him to the highest levels of power in the land," meaning his friendship and influence with Lincoln. He had "travelled much," and throughout his "many fiery ordeals," he said he had "always been proud to acknowledge that I was an Israelite."

As someone who well knew from his own experience that a good deed nearly always came at a price, Issachar thanked them for the testimonial. He was sure, he said, they didn't expect anything in return. "I am sure that none of you expect my favors from a humble individual like myself, I therefore know it comes from the purest motives." Issachar then invited his guests to his dining room, where "a sumptuous collation was prepared."[12]

Months later, the *New York World*, the voice of the Democratic Party, was far less complimentary. Its article titled "Mr. Lincoln's Unionism and Bunionism" derided "Dr. Zacharie … as a man who had been courted and flattered by high officials because of his intimacy with the President." He "has often left his business apartment to spend an evening in the parlor with his favored bunionist." Zacharie enjoys "Mr. Lincoln's confidence perhaps more than any other private individual." Broadly intimating Mordecai's release was obtained after a bribe, the *World* ventured, "there must be a reason for this remarkable intimacy between an obscure toe-nail trimmer and the Chief Executive of a great nation."[13]

* * * * * * * *

Meanwhile, Banks' ambition to replace an unpopular Lincoln through military victory faltered once again. Banks was a political general. He had had no formal military training, and his record showed it. He had been beaten, and beaten badly, in every military engagement he had led. If he were to be a serious contender for the Republican nomination, he needed a battlefield victory. Lincoln and his army chief of staff Henry Halleck wanted to drive an opening through Confederate-held Louisiana into Texas and its cotton. The first goal of the offensive was to capture Shreveport, the Confederate capital of Louisiana, and use it as a base from which to invade Texas. General

20. "Done things for me that would astonish you"

Sherman wanted to be in charge, but General Grant needed him to head the upcoming Atlanta campaign. Once again, Banks showed his ineptitude as a military commander. The campaign was a disaster. Banks was humiliated.

On his way back to New Orleans, he was informed General Edward Canby was taking over his military duties. His authority in the Gulf Department was now confined to only civil duties. His primary duty was to oversee elections in Louisiana. In September 1864, Lincoln summoned Banks to Washington to lobby Congress for allowing Louisiana's two newly elected congressmen to take office. Radical Republicans refused to seat them.

His political aspirations dashed, Banks asked for a leave of absence, which Lincoln granted. Banks later tendered his resignation to Lincoln, who denied his request and sent him back to New Orleans to resume his administrative duties under Canby. Banks remained in New Orleans until after the war. He went on to resume his political career in Massachusetts. After Banks' Red River debacle, Issachar no longer pinned any hopes on a Banks presidency. His influence with the Jewish community and with Lincoln, on the other hand, was in no way over.

* * * * * * * *

In July 1864, Issachar received yet another personal plea for him to intervene with Lincoln. This time, the request came from Rabbi Raphall on behalf of his son-in-law, Assistant Quartermaster Captain Cheme M. Levy. In a note to Secretary Stanton on November 4, 1862, Lincoln said (incorrectly), "I believe we have not yet appointed a Hebrew" to the post. Levy, an Orthodox Jew, was "well vouched as a capable and faithful man."[14] Almost a year later, in October 1863, Levy was court-martialed and cashiered from service. The charge was "conduct prejudicial to good order and military discipline" and "signing a false certificate relating to the pay of men under his command." The "prejudicial conduct" and "false certificate" involved his submitting a voucher for $100 to be paid to his clerk, but only paying him $50.[15] Levy was stripped of his command, but he continued to protest his innocence.

Raphall first appealed for Kansas Senator Samuel Pomeroy to ask Lincoln to look into the accusation. Lincoln declined to intervene. In a secret memorandum (the "Pomeroy Circular") that didn't remain secret for very long, Pomeroy had blasted Lincoln's reelection as "practically impossible." He wrote Pomeroy that Levy's case "makes too bad a record to admit of my interference … to interfere under the circumstances would blacken my own character."[16] Lincoln was not concerned with having his character blackened. He was not inclined to do Pomeroy any favors. Earlier that year, Pomeroy had spearheaded a movement to replace Lincoln with Treasury Secretary Chase.[17]

The appeal from Pomeroy having fallen on deaf ears, Raphall asked for a meeting with Lincoln to plead his son-in-law's case. After listening to

Raphall, Lincoln reconsidered his decision and recommended his reinstatement to the Senate. Raphall wrote him thanking him for "the generosity and justice with which you have treated my son-in-law Captain C(hene). M Levy."[18] Secretary of War Stanton refused to comply. A military court had ruled he was "forever disqualified to hold any office of trust or profit in the United States." To Stanton, "forever" meant "forever."[19]

In August 1864, Lincoln wrote an introductory letter for Issachar to Secretary of the Treasury William P. Fessenden. "Allow me to introduce Dr. Zacharie of New York, whose acquaintance I have made since residing here, and who has been known, and in some instances, use to me. Any kindness you may find it convenient to show him will be appreciated by me."[20] Why Issachar wanted to meet with Fessenden and the outcome of their meeting isn't known.

With nowhere else to turn, Raphall asked Issachar to use his influence with Lincoln to have him intercede on Levy's behalf. This time, Issachar sent Lincoln a basket of bananas before their meeting.[21] Lincoln thanked him "again for the deep interest you have constantly taken in the Union cause. The personal matter on behalf of your friend (Rabbi Raphall) which you mentioned, shall be fully and fairly considered when presented."[22] Levy was subsequently reinstated.[23]

* * * * * * * *

Issachar was now the toast of New York, hosting lavish banquets every night at his new "splendid mansion, near Fifth Avenue and Fiftieth Street" for "the most prominent men in New York, in business, in social life and in politics." The *New York Herald* told its readers, "the fashionable chiropodist who attended to the pedal needs of the most noted beaux and belles of the day" was also "a gourmet who kept open house, a wit and an eccentric." A dozen seats were always vacant for uninvited friends to drop by unannounced.[24] "The doctor had the reputation of being the greatest connoisseur of wine in the country. He always served the choicest liquors and the most delicate and original dishes. Not a dish could be concocted in Europe which did not find an early reproduction on his table."[25] Issachar's reputation as a gourmand was so well-known that even men like "Sam" Ward, known for his sumptuous dinners combining "food, fine wines and conversation to create 'social lobbying' in Washington, D.C., consulted him about the proper menu for banquets, public or private."[26]

* * * * * * * *

By now, Issachar's relationship with Lincoln was so well known there was no need to explain who he was to the readers of a humorous parody, *The War Letters of a Disbanded Volunteer*.[27] Written in fractured English, the

20. *"Done things for me that would astonish you"*

anonymous author (Joseph Barber), calling himself "Disbanded Volunteer," said he was calling his "vollum" *The War Letters of a Disbanded Volunteer* "bekase the most of the epistols has been written senst the war commenst, tho it will be seen that they begin immediately arter the elecksin of my ilustrus friend…. His 'idee in publershin the letters n a collected form,'" was to place "the karrickter and services of that Distingwished Statesman … with a view to biass and inflewence thar feelins and judgments, when they go to the poles in November next."

As a way of illuminating Lincoln's "karrickter and sarvices," "Disbanded Volunteer" jabbed obliquely at Lincoln's relationship with Issachar.

> It is as difficult for the solider troubled with warts to handle his arms, as for the soldier with corns to handle his feet. Even Dr. Zacharie must admit this. as new lether is apt to dror the feet and corn salve is sed to be getting skarse in the Union ranks, a ginral forrard moovement (against Richmond) may possably be postponied until arter the result of the November elecskins is known. I believe this is the opinyun of Dr. Zacharie and uther imminent shyrapidists, and they oughter no. Wunderful! isent it, on wot seaming trifuls the most important events depends.[28]

"Disbanded Volunteer," dedicated his book, "To Abrham Lincoln Of Illannoy, The Loftiest of Livin Statesmen, Renouond Alike For His Great Milentary Talons. Firm Adhearance To The Constitooshin, And Fidelity To HIs Inaugerashin Oath."[29]

21

"Can't go Lincoln"

Although the North had won impressive victories at Gettysburg, Vicksburg, and the Shenandoah Valley in 1863, the Confederacy showed no sign the fight had gone out of it. The spring of 1864 had seen some of the bloodiest battles of the war. An estimated 32,000 Union soldiers were killed at the Battles of the Wilderness (May 5–7, 1864) and Spotsylvania (May 8–12, 1864). Another 13,000 were butchered at Cold Harbor (May 31–June 12, 1864). The *New York World* howled the stalemate was "a national humiliation."[1] The war, as it was now being prosecuted, was a failure. After Lincoln issued a call for 500,000 more volunteers, the *Pittsburg Daily Post* blamed him "for the terrible and unavailing waste of life which renders five hundred thousand new men necessary so soon after the opening of a campaign that promised to be triumph?"[2]

Lincoln knew he was in trouble. The grumbling in the heartland that the war had gone on far too long and couldn't be won militarily was loud enough to be heard in the nation's capital. Washington's politicos, even those loyal to Lincoln, told him he would only carry three states in the upcoming November election. If he didn't bow out of the nomination at the Baltimore Convention in June, he was assured he would lose the election, and Republicans in both the House and the Senate would also lose their seats.[3]

It was not just that the North was discouraged. To many, Lincoln's Emancipation Proclamation had turned the war from a fight to restore the Union to one of eradicating slavery. "[Lincoln] cannot be elected," declared *New York Tribune*'s Horace Greeley. "We must have another ticket to save us from overthrow."[4] Generals Grant, Butler, or Sherman, Greely opined, would be stronger presidential candidates. Thurlow Weed, publisher of the *New York Enquirer* and a confidant of Secretary Seward, told him in no uncertain terms that Lincoln's reelection was "an impossibility."[5]

Radicals within the Republican party wanted no more of Lincoln. He was too moderate for their taste. In early December 1863, without consulting his cabinet, Lincoln had issued a "Proclamation of Amnesty and Reconstruction," known as the Ten Percent Plan. The plan offered pardons and restored

21. "Can't go Lincoln" 143

their property to Confederates who took the oath of allegiance to the United States, excluding its military leaders and high-ranking officials. When 10 percent of eligible voters enumerated in a state's 1860 census took the oath, the state would be allowed to rejoin the Union. Lincoln's "ten percent" policy toward a post-war South was far too lenient for the Radicals. Most felt the same as Kansas' Republican Senator Jim Lane, who hoped to "live long enough to see every white man in South Carolina, in hell, and the negroes inheriting their territories." It wouldn't wound his feelings, he said, "to find the dead bodies of rebel sympathizers [his term for the Democrats] pierced with bullet holes in every street and alley of Washington."[6]

Radicals in Congress passed the Wade-Davis Bill (named after Ohio Senator Benjamin F. Wade and Maryland Congressman Henry Winter Davis) as an alternative to Lincoln's Ten Percent Plan. Under its provisions, readmission to the Union by former Confederate states would not be as easy. A majority in each of the seceding states would have to swear they had never supported the Confederacy and had to ban slavery in their state's constitution. Lincoln torpedoed the bill by a procedural tactic called a "pocket veto."[7] Infuriated, on August 4, 1864, Wade issued a blistering "Manifesto" "To the Supporters of the Government," accusing Lincoln of "anarchy" and "dictatorial usurpation."[8]

By May 1864, feuding between the Radical and moderate wings of the Republican party was so embittered that the party split. The Radicals formed a splinter party called the Radical Democracy Party and nominated General John C. Frémont as their candidate for President when they convened in Cleveland.[9]

Frémont was the Radicals' darling. As commander of the Department of the West, headquartered in St. Louis, he had on his own accord instituted martial law in Missouri. He ordered confiscation of all property belonging to secessionists and emancipation of all slaves in his department. When Frémont refused to obey Lincoln's order to rescind his emancipation order (Lincoln was leery of alienating slave-holding border states), Lincoln stripped him of his command. Bowing to political pressure from Frémont's supporters, Lincoln gave him command of a minor department in West Virginia. Frémont was subsequently reassigned after the army was reorganized and placed under the command of General John Pope.

Republicans loyal to Lincoln joined with disaffected Democrats to form a reconstituted Republican party, called the National Union Party. At its convention in Baltimore, on June 7, 1864, they re-nominated Lincoln for President. Andrew Johnson was chosen as his running mate. The Democrats were also divided. The "Little Giant," Stephen A. Douglas, had been the party's acknowledged leader for more than a decade. When he died in 1861, Democrats had no clear spokesman. Even if it meant continuing the war, many former Democrats allied themselves with Lincoln's National Union Party. Peace Democrats, denounced as "Copperheads" by their opponents,[10] favored a quick negotiated end to the war, including a return to conditions before the war, including slavery.

Peace Democrats had high hopes of winning the election. The Republicans were divided. Lincoln was unpopular. The North was war weary. Several names were floated for the nomination, among them General Butler, Treasury Secretary Salmon Chase, Lincoln's Vice President Hannibal Hamlin, and General Grant. They chose General George McClellan on the first ballot and Ohio Congressman George H. Pendleton as vice president. McClellan supported the continuation of the war, but promised to end it by any means, even to the point of recognizing Southern independence.

Lincoln was not optimistic about being reelected. After Frémont withdrew his candidacy for President and endorsed Lincoln, Radical Republicans grudgingly backed Lincoln. They were pessimistic. The feeling throughout the North was that Lincoln had mismanaged the war effort. A war everyone had expected to be over in 90 days was now in its third year. The Confederates had been turned back at Gettysburg, and Vicksburg had been captured, but the South seemed as determined as ever to fight on. Peace Democrats campaigning for a negotiated settlement with the Confederacy and abandonment of emancipation had made significant Congressional gains in the 1862 elections. Twenty-two Republicans were defeated in Congress, while the Democrats picked up 28 seats. What was once a Republican majority in Congress was now a Democrat majority. Many anticipated a similar outcome in the upcoming Presidential election.

Facing what seemed inevitable defeat, Lincoln approved of a second unofficial peace mission to Richmond by Colonel Jaques and journalist Richard Gilmore to stop "Christians killing Christians." Jaques and Gilmore met with Jefferson Davis and Judah Benjamin in Richmond in July 1864. Gilmore conveyed Lincoln's terms for peace: immediate dissolution of the Southern Government; disbandment of its armies; recognition of the supremacy of the Union; and total, absolute, and perpetual abolition of all slavery. In return, Lincoln promised complete amnesty to all engaged in the rebellion, restoration of seceding states to the Union, and compensation to slave owners on the basis of one-half the value of slaves in 1860. Davis rejected Lincoln's offer outright. Amnesty, he said, implied Southerners were criminals. "This war must go on till the last of the generation falls in his tracks and his children seize the musket and fight our battles unless you acknowledge our right to self-government. We are fighting for independence, and that, or extermination we will have."[11]

Lincoln was not surprised at Davis' reaction. He had counted on it. The Peace Democrats had howled he would reject any negotiated settlement.

News of the failed Jaques-Gilmore effort showed Lincoln was willing to negotiate. It was Davis who was intransigent. The failed attempt showed Northerners there was no middle ground for peace.[12]

Humorist Charles Graham Halpine poked fun at Jaques' mission by reminding his readers of Issachar's previous failed venture. In his *Life and Adventures of Private Miles O'Reilly*, Halpine implied Lincoln wanted to send Issachar back to Richmond instead of Jaques, but Dr. Zacharie, "the celebrated corn-cutter and international negotiator," had turned down a second invitation.

Issachar's decision, Halpine said, had to do with his being Jewish. The "pickled pig's head at the top of the table, pickled pig's feet at the foot, and four thin slices of broiled bacon" served at the negotiating table at his last visit, said Halpine, "did not by any means form a pretty feast to set before a gentleman of his character."[13]

* * * * * * * *

On August 23, six days before the Democrat's Chicago convention on August 29–31, a grim Lincoln handed a sealed envelope to his cabinet asking them to sign it without showing them its contents. Possibly it was to avoid Secretary of the Interior John Palmer Usher, a paunchy gregarious "great lover of gossip," from leaking it.[14] Lincoln handed the signed envelope to Gideon Welles, Secretary of the Navy, instructing him not to open it until after the election. The note predicted his defeat:

> This morning, as for some day's past, it seemed improbable that this administration will be re-elected. Then it will be my duty to co-operate with the President-elect so as to save the Union between the election and the inauguration, as my successor will have secured his election on such grounds, that he cannot possibly save it afterwards.[15]

Although the Democrat convention in Chicago was still six days away, Lincoln was aware McClellan would be nominated, and he anticipated his victory. Had the election occurred soon after McClellan's nomination, McClellan would likely have won. Days later, the political tide changed in Lincoln's favor.

On September 2, 1864, General Sherman captured Atlanta, the "Gate City of the South." Atlanta had been a major industrial center in the Confederacy and a railway hub for the deep South. Sherman burned every munitions factory, foundry, warehouse, and any other building or structure in Atlanta that had contributed to the Confederate war effort. Union successes in the Shenandoah Valley in late September and early October raised Northern hopes the war was nearing an end.

But the election was still far from in the bag. Lincoln knew from his own experience there were no guarantees in politics. No one had given him a chance to be the Republican nominee at the Chicago convention in 1860, when William Seward had been the odds-on favorite. Yet here he was President, and Seward was his secretary of state.

An editorial in the Clearfield *Pennsylvania Republican* two weeks after Atlanta's capture claimed one of every four Republicans "Can't go Lincoln":

> The people are tired of war. They are for peace, for settlement, for a restored Union, for reduced taxes, for a return to the Constitutional currency. They know Lincoln's re-election would defeat all these darling objects. They are opposed to a national debt, and particularly to a further increase of our present one. They know that this can only be prevented by the success of the Democratic party. Is it strange, then, that they "can't go Lincoln?"[16]

* * * * * * * *

On September 19, 1864, Issachar received a brief note from Lincoln thanking him "for the deep interest you have constantly taken in the Union Cause."[17] Issachar read the note not as a thank you, but as a request for him to stump for Lincoln. Two days later, he wrote Lincoln he was leaving New York the next day for the interior of Pennsylvania and "might go as far as Ohio."[18]

That same day, Issachar sent a similar note to Secretary Seward, likewise advising him not to take Lincoln's reelection for granted. "I finde when men are to sure of any thing—that is the very time they fail. Now if they relax their Efforts *at any time before the 8th of Nov.* we are gone. They must work and keep on working until he is Elected. I am doing what little I can, and now leave, to work in Pennsylvania. May visit Ohio. 'We must carry Pennsylvania & Ohio' to succeed—and Mr. Lincolns Friends—are to sure, to suit me. I therefor beg of you—to speak to them and spur them up." The "friends" could only

Zacharie in later years. "I find when men are too sure of anything—that is the very time they fail" (courtesy American Jewish Historical Society).

have been Jews who might be wavering to the Democrats. With whom else did he have any influence? Although they were relatively few in the overall population, in a narrow election, they could sway the vote.[19]

In lecturing Seward, a seasoned politician on strategy, Issachar saw himself as Lincoln's strategist. The "me" was pure conceit. Pennsylvania's and Ohio's 26 electoral college votes each could not be ignored. But for Issachar, New York's 33 votes were the key to winning the election. Issachar believed the outcome in New York would heavily depend on the city's Jews.

New York City belonged as much to the South as to the North. Its economy, its political endorsement of unrestricted immigration, and its pro-slavery position put it squarely in the Democrat camp. By 1860, its garment industry had produced almost 50 percent of the country's clothing, including the clothes worn by Southern whites and slaves. Although it still manufactured uniforms and other clothing, peace with the South would bring even more wealth to its merchants. Fearing losing their jobs to freed slaves, New York's newly arrived German and Irish immigrant laborers were strongly Democrat.

Jewish lawyer Abram J. Dittenhoefer recalled how pressured he felt as a 20-year-old to join the Democratic party. "My father, who was a prominent merchant of New York, and very influential with the German population … urged me to become a Democrat." Dittenhoefer's father warned him if he allied himself with the Republicans, public office "would be impossible in the city of New York." On the other hand, if he joined the Democrats, he was assured "in a few years [he] undoubtedly would become judge of the Supreme court; later on, I might go still higher up." Dittenhoefer's decision to join the Republican party and his decision to campaign for Lincoln in the upcoming election[20] subjected him "to obloquy from and ostracism by my acquaintances, my clients, and even members of my own family."[21] Lincoln won the state by a narrow margin of 50.5 to 49.5 percent. He only won 33 percent of the city's vote.

* * * * * * * *

Issachar never made it to Pennsylvania. Around 10 o'clock on the morning he was supposed to leave, he lay wounded on the floor of his apartment in New York, shot in the face, a bullet "entering at the right of the nose."[22] The gunman was Issachar's junior partner at his Chestnut Street office in Philadelphia, 32-year-old Dr. Samuel M. Barnett.[23]

Brought before a judge, Barnett claimed he had shot Zacharie, whom he characterized as a "desperado," in self-defense. He said the two had had a falling out and quarreled when he had gone to Issachar's home to reclaim his possessions. Issachar had become irate and insulted him, he said, calling him a damned puppy and a son of a bitch. When Issachar advanced toward him, Barnett believed Issachar intended bodily harm and shot him in self-defense.²⁴ Issachar had a different explanation. With his ever-inflated sense of self-importance, he said Barnett was a spy "in the employ of the Confederate States Army." Issachar was implying he was so important the Confederate government had sent Barnett to assassinate him because of his clandestine activities on Lincoln's behalf.²⁵ There are no further reports of whether Barnett was charged with attempted murder and brought to trial, and nothing more was ever heard about him.²⁶

In the course of reporting the shooting, the *New York World* informed its readers the Jewish foot doctor "is a man who has enjoyed Mr. Lincoln's confidence perhaps more than any other private individual. Dr. Zacharie is perhaps the most favored family visitor at the White House, and has often left his business apartment to spend an evening in the parlor of his favored bunionist."²⁷ The *Daily Ohio Statesman* described Issachar as "one of the boon companions of Lincoln and a great favorite with him."²⁸

The incident eventually attracted the attention of the *Lancet*, a prestigious medical journal. The editor chuckled that the shooting lowered the dignity of chiropody even more. It also noted, mistakenly, that Lincoln had appointed "Dr. Issachar Zacharie, of New York" with the "lofty sounding title, 'Chiropodist-in-chief' of the United States Army!" Although the recent "difficulty" lowered "the newly-obtained dignity of corns and chiropody," nevertheless, the United States was rejoicing in its newly appointed chiropodist-in-chief.²⁹

22

"I promised I would elect you"

About a month after he was shot, Issachar felt well enough to resume his intended campaign itinerary. He decided there wasn't enough time now for him to stump Ohio as originally planned and instead, he focused on Pennsylvania, a battleground state.

Pennsylvania's Republican governor Andrew Curtin was a staunch supporter of Lincoln. When Curtin was running for reelection in 1863, Lincoln gave government clerks in Pennsylvania and Ohio leave for 15 days and had the railroads issue them passes so they could return home to vote Republican. Lincoln also authorized officers to issue furloughs to soldiers from Pennsylvania so they could go home to vote. Democrats groused Lincoln had furloughed so many men that he had imperiled General George Meade's army.[1] Despite Lincoln's help, Curtin only narrowly beat his Democrat opponent, but the Democrats won the Senate race.[2]

Issachar believed if anyone could swing the vote in Lincoln's favor, it was him. And he believed he could do it by getting out the Jewish vote for Lincoln. As the 1864 election approached, there were about 150,000 Jews in the United States. Most of them lived in New York City, Philadelphia, and Cincinnati. Issachar's hustling was aimed at getting the only bloc he had any influence over out for Lincoln.

Lincoln never publicly admitted he was interested in any particular group, but as early as 1858, Illinois politician Abraham Jonas, Lincoln's Jewish friend who had worked for Lincoln's nomination, urged him to court "the Israelites" as well as "liberal and freethinking Germans."[3]

While Jews zealously sought voting rights and aspired to public office, prior to the Civil War, Jewish leaders generally discouraged their political involvement as a group. Many of those leaders had recently come from Europe. They had had personal experience with anti–Jewish hatred and sought to keep a low profile for their minions. During the debate over tariffs and nullification raging in Charleston, the city's Jews were rumored to have petitioned the state legislature for representation "as a religious sect."[4] Nervous over possible political repercussions, 80 of Charleston's Jews publicly denied partisan allegiance. Charleston's Jews, they said, supported both parties. "We wholly disclaim any wish or intention to be represented as a peculiar community ... the perfect independence of the Israelite of Charleston, is beyond the control of any individual, it matters not to what sect or party he may be attached."[5]

Jewish leaders had another good reason to be concerned about taking sides. Protestant Know-Nothings had venomously attacked Catholics as un–American for allegedly voting for Whig candidates.[6] If Jews sought influence as a religious group, they too would be branded as un–American, they said. Their efforts would invite a backlash of anti–Semitism similar to anti–Catholic bigotry.[7] From recurring editorials in prominent Jewish periodicals advocating neutrality, however, it was evident for the most part, most of their Jewish followers ignored their admonitions.[8]

Jews in the North had mixed feelings about Lincoln. Jewish middle-class garment makers and their Jewish employees felt the same as their German and Irish counterparts did about their jobs. Others were strongly in Lincoln's camp in the run-up to the 1864 election. Lincoln had appointed Jews as military chaplains and officers in the army and had countermanded Grant's "Jew order." But there was a strong undercurrent of anti-Semitism in the Republican party, especially among Radicals.

As noted, Illinois Congressman Elihu Washburn, a close friend of Lincoln's, had written him he hoped the report of Lincoln's revoking Grant's expulsion order was incorrect.[9] Massachusetts Senator Henry Wilson (Grant's future vice president) blamed Jewish cotton brokers for starting the war and supported their expulsion from America.[10] Seething with indignation at Wilson's slur, Isaac Meyer Wise, editor of *The Israelite*, retorted that the race he had insulted "has produced greater statesmen and better men than you ... a ward politician."[11] Ohio Senator Ben Wade called Judah Benjamin an "Israelite with Egyptian principles."[12] Benjamin replied, "it is true that I am a Jew, and when my ancestors were receiving their Ten Commandments from the immediate hand of the Deity, amidst the thunderings and lighting of Mount Sinai, the ancestors of my opponent were herding swine in the forest of Great Britain."[13]

Republicans called August Belmont,[14] the chairman of the National Democratic Committee and a strong supporter of General George McClellan for President, the "Jew Banker of New York." The *Chicago Tribune* claimed "Belmont, the Rothschilds, and the whole tribe of Jews" were financing McClellan's campaign because they had "invested in Confederate bonds and stood to lose a lot of money if the Confederacy went down."[15] It didn't matter that Belmont, a Sephardic Jew by birth, had converted and married a

Christian woman in an Episcopal church and had never had any association with the Jewish community. The *Philadelphia Illustrated New Age* opined Belmont was being abused not because he was a Democrat, but because he was a Jew.[16]

Ohio Republican governor John Brough ridiculed Benjamin as untrustworthy because he was "a Jew by birth and (hypocritically), a politician by trade,"[17] Rabbi Isaac Mayer Wise, editor of *The Israelite*, reminded Brough there was a sizable Jewish vote in Ohio. "There are 2,000 and more Jewish voters in Cincinnati, and about 3,000 to 4,000 in the state of Ohio, who might feel offended at that uncalled-for remark." If Brough and others persisted in demeaning their Jewish fellow-citizens, Wise said, "we will certainly feel obliged ... [to] show them how many thousand votes we can kill for them."[18]

Jews had yet another reason to vote Democrat. When Lincoln's vice presidential running mate Andrew Johnson was in the Senate, he had lashed out against Jewish senator David Yulee of Florida, calling him "the contemptible little Jew" and a "despicable little beggar." Johnson had also sneered that Judah Benjamin was "a sneaking, Jewish unconscionable traitor. He looks on a country and a government as he would on a suit of old clothes ... one who belongs to that tribe that parted the garments of our Savior.... He sold out the old one; and he would sell out the new if he could in so doing make two or three millions."[19] Republican Herman Moos, literary editor of *The Israelite*, fretted that Johnson's remarks and similar screeds "'against my race will deprive us in the coming presidential election of ten thousands of votes.'"[20] When Moose asked Johnson about his "loose and uncalled for remark's," Johnson sidestepped the accusation. If he had had ever made derogatory remarks about the Israelites, Johnson said he didn't remember the time or the place.[21]

Many Jews were also inclined to vote for McClellan because his running mate, George Pendleton, had been one of the few members of the House of Representatives to publicly come out against Grant's "Jew order."[22] Another Democrat, Clement L. Vallandigham, had been the only gentile in Congress to protest the July 1861 requirement that only "a regularly ordained minister of some Christian denomination" could serve as a chaplain in the Northern army.[23]

Issachar was aware, as was every Jew, that neutrality was a fiction. Republican slurs directed at Judah Benjamin, David Yulee, and August Belmont, Grant's "Jew order," and every snub, taunt, abuse, invective, and slander vilifying a prominent Jew, no matter how indifferent to Judaism and the Jewish community, was an aspersion on every Jew. Despite such animosity, Issachar was confident he could sway Jews to vote for Lincoln in bloc in 1864. If he did nothing, their votes would go to McClellan.

Issachar was not the only one making promises to deliver the "Jewish vote" to Lincoln. A. S. Cohen, editor of the *Jewish Record*, wrote to Lincoln in September 1863 that a number of his subscribers had asked him to pass on a message. They "could use considerable influence by money and votes to secure your success … through an organization known as the Bnai Berith which has branches in every town and City in the Union."[24]

Thirteen Jewish spokesmen, 12 from New York and Pennsylvania and one from Illinois (their letterhead said Indiana) who called themselves the Jewish Union Republican Association also saw themselves as get-out-the vote advocates for Lincoln. "To Our Jewish Brethren," its lengthy broadside began, "in the political affairs of our adopted country, very few members of our persuasion have hitherto been led to take an active part…

> It [now] becomes imperative upon every honest-minded responsible Jew as well as Gentile, in the interests of humanity, patriotism and the preservation of the National existence, to well and impartially weigh the respective merits of the two candidates for the Supreme Executive Power in the American Republic…
>
> One more effort, strong, united and determined, and the Champion of Freedom, the Emancipator of the Slave and the preserver of his country will be reelected to the power he has so wisely and justly wielded during four years of civil war and political disorganization. We call earnestly upon our Jewish brethren to bring heart and soul, influence and wealth to this great movement.
>
> Unity is strength—Combine strongly, act energetically and unitedly, and the votes of the immense number of Jewish citizens will go far to determine the re-election of Abraham Lincoln to the presidency in November next, in other words, the salvation of the republic…

Lincoln and Union! McClellan and Disunion![25]

On October 23, 1864, Lincoln had a face-to-face meeting with "certain gentlemen of the Hebrew faith." The delegates claimed it represented "the Israelites of New York or the United States" and assured Lincoln they could deliver the "Jewish vote" his way. Myer Samuel Isaacs, secretary of the Board of Delegates of American Israelites and co-editor of New York's *Jewish Messenger*, was outraged to hear that New York Jewish leaders were claiming to represent Jews at large and had told Lincoln they could get them to vote for Lincoln. Isaacs didn't know exactly what was said at the meeting, but three days later, on October 26, 1864, he dashed off an angry letter to Lincoln, challenging any promise of a Jewish vote.

> As a firm and earnest Union man, I deem it my duty to add a word to those that have doubtless communicated to you from other sources, with reference to a recent "visitation" on the part of persons claiming to represent the Israelites of New York or the United States and pledging the "Jewish vote" to your support, and, I am informed, succeeding in a deception that resulted to their pecuniary profit.
>
> Having peculiar facilities for obtaining information as to the Israelites of the United States from my eight years' connection with the Jewish paper of this city and my

position as Secretary of their central organization, the "Board of Delegates" ... I feel authorized to caution you, sir, against any such representations as those understood to have been made ... the Israelites are not, as a body, distinctively Union or democratic in their politics.... Jews as a body have no politics.

"There is no 'Jewish vote,'" he bristled, "if there were, it could not be bought."[26] Two days later, Isaacs followed up his letter to Lincoln with an editorial in the *Jewish Messenger*. "Nobody is authorized to speak for our co-religionists on political questions. There is no such thing as 'a Jewish vote.' Israelites will indorse Mr. Lincoln or Gen McClellan according to their individual judgments."[27]

Lincoln could not ignore Isaac's warning. If Isaacs believed Lincoln could be bought, he might rail against him in his newspaper. If so, it could cost him the very Jewish bloc of votes Issachar had assured him did exist. Lincoln instructed John Hay, his private secretary, to write Isaacs to assuage his concerns. Hay's letter, dated November 1, 1864, didn't deny Lincoln had met with "certain gentlemen of the Hebrew faith." Those gentlemen had made "no pledge of the Jewish vote" to the President, and the President had not given them any "inducements or promises." "You are in error in the assumptions you make in regard to the recent interview to which you refer." They had claimed no such authority and had "received no such response as you seem to suppose."[28]

Even though Issachar was far away in Pennsylvania stumping for Lincoln, he had a subscription to the *Jewish Messenger* and read Isaac's editorial. Issachar was also concerned about promises of a Jewish vote, but for a different reason—someone or some other group might claim credit for delivering it. Issachar wrote his friend Samuel L. Lewis, urging him to write Lincoln about not being taken in by this other group. He could have written the admonition himself, but instead he asked Lewis to write it. Perhaps he thought the concern would seem more genuine if it came from Lewis because Lewis was indebted to Lincoln for arranging the release from prison of his soon-to-be son-in-law, Goodman Mordecai, who been arrested as a Confederate agent.

Heading his letter "having understood through our friend Dr. Zacharie that some parties representing themselves as 'a committee from the Jews'" had called on Lincoln soliciting a bribe for their support in getting out the Jewish vote for him, Lewis assured him they did not represent America's Jewish community. Speaking on Dr. Zacharie's and his own behalf, "I hasten to inform you that it is entirely against the wish of your Jewish friends here to take any money from outside committees or others ... [we] Jews propose to give not take." If any other Jewish group called on the President, Lewis said, "send them to me." Then in an about-face, he offered to bribe them. "I will furnish them such amounts as we can see can be used to advantage. Nothing shall be wanting," he assured Lincoln, "on the part of your friends here towards carrying the Union Cause."[29]

On November 3, 1864, five days before the November election, Issachar was back in New York, just returned from stumping for Lincoln for nine days. He was happy to inform him, he puffed, "that I have done much good. I now think all is Right," meaning the election would go Lincoln's way. "As regards the Israelites [sic]—with but few exceptions they will vote for you…. I understand them well, and have taken the precaution—to see that they do as they have promised. I have secured good and trustworthy men to attend to them on Election Day—My Men have been all week seeing that their masses are properly Registered—so that they will go right on the 8th inst."[30]

"I flatter myself I have done one of the sharpest things that has been done in the campaign," he continued, promising to explain exactly what he had done the next time they met. Then he outdid even himself, hyperbolically claiming he was a king-maker. "3 years ago, I promised I would elect you, and if you are not it shall not be my fault." Issachar ended his letter sending his regards to Mrs. Lincoln and saying he was looking forward to seeing him "after the fun is over, when I hope you will say, 'Well done, my good and faithful Servant,'" adding in a P.S. "Did you receive the oranges."[31]

"Election day," writes historian Allan Nevins, "was filled with anxiety and tension in the largest cities, especially in New York."[32] General Dix, commanding the Department of the East, charged General Butler with keeping the peace. Butler stationed men at strategic points in the city. Saloons were shuttered to prevent drunken violence. Rain and fog that day defused partisan animosities among voters who waited patiently, some for as long as two hours, to cast their ballots.[33]

Lincoln won the electoral college vote by 212 to 21, winning all but three states (Delaware, Kentucky, and New Jersey), and the national election by more than 400,000 votes. Had the election been decided by New York City alone, Lincoln would have lost. The city went against him two to one (66.8 percent to 33.2 percent). He barely won the state as a whole by a 50.5 to 49.5 percent margin. Lincoln's support came mainly from native-born citizens in the farmlands and the skilled workers, merchants, and professional classes, whereas McClellan's primary support came from the immigrant working class. Most Protestants voted for Lincoln, while Irish Catholics voted for McClellan.

Historian Howard Rock contends Jews were similarly split. Ignoring the goodwill Jews may have felt toward Lincoln for his appointment of Jewish chaplains and his rescinding Grant's anti–Semitic fiat, Rock instead focused on economic issues. Jewish industrialists and merchants and garment manufacturers had made fortunes before and during the war supplying the army with its needs and were solidly in Lincoln's camp. New York's working and middle-class Jews, many of whom had emigrated from Germany, voted Democrat. Wages increased during the war, but so did inflation. Prices for sugar doubled, and coal and flour prices rose by a third. Jewish immigrants from Germany continued speaking in their native language for decades after their arrival, mingled freely with gentile Germans, and experienced the same economic hardships and resentments. The Irish and German wards came out strongly for McClellan, giving him 69 percent of its votes. Since Jews did not live in separate enclaves from their gentile German neighbors, they voted the same way as their working-class neighbors.[34]

23

"My family are crazy with joy"

Five days after General Sherman sent Lincoln the city of Savannah as a "Christmas gift,"[1] Issachar wired Lincoln his congratulations, adding his family (his father and sisters and their husbands in Savannah) "are crazy with joy."[2] Either Issachar was expressing what he felt were his family's sentiments, or more intriguing, someone in his family had been able to telegraph him now that the city was in Union hands and knew where to find him. It also meant Issachar had somehow maintained contact with them during the war, despite restrictions on communications.

With Savannah under Union control, Issachar now had an opportunity to visit his family. From New York, he wrote Secretary of War Stanton requesting a pass to allow him passage through the Union lines. Issachar expected Stanton would not object. He and Stanton were both Masons, and Issachar had treated Stanton's corns in Washington. Stanton had also not objected to his heading up a "chiropody corps" for the army (the appointment was rejected by Surgeon General Hammond). But Stanton refused to issue the necessary pass.[3]

Never one to take no for an answer, the next day, Issachar called on Lincoln. After some brief pleasantries, Issachar reminded Lincoln of a promise he had made about allowing him to visit his family once Savannah was under Union control. If Issachar mentioned Stanton's refusal to give him the pass, which he probably did, there is no mention of it in any of their correspondence. Despite anticipating angering Stanton for pulling rank, Lincoln told Issachar he would have the pass sent to him the next day. Issachar asked for one more favor. Could he also have a pass for his nephew, Jacob G. Cohen, his sister's son? Lincoln had earlier arranged for Cohen's release when he was detained after fleeing the South. Lincoln nodded agreement.[4]

Lincoln issued the pass for Issachar and his nephew[5] as asked, and also wrote a letter of introduction for Issachar to show General Sherman.

Allow me to introduce Dr. I. Zacharie, of New York who visits his father & friends at Savannah, when the Dr. is well acquainted, and when very likely he could be of (unreadable) to you in some matters—He is entirely loyal and devoted to the Union Cause.[6]

A few days later, Issachar wrote Lincoln he was leaving for Savannah "where I hope to find my Dear old Father and friends—if you have any matters that you would have properly attended to, I will consider it a favour to let me attend to it for you." Issachar ended his brief letter with a P.S: "please informe me if you [received] the Bannas."[7] Always alert to Issachar's activities, the newspapers assumed some clandestine reason behind his trip south. Dr. Zacharie had been appointed by Lincoln to go to Savannah, readers were told, "upon an important mission."[8]

By coincidence, Stanton was on his way to Savannah at the same time as Issachar. Stanton's asthma was especially bad during the winter, and Surgeon General Joseph Barnes had strongly urged him to take the trip to give him some relief.[9] Anticipating adverse publicity over using military resources for a health trip, Stanton had given out that the purpose of his trip was to consult with Generals Grant, (John Gray) Foster, and Sherman. They were to discuss prison exchanges, "the organization of colored troops; raising the blockade of Savannah," opening Savannah to free trade, and seizure of rebel property.[10]

Issachar arrived at Hilton Head, South Carolina, on his way to Savannah, a few hours before Stanton. "The distinguished statesman" (Issachar, not Stanton), the *New York Herald* reported, was accompanied by two other men, "one doubtless of the legation (Issachar's nephew), and the other holding the position of confidential secretary (Charles Johnson) to the envoy extraordinary."[11] The implication was there was more to Issachar's visit than just his visiting his family.

As soon as Issachar's steamer docked, "the celebrated chiropodist and distinguished diplomatist" called on General Foster, the officer in charge of the Department of the South, and showed him his pass along with Lincoln's introductory letter to Sherman. The two men then sat down and chatted for several hours. Foster asked him about Lincoln, obviously aware Issachar was on intimate terms with the President. Born in New Hampshire, Foster was a career military officer. He had served as an engineer during the Mexican American War and had been an instructor at West Point. Foster was one of the engineers who constructed Fort Sumter. He'd been second in command to Major Robert Anderson when he surrendered the fort. In 1864, Foster was put in charge of the Department of the South and had aided Sherman in capturing Savannah.[12]

"The doctor was in his glory," the *New York Herald's* correspondent reported, "brisk and blithe as a bird in full plumage, in the June sunlight." But the "bird" was cut "down while he was in full blossom." A few hours later,

Stanton's steamer, the *Nevada*, arrived. As soon as General Foster was notified of Stanton's arrival, he immediately went to greet him. Without a second thought, Foster asked Issachar if he'd like to accompany him. Even though his last meeting with Stanton had not turned out well, Issachar went along.

Stanton was livid at seeing Issachar standing beside Foster. Lincoln had obviously gone over his head and issued Issachar a pass. After Foster and Stanton shook hands, Issachar held out his hand. Stanton stared at Issachar for a moment and briskly turned away, saying, "I want nothing to do with that man." Stanton ordered him off the ship. Issachar stood speechless and dumbfounded. Everyone on board held his breath. "It was a moment big with import," wrote the *Herald*. "It settled the diplomatic mission of the Doctor. He was not to be permitted to go to Savannah and meet with Sherman."[13]

Issachar left the ship wondering what to do next. He didn't have to think about it for long. Humiliation over being ordered off the ship was only the beginning of his problems. Moments later, an officer informed him he "had a disagreeable duty to perform." Issachar's eyes widened in fear as the officer told him he had been "ordered by the Secretary of War to place you under arrest, with a sentry at your door. It is a disagreeable duty, but must be performed." The officer then escorted him to the provost guard house.[14] "It is understood that the Secretary will send him North by the first conveyance and with him his two secretaries," the *Herald* reported. With obvious sarcasm, the *Herald* scoffed, "Dr. Zacharie will hereafter add the proud title of martyr to the equally distinguished and proud appellations of chiropodist and diplomat."[15]

Two days later, the *Herald* gleefully ran the exact same story with a different headline: "Dr. Zacharie, Chiropodist and Diplomatist, Becomes a Martyr."[16] The story became a lead article in newspapers as far west as San Francisco.[17] Bennett correctly speculated Stanton had had Zacharie arrested because Issachar had gone around him and had obtained the pass to Savannah after Stanton had refused to give it to him. Stanton could be vindictive. Just before leaving for Savannah, Stanton had General Butler transferred to Lowell, Massachusetts, "a decree of meanness that is worthy of our small secretary." Before the war, Butler had been beaten and given a black eye before the war by a local bricklayer in Lowell. "To send him to this town where he will daily be in danger of meeting the brick layer ... is perfectly terrible."[18]

Major John Chipman Gray, the judge advocate for the Department of the South under Foster,[19] had a different explanation for Stanton's "arbitrary" behavior. According to Gray, who was on board when Issachar was arrested, Stanton didn't want anything to do with Jews, and Issachar was a Jew. Gray was quite open about his own anti-Semitism[20] "This man Zachary is in appearance the lowest and vulgarest of Jew peddlers and it is enough to condemn Mr. Lincoln that he can make a friend of such an odious creature. He came with letters to General Foster but Mrs. Foster absolutely refused to sit at the same table with him."[21]

It was Gray's anti–Semitism, not Stanton's, that prompted his explanation. Stanton had no personal animosity toward Jews or Issachar prior to their Hilton Head confrontation. Earlier in his career, Stanton had defended Florida's Jewish elected Senator David Yulee's right to a seat in the Senate in a contested election.[22] He also ignored the attempt on the part of General Stephen A. Hurlbut to deflect corruption charges against him by forwarding the agreement between "the celebrated Chiropodist Dr. Zacharie" and Betterton, along with letters Issachar had written for him allegedly implicating Issachar in smuggling.[23]

Stanton was well aware of Issachar's activities when he was in New Orleans and did not respond. Stanton's absence of anti–Semitic bias was also indicated when he ordered another Jew, Simon Wolf, freed after Union spymaster Lafayette C. Baker arrested Wolf for meeting with a Southern refugee in Philadelphia. A lawyer and prominent member of the B'nai B'rith in Washington, Wolf often represented other Jews in similar circumstances. Baker had charged him with being an enemy agent: "You belong to the Order of B'nai B'rith, a disloyal organization which has its ramifications in the South, and ... helping traitors."[24]

Shortly after Stanton left for Washington after his meeting with Sherman, Issachar was freed and escorted aboard a steamer back to Washington without meeting his family in Savannah. By then, his entanglement with Stanton had made him such a national figure that the *New York World's* correspondent, who had sailed on the *Fulton*, the same steamer Issachar took to Hilton Head, wrote an amusing tongue-in-cheek spoof of Issachar's wayward journey.

He had tried to book a stateroom for himself and his companions on the trip to Hilton Head, he said, but was told it belonged to Dr. Zacharie. Seeing the journalist's dismay, Issachar asked if there was anything he could do for him, and the journalist told him he needed a berth for him and his friends. The journalist said Issachar smiled back at him and told him he couldn't oblige, "for I have refused it to two brigadier-generals, three colonels, and five captains, who are now sleeping on the floor." Issachar offered him some brandy, "the same brandy which I have sent as a gift to General Sherman and to General Foster," he said. "The demijohns are now on the deck with the labels on They cost me three hundred dollars apiece, and are of the finest quality I could find in New York."

The doctor had not exaggerated its merit, said the correspondent. "This indeed is a very fine liquor, doctor; I do not suppose Mr. Lincoln drinks any better in the White House."

"The same sir, the same sir, I gave him the address of the importer myself," Issachar beamed. "Mr. Lincoln is my friend, and I should be sorry to see my friends drink worse liquor that I drink myself." (Lincoln in fact was a teetotaler.)

Issachar then pulled out a letter from his pocket and handed it to the correspondent. It was supposedly Lincoln's letter to Sherman, introducing "Dr. Zacharie, my friend who is going to Savannah on some important business. You will find him a pleasant and very useful gentleman. I ask for him your kinds regards and attention."

That "is certainly as high a recommendation as any one can wish," the correspondent said, handing the letter back.

"Is it not," said Issachar with "another smile of satisfaction." "Well, gentlemen, I could show you many letters, just as strong from every distinguished man in the country." As proof, Issachar showed him a pocketbook with similar letters (Issachar's well-known certificate book). Hearing the dinner bell, Issachar invited him to dinner.

"No one, then contemplating so much wealth, so much brandy, and so much impudence," he said, could have anticipated the "sad fate" about to unfold.

On the way back to Washington after Issachar's humiliation, the correspondent wrote Issachar seethed with anger at Stanton. "I will slap his jaw, I will have him turned out of the cabinet, I will ruin him in the eyes of the people."[25] Believing the correspondent's farfetched recital of the incident, the *Columbia* (Connecticut) *Register*, no friend of Stanton's, said "it is to be hoped he (Issachar) may get it (his vengeance)."[26]

Back in Washington by January 25, Issachar related his reception and subsequent arrest to Lincoln. Lincoln immediately dashed off a memorandum to Stanton. It began, seemingly enigmatically, "About Jews." Lincoln asked Stanton to issue Issachar a second pass for him to go to Savannah for a week and return, "bringing with him, if he wishes his father and sisters or any of them. This will spare me trouble and oblige me—I promised him long ago that he should be allowed this whenever Savannah should fall into our hands."[27]

Historian Bertram Korn inferred that when Lincoln wrote "about Jews," he was reacting to Stanton's dislike of Jews and Issachar in particular because he was Jewish. But as noted, Stanton had no personal animosity toward Jews or to Issachar prior to their Hilton Head confrontation. The reason the letter began "about Jews" was that in the same letter, Lincoln referred to another Jew, Major Leopold Blumberg, who had been summarily dismissed from service for alleged "cruelty in gagging men to make them confess they were deserters."[28] Lincoln asked Stanton to give him a "hearing" to defend himself. "He (Blumberg) has suffered for us (he had been 'crippled' at the Battle of Antietam) & served us well (after Antietam he was appointed Provost Marshall of Maryland's Third District)—had the rope around his neck for being our friend—raised troops—fought, and been wounded. He should not be dismissed in a way that disgraces and ruins him without a hearing."[29]

Stanton could read Lincoln's anger between the lines. He dashed off a reply to the President that same day. "An order for leave to Zacharie as directed by you has been issued & sent to Mr. Nicolay."[30] As to Blumberg, Stanton said he hadn't known anything about his case beforehand. After looking into the matter, he had been informed Blumberg had been dismissed for reasons besides gagging men to make them confess. Blumberg was later cleared of all charges. After the war, he was reinstated and promoted to brevet brigadier general.[31]

Issachar departed for Savannah the following day. Before leaving, he wrote a brief note to Lincoln, calling him "My Dear Friend." Issachar said he hoped to "find my Dear old Father and Friends" and would be more than happy to attend to any matters for Lincoln he might have in the city. He ended the letter with "God Bless you," and asked whether he had received the bananas he'd sent him earlier.[32]

Under the headline "Movements of Dr. Zacharie," the *New York Herald* whimsically reported, "Dr. Zacharie, whose return from Savannah, by request of Secretary Stanton, was rather sooner than anticipated, leaves again for that point, having today received the necessary authorization for the purpose from the Secretary of War."[33] What happened after Issachar left for Savannah isn't known. There is no record of his meeting with General Sherman or of his seeing his family. His thank-you to Lincoln for reissuing his pass was the last known correspondence he ever had with Lincoln.

PART FOUR

Later Years

24

"Surely you don't intend to go for Grant"

After Lincoln's assassination, Issachar busied himself with his chiropody practice in New York and Philadelphia[1] and with marketing "Italian Lotion. For the Complexion. Prevents sunburn, freckles and pimples" as a new sideline.[2] He didn't need the money. Issachar hadn't exaggerated when he told Lincoln he had no need for bribes. According to the *New York Evening Telegraph*, he owned $10,000 in diamonds, putting him high on the list of "principal Diamond Owners in New York."[3]

In 1868, Issachar moved his family into a mansion on 51st near Fifth Avenue.[4] The new address was more prestigious than Broadway. It was also larger and needed more servants to properly host the "nightly banquets" he gave for "the high-rollers of that city."[5] It wasn't just New York's elite who were guests at the Zacharie mansion. Issachar kept in touch with General Banks, who was still popular enough in his home state of Massachusetts to be reelected to Congress and was serving as chairman of the House Committee on Foreign Affairs. When Banks visited New York, Issachar invited him to dinner at his new residence at number 16 on 51st street, a few doors west of 5th Avenue.[6]

Nothing much is known about Issachar's personal life. Did he have any close friends? Was he a faithful husband? His and Mary Ann's marriage seemed happy enough. Had there been any strain in their marriage, Mary Ann could have sought divorce, but they stayed married. Was Mary Ann religious? Did she take her children to church? Did they go to Sunday school? Did he ever speak to them about his own religion?

Issachar's children began leaving to start their own families in 1871, when 19-year-old Amelia, Issachar's eldest daughter, married Joseph Edward Hughes and left to live with her husband in England.[7] That same year, his son Charles Lawson Zacharie married Florence Cowing. (Their son, Charles C. Zacharie, born two years later, served as a physician in the American army during World War II and died in 1948.)

* * * * * * * *

24. "Surely you don't intend to go for Grant" 165

Like the rest of America, Issachar read about the political drama evolving after Andrew Johnson became President. When Johnson took office, Radical Republicans were overjoyed that one of their own was in the White House as President and would go along with their intentions to punish the South for the war. But Johnson had his own ideas about Reconstruction that were much more lenient. When Johnson refused to budge, the House considered impeaching him, but couldn't come up with sufficient grounds. The House finally found a cause after Johnson asked Secretary of War Stanton, whom he suspected of conspiring with the Radicals, to resign. When Stanton refused, Johnson suspended him when Congress was not in session and appointed General Grant as interim secretary. When the Senate returned, its members insisted Stanton could not be fired. Grant resigned to avoid becoming entangled in the dispute. Johnson wouldn't back down. He accused Grant of reneging on his promise to continue as an interim cabinet member until the Supreme Court weighed in on the constitutionality of his firing Stanton. Grant said he had given him no such assurance. Johnson then appointed Major General Lorenzo Thomas Secretary of War. Impeached by the House, Johnson narrowly avoided conviction in the Senate by a single vote.[8]

There was no chance Johnson would be reelected in 1868. Issachar would have been ecstatic had Banks been the Republican party's nominee, but Banks' time had come and gone. General Grant was the obvious choice to succeed Johnson. Issachar kept in touch with Banks and invited him to call on him "when convenient,"[9] but Issachar no longer had any illusions of riding back to fame on Banks' coattails.

Ulysses S. Grant was not a politician. He had never held public office. He knew war and horses. A political naif, he lacked the acquired instincts of the wily politician.[10] Grant was a modest man not prone to bombast. His simple presidential message was, "let us have peace,"[11] by which he meant reconciliation between North and South and black and white.[12] Grant favored black manhood suffrage in the former Confederate states, but left the issue up to the states in the rest of the country. Promises aside, Grant's strategists knew one thing: Grant was a revered hero. "Waving the bloody shirt," they reminded the country Grant had defeated the enemy and restored peace, despite Democrats' opposition.

Grant's Democrat opponent in the 1868 election was New York State's former governor, Horatio Seymour. Seymour had not been one of Lincoln's admirers. When Lincoln issued his Emancipation Proclamation, Seymour lambasted it as a "proposal for the butchery of women and children, for scenes of lust and rapine, and of arson and murder."[13] Seymour's vice presidential running mate, Francis Preston Blair, Jr., promised, when elected, to "prevent the people of our race ... from being driven out of the country or trodden under foot by an inferior and semi-barbarous race."[14]

America's Jews were conflicted.[15] Like the rest of the North, they revered Grant as a war hero, but the memory of Grant's infamous order expelling all Jews from his department was still vivid in their minds. Myer Samuel Isaacs, editor of the *Jewish Messenger*, wasn't dismissive of Grant's egregious fiat, but insisted, as he had in the 1864 election, America's Jews would vote as individuals on the basis of their ideals, not as a Jewish bloc. "Judaism," he insisted, "has nothing in common with partisan politics."[16]

How Jews voted in the 1868 election is guesswork. Jews were only a small minority, numbering no more than 150,000 to 200,000, but that included women and children and recent immigrants who were ineligible to vote.[17] If the outcome were based solely on the popular vote, in a close election, they might have made a difference. But the electoral college determines the winner. In 1868, America was still mostly farmland and rural. Most of America's Jews lived in the larger cities of New York, Baltimore, Chicago, Cincinnati, and Philadelphia. Their votes would not count for much in the electoral college.

Grant easily won the electoral college, 214 to 80. He carried the popular vote by the narrower margin of 3 million to 2.7 million votes. In New York, Grant lost by 10,000 votes.[18] The *New York Times* opined that because of the lasting "enmity" over Grant's "Jew order," "the entire body of voting Israelites" marked their ballots for Seymour.[19] Sarna and Chernow speculate Grant would have lost the popular vote were it not for the more than 500,000 African American voters who supported him.[20] At 46, Ulysses S. Grant was the youngest Presidential candidate ever elected, until John F. Kennedy at 43.

Issachar had no personal influence or connection with Grant or Seymour or any of their supporters, but he had hardly been forgotten. In the aftermath of the 1868 election and Grant's mantra, "let us have peace," *Galaxy* magazine reminded its readers of Issachar's peace mission to the South, not to praise, but to blister him for "meddling in public business, pretending to do something when doing nothing … then telegraphing it to the newspapers?" Wagging a finger at "Mr. Lincoln's corn-doctor," it asked what "was the State business requiring so queer an ambassador as this reaper and mower of corns, and soother of in-grown toe-nails?" The "worthy corn-doctor" used the notoriety he got by his "diplomatic functions" well. "He is now doing a thriving trade in salves and toe lotions up in Broadway, in a museum of monstrous corns and abnormal bunions, to which he will add yours, gentle reader, at a reasonable rate."[21]

Issachar was in fact "doing a thriving trade." He'd relocated his storefront in Philadelphia to 1011 Chestnut and was still selling his Italian lotion from his Broadway building,[22] Issachar had also rented out part of his business space at his Broadway location to an M. Lausson who offered to enhance faces by enameling them "in the most exquisite style, so as to last for one day or one year. The preparation used is purely vegetable and warranted not to injure the skin. Eyelashes trimmed and eyebrows arranged so as to add much to the appearance of the face.... All communications strictly confidential."[23]

* * * * * * * *

The year 1872 was another election year. Grant told a reporter he wasn't anxious for a second term. He said he had decided to run to learn whether the country really believed all that was alleged against his administration and himself personally. Grant was aware of the animus many Jews still harbored against him because of his expulsion order, but he had done much to undo that bitterness.[24]

Grant's opponent this time was the *New York Tribune*'s prickly Horace Greeley, who was backed by an unholy alliance between the Liberal Republican Party, splintered from the Republican Party, and the Democrats. Liberal Republicans balked at Grant's Reconstruction policies, including his promotion of black suffrage, and the "Grantism" that characterized his administration.

"Grantism" became a generic term for the scandals and corruption for the era known as the "Gilded Age." The "Gilded Age" was Mark Twain's cynical label[25] for the "shiny and prosperous on the outside, but rotten on the inside" years that began with Grant's first term as President, an administration mired in mismanagement and corruption. Initially inclined to be lenient toward the postwar South, Grant changed his attitude after scheming politicians with more punitive ideas plied him with expensive wines and cigars and fast horses.[26]

Dishonest politicians and businessmen became multimillionaires during Grant's administration while millions of others struggled to keep food on the table. A year into Grant's presidency, his administration was racked by "Black Friday," the first of its major scandals. Millionaires Jay Gould and "Jubilee Jim" Fisk cornered the gold market, buying enough gold and stock to send gold prices soaring, and then sold it for a huge profit. The scheme worked because Gould and Fisk bribed Grant's brother-in-law, Abel Corbin, to persuade Grant not to let the Federal Treasury sell its gold. When the Treasury finally released its gold, the price for gold plummeted. A Congressional investigation concluded that Grant was stupid, but not crooked.[27]

* * * * * * * *

Issachar had sat out the 1868 election. Like many, he was fed up with the scandals that dominated the newspapers. He felt certain Grant would not be reelected and sensed this might be an opportunity for Banks and himself, as Banks' self-appointed advisor, to regain the national spotlight. When Issachar read Banks was considering supporting Grant, he dashed off a letter to the General.

Surely you don't intend to go for Grant. You are too young a man to choose deliberately to go on the losing side, when both your principles and our feelings can be better served by going on the winning side. We know here that the indorsement of Greeley or a Brown (Benjamin Gratz Brown, Greeley's running mate) by the Democratic convention is as certain as anything in the political future can be. With that indorsement, and with the support he already has from the Liberal Republicans especially from the Irish and Germans, there can be scarcely a reasonable doubt of his election.[28]

Despite his initial support for Grant, Banks was disappointed Grant had ignored him after the 1868 election. He had expected Grant to offer him a cabinet position or a foreign ministry.[29] Grant had also ignored Banks' patronage requests,[30] but Banks wasn't yet ready to sever his loyalty to the Republican party he had helped organize. "Waiting on the Lord" to see in which direction the electoral wind blew, Banks procrastinated about lending his name to the Greeley campaign.[31]

Issachar intimated that Banks could expect a cabinet appointment or at least patronage appointments in return for supporting Greeley. "If political gratitude amounts to anything, you could hardly in any other way command yourself so well to the Administration that is for the next four years to rule."[32] By early July, Banks was rumored to be leaning toward Greeley.[33]

There is no longer "the slightest doubt that General Banks has determined to abandon the administration, and array himself on the side of the democracy and liberal republicanism," the *Brooklyn Daily Eagle* told its readers. "Of course, this movement destroys his chances for reelection to Congress (Republicans would turn against him) but it may be possible that the General is willing now to terminate his Congressional career and take the chances of a cabinet position or a foreign Ministry under the government to come."[34]

"Not a sorehead," the *Chicago Post* crowed about Banks' silence, surmising it amounted to a denial of apostasy. "He [still] adheres to the Republican party."[35] Banks had "positively denied the rumors in regard to his being a supporter of Horace Greeley," trumpeted the *Boston Traveler*. "This is decisive. General Banks' friends never doubted his fidelity."[36] General Banks is "too shrewd a man to step outside of an organization which has given him so much more than he deserves," said the *Sacramento Daily*.[37]

"I have tried to serve you," Issachar chastised Banks after he failed to show up at a meeting Issachar had arranged for him to meet with Greely and a "few prominent friends." "Without further explanation from you," he said, he will not again allude "to the subject in which I have taken a deep interest," implying Banks was wasting Issachar's time. Issachar scolded Banks as if he were a disobedient child. "I do all for your good but I fear that you as usual procrastinate." "I have done my duty towards you as I would expect any friend to do towards me. If I have failed it is not my fault. I fear you will come out too late. Now is the time or never."[38]

24. *"Surely you don't intend to go for Grant"*   169

On July 31, Banks finally announced he was supporting Greeley. "No personal feeling of any character" influenced his decision, he said, by which he meant Grant. "My duty to myself and my country requires me to give him [Greeley] my support."[39]

Just as it had been in the 1868 election, Grant's General Orders No. 11 was weaponized, this time by the Greeley camp. Greeley's *New York Tribune* published a letter from a reader saying it seemed odd to him that the Jewish press, with one exception, had been ominously silent on the election. If the controversy merely involved political questions, there might be a reason to keep aloof. But "we know that both Grant and (Henry) Wilson (his vice-president running mate) ... are both enemies to the Jews.... What Grant has done against us we all but too well know, he having issued that infamous order, banishing the Jews as a class from his district, because, forsooth, a few of them were petty traders."[40]

By 1872, however, the animus many Jews felt toward Grant had lost most of its sting. In a letter to a former Congressman, Isaac Morris, that was purposely leaked to the press, Grant said he had issued the expulsion order "without any reflection and without thinking of the Jews as a sect or race ... but simply as persons who had successfully (I say successfully instead of persistently because there were plenty of others within my lines who envied their success) violated an order, which greatly inured to the help of the rebels."[41] It was a transparently feckless denial. Nonetheless, many Jews accepted the halfhearted apology, especially when Grant added he had "no prejudice against sect or race, but want each individual to be judged by his own merit." Grant admitted Orders No. 11 didn't support his statement. "But then I do not sustain that order. It would never have been issued if it had not been telegraphed the moment it was penned, and without reflection."[42]

To prove he had no animus against Jews, Grant appointed Jews to public office, opposed a Constitutional amendment explicitly acknowledging "the Lord Jesus Christ as the Ruler among nations," publicly protested pogroms in Russia and Romania, and appointed a Jewish consul-general to Romania.[43] Countering the accusations of Grant's anti–Semitism, the pro–Grant *New York Times* accused Greeley of ridiculing a sacred Jewish rite. According to the *Times*, after some Indians had fled to Canada after a rabbi had allegedly forcibly circumcised them as the lost tribes of Israel, Greeley supposedly said that when he got to be President, "I'll send a lot of these rabbis out there" to get the redskins to leave the country.[44] During the war, Greeley had also disparaged Jews as "the most persistent and cunning contrabandits."[45]

As he had in the 1864 and 1868 elections, the *Jewish Messenger's* editor, Samuel Myer Isaacs, berated the partisan newspapers for urging Jews to vote as a bloc, this time against Grant. "While some Israelites may not have forgotten that indefensible action (Grant's Orders No. 11), many have long ago forgiven Grant, and have buried their private feelings in consideration of the General's public services.... It is absurd for the managers of either party to imagine that 'Jewish votes' can be bought or sold," he blustered. "There are no 'Jewish votes.' Let there be an end to these newspaper efforts to embroil American Hebrews in political controversy."[46] For his part, throughout his stumping for Greeley, Banks never mentioned Grant's order or made any overtures to win the "Jewish vote." Strangely, neither did Issachar. During the 1864 election, Issachar had prided himself on allaying America's Jews on Lincoln's side. This time, Issachar was strangely silent about getting out the Jewish vote for Greeley.

The day after Banks came out publicly for Greeley, Issachar congratulated him on his decision. "Well done my good friend. I know you will never regret coming out for Greeley."[47] A day later, Issachar wrote him he had heard from "several prominent men" about what they thought about Banks' letter. Issachar had lost none of his self-serving sycophantism. "I can say with satisfaction to myself and friends and with honor to you, that it is one of your master letters." He had spoken with Greeley in his home the day before, and Greeley asked Issachar to thank Banks. Greeley told him Banks' letter clinched his election. He hoped to meet him soon and thank him personally.[48] Continuing to praise Banks for his "manly letter," Issachar gloated with satisfaction and pride that his efforts to persuade Banks to support Greeley had not been in vain. "Keep it up," he beamed with anticipation, "and N.P. Banks will yet pull the strings of government."[49]

Just as he had boasted to Lincoln years before that he would guarantee his reelection if he followed his advice, Issachar ended his letter by praising himself for putting Banks "on the right path," telling him to "only take my advice" and his future would not "slip through your fingers." Ironically, Issachar cautioned Banks to "trust no man, they will deceive you." He himself had induced Banks to go into this campaign, he said, "from the purest of motives." Should Greeley lose the election, "I hope you will not blame me for persuading you to break ranks with the Republicans and support him."[50]

A day later, flush with enthusiasm, Issachar wrote Banks he had picked up some gossip the night before at Democratic Headquarters. One of the delegates had said Banks was "the biggest gun that Greeley has" and hoped one day to vote for Banks for President.[51] Feeling he could once again be Banks' puppet master, Issachar wrote he was too busy seeing patients to call on him at Banks' room in New York, but if Banks could come to his office, "I think it will be to your advantage."[52]

It was no contest. Grant won 31 of the 37 states, including several Southern states, the electoral vote, 286 to 3, and the popular vote with 55.6 percent to Greeley's 43.8 percent (other candidates won the remaining 0.6 percent). Just before the electoral college cast its votes, Greeley unexpectedly died.

24. "Surely you don't intend to go for Grant" 171

Banks' support of Greeley cost him his own state congressional seat. But Banks was not ready to retire. Two years later, Banks again ran for Congress. Despite the disastrous outcome of the national election and his costly advice to Banks' career, Issachar once again offered to help Banks in his reelection bid. Telegraph me immediately, he wrote Banks, "and I will be on hand.... Never Say Die."[53] Banks did not take him up on his offer and regained his seat in the midterm election on his own.[54]

* * * * * * * *

Issachar had finally closed his business in Philadelphia in 1872. In 1873, he relocated his residence to 27 Union Square East in New York, one of the streets surrounding the Union Square Park.[55] Union Square was a much more prestigious address than Issachar's former location farther down on Broadway. The streets surrounding the park were paved, and the streets were lined with trees, posh hotels, and upscale businesses like the first Tiffany & Co.

Issachar was nothing if not resilient. Whatever animus he may have had toward Grant, Issachar didn't let it get in the way of an invitation on Grant's part for him to come to Washington to remove Grant's corns. As was his usual custom, he asked Grant for a testimonial. The autographed note, dated Washington, January 15, 1874, stated "Dr. I Zacharie M.D. has extracted from my feet corns of long standing without producing the slightest pain and the work is done in the most effectual manner."[56]

Grant's testimonial caught the attention of journalist George Alfred Townsend. Best known as John Wilkes Booth's first biographer, Townsend, writing under the pseudonym Gath, visited the "celebrated corn doctor" under the pretense of ridding himself of bunions. What he was really interested in was "making some inquiries about the footprints of statesmen. So, with all my antennae out, I dropped, in an indifferent way, into the sanctum of our greatest corn-surgeon, and asked him to cut four dollars' worth off, but not to hurry about it." Townsend embellished his description of his visit for his readers, but despite his elaborations, his is the first and only insight into Issachar's personality and business.

Issachar showed him a "luxurious chair" and told him to sit and relax while he "prepared some occult salve." While he was busy preparing the ointment, Issachar gave him a large pile of corns to examine. Years earlier, *Galaxy* magazine had referred to Issachar's "museum of monstrous corns and abnormal bunions":

> He had about one thousand hard corns of all sizes strung upon wire, as a merchant keeps his bills or charges on file. Some were nearly an inch square and looked like a section cut out of a horse's hoof; others were little delicate corns no larger than those raised upon the branching feet of a young robin; others were clear as glass ... while some were dark and muddy, and the coagulated blood at their center made them

resemble ossified violets…. What a memorandum of mankind and womankind it was! The story of torture for vanity's sake; of high heels consented to the sacrifice of love; of man's pursuit of wealth, all day upon his feet, and these horny milestones, the silently accumulating measure of his journey; of weary postmen bearing out letters from door to door, while the long, poignant ache rested within the boot unnoticed of soldiers marching into the jaws of death but reckon less of the enemy's Minnie balls than of those missiles which crush their feet at every stride. Here it was, the intensest epitome of woe ever hung up in a business museum.

Townsend asked Issachar why he kept them. "Curiosity," Issachar answered, and also as evidence he had not lived in vain. "If the man who gives a cup of cold water to one of these little ones, expects to be remembered in Heaven, what will they say up there when I appear with my linear half mile of such corns as this?"

"So, you think there is a religious aspect to your business," Townsend asked?

Issachar nodded. "Yes, I like to think so. So does everybody like to think that he is necessary and comfortable to have round. Yesterday there was a young lady here, whose foot looked like a slim new moon made out of ivory, with a corn peeping out behind it like a star. I cut it off for her, and she said: 'Oh! Doctor, I feel as if I could fly.' And the young man who came with her asked me to give him the corn to put in his watch seal."

Some of his patients were less grateful when he handed them his bill, said Issachar. Reaching out for a "corn which looked like three silver half dollars that had been run over by a locomotive," Issachar smiled. "Didn't that one make him 'ouch,'" he said. Then in all seriousness, "that disagreeable and ungrateful fellow" complained about Issachar's bill. "No sooner shed that corn that he turned round, and says: 'If I knew you'd a charged two dollars I'd walked with it half a century first.'"

Issachar then took Townsend's foot "very much as if he were picking at the flint of an old-fashioned musket, and, having moistened the corn, proceeded with three sorts of knives alternately to quarry off the capstone. Then he cut all my nails with a machine which seemed to be a sort of juvenile guillotine, and having set a plast upon the spot showed me through the glass a corn like a limekiln."

After more light banter, Townsend edged the conversation to the reason he had come to see Issachar. "Doctor, do any of the great politicians come here?"

Issachar showed him corns he had cut from General George H. Thomas, "a little fellow," and then showed him corns he had removed from Generals Sheridan and McClellan and Lincoln, "the whole set. It's the only collection in the United States." Then with no little pride, Issachar showed him a corn he'd "cut off the little toe of Grant after Lee's surrender. It's the only wound

24. "Surely you don't intend to go for Grant"   173

he ever received in the war; and I've been offered twenty-five dollars for it." (Did Issachar treat Grant when he was in Washington just before Lincoln's assassination?)

Townsend was excited. He was now getting down to business. Here was what he came for. "Doctor, what sort of foot has Grant?"

"A solid sort of an edifice," said Issachar. "He's well sot on his astragali, but horseback has given him a pigeon-toed tendency. When he stands up and ain't thinking, the axes of his feet, if prolonged, pass through each other a rod ahead of him. He's a better officer than ossifier."

As Townsend paid his bill and left, Issachar told him his "corn has gone into the American National Pedalion collection, and will be preserved for the benefit of posterity."[57]

25

"Republics are unquestionably ungrateful"

General Banks owed his reelection in Massachusetts in the middle of Grant's second term to a Democrat resurgence in the wake of government scandals and a financial crisis rocking America. The years immediately after the war had been a boom time in America, fueled in large part by rapid growth in railway construction. Between 1868 and 1873, more than 30,000 miles of new track were laid.[1] Owing to government land grants and subsidies, the railroad industry and its ancillary industries became the country's second largest employer next to farming. Thousands of factories opened. The stock market soared.

The bubble burst when profits didn't match expectations. Much of the expansion had been fueled with borrowed money. The most powerful banking firm in the country, Jay Cooke & Company, which had invested millions of dollars in railway industry, couldn't sell its bonds and declared bankruptcy. It was the end of a lovely summer holiday, said financier Andrew Carnegie. "All was going well when one morning in our summer cottage … a telegram came announcing the failure of Jay Cooke & Co. Every hour brought news of another bank and investment firm's collapse." At the same time, Congress tightened the money supply. Businesses that had to borrow at the higher interest rates closed. The New York Stock Exchange shut its doors for 10 days. About 14 percent of the workforce was suddenly unemployed. Workers who didn't lose their jobs took pay cuts. "Every failure depleted the resources of other concerns," said Carnegie. America was in the grip of "a total paralysis of business."[2] The country was in the midst of what was called the "Great Depression," until the depression of the 1930s took over that unwanted title.

In July 1864, Congress created a committee to provide payment for debt the federal government owed to loyal citizens in states not in rebellion for their property losses. In 1873, the name of the committee was changed to the Committee on War Claims. During its tenure, the committee examined 2,407 claims for over $5 million in compensation. Of these, 1,244 were disallowed.

25. "Republics are unquestionably ungrateful" 175

The final bill only came to $770,711 (approximately $16.5 million in today's money).

To qualify for compensation, petitioners had to prove they had been loyal to the Union cause and had to provide documents supporting their petitions. Every petitioner had to answer 43 questions, among them:

> Where were you born? If not born in the United States, when and where were you naturalized? Produce your naturalization papers if you can.
> Did you ever do anything for the Union cause or its advocates or defenders? If so, state what you did, giving times, places, names of persons aided, and particulars. Were the persons aided, your relations?
> Were you in the service or employment of the United States government at any time during the war? If so, in what service, when, where, for how long, under what officers, and when and how did you leave such service or employment.
> Did you ever voluntarily contribute money, property, or service to the Union cause; and if so, when, where, to whom, and what did you contribute?
> What favors, privileges, or protections were ever granted you in recognition of your loyalty during the war, and when and by whom granted?[3]

Most of the claims were disallowed because the claimants had served in the Confederate army, had sent a substitute, were in the Confederate civil service, had voted for secession, were not American citizens, or were not in the service or employment of the government.[4]

The committee's most sensational claimant was Dr. Issachar Zacharie. Stating he had operated on the bony excrescences of not less than 5,000 soldiers at Fortress Monroe, 6,000 men in New Orleans preparing for the Red River campaign, and, 4,000 men in the capital and Baltimore and surrounding areas after returning to Washington, Issachar asked for reimbursement of $45,000 (about $960,000 and $60, respectively, in today's money), charging $3 for two feet.[5]

To support his petition, Issachar sent the committee the testimonials Lincoln and Seward had signed on September 23, 1862, stating from personal experience they had benefited from his skill in treating various "troubles of the feet" and "we desire that soldiers of our brave Army may have the benefit of the doctors' surprising skill."[6] He also submitted Stanton's order giving him the freedom to operate on the feet of soldiers around Washington and on the Potomac for 30 days[7] and its continuance, for another 60 days, that was signed by General Tucker Black, Stanton's assistant secretary of war.[8] Issachar would have asked Lincoln, Stanton, and Seward to testify or write additional letters on his behalf, but they were all dead—Lincoln in 1865, Stanton in 1869, and Seward in 1872. The only other high-ranking official still alive who could support his claim was General Banks.

So certain Banks' testimony would convince the committee his claim was legitimate, Issachar wrote asking for his help, offering to pay all his expenses if he went with him to Washington (Banks was at the time senator in the Massachusetts legislature) to appear before the committee. "Your position alone will assist me," he pleaded. "I have all the Evidence. Still they want to know if [I]was with you in New Orleans. I do hope you will do all you can for me. I think there will be no doubt that a favourable report will be made, and a few words from you will assist me very much."[9]

Banks had had enough of Issachar. He had lost his seat in Congress because he had followed Issachar's advice and supported Greely in the 1872 election. Banks answered a few days later. His duties in the state legislature, he said, made it "imposable" for him to appear before the War Claims Committee in Washington at the present time. There was no doubt, he said,

> you was operating upon the feet of our soldiers. When I was in Command of Washington in 1862, and that when I was ordered to the Department of the Gulph, that the President ordered me to take you with the Expedition … no one will doubt but that you did good Service, and must of operated upon several thousand of our brave Soldiers during the War. I am satisfied had Mr. Lincoln had lived, that you would of received your pay for operating upon our Army long ago. Hope that you will now receive your just claim.[10]

Despite Banks' support, the committee denied Issachar's claim. It could have dismissed it outright because claimants had to be U.S. citizens. Issachar was not born in the United States and had not been naturalized. He was still a British citizen. For some reason, the committee did not take his citizenship into consideration. Instead, it said Issachar hadn't produced any evidence from soldiers "whose pedal extremities are alleged to have been operated on…. It is not even pretended by Zacharie that the corns and bunions on the feet of the soldiers of the Army of the Potomac operated by him were the result, either of the active military operations" or were preexisting conditions. As far as the committee knew, he might have been paid by the soldiers themselves when he treated them.

The committee also turned him down because it said it only had his word he had operated on 15,000 men. He hadn't submitted any account whatever to the commanding officers of the units he said he had treated. Had he done so, it would have been a valuable addition to the "Army Medical Museum." The information gained from those records could have been provided a way of "recoupment, or set-off" for his claim. Besides, he did not have a formal contract from the government. If he had, he would be due the money he claimed. Issachar answered that although he had worked *pro bono publico*, "a great, powerful, and just Government should, in the consideration of a claim like his, lay aside the legal technicalities that surround the case, as well as mere formalities, and, considering only the results attained, decide the case in his favor."

The committee answered that if it honored Issachar's claim, based solely

25. "Republics are unquestionably ungrateful" 177

on his word, it would establish a principle that the government was bound to remove the corns and bunions of its soldiers during the war. "If soldiers were entitled to such relief at Government expense, why not sailors? If sailors, why not civilian employees? Congress would be flooded with so many claims it would have to appoint 'a standing committee on corns and bunions.'"[11]

Newspapers around the country had a field day mocking Issachar's failed bid for reimbursement. The Chicago *Daily Inter Ocean* questioned his motives. Dr. Zacharie had treated the army's foot soldier out of "lofty patriotism," it said. Now he was asking the government to pay for what he had offered *pro bono*.[12] The New York *Daily Graphic*'s coverage was sarcastic. It restated Issachar's evidence and said the Committee on War Claims had treated Dr. Zacharie as though corns were a joke and a chiropodist a confirmed humorist. "Republics are unquestionably ungrateful, and this particular Republic evidently doesn't feel the slightest gratitude for the elimination of military corns."[13]

The *Indiana Herald* criticized the committee's decision for the same reason. "Republics are unquestionably ungrateful, and this particular Republic evidently doesn't feel the slightest gratitude for the elimination of its military corns."[14] The *Biloxi* (Mississippi) *Herald* stated that Zacharie's claim amounted to a "Pretty costly corn crop for our Uncle Samuel."[15]

The most biting commentary came from the *Cincinnati Commercial*. In a widely reprinted editorial headlined "Concerning Corns." the *Commercial* called Issachar, "A Quack Patriot … an official excrescence exterminator of the army in the times that tried men's soles." Citing verbatim parts of the War Claims Committee's summary of Issachar's evidence, including his "alleged" documents, the *Commercial* tore into his claim for reimbursement for having done "his part toward the stamping out of the rebellion." "Fifteen thousand stamps would otherwise have been in hospitals hobbling about on crutches, consuming rations and hospital stores instead of serving at the front, had it not been for his efforts." The reason he was asking for compensation now, the *Commercial* mused, was Dr. Zacharie had decided to wait "until the war was over, the negroes freed and habilitated as citizens, the work of reconstruction about completed and, the national debt in process of reduction." The paper mockingly accused the chairman of the committee of having turned Issachar down because, not having corns or bunions or other painful extremities himself, he didn't know what it was like to suffer.

Dr. Zacharie needn't despair, the *Commercial* continued. He should renew his petition when the new Congress takes over. If he failed there, "it is the duty of the rich and powerful municipality of which he is an honored resident, to erect to his memory, and in recognition of his patriotic services, a towering monument in Central Park." The appropriate design for the monument would be a colossal corn surrounded by a gigantic statute of the famed chiropodist.[16]

Twenty years later, an editorial in the *New York Times* cited Issachar's claim as one of a number of "Freaks of Legislation. Odd Bills and Reports to Congressional Committees.... There was perhaps no better example of one of these doubtful and musing claims," it chuckled, "than that of Issachor Zacharie, a gentleman learned in the profession of extracting corns, who plied his trade during the war of the rebellion." To illustrate how "freakish" his claim was, it reproduced much of the War Committee's report verbatim.[17]

26

Return to England

In the second year of the "long Depression" which began in 1873 and lasted until 1879, Issachar left America for good to join his family. The *London Morning Post* informed its readers, likely repeating what it was told by Issachar himself, that Dr. Zacharie had been "induced to return to the country of his birth by some of our most influential men."[1]

In late 1874, he immediately set up an office in London where his wife and daughter Clara had moved into in an elegant 11-bedroom, three-bathroom, four-story building at 80 Brook Street at the corner of Brook and Gilbert streets in Grosvenor Square. Issachar's office was in one of the three ground floor reception rooms. The *Business Directory of London* for 1884[2] listed him along with 31 other chiropodists in the city. By then, chiropody had become a respectable profession. One of those also listed in the *Business Directory* was Frederick Bearnard, "Surgeon Chiropodist to the Royal Family." Another directory, *Webster's Royal Blue Book: Fashionable Directory and Parliamentary Guide*, listed "Dr. Zacharie" among "the names and addresses of (London's) better class private residents."[3]

Grosvenor Square, where Issachar had his new home, was located in London's exclusive Mayfair District. Lord North, the prime minister, lived there during the American Revolution, as had many of England's elite. In *Pride and Prejudice*, Jane Austen alludes to its posh residences. Oscar Wilde lived there in the 1880s and referred to it in four of his plays. Grosvenor Square, the "little America in London," has traditionally been America's diplomatic home site ever since John Adams lived from 1785 to 1788 at 9 Grosvenor Square at the corner of Brook and Duke streets. Adams' wife, Abigail, said their home was opposite Lord North's. General Eisenhower had his headquarters in Grosvenor Square during World War II. At one time, George Frederic Handel, guitarist Jimi Hendrix, and the Bee Gees all lived on Brook Street.

Modesty or veracity rarely being among Issachar's virtues, he now advertised his past professional standing as "late Chiropodist-General of the United States Army."[4] A year later, the *London Morning Post* spotlighted his return with a lengthy and largely exaggerated profile that could only have

Zacharie's home at 80 Brook St., London, "Among the names and addresses of (London's) better class private residents" (photograph by author).

come from Issachar himself. "Although of American reputation," the *Post* beamed with pride, "this justly-celebrated practitioner is an Englishman." He emigrated to America when a "mere boy," but before leaving, he had been a pupil "of our celebrated St Astley Cooper." Once his family settled in Philadelphia, he studied surgery under "the famous Dr. Mutter."[5] In 1862, the *Post* con-

26. Return to England

tinued, he was appointed "Chiropodist-General to the United States Army" and "served during the whole of the campaign under Generals M'Clellan, Banks, Burnside and Grant." He was a confidant of President Lincoln and Secretary William Seward, "who appointed him Minister Plenipotentiary to the Department of the Gulf." In 1864, "he was sent as peace commissioner to the Southern Confederacy ... the result of which (as far as the doctor was concerned) was highly satisfactory to both parties."

Other than his being Lincoln's confidant, none of the story was true. What was true was that since arriving back in England, he "has already performed some wonderful operations with great skill and dexterity. He operates we are informed, without pain of the slightest kind, and without drawing a drop of blood."[6]

Issachar relished London society. He became widely known for his lavish dinner parties, at which he hosted the "elite of Masonry" and "frequently many of the worthiest of England's nobility."[7] A contemporary recalled his mother telling him about a patient of hers (she was also a chiropodist) who complained that although "you make me quite comfortable ... you do not ask me to dinner. Now if I went to a certain chiropodist in Brook Street, I might be asked to dinner and perhaps to a game of cards."[8]

"Under the influence of the cheery glass," Issachar was wont to "unlock the stores of his memory" of his exploits in America. With typical immodesty, he bragged to his guests about how he had been responsible for "the disbursal of large secret service State funds, necessary to effect certain operations arising during the internecine conflict" (the Civil War) and regaled his dinner companions with stories about the "friends he had on both sides. He and he alone," he said, had been able to "gain a hearing from the leaders when their ears were closed to every other voice."[9]

Although he had left the United States, Issachar was still newsworthy there. American newspapers continued to report on his activities in England, especially when there was anything offbeat about the flamboyant chiropodist. In the March 1880 edition of the *Washington Evening Star*, under the ominous headline, "Thirteen at Table," it reported Queen Victoria's personal physician, Dr. Fairbank, had mysteriously died the day after dining at Issachar's home, intimating some supernatural involvement in his death.

According to the news report, Issachar had invited 15 of London's elites to a dinner party at his home. On the morning of the day of the party, two of the guests cancelled. Since that would leave 13 guests, the superstitious host was about to invite an intimate friend to avoid the unlucky number when he received a telegram from another expected guest saying he also couldn't make it. With his guest list down to 12, Issachar went about taking care of other things he had to do that day. As the guests arrived, the man who had sent the telegram unexpectedly appeared, having cancelled his previous engagement.

Gazing around the table, it quickly dawned on the guests there were 13 of them. "Presently everybody remarked upon the ominous number present." There was another superstition attached to the "thirteen at table" that the guests were all aware of—the first one to sit down was destined to die shortly.[10]

Dr. Thomas Fairbank, a 36-year-old obstetrician, dismissed the superstition as foolishness. He was about to sit when Issachar warned him about the fatal prediction. Fairbank laughed, although before sitting down, he confided to one of the other guests he didn't feel in a dinner mood. He died unexpectedly the next day.[11]

A month later, an editorial regarding Fairbank appeared in the *London Medical Press and Circular*. The

> morbid curiosity for petty details of purely personal and private matters which the so-called "society" journals have carefully fostered and now live, by gratifying, is extending its unpleasant inquisitiveness into the ranks of our profession. We fail to see why the fact should be trumpeted forth to the world through the press. We notice, however, "Dr." Zacharie's address is carefully recorded. Is it possible the eminent "orthopeaedist" is in want of an advertisement, and secures it cheaply by asking an editor to dine with him?[12]

Issachar had become such a prominent social figure in London that he was invited to elegant banquets given in honor of prominent figures in England. At one such banquet at London's posh Metropole Hotel, he sat at the table with an English lord, several high-ranking military officers, the United States consul to London, France's Prince Camille de Polignac, and more than a hundred other dignitaries.[13] De Polignac had been a major general in the Confederate army. When he died in 1913, he was the last surviving Confederate major general.

Anything remotely involving Issachar was reported, even domestic disputes among his employees. When Issachar's cook was arrested for assaulting Issachar's footman, "a lad of colour," "both in the service of Dr. Issachar Zacharie, orthopedist," the incident was reported in both the *London Morning Post* and *Lloyd's Weekly Newspaper*.[14]

* * * * * * * *

Very little is known about Issachar's personal life in England apart from his activities as a Mason.[15] In 1887, several members of his Masonic lodge met at Issachar's home and resolved to form a new chapter of the Order of the Secret Monitor Issachar had founded in California.[16] Issachar was nominated as its first Supreme Ruler. Mary Ann and her daughters arranged the tailoring for the robes Issachar wore at its first meeting.

His greatest pleasure was still entertaining guests at his home. Although he never denied his religious heritage, it ceased to be of any importance to him. Very often, he attended Sunday services at Westminster Abbey. Afterwards, he invited fellow Masons and their wives to his home for dinner. "The dinner was a beautiful one," one of the guests recalled. It was "bountiful ... and beautifully served in courses, embracing the choicest viands of the season. Bro. Dr. Zacharie is a whole-souled host, enjoying his guests as much as they enjoy his hospitality and *bone-hommie*."[17]

By 1895, Issachar's health was failing, and he resigned his position as Grand Supreme Ruler of the Order of the Secret Monitor, but he continued to see patients.[18] When he was just starting out, he had sold patent medicines, some of which he claimed to have created on his own. At this late stage in his life, he latched on to the dieting craze that had started several years before with the first low carbohydrate diet book, the Banting Diet.[19] Catering to a public he believed would prefer an easier and quicker weight loss method, Issachar capitalized on another fad—magnetism. Applying magnets to the body was ballyhooed as a cure for any and all ailments. Issachar decided to get into the weight loss business and advertised he was selling the "Magneticon," a magnetized belt heralded as a way of reducing abdominal corpulence without dieting.[20] When even that became too onerous, he turned over "his most extensive practice" to his student, W. Prince Mumford.[21]

27

Death of an Eccentric Man

Issachar Zacharie died on September 16, 1900, at his home. at 80 Brook Street. He was 74. He was buried in Highgate Cemetery in the outskirts of London. The same cemetery housed the bodies of Karl Marx, novelist George Eliot, poet Christina Rossetti, artist John Singleton Copley, scientist Michael Faraday, and philosopher Herbert Spencer. Mary Ann died six years later. She was buried alongside Issachar.[1] Issachar's brother, Eleazar, called Elly, married Ann Hutchings, a New Jersey girl, in 1853. Eleazar died in June 1903 in Chicago.[2]

Nothing is known about Issachar's family life. His and Mary Ann's marriage seemed happy enough. Their daughters' and grandchildren's married lives were less than happy.[3] Amelia, Issachar's eldest daughter, was divorced. She'd married Joseph Hughes in 1871 when she was 19. Fourteen years later, in 1885, Hughes divorced her on grounds of adultery. Amelia had had an affair with Hughes' brother John.[4]

Clara Louise stayed in New York after her parents left. A year later, she married Francis Bulley in February 1876, in a Dutch Reformed Church ceremony.[5] Their son, William, was born in November, eight months later.[6] Their marriage was not a happy one. Clara left Francis and went to live with her parents. She filed for divorce in 1883.[7]

Ten years later, in 1893, the *Boston Globe* reported Clara, "Daughter of Dr. Zacharie of London" was engaged to "Morland Dessau of Boston."[8] How Clara and Morland met or how they became engaged isn't known, but the Zacharies and the Dessaus were long-time friends. In 1843, Issachar's sister Amelia Lavinia married Jacob Dessau in Charleston. In 1891, two years before Clara's and Morland's engagement announcement, Issachar testified at an inquest in a London suburb about the death of David Dessau. Issachar told the inquest he'd been an intimate friend of the deceased who had been staying with him for several weeks before his death.[9]

Morland's wife, Katherine Bray, "a fair-featured good-looking woman of rather heavy build," was startled when she read the engagement announcement in the *Boston Globe*. Braving a storm at night, she made her way to the

Globe office. Wiping the rain from her forehead "with an elegantly embroidered, sweetly perfumed handkerchief, she told a tale of domestic infelicity that would move to pity a granite statue."[10]

Morland had left her with only a dollar to her name, a bill for rent, and a grocery man clamoring for money she owned him. Her married life had been a nightmare. At one time during their marriage, he had tried to have her incarcerated in an asylum. Another time, when he was short of money, he doused himself with kerosene and lit himself on fire to claim accident insurance. He was badly burned before the fire was put out. The insurance company paid him over $200. He had never been faithful. She knew he had "made love to several young women in and around Boston." She was "glad to get rid of him."[11] "Let that poor woman over there know what sort of a person she had promised to marry."[12]

The scandal ended Clara's and Morland's engagement. When Morland returned to Boston, he pleaded for his wife to take him back. He promised he would never treat her badly again or desert her. Mrs. Dessau had had enough. She now only felt contempt for Morland. She told him she was divorcing him.

Clara never married again. Her name appears in the 1901 England census with only Mary Ann's name as "parent or spouse." In a 1903, she filed a negligence suit against two pharmacists for incorrectly labeling her medicine. Clara claimed the error had caused her to overdose on mercury pills. A jury awarded her £150.[13] She died in 1928 in Brighton, England.[14]

Mariposa, Issachar's and Mary Ann's youngest daughter, married London-born Marcus Arthur Blumenthal in 1881.[15] Marcus was a bullion dealer and banker. Mariposa died in 1899 when she was only 39. Although they had three children, it may not have been happy marriage. Within months of Mariposa's death, Blumenthal married Agnes Cage in Kent, England, in an Anglican ceremony.[16]

The marriage of Issachar's granddaughter, Amelia's daughter Edith, did not turn out much better than her aunts'. In 1894, she married Hector Gammell.[17] The newspaper tactfully omitted reporting Mary Ann's mother's name. The bride was elegantly attired, the *Bristol Mercury* told its readers. Her wedding gown was a gift from her grandmother, Mrs. Issachar Zacharie. The wedding reception at the Zacharie home was held a day after Issachar's and Mary Ann's golden wedding anniversary.[18]

In 1905, the Gammells moved to Saskatoon in the midwestern Canadian province of Saskatchewan, where Hector had been hired as an engineer. When Edith discovered Hector was having an affair with a Saskatoon woman, she left Saskatoon and filed for divorce in Toronto on grounds of adultery. The marriage was formally dissolved by an act of Parliament in 1908.[19]

Issachar's two sons Charles and Samuel earned medical degrees and remained in the United States. In 1873, Charles married Florence Cowing, a girl from Seneca Falls. The couple had four children they named after themselves and family members.[20] In 1901, while their son Charles C. was living in White Plains, New York, the *New York Tribune* informed its readers he had inherited $25,000 from his grandfather Issachar's estate, mistakenly reporting he had received the inheritance "through the death of an uncle in London last January."[21] Less is known about Samuel except that in 1886, Issachar assigned patent rights to an "orthopedical appliance" to Samuel.[22]

Although Issachar had willed $25,000 to his grandson Charles, his officially reported estate was valued at only £276, 14s (approximately $43,000 in today's money)[23] The wily Issachar had somehow hidden his assets or had placed them in his wife's name before he died.

* * * * * * * *

Despite having disappeared from public notice in America for more than 25 years, newspapers across the country carried lengthy obituaries of Issachar's career. Headlines announced his death in large block headlines and brief subheads. The longest tribute appeared in his former nemesis, the *New York Herald*.

DR. I. ZACHARIE, OLD NEW YORKER, IS DEAD

For a Quarter of a Century One of the Best-Known Characters Of This City. He had for Many years Lived in London, Where He passed away.[24]

Other papers carried similar, albeit less flamboyant headlines:

WAS FAMOUS IN WAR TIMES

Death in London of Dr. Zacharie, Who Was a Noted Chiropodist and Bon Vivant.[25]

DEATH OF AN ECCENTRIC MAN

Wanted To Raise A Corps of Chiropodists For Army[26]

DR ISACHAR ZACHARIE DEAD.

A Famous Army Chiropodist And A Friend of Lincoln[27]

Most of the papers covering the story reprinted the *New York Herald's* obituary For almost a quarter century, the "fashionable chiropodist attended the pedal needs of the most noted beaux and belles of the day" at his "magnificent offices at No. 760 Broadway, near Bond Street and Washington Square," the aristocratic quarters of the town. Issachar's offices were convenient to both. "Fame and money rolled in upon him."[28]

"He was also a gourmet, a wit, and an eccentric." He hosted "magnificent banquets at his splendid mansion near Fifth Avenue and Fiftieth street every night." He invited "the most prominent men in New York, in business, in social life, and in politics," and "they were glad to accept." A dozen seats

27. Death of an Eccentric Man

were always left vacant for uninvited friends to drop by, and they did. He had the choicest liquors on hand. He was reputed to be "the greatest connoisseur of wine in the country." He served his guests the most delicate and original dishes. He was a "bon-vivant" in New York and no less in London after he moved there in 1874.

Issachar's failed attempts to raise "a corps of chiropodists to accompany the various armies" and his grandiose scheme for ending the Civil War and expelling the French from Mexico were also reported in detail. He was ridiculed and made a laughingstock, but he "stood this fun good naturedly," said the *Herald*.[29]

Obituaries in Masonic newspapers credited him with nonexistent military associations and achievements. "Under the influence of the cheery glass,"[30] they said he regaled not just "many of the elite of Masonry" with his exploits, "but frequently many of the worthiest of England's nobility."[31] "While yet a boy," he was said to have been appointed a medical officer "in the U.S. Army of the West Californian region," after which he was "attached to Grant's division, and was Lincoln's 'shrewd ambassador.'"[32] "Naturally qualified, he came to be a diplomat of no mean ability, and an astute and dexterous mediator. Many social and state secrets, were said to have been confided to his care."[33] "Numerous are the occasions when his astuteness, dexterity and high diplomatic qualities" patched up social quarrels.[34]

"One seldom sees so many and such lovely floral tributes" as those at his grave site in Highgate Cemetery, the *Freemason and Masonic Illustrated* told its readers. "The beautiful wreaths at his headstone were 'most striking' ... one wreath bore the legend 'Great Grandpa.' Others bore the names of intimate and distinguished private friends and relatives."[35] Notably, the burial service was performed by a Christian minister, not a rabbi.[36]

A month later, a memorial service in his honor was held at London's posh Hotel Cecil. "A semi-public Masonic Memorial is a very rare thing in England," the *Freemason's Chronicle* noted.

> On this occasion no jewels or Masonic clothing were worn. The whole ceremony was simple to a degree. The raised catafalque in the middle of the room was covered with a purple pall. On it were photographs of the deceased member, illuminated and framed testimonials, and an album presented to him on his golden wedding anniversary. Nearly all the members of his family, attired in deep mourning, were present.[37]

28

Aftermath

In the 1880s, thousands of Jews from eastern Europe and Russia began immigrating to America. The soaring wave of "huddled masses yearning to be free" touched off a new wave of nativist resentment, hostility, and derision. Christians denounced these highly visible newcomers' "unmannerly habits in walking, talking, and acting" as clannish, unassimable, and "undesirable."[1] By implication, so were all American Jews.

These immigrant Jews were painted as no different from the Jews who had supported the Confederacy during the war; a people without allegiance or loyalty. German Jews who had come before them and had fought in the war worried these newcomers might cause them to lose the gains they had made in America.[2] If the German establishment was not to lose its good reputation, the newcomers had to be integrated into American Jewry.[3] Jews had to be recognized as "Americans in every respect." Only then would prejudice against them end.[4] In this country, which is the promised land, said Simon Wolf, a vocal spokesman for American Jews, "the Israelite must, in common with his fellow-citizens, contribute to the political and social formation of the state" as Americans, not as Jews.[5]

The Civil War and the post-war elections of 1868 and 1872, had given American Jews a new sense of political consciousness. If they were ever to be accepted and become socially respectable, they needed to assert they were not strangers in a strange land. To meet that need, Jewish journalists and amateur historians began writing articles and books that emphasized Jews had been coming to America for hundreds of years. Jews had been a vital part of America's emergence and stature as a nation. These articles gave American Jews a sense of pride in their accomplishments. They instilled a sensibility of a common past with their predecessors. Equally important, they counteracted unfavorable perceptions of otherness and disloyalty, particularly with respect to Jewish participation in the Civil War.

The earliest of the Jewish writers to instill a consciousness of the positive role of Jews in conflict was Isaac Markens, who in 1888 self-published *The Hebrews in America*.[6] Markens was a journalist, not a professional historian,

28. Aftermath

and relied on newspapers for his information. Setting a pattern that would be followed for more than 50 years, Markens highlighted Jewish participation in the war, listing the names and regiments of Jewish officers and episodes of Jewish bravery,[7] but failed to mention Issachar, the second most famous Jew in the war next to Judah Benjamin. Twenty years later, when Markens published a lengthy article specifically about Lincoln's dealings with Jews before and during the war, he briefly mentioned their relationship.

Issachar was similarly ignored in Simon Wolf's 1895 *The American Jew as Patriot, Soldier and Citizen*. Simon had written his book after reading an article in the 1891 *North American Review*, a popular newsmagazine of the day, claiming Jews had shirked military service during the war. A few months later, a letter to the *Review* by a gentile Civil War veteran claimed he had never seen a Jew in uniform during the war and that Jews had been either illegal traders or Confederate spies.[8] Incensed at what he and many other Jews regarded as an outright instance of anti–Semitism, Wolf devoted three years to compiling 10,000 names of Jews who had participated in the war, 7,000 in the Union and 3,000 in the Confederacy, in his *American Jew as Patriot*, but Issachar was not included in his compendium.[9]

Not until Isaac Markens' 1909 article "Lincoln and the Jews" was published was Issachar's name mentioned. Even then, Markens had less to say about Issachar than he had about Abraham Jonas, Lincoln's Jewish friend in Illinois before his presidency. Markens said he was relying almost solely on information from American newspapers, which he said gave "special prominence ... to his (Issachar's) relations to Lincoln."[10] Based on those sources, Markens described Issachar as "a young Englishman, who had attained considerable celebrity as a skillful chiropodist." He had been "one of the vast army of civilians attracted to Washington in the early days of the Civil War." By "some means," he was introduced to Lincoln, after which "friendly relations resulted in their intimacy."

Markens was skeptical about the depth of their relationship. Lincoln, he said, allegedly entrusted Zacharie with going to Richmond in the role of peacemaker, a statement Markens said "should be accepted *cum grano salis* (with a grain of salt)."[11] Although there was no doubt about their close relationship, Markens said he hadn't been able to find out if their relationship went beyond Zacharie's treating Lincoln's feet. The only evidence of their acquaintance Markens was able to discover was Lincoln's handwritten 1862 statement about Issachar's operating on his feet with "great success and considerable addition to my comfort."[12]

Markens also made note of the *New York Herald*'s October 1862 column "The Head and Feet of the Nation," characterizing Issachar as "a wit, gourmet and eccentric," his "splendid Roman nose" and "fashionable whiskers," his "perfect knowledge of his business," and "a plentiful supply of social and moral courage." Other than what had appeared in the *Herald* article, Markens had little else to add to what was known about him. Like most historians who wrote about Issachar, Markens had little information about Issachar's life before or after the war. With little to go on, he said Issachar left New York for London after the war, founded a branch of Free Masonry, and died in 1897, not 1900.

Five years later, Markens wrote a second article titled "Jews Close to Lincoln," mentioning an interview he had had with a little-known secret service agent, Louis Sterne, whom Lincoln had sent to the Baltic coast to prevent blockade runners from that area from smuggling equipment to the South. According to Markens, Sterne told him that in conversations he had had with Lincoln, the President had mentioned offhandedly he was bothered by corns on his feet and had employed a Jewish foot doctor, Issachar Zacharie, to relieve him of his discomfort.[13] Markens concluded his article with a comment that would be often heard with obvious irony: further research into Lincoln's life had "the appearance of a dreary waste."[14]

Two years later, Sterne published his own story of his life during the war. In a passing comment, he described the interview he'd had with Lincoln in more detail.

> I shall never forget that at one of the early interviews I had with him (Lincoln) he told me that he suffered from corns, and that he employed the best chiropodist obtainable, and had given him the post of Chief Orthopedist [sic] to the army. The President declared that no man can do good marching if he suffers from this cause. Issachar Zacharie was the name of the orthopedist in question, and he subsequently practiced in London with considerable success. This, l believe, is the only instance of such an appointment being made in connection with an army in the field.[15]

Since Lincoln never appointed Issachar "Chief Orthopedist," Sterne probably relied on one of Issachar's obituaries for his statement.

Nothing more was written about Issachar until the 1930s, when memory of the once-famed Jewish doctor was invoked. Like Anthony's eulogy over Caesar, it was to bury the man, not to praise him.

* * * * * * * *

America was in the grip of a world-wide depression. According to America's flourishing anti–Semites, it was brought on by an international conspiracy of Jewish bankers. Jews were accused of not only of causing the depression, but also of unduly influencing President Franklin Roosevelt, whose "New Deal" slogan was derided as the "Jew Deal."[16] Roosevelt was himself maligned as "Rosenfelt the Jew."[17] Roosevelt went on record as denying any physical relationship to the Jewish race.[18]

Anti–Semites also resurrected Issachar's relationship with Lincoln to

28. Aftermath

prove undue Jewish influence in American politics had deep roots, reaching back to the time of the Civil War. To blunt that assertion, journalist Bertram Jonas downplayed Issachar's political connections. In a three-column article titled "Exploding a Myth," Jonas scoffed at the "crop of fantastic and obviously ridiculous rumors ... accepted by a gullible and disturbed people." The most curious rumor, he said, "one widely accepted as true during Lincoln's lifetime, was to the effect that his most intimate unofficial backs-stage adviser, this one man 'brain trust' was Dr. Issachar Zacharie, a Jewish chiropodist." "Ill-informed historians," he said, had exaggerated Zacharie's influence on the basis of articles from the *New York Herald* ("Head and Feet of the Nation") and *New York World* ("Unionism and Bunionism") and on rumors Lincoln had sent Issachar on his secret unofficial mission to Jefferson Davis to discuss peace terms. Jonas especially singled out the *New York World* for creating the impression Lincoln was so reliant on the Jewish doctor he frequently left the White House to spend an evening discussing affairs of state with his bunionist. The *World* mistook those visits, said Jonas. Those nighttime calls, he said, were merely professional visits. Lincoln was so busy prosecuting the war he didn't have time to have his feet treated during the day.[19]

Jonas also contended Lincoln's pardoning of Mordecai, a Jewish officer in the Confederate army, was not the direct result of Issachar's intervention. "Students familiar with Lincoln's character," said Jonas, "knew the pardon was not the result of Zacharie's influence but simply one of a thousand cases of Lincoln's good nature and desire to re-unite families separated by war." This incident "merely increased the extravagant tales regarding Zacharie's influence over Lincoln." The best Lincoln authorities, he said, "are agreed that between Lincoln and his Jewish chiropodist there was nothing more than the ordinary relationship between doctor and patient and possibly a mutual interest in witticisms which may or may not have prompted the President to seek out his toe doctor for occasional social diversion."[20]

Jonas' final argument denying Issachar's influence on Lincoln was his letter to Secretary of War Stanton, telling him to issue Issachar a pass to visit his family in Savannah. The letter, Jonas contended, was "something in the nature of a reward for faithful work done by the Jewish doctor during the period of the war. It proved quite conclusively that the great influence attributed to Zacharie was a myth. If the Jewish doctor were really such a close confidante of the President and his cabinet," said Jonas, "Zacharie could easily have obtained the pass without troubling Lincoln about it."[21]

Jonas ended his long discrediting of Issachar's and obliquely other Jewish influences on Lincoln by noting Issachar was not the only Jew Lincoln knew. "He had numerous Jewish friends, and on several occasions, went out of his way to befriend the Jewish People.... Suffice to say that in Abraham Lincoln the Jews of the United States had a staunch and sympathetic friend.

In turn Jews were his strongest and most loyal supporters, for they saw him as spiritually one of them."²²

Ignoring the anti–Semitic defamation of one of their own, a number of Jewish chiropodists, proud a Jewish chiropodist had been socially intimate with the revered President, planned to erect a monument to Dr. Zacharie, "the great emancipator's chiropodist [and] a confident who was entrusted with several important missions during the civil war."²³ In support of the tribute, a Pennsylvania chiropodist noted the National Association of Chiropodists was currently attempting to have Congress establish a chiropody corps to accompany Northern armies in the field, just as the "far-sighted Jewish doctor of Civil War days had proposed."²⁴

The *Boston Jewish Advocate* said it couldn't feel any enthusiasm for memorializing the Jewish chiropodist. Even if he had been Lincoln's foot doctor, "it is not very difficult to think of many much more suitable subjects for memorialization in American Jew history."²⁵ No monument was erected to Issachar, but he was "memorialized" in the 1939 *Jewish Contributions to Medicine in America*, albeit as a largely forgotten historical anecdote as Isachar Zacharie, "reputed to have been a skillful chiropodist, who attended the martyred President, Abraham Lincoln, and members of his cabinet."²⁶

Although the statue was never erected, the publicity surrounding it created renewed interest about Lincoln's Jewish foot doctor. A year later, the *Pittsburg Post-Gazette* and many other papers carried a short article on Issachar's relationship with Lincoln, and reprinted Lincoln's comment about Issachar operating on his feet.²⁷ Dr. Zacharie's urging Lincoln to have trained chiropodists attached to each regiment in the army was a worthy idea, said the paper. The army "had chaplains take care for the souls of the soldiers, why not chiropodists to look after their soles!"²⁸

Once World War II was over, Issachar's special relationship with Lincoln was again celebrated and oftentimes embellished. The *Wisconsin Jewish Chronicle* seriously claimed Lincoln relaxed from the heavy duties of the Presidency by playing a nightly game of pinochle in the White House with "his close friend, Dr. Isachar Zacharie, a Jewish chiropodist."²⁹ Other Jewish writers got carried away, inventing more intimate moments between Issachar and Lincoln. David Schwartz in *The Sentinel* imagined Lincoln "reposing on his bed and Dr. Zacharie working on his feet" while discussing Issachar's plan to meet with Confederate leaders to end the war. In their imaginary conversation, Lincoln asks Issachar, "why do you think an attempt to bring about peace now would succeed? And why do you think you would succeed at it? After all, you are a chiropodist, not a diplomat." "Mr. President," Issachar answers, "the present condition of things" stemmed from "the callousness of the people and you know we chiropodists are always dealing with callouses."³⁰

Ten years later, in a longer essay, Schwartz affected a semi-serious tone.

28. Aftermath

"We are apt to be a little contemptuous about toe doctors," he burbled. "We almost become mirthful at the mention of them, but Abe Lincoln was probably an exception in this regard. We know he had a decent respect for the position of the toe in society, as one should have." Schwartz imagined Issachar telling Lincoln, "this war is just caused by the North and South stepping on each other's toes." Lincoln was very conscious of this part of the anatomy, said Schwartz. "I think it was this foot consciousness (that led to his relationship with) Dr. Issachar Zacharie, the Jewish toe doctor of New York" and eventually to Lincoln sending him to talk peace with Judah Benjamin, the Confederate Secretary of State, "who was also Jewish."[31] "Dr. Zacharie did not deliver a country, but who knows, he might conceivably have done so, if his advice had been followed. Anyway, he tried hard."[32]

Issachar resurfaced again in the 1950s following his prominent place in Bertram Korn's *American Jewry and the Civil War*. Korn wrote a lengthy biography of Issachar and reproduced many of the letters Issachar wrote to Lincoln and vice versa.[33] Citing Korn's book, podiatrist Eugene Friedberg beamed, "much new material has been brought to light recently concerning Dr. Issachar Zacharie, Lincoln's chiropodist, who was one of the most colorful figures in chiropodical history."[34] Friedberg said he couldn't point to any tangible effects Issachar had on podiatry because of the major improvements in the profession since his time. "Nevertheless, the great amount of sound publicity he obtained materially helped our profession to sink a firmer and deeper root than would have been possible otherwise."[35]

In 1950, a series of articles in the newspapers dwelled on what seems to have been a growing problem with the nation's feet. The *Honolulu Star-Bulletin* ran a page one story headlined "It Seems Abe Lincoln Had Foot Trouble, Too."[36] The same story was headlined "Abe Lincoln's Feet Hurt Too" in the *Bloomington* (Indiana) *Pantagraph*. Lincoln had so many corns and calluses, said the *Pantagraph*, he had a personal foot doctor, "a chiropodist named Zacharie."[37] Other papers noted Issachar giving "the President great relief by a foot operation in 1862."[38]

Issachar also made a brief appearance in 1955 in Christopher Morley's comical article "Lincoln's Doctor's Dog" in *The Saturday Review*. Lincoln's family physician, Dr. Stone (his real-life doctor), confides to Lincoln he wasn't as sensitive about feet as he used to be "since that corn-doctor, Dr. Zacharie was here." Recounting the exaggerated claims of other chiropodists, Stone praises Dr. Zacharie as having come "here with an introduction from Napoleon III" and having "attended all the crowned heads of Europe." "I wanted to tell him," says Stone, "he must mean the crowned feet, but I was too polite."[39]

Issachar was never memorialized in bronze, but he was memorialized in a different way. In 1960, the California Podiatry College established an annual four-year tuition scholarship, "Zacharie Scholarships in Podiatry," "to honor

Dr. Zacharie, Chiropodist General to the United States Army as appointed by President Abraham Lincoln."⁴⁰

Schwartz continued writing about Lincoln's ties to America's Jews, and Issachar in particular, in the 1960s. "Everybody wants to get into the act and stake a little claim on Lincoln.... We Jews would claim Lincoln as a Jew," he quipped, "except for the fact that we know if he had been a Jew, his name would have been Arnold Lincoln." As far as he was concerned, Schwartz took "pleasure in the fact that Lincoln's corn doctor Dr. Isodore Zacharie, was a Jew." "I would build a monument to him," he mused, not knowing a monument had been planned but had never materialized. "I am tired of all of these monuments to military heroes and even to many of the so-called statesmen, standing with their arms against their breasts. Give me the stature of a corn doctor."⁴¹

As part of the Civil War centennial observance, several papers carried articles about the role of Jews in the Civil War, including Lincoln's unique relationship with Issachar. "With all the excitement over the Civil War Centennial," the *Fort Myers News-Press* editorialized, "it probably is inevitable that we would at last work our way around to Abraham Lincoln's corn doctor."⁴² The *Rapid City* (South Dakota) *Journal* told its readers, "Lincoln's Corn Doctor Gets Recognition He Deserved."⁴³ The *Palm Beach Post* proclaimed "Abe Lincoln's Corn Doctor Played Key Civil War Part."⁴⁴ In punning headlines, newspapers around the country heralded Dr. Zacharie, the corn doctor who "Kept Lincoln on Firm Footing,"⁴⁵ the "Expert Corn Surgeon (who) Got Himself on Good Footing with Lincoln,"⁴⁶ and the "Corn Doctor [who] Used Abe's Feet to Prove His Worth."⁴⁷

Except for a few brief notices, Issachar again slipped into obscurity during the rest of the 1960s and 1970s. An item in the *Arizona Republic* informed its readers "the tall president was miserable until a person who is identified only as a Dr. I Zacharie came along to ease his pain." In return, the grateful President, the *Republic* mistakenly said, appointed Dr. Zacharie "the first (and, insofar as we know) the only Chiropodist General to the United States Army."⁴⁸

A decade later, the *Indianapolis Star* was more critical, calling Issachar "something of a celebrity-hound foot doctor among the Washington set. Zacharie's reputation probably gained more than Lincoln's feet."⁴⁹ The indefatigable David Schwartz, who invented conversations between Lincoln and Issachar, lamented "the name Dr. Issachar Zacharie may arouse little in today's average American."⁵⁰ Reviewing Issachar's career as a chiropodist and spy, Harry Bloch, M.D., wrote in the *Journal of the American Podiatry Association*, that Dr. Zacharie "was not lacking in ambition and aggressiveness" and "possessed a flair for heroics."⁵¹

Noting Philadelphia was the birthplace of American podiatry, the *Phil-

28. Aftermath

adelphia Inquirer reported Dr. Zacharie was "one of the first and certainly the most zealous of podiatrists." "Lincoln sent him into the field ostensibly to treat generals' feet," said the *Inquirer*, surmising "podiatrists, like hairdressers hear all the gripes of their clients."[52]

The Civil War sesquicentennial anniversary once again put Issachar in the limelight as the most famous Northern Jew of the war. This time, Issachar's day was due to his prominent place in *Lincoln and the Jews*, a lavish and meticulously researched book by American Jewish historian Jonathan D. Sarna and Lincoln ephemera collector Benjamin Shapell. Among the many engaging aspects of their richly illustrated book are the high-quality reproductions of letters in Lincoln's own handwriting on behalf of Jews and to individual Jews, including Issachar, who Sarna and Shapell characterize as a man of "many mysteries."[53] Since the book is not solely about Issachar, much of his life before and after the war are only briefly mentioned, but his wartime activities, especially his espionage and diplomatic activities, are recounted, although often without context.

Steven Spielberg's 2012 movie, *Lincoln* and Sarna and Shapell's 2015 book created a posthumous fan club for Issachar. Since then, Issachar's grave site has become a tourist destination in London's Highgate Cemetery, where Issachar is buried. His monument is now in listed in the cemetery's guide, along with Karl Marx and George Eliot.[54]

* * * * * * * *

"What manner of man," Bertram Korn, author of *American Jewry and the Civil War*, asked, "was this chiropodist-envoy who sent baskets of bananas, oranges, and pineapples to the White House, conveyed his 'kind regards' to Mrs. Lincoln, and after two years of correspondence, began to address the President as 'My Dear Friend.'"[55] Issachar obviously possessed considerable personal and political skills. He was a prosperous businessman. He was a highly sought after in his profession. He was an epicurean, a connoisseur of fine wines. He was a high-ranking Mason. He was a liar and a self-promoting opportunist. He was a man who desperately wanted to be noticed.

Historical characters rarely warrant biographies if they are not complex and enigmatic. They have to be out of the ordinary. They have to have had flaws as well as accomplishments. They have to pique a biographer's curiosity to spend years trying to figure out "what manner of man (or woman)" they were.

Lincoln had never heard of Issachar before he met him, and he only met him because he was pained by his corns. In the course of treating him, Issachar charmed him. Lincoln was not naïve. He was a fairly good judge of character. He had to have been aware Issachar was no paragon of virtue. He had only to look at him with his diamond stickpin to know the man was vain and meticulous about his image. From their conversations, Lincoln would have sized Issachar up as a political opportunist. So why did he befriend him? That inconsistency, writes historian Charles Segal, is one reason Issachar Zacharie is so enigmatic for Lincoln scholars and writers, especially in the field of American Jewish history.[56]

One reason Issachar was "the most favored family visitor at the White House"[57] is that Lincoln liked Issachar's bonhomie and wit. He had an innate sense of comfort that put him at ease with others. Issachar's wit was not as earthy as his own, but was still amusing enough for Lincoln to have liked Issachar's company. "Perhaps I'm somewhat like the Irish Biddy who remarked to the lady of the house," Issachar joked, by way of assuring Lincoln of his sincerity, "'Shurr Mistress darlent a poor gal that works hard likes to know if she gives satisfaction to youz.'"[58]

Issachar's humor and wit were touted as far away as Australia. Dr. Zacharie, the *Melbourne Argus* reported, was "a person of varied attainments, of refined manners, and of a persuasive address, with materials enough at the tip of his tongue to add a few supplementary sheets to the next edition of *Joe Miller's Jests* that any enterprising bookseller in the Old World or the New may think it profitable to publish. It is, perhaps, the last of these accomplishments that has recommended him to the congenial President."[59]

Issachar could not have gained the trust of the President of the United States merely by amusing him or offering free corn and bunion snips. Beyond Issachar's wit, charm, and glibness, Lincoln saw a Jew not unlike his Illinois friend, Abraham Jonas, someone with intelligence and ambition, someone Lincoln must have felt could be of use to him.

Issachar was no paragon of virtue. He could be "obsequious, oleaginous, and painfully solicitous," writes historian Gary Zola. "At other times, he could be self-congratulatory, petty, and critical."[60] Charles Segal had a similar unflattering estimation of Issachar. Dr. Zacharie, he writes, was "morally flawed."[61] Mitchell Abidor censured him for the "magnificent claims about his education" that were false and for plagiarizing another author's book on chiropody and replacing the author's name with his own. He was a salesman, says Abidor, whose main stock-in-trade was himself.[62]

Despite his flaws, writes historian Zola, Issachar Zacharie was nonetheless "a man of exceptional talent."[63] He lied about his training and his medical education, yet there is no doubt about his abilities as a chiropodist. His skills were endorsed by U.S. Senators like Henry Clay of Kentucky, John C. Calhoun of South Carolina, Lewis Cass of Michigan, Generals McClellan, Burnside, and Banks, Secretaries Seward and Stanton, and of course, the President of the United States. If those endorsements were not enough, the "proof of the pudding" was his lucrative practice. Neither could anyone deny his extraordinary intimacy with the President of the United States.

28. Aftermath

Issachar was a man with little or no introspection. He was so self-absorbed he never took time to reflect on his drive for recognition. On one of the few occasions in which he offered any glimpse into his own personality, he told a group of friends and admirers gathered to honor him that he had been "launched out into thse world a poor boy, with no friend save my God, without a penny in my pocket, and deprived of that which is so essential to the elevation of man in this world, education." Like his professional exaggerations, it was an exaggeration. He was not "launched" into the world a poor boy. He came from humble beginnings, but his family was middle-class. They had enough money to set him up in business when he was still a teenager. He chose to leave his family to pursue his career.

What was true, what he deeply felt, was his lack of education. He referred to it on more than one occasion. It was the reason he invented fictional apprenticeships with Aston Cooper and Valentine Mott. It was why he plagiarized his books. He was fully aware of his educational shortcomings, and he did his best to hide them. For Issachar, "The past is never dead. It's not even past."[64] Despite his fabrications about his professional medical training and books, no one denied his skill in treating foot problems.

What drove whatever successes Issachar had accomplished in public life, he said, was due to his boundless energy and ambition for recognition. Issachar's ambition in promoting himself goes to the heart of his character. He did not crave power. He craved recognition and admiration from those in power and from a grateful public at large. His ambition fed a growing sense of importance. He fantasized himself a kingmaker, bolstering General Banks' own presidential ambitions. When he first met Lincoln in 1862, he boasted he would get him reelected. If he wasn't reelected, Issachar said it would not be his fault.

Issachar felt he was destined for a much greater future than merely a confidante or "favored family visitor at the White House." He had so much energy and self-confidence, he believed he could do anything he set his mind to. When General Banks seemed to have a chance at being the Republican nominee in the 1864 election, despite his indebtedness to and friendship with Lincoln, Issachar saw an opportunity for fame and recognition and high political office, not unlike Judah Benjamin. Banks hoped he could realize his ambition through a military process. Military failure kept him from ever realizing his dream. Issachar felt he could achieve fame through negotiation. When Banks' prospects fizzled, Issachar threw himself wholeheartedly behind Lincoln in the upcoming election.

Issachar was an opportunist and a self-promoter. He had fortitude and ingenuity. Even though he had no formal education, he innately knew how to ingratiate himself with others. He too was large. Like Walt Whitman, he could say he celebrated himself and sang of himself. Like Whitman, he congratulated and humbled himself.[65] He learned a profession and worked on getting his name out as a corn cutter and more. And like Whitman, he concocted testimonials to himself.⁶⁶

Had he been content merely to stand at the sidelines, history would never have heard of Issachar Zacharie. His ambition drove him. It made him friends as well as enemies. His ambition, his determination, his ingenuity, and his resilience made him the man he was. When he made his mind up, he refused to take "no" for an answer. His ambition led him to lie about his mentorship and his medical training. But he wasn't any more deceitful than Whitman, or his competitors, or present-day politicians, CEOs, bureaucrats, university deans, or football coaches who have padded their resumes with fake diplomas, or, for that matter, university coaches who took bribes in exchange for recruiting students as athletes, or the parents of those students who paid those bribes.⁶⁷ Compared to those captains of industry and education, Issachar's fabrications seem benign.

Issachar was undeniably a flawed character, but that is what makes him so interesting for a biographer. It is not his flaws that are celebrated, but his celebrity. In his own time, Issachar was talked about in some of the country's major newspapers. His death was likewise noted in newspapers across the country. Mitchel Abidor considers him merely a "minor sideshow" in the whole scheme of the war. For a minor sideshow, he certainly garnered considerable news coverage in his own lifetime and beyond. Few figures from the Civil War, other than those in government or the military, have had as much written about them in his own time. His efforts did come to naught. So eventually did Judah Benjamin's and the efforts of many of the country's leading generals. Like Judah Benjamin, "navigating affairs of state for a responsive President,"⁶⁸ Issachar asked why, "in this republican and enlightened country," shouldn't an Israelite "be elevated to a high position by his government."⁶⁹ It is very much the question behind the story of the Jews in America.

Issachar was an "Israelite" in solidarity, not belief. He was never observant. He married a gentile girl. He did not raise his children as Jews. With one exception, none of his children married Jews. He is not known to have contributed to any Jewish benevolent society. He is not buried in a Jewish cemetery. But he always considered himself an "Israelite"⁷⁰ and was always described as such by his detractors.

More than any other Jew of his day, Issachar was the visible embodiment, the public face, of the integration of the Jew in America. At a time when influential leadership roles were denied them in other parts of the world, writes historian Zola, Issachar's extraordinary relationship with President Lincoln made him a *beau ideal* for Jews then and an exemplar to Jews today. Lincoln's befriending and selecting an immigrant Jew as a high-level envoy and reconnaissance agent for the good of the country demonstrated that Jews "could achieve a political distinction in America that was denied them elsewhere."⁷¹

Appendix: Zacharie's Accounts

The United States

In Account with I. Zacharie M.D.

1862				
Decr.	26		For expenses	6.00
	27		" Do	5.00
	28		" Pr. Services	10.00
	"		" Expenses	5.00
	29		" Pd. girl for information	10.00
	30		" Expenses	4.00
1863	"		" Pd. for information	10.00
Jany	1		" Expenses	3.50
	2		" Do	4.50
	3		" Pd. for information	10.00
	"		" Expenses	1.50
	4		" Do	2.00
	5		" Do	5.00
	6		" Pd. Marquis Men	10.00
	7		" Expenses	4.50
	8		" Do	3.00
	9		" Do	2.50
	10		" Do	1.50
	11		" Do	3.00
	12		" Do	1.00
	13		" Do	1.00
	15		" Do	3.25
	16		" Expenses	2.00
	19		" For information at Lake	5.00
	21		" Pd Marques men	10.00
	23		" Expenses	3.00
	24		" Do	1.00
	25		" Do	1.50
	26		" Do	2.00
	28		" Do	3.50
	29		" Do	1.00

30	" Do		1.50
31	" Do		1.50
"	" Pd. board as per bills		117.00
"	" " Lewis Bach for services		100.00
"	" " C. Johnson "		150.00
"	" " Services of self to date		300.00

$800.50

Approved
    N.P. Banks M.G.C.
                      Received payment
                          I, Zacharie

1863
July 1st   For 2 months & 13 days services
                From April 17 to date   730.00
           For 2 months & 13 days services
                Of C. Johnson as secretary   365.00
           For rent of rooms & board as
                Per bills   342.00

$1,437.00

Received the above in full
    (signed)   I. Zacharie
Approved N. P. Banks, M. G. C.   2nd July 1863

                        New Orleans March 6th 1863

1863
Feby 4	For amt. paid Mr. Collins, trip to Mobile	100.00
20	" " for information respt. salt	10.00
Mar 6	" " bills St. Charles Hotel	121.00
"	" " Chas. Johnson services	150.00
	" " services of self to date	360.00

$741.00

Approved N. P. Banks M. G. C.
    Received payment
        Zacharie

Chapter Notes

Abbreviations

ABL LOC Abraham Lincoln Papers at the Library of Congress. The papers are online at https://memory.loc.gov/ammem/malquery.html.
AJA American Jewish Archives
CW Collected Works of Abraham Lincoln
LOC Library of Congress
NA National Archives
OR. Official Records of the War of the Rebellion
PSUG. Papers of Ulysses S. Grant
RRL Rush Rhees Library, University of Rochester

Chapter 1

1. Joan Ryan, *Women Naval Dockyard Workers in Two 19th Century Dockyard Towns: Chatham and Plymouth* (M. Ph., University of Greenwich, 2011), 24.
2. Robert George Hobbes, *Civil Service in Sheerness and Chatham Dockyards. Home and Foreign Travel* (London: Elliot Stock, 1895), 103. (Although published in 1895, the chapters on Chatham are dated much earlier in 1848.)
3. U.S. Census, 1850.
4. Haumann, Heiko, *A History of East European Jews* (New York: Central European University Press, 1990), 71, 94–95; Thomas Nickol and Curt Gerhard Lorber, "Germany between 1780 and 1810," in Christine Hillam (ed.), *Dental Practice in Europe at the End of the 18th Century* (Amsterdam: Rodopi B. V., 2003), 367.
5. Lucien Wolf, "The Origins of Provincial Anglo-Jewry," in Aubrey Newman (ed.) *Provincial Jewry in Victorian Britain* (London, 1975), https://www.jewishgen.org/jcr-uk/Provincial_Jewry_Victorian.htm, accessed January 22, 2018.
6. Medway Archives and Local Studies Center, http://discovery.nationalarchives.gov.uk/download/GB1204%20DE%202023; http://discovery.nationalarchives.gov.uk/download/GB1204%20DE%20202; *Records of Chatham Memorial Synagogue and the Chatham Hebrew Congregation 1834–1972*, Chatham Memorial Synagogue, http://www.jewishgen.org/jcr-uk/Community/ch/history1.htm; accessed May 3, 2015.
7. Charles Dickens, *The Pickwick Papers* (originally published, 1837; New York: Books, Inc., 1867), 14.
8. R.G. Hobbes, *Reminiscences of 70 Years' Life, Travel & Adventure; Military and Civil, Scientific and Literary* (London: Elliot Stock, 1893), Vol. II, p. 94; Charles Dickens, *The Uncommercial Traveler and Additional Christmas Stories* (Boston: Houghton, Good and Co., 1879), 256.
9. *The Weekly Gleaner, A Periodical Devoted to Religion, Education, Biblical and Jewish Antiquities, Literature and General News*, 1 (January–December 1857), n.p.
10. Michael Shekel, *The Jewish Lifecycle Book* (Ktav Publishing, 1989). 21; Alisa Leebo, *First Person Jewish* (Minneapolis: University of Minnesota Press, 2008), 66.
11. *South Carolina Courier*, October 19, 1843, 3.
12. Buried in the hoary pages of the *Sangre Judia* ("Jewish Blood"), the Spanish Inquisition's records of known *conversos*, are the surnames Zacarias and Zaccheria, variants of Zachariah. The *conversos* were Jews who stayed behind and went through the motions of conversion to Christianity, but some secretly practiced their previous religion.
13. Halm F. Ghiuzeli, "The Jewish community of Zamosc," http://www.bh.org.

il/jewish-community-zamosc/, accessed September 12, 2015).
　14. http://esefarad.com/?p=79424; http://www.sephardicgen.com/names.htm, accessed September 12, 2015.
　15. *Records of Chatham Memorial Synagogue*.
　16. *Ibid*.
　17. In October 1831, a Charles Leary was arrested for stealing two jackets, valued at 10 shillings, from Jonathan's store. *South Eastern Gazette*, October 25, 1831.
　18. Frank I. Schecter, "An Unfamiliar Aspect of Anglo-Jewish History," *American Jewish Historical Quarterly*, 25 (1917), 67.
　19. Medway Archives and Local Studies Center.
　20. The names and ages of the Zachariahs are taken from passenger lists on their arrival in the United States (Elizabeth P. Bentley, *Passenger Arrivals at the Port of New York 1830–1832* (Baltimore: Genealogical Publishing Co., 2000), 1102–1103.
　21. Robert Justin Goodman, *Political Repression in the 19th Century Europe* (London: Routledge Taylor & Francis, 2013), ch. 4.
　22. Phillip MacDougall, *Chatham Dockyard, 1815–1865. The Industrial Transformation* (Surrey, UK: Ashgate Publishing, 2009), xvi.
　23. *The London and Paris Observer*, November 27, 1831, 1. Cholera is an acute diarrheal disease that induces severe dehydration. A death spiral ensues from the loss of minerals in the blood that maintain the body's balance of fluids. Charles E. Rosenberg, *The Cholera Years. The United States in 1832, 1849, and 1866* (Chicago: University of Chicago Press, 1987), 2–4.
　24. Quoted in Elizabeth Jane Errington, *Emigrant Worlds and Transatlantic Communities: Migration to Upper Canada* (Montreal, Quebec: McGuill-Queen's University Press, 2007), 54.
　25. Bentley, *Passenger Arrivals*, 13–14.
　26. Edwin Williams, *The New York Annual Register*, March 10, July 10, and November 10 (New York: J. Seymour, 1832), 226.
　27. *Norwich Mercury*, March 20, 1830, "Maritime Newspaper Articles, 1830," https://immigrantships.net/newsarticles/1830_newsarticles.html, accessed August 14,2017; https://alookthrutime.wordpress.com/tag/cost-of-third-class-titanic-ticket/, accessed August 14, 2017. A first-class cabin aboard the *Titanic* cost $50,000 in today's money. https://alookthrutime.wordpress.com/tag/cost-of-third-class-titanic-ticket/, accessed August 14, 2017.
　28. *Norwich Mercury*, March 20, 1830. Steerage aboard the *Titanic* was about $700 for adults and $300 for children.
　29. Tyler Anbinder, *City of Dreams. The 400-Year Epic History of Immigrant New York* (Boston: Houghton Mifflin Harcourt, 2016), 135.
　30. Damon Veach, "N.Y. ship lists transcribed from originals," http://www.nola.com/ancestors/archive/1999/la032199.html, accessed May 20, 2015.
　31. Bentley, *Passenger Arrivals*, 13–14.
　32. Jack Lynch, "A Guide to Eighteenth-century English Vocabulary," http://andromeda.rutgers.edu/~jlynch/C18Guide.pdf, accessed December 26, 2015.
　33. Bentley, *Passenger Arrivals*, 13–14. The "Find a Grave Memorial Site" incorrectly gives his birth year as 1827, based on his age of 73 when he died in 1900. The Passenger List and U.S. Census data list it as 1825.
　34. Charles Knight, *The British Mechanic's and Labourer's Handbook, and True Guide to the United States: With Ample Notices Respecting Various Trades and Professions* (London: C. Knight, 1840).
　35. *Ibid.*, 20.
　36. Gary Gorton, "Ante Bellum Transportation Indices," unpublished article, Wharton School, University of Pennsylvania, August 1989, n.p.

Chapter 2

　1. Jonathan D. Sarna, "Port Jews in the Atlantic: Further Thoughts," *Jewish History*, 20 (2006), 214, 213–219.
　2. Irwin Lachoff and Catherine C. Kahn, *The Jewish Community of New Orleans* (Charleston, SC: Arcadia, 2005), 1.
　3. *Daily Pennsylvanian*, August 24, 1836, 2.
　4. *M'Elroy's Philadelphia Directory, for 1839* (Philadelphia: A. M'Elroy, 1839), 62.
　5. *Charleston Courier*, December 23, 1843, 2.
　6. Rudolf Glanz, *Studies in Judaic Americana* (New York: Ktav Publishing House, 1970), 63.
　7. Quoted in Ester L. Panitz, *Simon Wolf*

(Cranbury, NJ: Associated University Press, 1987), 19.
  8. Glanz, *Studies*, 104–121.
  9. U.S. Census, 1850, 1860.
  10. Glanz, *Studies*, 56.
  11. E. Digby Baltzell, *Philadelphia Gentlemen* (New Brunswick, NJ: Transaction Publishers, 2004), 279.
  12. Leeser organized Philadelphia's first Jewish parochial school at Mikveh Israel and edited *The Occident and American Jewish Advocate*, the first Jewish monthly periodical in America, and the American Jewish Publication Society. He was also one of the founders of America's first rabbinical college and the Board of Delegates of American Israelites, the first association of Jewish congregations. Lance J. Sussman, *Isaac Leeser and the Making of American Judaism* (Detroit: Wayne State University Press, 1995; Korn, American Jewry, 6–7.
  13. The split was inevitable. Sephardic prayers and rituals were different from the Ashkenazis' synagogue prayers and rituals. Sephardim pronounced Hebrew differently and chanted different melodies. Rodeph Shalom was the first of many splinterings within American Jewish communities. Henry Berkowitz, "Notes on the History of the Earliest German Jewish Congregation in America," *Publications of the American Jewish Historical Society*, 9 (1901), 125.
  14. Edwin Wolf and Maxwell Whiteman, *The History of the Jews of Philadelphia* (Philadelphia: Jewish Publication Society of America, 1975), 234. To encourage members to attend Friday night and Saturday morning services and remain until the end of services, Rodeph Shalom imposed a fine of 25 cents for missing services; the only excuse was if a member were out of town or ill. Members leaving services early were also fined 25 cents (Berkowitz, "Notes," 126).
  15. Wolf and Whiteman, *History of Jews*, 234.
  16. *Daily Pennsylvanian*, April 11, 1837, 1.
  17. A. M'Elroy's Philadelphia Directory, for 1839 (Philadelphia: A. M'Elroy, 1839), 284. Cedar/South Street became the core Jewish neighborhood in the 1880s, when it became known as "the great Street for Polish Jews and huckstering of every variety." Harry Bonin, "The Jewish Quarter of Philadelphia," https://www.phillyhistory.org/blog/index.php/2008/03/the-jewish-quarter-of-philadelphia/.

  18. A. *M'Elroy's Philadelphia Directory, for 1840* (Philadelphia: A. M'Elroy, 1840), 283.
  19. *M'Elroy's Philadelphia Directory, for 1839*, 62.
  20. *M'Elroys Philadelphia Directory*, 1840, 142.
  21. Caroline London, "The Marie Antoinette Dress that Ignited the Slave Trade," https://www.racked.com/2018/1/10/16854076/marie-antoinette-dress-slave-trade-chemise-a-la-reine, accessed February 10, 2018.
  22. Ibid.
  23. Thomas W. Knox, *Camp-Fire and Cotton-Field* (New York: Blelock and Co., 1865), 380.
  24. James William Hagy, *Directories for the City of Charleston, South Carolina for the Years, 1849, 1852, and 1855* (reprint, Baltimore, MD: Genealogical Publishing Co., 1998), 47. There are no city directories for Charleston for 1840 to 1848.
  25. *Charleston Courier*, October 17, 1849, 3.
  26. *Charleston Courier*, January 19, 1843; October 19, 1843, 3; October 21, 1843, 3; April 15, 1844, 3; October 16, 1849, 3.
  27. Reznikoff, *Jews of Charleston* (Philadelphia: Jewish Publication Society of America, 1950), 71.
  28. *City Council of Charleston vs. Sa. A. Benjamin*, March, 1847; http://www.jewish-history.com/occident/volume4/mar1847/sunday.html, accessed July 7, 2018. The constitutionality of the ban was challenged in 1848, in the Court of Errors in Charleston and upheld. The full text is available at http://www.jewish-history.com/occident/volume5/mar1848/sunday.html.
  29. Stephanie E. Yuhl, "Hidden in Plain Sight: Centering the Domestic Slave Trade in American History," *Journal of Southern History*, 79 (August 2013), 597.
  30. U.S. Census, 1850.
  31. Quoted by Jason H. Silverman, "The Law of the Land Is the Law," in Jack Salzman and Cornel West (eds.), *Struggles in the Promised Land* (New York: Oxford University Press, 1997), 81
  32. Rosengarten and Rosengarten, *A Portion of the People* (Columbia, SC: University of South Carolina Press, 1002), 63.
  33. Bertram W. Korn, *Jews and Negro Slavery in the Old South, 1789–1865* (Elkins Park, PA: 1961), 26. Issachar rarely expressed any views about slavery, but on the one occasion he did, it was derogatory.

Letter of Zacharie to General Nathaniel Banks, January 25, 1863, Nathaniel P. Banks papers, LOC (henceforth Banks Papers), Box 79.

34. Silverman, "The Law of the Land," 73.

35. James William Hagy, *This Happy Land: The Jews of Colonial and Antebellum Charleston* (Tuscaloosa: University of Alabama Press, 1993), 91.

36. *Ibid.* 93.

37. Rosen, *Jewish Confederates*, 16, 382, n23.

38. U.S. Census 1850. The parish was the local government unit. The two separate parishes were combined for voting purposes.

39. Rebecca married Abraham Dessau, a "trader," in 1836 in Philadelphia; Amelia Lavenia married Jacob H. Dessau, a "dry goods" merchant, in Charleston in 1843 (Elzas, *Jewish Marriage Notices*, 21); and Jane married Abraham Backer in 1848 and was living in Columbus, Georgia (*Charleston Courier*, March 13, 1848, 2).

40. U.S. Census 1850.

41. Although listed in the 1850 census, they are not listed in Hagy's *Happy Land* appendix of Charleston's Jews (277–414).

Chapter 3

1. *Charleston Southern Patriot*, April 28, 1843, 1.

2. *Ibid.*

3. *New London Connecticut Daily Chronicle*, May 12, 1862, 2.

4. "Words" *The British Medical Journal*, 1 (No. 6166) (March 24, 1979), 814, 1; (No. 1522) (March 1, 1890), 489.

5. Littlefield and Westervelt advertisement, *New York Herald*, May 6, 1858, 9.

6. *Alexandria Gazette*, March 6, 1860, 6.

7. John Pearson, "A Brief History of Chiropody and Podiatry," https://johnrpearson.wordpress.com/tag/a-brief-history-of-chiropody-and-podiatry/; Cameron Kippen," A Potted History of Professional Foot Care," http://foottalk.blogspot.com/2008/12/potted-history-of-podiatry.html, accessed May 25, 2015.

8. Ben Jonson, *Bartholomew Fair* (1614), quoted by Pearson, "Brief History."

9. Pearson, "Brief History." The full title of Low's book was *Chiropodologia, Or a Scientific Enquiry into the Causes of Corns, Warts, Onions and Other Painful or Offensive Cutaneous Excrescences: Confirmed by the Practice and Experience of D. Low*.

10. Maurice Marks, "Recent History of Chiropody," in Maurice J. Lewi (ed.), *The Text Book of Chiropody* (New York: School of Chiropody, 1914), 70.

11. Pearson, "Brief History."

12. *Ibid.*

13. Kippen, "Potted History."

14. *Ibid.*

15. Lewi, *Text Book*, 103.

16. J. Colin Dagnall, "The English Influence on the Beginnings of American Podiatry," in Lisbeth M. Molloway, *A Fast Pace Forward* (Philadelphia, Pennsylvania College of Podiatric Medicine, 1987), 6–18; Kippen, "Potted History"; Lewis Durlacher's 1845 book, *A Treatise on Corns, Bunions, the Diseases of Nails, and the General Management of the Feet* (Philadelphia, Lea & Blanchard, 1845) was published within the year in Philadelphia. Malcolm Brown and Judith Samuel, "The Jews of Bath," *Jewish Historical Society of England* 29 (1982–1986), 157.

17. John Eisenberg, *Surgical and Practical Observations on the Diseases of the Human Foot; with Instructions for Their Treatment. To Which Is Added Advice on the Management of the Hand* (London: John Eisenberg, 1845).

18. Nehemiah Kenison, *The New Revelation; Or Dreams Relating to the Mysteries of the Soul* (St. Louis: Privately published, 1879), 8.

19. *Charleston Courier*, January 31, 1840, 3.

20. *Camden* (South Carolina) *Journal*, June 27, 1840, 3.

21. *Charleston Southern Patriot*, April 28, 1843, 1; May 30, 1843, 1; May 31, 1843, 3.

22. *Ibid.*, April 29, 1843, 4.

23. *Ibid.*, March 4, 1843, 4; April 6, 1843, 1.

24. *Ibid.*, July 15, 1843, 3.

Chapter 4

1. Samuel Wilson, Jr., and Bernard Lemann, *New Orleans Architecture* (Gretna, LA: Pelican Publishing Co., 1998), xiv.

2. J. Russell Smith, "Line Traffic in the United States Coasting Trade," *The Railroad Gazette*, 44 (March 1908), 377.

3. William I. Hair, "Stagecoaches and Public Accommodations in Antebellum Georgia," *Georgia Historical Quarterly*, 68 (Fall 1984), 326.

4. *Ibid.*, 327.

5. Everett Dick, *The Dixie Frontier: A Social History of the Southern Frontier from the First Transmontane Beginnings to the Civil War* (Norman, OK: University of Oklahoma Press, 1948), 211–212.
6. Gary Gorton, Ante Bellum Transportation Indices, http://faculty.som.yale.edu/garygorton/documents/AnteBellumTransportationIndices.pdf.
7. Lachof and Kahn, *Jewish Community of New Orleans*.
8. Louisiana State Museum, "Antebellum Louisiana III: Urban Life," www.crt.state.la.us/louisiana-state-museum/online-exhibits/the-cabildo/antebellum-louisiana-urban-life/index, accessed February 28, 2018.
9. Leo Shpall, "The First Synagogue in Louisiana," *Louisiana Historical Quarterly* 21 (1938), 518; Elliott Ashkenazi, *The Business of Jews in Louisiana, 1840–1875* (Tuscaloosa: University of Alabama Press, 1988), 105.
10. Knox, *Camp-Fire*, 392.
11. Peggy Scott Laborde and John Magill, *Canal Street. New Orleans' Great Wide Way* (Gretna, LA: Pelican Publishing Co., 2006), 31; Ashkenazi, Jewish Businesses, 10.
12. (New Orleans) *Times-Picayune*, January 15, 1843, 3.
13. *Ibid.*, March 9, 1841, 1.
14. *Ibid.*, September 6, 1843, 2.
15. His last ad appeared in the *Times-Picayune* on November 5, 1843, 1.
16. *Richmond (VA) Whig*, May 28, 1844, 2.
17. *A. McElroy's Philadelphia City Directory for the Year 1844* (Philadelphia: Edward C. Biddle, 1844). Coates was renamed "Fairmount Avenue." Neither Mary Ann nor Issachar are listed in the Philadelphia City Directories for 1845–1848, under Lawson or Zachariah.
18. *Philadelphia Dollar Newspaper*, September 18, 1844, 3.
19. Jacob Rader Marcus, *United States Jewry, 1776–1985* (Detroit, MI: Wayne State University Press, 1989–) Vol. 2:203.
20. Michael F. Barnes, "Presentation on the Order," www.orderofthesecretmonitor.co.unk/News_27.html, accessed July 19, 2015.
21. *New Orleans Daily Delta*, April 14, 1846, 3.
22. *Ibid.*; (New Orleans) *Times-Picayune*, April 14, 1846, 2.
23. *Ibid.*, April 15, 1846, 2.
24. *New Orleans Daily Delta*, April 17, 1846, 3.
25. *Baltimore American and Commercial Daily Advertiser*, June 8, 1846, 2.
26. U.S. Census, 1870.

Chapter 5

1. Sherry Olson, "Downwind Downstream, Downtown: The Environmental Legacy in Baltimore and Maryland," *Environmental History* 12 (October 2007), 845–866.
2. *Baltimore American Republic and Daily Clipper*, June 4, 1846, 2
3. *Ibid.*, June 4, 1846, 2. The three years he claimed to have been in Baltimore, he was living in Charleston and New Orleans. (Charleston) *Southern Patriot*, July 15, 1843, 3; (New Orleans) *Times-Picayune*, October 19, 1843, 3.
4. *Baltimore American Republic and Daily Clipper*, November 23, 1846, 3; December 12, 1846, 3.
5. *Baltimore Sun*, December 3, 1846, 3.
6. *Baltimore American Republic and Daily Clipper*, November 23, 1846, 3; December 12, 1846, 3.
7. *Washington (DC) Daily Union*, January 13, 1847, 1. The four physicians were W. W. Handy, a professor of anatomy at the Baltimore Dental College (Baltimore City Directory, 1845, 166); Nathan R. Smith, dean and professor of surgery at the University of Maryland who had an office and infirmary on Lombard Street in Baltimore (*Baltimore Sun*, December 30, 1846, 3); and Charles Bell Gibson, who was a professor of physics at Washington University in Baltimore. Gibson extracted a bullet from General Winfield Scott at Lundy's Lane during the War of 1812. During the Civil War, he was a surgeon in the Confederate army. Pierre Chatard was an obstetrician. He died two years after being cited in Issachar's testimonial list (Eugene F. Cordell, *Medical Annals of Baltimore* (Baltimore: Williams and Wilkins, 1903), 348). John Whitridge had a practice at 46 North Gay Street (Cordell, **Medical Annals**, 620). Obstetrician Ferdinand Chatard was the son of Pierre Chatard (Cordell, *Medical Annals*, 348).
8. *American and Commercial Daily Advertiser*, November 9, 1846, 4.
9. *Washington (DC) Daily National Whig*, December 3, 1847, 3; January 3, 1848, 3.

10. *American and Commercial Daily Advertiser*, April 12, 1847, 3. If there is any further need to doubt the credibility of these endorsements, there are noticeably different endorsements from some of these same doctors that Issachar collected in a book he kept of testimonials to his work (*Dr. I Zacharie, Corns Operations on the Feet [privately published]*, 2 hereafter "Corns"). A copy is in the National Archives (RG 112 Records of the Office of the Surgeon General. Central Office Correspondence 1818-1946, Z (July 8, 1830–December 8, 1870), Box No. 113). The original is in the Shapell Museum. Zacharie published a later compilation titled *Testimonials to I. Zacharie, Late Chiropodist General, United States Army* (London: S. Firth and Ellis, 187–?). Dr. Gibson's statement is dated March 31, 1848, two years after the newspaper endorsement. The testimonial in the book is to "Dr. Zacharie" and quotes Gibson as stating, "We have seen Dr. Zacharie, the Chiropodist, operate, and approve of his method, which is scientific and free from inconvenience or pain" (Zacharie, *Corns*, 3). In 1848, Issachar was still calling himself Dr. I. Zachariah Jr. He didn't drop the "Jr." and change the surname to Zacharie until the late 1850s. It is hardly believable that Dr. Gibson would have given him two testimonials. The name change was an obvious instance of backdating. Issachar resorted to the same sham for another of his books.

11. Eisenberg, *Surgical and Practical Observations*.

12. Editorial, "The Peerage and Its Corns," *The Spectator* 22 (1849), 299.

Chapter 6

1. Zacharie also cited Cooper's fake endorsement in *The Daily Union*, January 13, 1847, 1; February 18,1847, 3; March 5, 1847, 4; Zacharie, *Corns*, 2.

2. Sir Leslie Stephen and Sir Sidney Lee (eds.), *Dictionary of National Biography* (London: Oxford University Press, 1921–1922), Vol. IV, 1062–1064.

3. See, e.g., Gary P. Zola, *We Called Him Rabbi: Abraham Lincoln and American Jewry, A Documentary History* (Carbondale, IL: Southern Illinois University Press, 2014), 403.

4. Joyce Carroll Oats, *Soul at the White Heat* (New York: Harper Collins, 2016), 62.

5. Editorial, "The Peerage and Its Corns" *The Spectator* 22 (1849), 299.

6. *Hartford* (Connecticut) *Times*, February 11, 1843, 4.

7. *New Hampshire Sentinel*, Mary 17, 1841, 4.

8. *Baltimore Sun*, June 6, 1843, 2.

9. I. M. Rutkow, "Valentine Mott (1785–1865), the Father of American Vascular Surgery; A Historical Perspective," *Surgery* 85 (April 1979), 441–450.

10. "Obituary: Death of Dr. Valentine Mott," *New York Times*, April 27, 1865, 4.

11. Valentine Mott, "The Fractured Penis of Laceration of the Corpus Cavernosum Penis, Commonly Called Fracture of the Penis," *Transactions of the New York Academy of Medicine* 1 (1848), 99.

12. Mott quoted in Zacharie, *Corns*, 2.

13. I. Zacharie, *Surgical and Practical Observations on the Disease of the Human Foot* (New York: Charles D. Norton, 1860); (London: Adams Brothers, 1876).

14. Eisenberg, *Surgical and Practical Observations*.

15. *Columbia* (South Carolina) *Daily Phoenix*, November 23, 1865, 1.

16. *Washington* (DC) *National Republican*, January 25, 1862, 1.

17. *Charleston* (South Carolina) *Courier*, February 15, 1862, 3; *Daily* (Columbus) *Ohio Statesman*, May 25, 1861, 4.

18. *Richmond* (Virginia) *Daily Dispatch*, November 24, 1852, 4.

19. Quoted by Daniel Dorchester, *Latest Drink Sophistries versus Total Abstinence* (Boston: Frank Wood, 1883), 43; H., "The Pathology of Drunkenness or the Physical effects of Alcoholic Drinks, with Drawings of the Drunkard's Stomach," *Botanico-Medical Recorder*, 11 (1843), 115.

20. *Richmond* (Virginia) *Daily Dispatch*, May 22, 1852, 2.

21. *St. Louis Clinical Record* 3 (1877), 158.

22. The Abraham Lincoln Papers at the Library of Congress (ABL LOC). Copies of Issachar's correspondence with Lincoln at the Library of Congress are online at "The Abraham Lincoln Papers at the Library of Congress," https://memory.loc.gov/ammem/malquery.html.

23. Quoted in David Von Drehle, *Rise to Greatness: Abraham Lincoln and America's Most Perilous Year* (New York: Henry Holt Co., 2012), 165.

24. Zacharie, *Corns*, 5. Clay's statement also appears in a shorter version of Issachar's book, *Testimonials To I. Zacharie. Late Chiropodist General, United States Army* (London: S. Firth and Ellis, 187–?), 8.

25. Jonathan D. Sarna and Benjamin Shapell, *Lincoln and the Jews, A History* (New York: Thomas Dunne Books, 2015), 128.

26. *Corns*, 6; *Testimonials*, 9.

27. *Corns*, 5–6; *Testimonials*, 8.

28. *Corns*, 6; *Testimonials*, 9.

29. *Corns*, 6; *Testimonials*, 9.

30. *Corns*, 6; *Testimonials*, 9. Issachar's *Corns* also contains testimonials that year from Dr. Wm Gibson, dated March 31, 1848; Professor Hugh M. Maguire, November 1, 1848; and Dr. Thomas Hammond, October 27, 1848.

31. *Corns*, 3.

32. *Ibid.*, 6–7.

33. *Washington* (DC) *Daily National Whig*, January 4, 1848, 2; *Washington* (DC) *Daily National Intelligencer*, April 8, 1848, 1.

34. Charles M. Segal, "Isachar Zacharie: Lincoln's Chiropodist," *Publications of the American Jewish Historical Society*, 43 (December 1953), 73.

35. "This will assure those who may desire an operation upon their feet for Corns, that Dr. I. Zacharie has performed an operation upon mine with much success; he extracted one or two for me about one year ago, which gave me immediate relief at the time, and I have not been troubled since then." Sam'l D. Lecomptem [sic]. No date. *Corns*, 12.

Chapter 7

1. *New Orleans Weekly Delta*, May 14, 1849, 4; *Brooklyn* (New York) *Daily Eagle*, May 21, 1849, 2.

2. *Ibid*.

3. *Philadelphia Dollar Newspaper*, June 25, 1851, 2; *Boston Courier*, April 21, 1851, 2.

4. K. M. Nesfield, "The Jew from a Gentile Standpoint," *Overland Monthly and Out West Magazine* 25 (April 1895), 414.

5. Martin A. Meyer, *Western Jewry. An Account of the Achievements of the Jews and Judaism in California* (San Francisco: Emanu-el, 1916), 46.

6. Gustav Adolf Danziger, "The Jew in San Francisco. The Last Half Century," *Overland Monthly and Out West Magazine* 25 (April 1895), 385.

7. Jacob Voorsanger, *The Chronicles of Emanu-el* (San Francisco: Geo. Spaulding Co, 1900), 17; Myer, *Jews in California*, 46.

8. Marcus, *Western Jewry*, 2, 197.

9. Danziger, "The Jew in San Francisco," 385.

10. The 1850 U.S. Census lists Issachar (Issica Zackriah), age 25, living at his father-in-law's home with his wife, her three sisters, Fanny, 17, Frances, 12, Lavernia, 7, and Issachar and Mary's two children, Charles, 4, and Samuel, 2.

11. Danziger, "The Jew in San Francisco," 385. The other route, more costly and slower, but safer and more comfortable, was by sailing around Cape Horn. Slower steamers could take as long as six months. Clipper ships, the "ocean greyhounds" built for speed, could make the trip in three months.

12. *Daily Alta California*, June 14, 1850, 2.

13. *Ibid*.

14. *Rochester Daily Democrat*, July 25, 1850, 2.

15. Ava F. Kahn, and Adam M. Mendelsohn (eds.), *Transnational Traditions: New Perspective on American Jewish History* (Detroit: Wayne State University, 2014), ch. 2.

16. Charles Proctor Kimball, *The San Francisco City Directory* (San Francisco: Journal of Commerce Press, 1850), 66; *Daily Alta California*, January 30, 1850, 3.

17. Stockton California History 1846 to 1900, http://www.wrightrealtors.com/stockton/stockton_history.htm, accessed July 20, 2015.

18. *The Stockton Directory and Emigrant's Guide to the Southern Mines* (Stockton: San Joaquin Republican, 1852), 19.

19. *Sacramento Steamer*, October 31, 1851, 3; *San Francisco Daily Placer Times and Transcript*, August, 23, 1854, 2.

20. *San Francisco Weekly Pacific News*, February 15, 1851, 3.

21. *Daily Alta California*, March 1, 1852, 7.

22. *Elkton, Maryland Cecil Whig*, April 26, 1851, 1.

23. Abraham Abrahamsohn, *An Interesting Account of the Travels of Abraham Abrahamsohn to America*, reprinted in Ava F. Kahn (ed.), *Jewish Voices of the California Gold Rush. A Documentary History, 1849–*

1880 (Detroit: Wayne State University Press, 2002), 79.
 24. *Ibid.*
 25. George H. Tinkham, *History of San Joaquin Country California* (Los Angeles, CA: Historic Record Co., 1923).
 26. In 1855, it became Temple Israel, an Ashkenazi Congregation (Alexander Iser, *The California Hebrew and English Almanac for the Year 5612, Corresponding with the years 1851–1852* (San Francisco: Alexander Iser, 1851).
 27. Mrs. David "Bea" Schwartz, The Oldest Jewish Cemetery in the West, Stock, California (http://www.wsjhistory.com/oldest_jewish_cemetery.htm, accessed September 10, 2015; I. J. Benjamin, *Three Years in America, 1859–1862* (Philadelphia: Jewish Publication Society of America, 1956), *Three Years*, Vol. 2, 64.
 28. *Daily Alta California*, December 4, 1851, 2.
 29. U.S. 1870 Census.
 30. Jane, Issachar's sister, was 16 when she married Abraham Backer, 24, a merchant from Columbus, Georgia, in 1848. *Charleston Courier*, March 13, 1848, 2; 1860 U.S. Census.
 31. Eleazar was a permanent trustee of Stockton's short-lived Sephardic congregation, Shaar Hashamayim, the "Polish synagogue." Norton B. Stern, and William M. Kramer, "Sephardic Leadership of Early California Jewish Life," *Western States Jewish History* 17 (April 1985), 227.
 32. Saul Jacob Rubin, *Third to None. The Saga of Savannah Jewry, 1733–1983* (Savannah, GA: Self-published, 2013), 129.
 33. "Obituary," *The Weekly Gleaner as a Voice to Israel* (January—1857), n.p.; *History of San Joaquin Country*, 55. Jonathan's whereabouts for the next few years aren't known, other than his being listed in the Savannah Georgia voter records for 1856–1896. In the 1859 state and the 1860 federal census, he is listed as living in Savannah with his married daughter and other members of the Backer family.
 34. *The Ark, and Old Fellows' Western Magazine: A Monthly* 10 (August 1853), 257. *The Ark* listed his name as "I. Zachariah, Stockton."
 35. *An Illustrated History of San Joaquin County* (Chicago: Lewis Pub Co., 1890), 64.
 36. U.S. 1870 Census.

 37. *San Francisco Daily Placer Times and Transcript*, February 22, 1855, 2.
 38. It was a "side degree" that any Freemason who had received it could confer on anyone else. *Masonic Standard*, November 3, 1900, 19; Michael F. Barnes, Presentation on the Order; Albert C. Mackey, *Encyclopedia of Freemasonry and Its Kindred Sciences*, http://www.phoenixmasonry.org/mackeys_encyclopedia/s.htm.
 39. Charles E. Krausz, *A Fast Pace Forward: Chronicles of American Podiatry* (Philadelphia, PA: Pennsylvania College of Podiatric Medicine, 1987), 19.
 40. Harris, Bogardus, and Labatt, *San Francisco City Directory: For the Year Commencing October 1856* (San Francisco: Whitton, Towne & Co., 1856), 7; *San Francisco Bulletin*, May 2, 1856, 3.
 41. *Sacramento Daily Union*, November 12, 1856, 3; *San Joaquin Republican*, November, 15, 1856, 2.

Chapter 8

 1. J. F. Trow, *Trow's New York City Directory, 1857–1858* (New York: J. F. Trow), 911.
 2. Franklin Ellis, *History of Cattaraugus Co., New York* (Philadelphia, PA: L. H. Everts, 1879), 445.
 3. *New York Herald*, May 10, 1858, 5.
 4. *New York Evangelist*, January 8, 1857, 5; *New York Herald*, January 7, 1858, 6.
 5. Charles Mackay, *Life and Liberty in America* (New York: Harper & Brothers, 1859), 16–17. The *New York Times* editorialized that a New Yorker who returned after a five-year absence would hardly recognize the changes "in the business character of Broadway," the city's backbone.
 6. Burrows and Wallace, *Gotham*, 653.
 7. *Ibid.*
 8. Mackay, *Life and Liberty*, 18; *New York Tribune*, January 9, 1858, 3.
 9. *New York Tribune*, January 9, 1858, 3.
 10. *The Israelite*, June 24, 1864, 412.
 11. Burrows and Wallace, *Gotham*, 664.
 12. Mackay, *Life and Liberty*, 18.
 13. Robert Edwin Dietz, and Frederick Dietz. *1913: A Leaf from the Past. Then and Now* (New York: R. E. Dietz Company, 1914), 69.
 14. Walt Whitman, *Leaves of Grass*, "Mannahatta" (Philadelphia: David McKay, c. 1900), 161.
 15. *New York Times*, July 6, 1857, 1. The

Irish and Germans had their own tenement enclaves in the Bowery. The Irish lived in the very low part of the Bowery; the German neighborhoods were to the north. The middle classes lived above Bleeker Street; wealthy New Yorkers lived above 14th. JoAnne O'Connell, *The Life and Songs of Stephen Foster: A Revealing Portrait of the Forgotten* (Lanham, MD: Rowman & Littlefield, 2016), 308.

16. George G. Foster, *New York in Slices* (NY: W. F. Burgess, 1849), 13–146, quoted in Rudolf Glanz, *Studies in Judaic Americana* (New York: Ktav Publishing House, 1970), 163.

17. *Ibid.*, 127.

18. Quoted in *Alexandria Gazette*, October 22, 1858, 1.

19. *New York Herald*, May 6, 1858, 9; *New York Tribune*, April 30, 1858, 1.

20. *New York Times*, September 7,1859, 5.

21. David Brooks, *The Road to Character* (New York: Random House, 2015).

22. *Washington* (DC) *Daily Union*, January 13, 1847, 1.

23. Federal Trade Commission, "FTC Issues Facts for Business Guide on Avoiding Fake Degrees," February 2005, www.ftc.gov/opa/2005/02/diplomamills.htm.

24. Angelo Baracca, Jungen Renn, and Helge Vendt (eds.), *The History of Physics in Cuba* (New York: Springer, 2014), 75.

25. Zacharie, letter to General Banks, December, 28, 1863, Banks Papers, Box 30.

26. The Real Academia de Ciencias, Medicas, Physicas y Naturales de la Habana (Royal Academy of Medical, Physical and Natural Sciences of Havana). http://www.academiaciencias.cu/index.php?lang=en.

27. *Ibid.*

28. *New York Evening Post*, March 17, 1858, 3; *New York Times*, February 11, 1858, 3.

29. *New York Atlas*, August 29, 1858.

30. Zacharie, *Corns*, 8–9.

31. Gilbert H. Muller, *William Cullen Bryant: Author of America* (Albany, NY: State University of New York Press, 2008), 74.

32. Robert Michael and Philip Rosen, *Dictionary of Antisemitism: From the Earliest Times to the Present* (Lanham, MD: Scarecrow Press, 2007), 75.

33. *New York Evening Post*, February 19, 1859, 3. Issachar reproduced Bryant's article in Corns, 7–8.

34. *Ibid.*

35. *Ibid.*, December 5, 1859, 2.

36. *Washington* (DC) *Constitution*, January 8, 1861, 3.

37. I. Zacharie, *Surgical and Practical Observations on the Diseases of the Human Foot, with Instructions for Their Treatment. To Which Is Added Advice on the Management of the Hand. Illustrations with Six Colored Plates* (New York: Charles B. Norton, 1860).

38. *New York Daily Tribune*, August 22, 1860, 1; *Washington* (DC) *Constitution*, January 8, 1861, 3.

39. *New York Evening Post*, October 25, 1860, 1.

40. Durlacher, *A Treatise on Corns*.

41. John Eisenberg, *Surgical and Practical Observations*. For a detailed comparison of other portions Issachar plagiarized from Eisenberg, see Robert Schosteck, "Dr. Zacharie as an Author," *American Jewish Archives*, document SC-13336.

42. J. Colin Dagnall, "The history of Chiropodial Literature," *The Chiropodist* 20 (July, 1965), 173–184; J. C. Dagnall, "Issachar Zacharie (1827–1900)," *British Journal of Chiropody* 22 (1957), 228–231).

43. Glanz, *Studies*, 132.

44. Perhaps he would not have been so willing to change his name had he been aware that a "Doctor Zacharie" is a disreputable Jewish anatomist in a late 16th-century novel by Thomas Nashe.

45. Rudolf Glanz, "German-Jewish Names in America," *Jewish Social Studies* 23 (July 1961), 143–169.

46. Glanz, *Studies*, 292.

47. Hasia. R. Diner, "Buying and Selling 'Jewish.' The Historical Impact of Commerce on Jewish Communal life," in Jack Wertheim (ed.), *Imagining the American Jewish Community* (Waltham, MA: Brandeis University Press, 2007), 28, 41.

48. Leon Edel, *Henry James. The Untried Years* (Philadelphia: J. B. Lippincott, 1953), 57.

49. Timothy Noah, "When Junior is President, Part 1," http://www.slate.com/articles/news_and_politics/chatterbox/2000/10/when_junior_is_president_part_1.html, October 25, 2000, accessed August 6,2013.

50. *Daily Alta California*, April 27, 1850, 3.

51. *New York Herald*, October 3, 1862, 5; November 17, 1863, 7.

52. *Ibid.*, November 17, 1859, 6.

53. *Ibid.*, June 1, 1858, 8; June 14, 1858, 6; December 12, 1859, 7.

54. *Ibid.*, June 1, 1858, 8; June 14, 1858, 6.
55. *Ibid.*, January 29, 1859, 7; February 23, 1859, 7; May 20, 1859, 7.
56. *Ibid.*, August 26, 1858, 7; October 5, 1858, 8; December 7, 1858, 6; January 26, 1859, 7; October 21, 1859, 7.
57. *Ibid.*, February 4, 1859, 7; August 14, 1860, 6.
58. Gotthard Deutsch, "Mortara Case," *Jewish Encyclopedia* (New York: Funk and Wagnalls, 1905), Vol. 9, 36.
59. *New York Commercial Advertiser, The Evening Post, New York Herald, New York Journal of Commerce, New York Daily Era, New York Daily News, New York Journal, New York Transcript, The Sun, The New York Times,* and the *New York Tribune.*
60. "Payments," *The Jewish Messenger,* October 8, 1858, 62. The *Jewish Messenger* began publication in 1857 as a semi-monthly newspaper and quickly became a weekly. Edited by Samuel Myer Isaacs, it covered topics concerning Jews in America and Europe. It was anti–Reform in religious issues, and politically, strongly abolitionist.

Chapter 9

1. South Carolina (December 20, 1860), Mississippi (January 9, 1861), Florida (January 10, 1861), Alabama (January 11, 1861), Georgia (January 19, 1861), Louisiana (January 26, 1861), and Texas (February 1, 1861).
2. Roy Basler (ed.), *Collected Works of Abraham Lincoln* (New Brunswick, NJ: Rutgers University Press, 1953), Vol. 4, 254, 330.
3. Basler, *Collected Works,* 4:271. Lincoln refused to use the term "Confederacy," since that would give it some semblance of legitimacy.
4. *Ibid.*, 5, 241.
5. Virginia (April 17, 1861), Arkansas (May 6, 1861), North Carolina (May 20, 1861), and Tennessee (June 8, 1861).
6. Quoted in Rosen, *Jewish Confederates,* 1.
7. *Charleston Courier,* January 11, 1861; May 2, 1861; *Charleston Mercury,* November 29, 1861, 2.
8. *Charleston Mercury,* January 12, 1861, 2; "Charleston Under Arms," *Atlantic Monthly,* August 1861.
9. Rosen, *Jewish Confederates,* 393, n121. Valentine was killed in action in June 1862, as was Rabbi Poznanaski's son, Gustavus, Jr. Charleston *Mercury,* June 21, 1862, 2).

10. Rosen, *Jewish Confederates,* 2, 9.
11. *Charleston Courier,* December 11, 1861, 1.
12. Edward S. Shapiro, *We Are Many* (Syracuse, NY: Syracuse University Press, 2005), 171; Amos Oz and Fania Oz-Salzberger, *Jews and Words* (New Haven, CT: Yale University Press, 2012), 147.
13. The number of Jews who served in the Confederate army is estimated at 2,000 to 3,000. Jews serving in the Union army are estimated at 7,000. Simon Wolf, *The American Jew as Patriot, Soldier and Citizen* (New York: Brentano, 1895); Simonhoff, *Jewish Participants,* 21–28.
14. Rosen, *Jewish Confederates,* 382. The words are "Sh'ma Yisra'el, Adonai Eloheinu, Adonai Echad" ("Hear, Israel, the Lord is our God, the Lord is One").
15. Marcie Ferris Cohen and Mark I. Greenberg, *Jewish Roots in Southern Soil* (Waltham MA: Brandeis University, 2006), 114.
16. *Ibid.*
17. M. I. Greenberg, "Becoming Southern: The Jews of Savannah, Georgia, 1830–70," *American Jewish History* 86 (March 1998), 68.
18. Elliott Ashkenazi, *The Civil War Diary of Clara Solomon* (Baton Rouge: Louisiana State University Press, 1995), 264.
19. For Northern and Southern rabbis on the slavery issue, see Korn, *American Jewry,* 15–55.
20. Rosen, *Jewish Confederates,* 38; Jonathan D. Sarna (ed.), *Jews and the Civil War: A Reader* (New York: New York University Press, 2011), 231.
21. On Wise's views of slavery and abolition, see Sefton D. Temkin, "Isaac Mayer Wise and the Civil War," in Sarna and Mendelson, *Jews and the Civil War,* 161–180. Two weeks after Lincoln was elected in 1860, Wise said, the "the people of the United States just committed one of the greatest blunders a nation can commit." *The Israelite,* November 30, 1860, reprinted in Zola, *We Called Him Rabbi,* 201.
22. *Jewish Messenger,* June 7, 1861, 172.
23. Funeral Address By Rabbi Isaac M Wise, Delivered at Lodge Street Temple, Cincinnati Ohio, April 19, 1865, Jewish-American History Foundation, http://www.jewish-history.com/civilwar/lincoln_eulogy.html, accessed 12/1/2017.
24. Isaac Markens, "Lincoln and the

Jews," *Publications of the American Jewish Historical Society* 17 (1909), 109.

Chapter 10

1. Burrows and Wallace, *Gotham*, 868.
2. *Brooklyn Evening Star*, April 18, 1861, 1. The *Evening Star* added a footnote to the notice: "This is what we should call, 'Patriotism striking out a feet [sic].'"
3. Abel, Ernest L. "Maryland-born James Ryder Randall Penned One of the Civil War's Most Stirring Songs in Honor of His State," *America's Civil War* (July 1988), 78–82.
4. Burrows and Wallace, *Gotham*, 869.
5. *Indiana State Sentinel*, May 20, 1875, 6.
6. Gilbert H. Muller, *Abraham Lincoln and William Cullen Bryant: Their Civil War* (Palgrave Macmillan, Cham, Switzerland: 2017), 24.
7. Bryant to Lincoln (August 21, 1862), reproduced in Heritage Auction Gallery Heritage Auction Gallery, "Dr. John K. Lattimer Collection of Lincolniana" (Dallas, TX: 2008), No. 61022. The letter is now part of the Shapell Manuscript Collection and is reproduced in Sarna and Shapell, *Lincoln and the Jews* (New York: Thomas Dunne Books, 2015), 130–131.
8. Bryant to Stanton (August 21, 1862). Parts of the letter are quoted in Sarna and Shapell, *Lincoln*, 129.
9. *New York Evening Post*, August 22, 1862, 2. Bryant possibly had in mind Confederate General Thomas "Stonewall" Jackson's "foot cavalry," renowned for the distances they covered in a day's march. None of the Confederacy's generals relied on a chiropodist in his command.
10. Ibid.
11. *Buffalo* (New York) *Commercial*, August 25, 1862, 2.
12. *New York Herald*, August 26, 1862, 4.
13. *Boston Daily Advertiser*, September 8, 1862, 2.
14. *New York Herald*, August 26, 1862, 4.
15. Zacharie to Stanton, August 26, 1862. Letters received files, August 27, 1862, Records of the War Department (RG 112), Office of the Surgeon General, National Archives and Records Administration (NARA), Box 113.
16. Zacharie to Hammond, August 27, 1862. Ibid.
17. James L. Huston, *The Panic of 1857 and the Coming of the Civil War* (Baton Rouge, LA: Louisiana State University Press, 1987), 91.
18. After the Convention, Opdyke had gone to Springfield in early 1861, to ask for a patronage job as collector of customs in New York. Lincoln turned him down. Opdyke went back to New York and won the mayoral election.
19. *The Inland Printer, A Technical Journal Devoted to the Art of Printing* 21 (April 1898–September 1898), 71.
20. Opdyke to Lincoln (August 28, 1862), Heritage Auctions Catalogue, "The John Lattimer Collection of Lincolniana, #6014, 2008." A partial copy of the letter in Andrew's handwriting is reproduced in Sarna and Shapell, *Lincoln and the Jews*, 131.
21. Andrews to Abraham Lincoln, August 29, 1862, copy in Sarna and Shapell, *Lincoln and the Jews*, 131.
22. *New York Times*, August 30, 1862, 3.
23. Alonzo Rothschild, *Lincoln, Master of Men: A Study in Character* (Boston: Houghton Mifflin Company, 1908), 227.
24. Stanton was a formidable defense lawyer. In 1859, Stanton got Dan Sickles off after he had murdered his adulterous wife by arguing Sickles had suffered from temporary insanity. It was the first time that defense was successfully used in the United States to exonerate someone about whose guilt there was no doubt.
25. Ernest B. Furguson, *Freedom Rising: Washington in the Civil War* (New York: Vintage Books, 2004), 110.
26. Frank Abial Flower, *Edwin McMasters Stanton: The Autocrat of Rebellion, Emancipation and Reconstruction* (Akron, OH: Saalfield Publishing Co., 1905), 125.
27. Edwin McMasters Stanton to Charles Dana, January 24, 1862, Rosenbach Collection, www. http://civilwar.rosenbach.org/?p=3962, accessed October 24, 2017.
28. Benjamin Thomas and Harold M. Hyman, *Stanton: Life and Times of Lincoln's Secretary of War* (New York: Alfred A. Knopf, 1962).
29. McClellan testimonial, Zacharie, *Corns*, 6. While there is no record of McClellan's doing or saying anything about Jews during the war, while he was travelling back from Germany in 1875, he wrote, "We have lots of Germans and Jews on board—but fortunately there are enough Christian gentiles to make it pleasant for us [so as to]

enable us to be quite independent of the sons of Jacob." "American Civil War Union General George McClellan's Anti-Semitic Letter," Shapell Collection, http://www.shapell.org/manuscript/anti-semetic-civil-war-union-general-george-mcclellan, accessed January 3, 2016.

30. Burnside, Cadwalader and Banks testimonials, *Corns*, 7.

31. *Boston Daily Advertiser*, September 8, 1862, 2. Ordinarily, soldiers marched an average about two miles an hour a day. In forced marches, for 20 or at least 10 miles, they averaged three miles an hour. OR Series 1, Vol. 16, pt. 1, 56.

32. *Newport* (Rhode Island) *Mercury*, September 13, 1862, 2.

33. *New York World*, September 19, 1862, 2.

34. *Frank Leslie's Illustrated Newspaper*, September 20, 1862, 4.

Chapter 11

1. *New York Herald*, October 21, 1863, 6. The *Herald* described Issachar's nose as "splendid Roman."

2. Russell Freedman, *Lincoln: A Photobiography* (New York: Clarion Books, 1987), 1.

3. See Figure 1.

4. *New York Herald*, October 3, 1862, 2.

5. Corns and bunions can make the natural gait (how a person walks) stiff and ungainly. Albert F. Blaisdell, *Our Bodies and How We Live: An Elementary Text-Book of Physiology* (Boston: Lee and Shepard, 1891), 33.

6. Bryant had likely told Issachar that Lincoln was bothered by corns.

7. Peter Kahler, *Indianapolis Star*, February 10, 1924, 2.

8. The shoes can be seen at http://www.neatorama.com/2014/07/01/President-Abraham-Lincolns-Slippers/.

9. According to A. A. McQuesten, who sold shoes to Lincoln in Springfield, Lincoln did not wear socks (*Ottawa* [Kansas] *Herald*, September 4, 1902, 8.

10. Jonathan D. Sarna and Benjamin Shappell, *Lincoln and the Jews, A History* (New York: Thomas Dunne Books, 2015) reproduced the testimonial in Lincoln's own handwriting, 133.

11. Lincoln had informed his cabinet in July 1862, that he would be issuing a proclamation to free slaves. On Secretary Seward's advice, he held off making a formal announcement until after the Union victory at Antietam on September 17, 1862, which was considered decisive enough to give the proclamation the gravitas it needed.

12. Lincoln had hurt his back and wrist several days earlier.

13. The testimonial in Lincoln's own handwriting is reproduced in Sarna and Shapell, *Lincoln and the Jews*, 133.

14. The *New York Herald* (October 3, 1862, 4) reported that Issachar had treated Seward and members of Lincoln's cabinet.

15. *Congressional Series of the United States Public Documents*, Volume 1627, 43rd Congress, House of Representatives (HR), Committee on War Claims, Report No. 817, 1.

16. *HR Committee War Claims*, 123.

17. The pass was renewed for 60 days on November 21, 1862, by General Tucker, Assistant Secretary of War (*HR Committee War Claims*, 123).

Chapter 12

1. Quoted in Harold Holzer, *Lincoln and the Power of the Press* (New York: Simon and Schuster, 2014), 27.

2. David Von Drehle, *Rise to Greatness: Abraham Lincoln and America's Most Perilous Year* (New York: Picador, 2013), 298.

3. Ted Widmer, "Yacht for Sale," *New York Times*, April 21, 2011, 16.

4. George Templeton Strong, quoted by Widmer, "Yacht for Sale."

5. *New York Herald*, May 22, 1860, 7; May 23, 1860, 6.

6. Von Drehle, *Rise to Greatness*, 298.

7. *Ibid*.

8. *New York Herald*, October 3, 1862, 2.

9. *Ibid*.

10. *Ibid*.

11. *Ibid*.

12. *Ibid*.

13. *Ibid*.

14. Markens, "Lincoln," 138.

15. *Daily* (Columbus) *Ohio Statesman*, September 29, 1864, 2.

16. "Ode to Dr. Zacharie," *Vanity Fair*, October 1862, 190.

17. *Ibid.*, October 18, 1862, 186.

18. *Yorkville* (South Carolina) *Enquirer* (October 29, 1862, 2) reported that the War Department "had engaged Dr. Zacharie" and described him as "a celebrated chiropodist of New York."

19. Philadelphia *Public Ledger*, October 11, 1862, 1; *New York Times*, September 28, 1862, 4.

20. The original broadside is reproduced in Zola, *We Called Him Rabbi*, 58, and Jonathan D. Sarna and Benjamin Shapell, *Lincoln and the Jews, A History* (New York: Thomas Dunne Books, 2015), 137.

21. In 1866, President Johnson appointed Dix U.S. Minister to France. He was elected governor of New York in 1873, but lost election as mayor of New York three years later. Fort Dix in New Jersey is named after him.

22. Two years later in September 1864, Dix wrote a letter of introduction on Issachar's behalf to General John G. Foster, stating that Issachar was on his way to Savannah to visit family. "Any favor you can extend to him will be appreciated." Brown University, https://repository.library.brown.edu/studio/collections/id_572/?selected_facets=genre_aat%3Anotes&view=list.

23. Zacharie, *Corns*, 8; HR Committee on War Claims, 124.

24. William A. Hammond, *A Statement of the Causes which led to the Dismissal of Surgeon-General William A. Hammond from the Army* (New York: Hammond, 1864), 52.

25. Ibid.

26. Margaret Leech, *Reveille in Washington* (New York: Harper & Brothers, 1941), 267–268; Frank R. Freemon, *Gangrene and Glory* (Urbana, IL: University of Illinois Press, 2001), 143.

27. Hammond, *Statement*, 52.

28. Peter Adams, *Politics, Faith and the Making of American Judaism* (Ann Arbor, MI: University of Michigan Press, 2014), 40. To meet demand for blankets, uniforms, and similar necessities, textile mills began cutting corners, turning out material made from shoddy, compressed fibers swept up from shop floors. Shoes, overcoats, and blankets made from such materials disintegrated into rags with days of use. Some blankets were so thin a finger could poke through them.

29. Hammond, *Statement*, 52; *The Medical Times and Gazette*, December 31, 1864, 706.

30. *The Medical Times and Gazette*, December 31, 1864, 706.

31. Quoted by Rosen, *Jewish Confederates*, 275; Frederick Cople Jaher, *A Scapegoat in the New Wilderness. The Origins and Rise of Anti-Semitism in America* (Cambridge, MA: Harvard University Press, 1994), 225.

32. *New York Tribune*, October 7, 1861, 6.

Chapter 13

1. Jonathan D. Sarna and Benjamin Shapell, *Lincoln and the Jews, A History* (New York: Thomas Dunne Books, 2015), xii.

2. Yoskowitz distinguishes between "Zionistic," the 19th-century sentiment favoring the return of Jews to the Holy Land, and "Zionism," the late 19th- and early 20th-century idea of Jewish statehood. Herbert A. Yoskowitz, "British Zionistic Writings Revisited," *European Judaism* 13 (1979), 45.

3. Quoted in Richard S. Lambert, *For the Time Is at Hand* (Toronto: Andrew Melrose, 1947), 82.

4. Abraham Lincoln to Abraham Jonas, Springfield, February 4, 1860, in Basler, *Collected Works of Abraham Lincoln*, Vol. 3, 516. On Lincoln's relationship to Jonas, see Markens, "Lincoln," 123–128.

5. Markens, "Lincoln," 127; Korn, *American Jewry*, 194.

6. Charles later wrote a letter thanking him for letting him be at his father's side "in time to be recognized and welcomed by him." A few days later, Lincoln appointed Jonas' wife to serve out his unexpired term as postmaster (Markens, "Lincoln," 127–128).

7. *New York World*, September 24, 1864, 4.

8. Segal, "Isachar Zacharie," 71.

9. The chaplaincy controversy is detailed in Korn, *American Jewry*, 56–97; Zola, *We Called Him Rabbi*, 72–90; Sarna and Shapell, *Lincoln and the Jews*, 103–11.

Chapter 14

1. Elisabeth J. Doyle, "Greenbacks, Car Tickets, and the Pot of Gold," *Civil War History* 5 (December 1959), 348; Daniel W. Howe, *What Hath God Wrought, The Transformation of America 1815–1848* (New York: Oxford University Press, 2009), 671–700.

2. Doyle, "Greenbacks," 348.

3. Mark Scroggins, *Hannibal: The Life of Abraham Lincoln's First Vice President* (Latham, MD: 1994), 204.

4. Quoted in Darcy G. Richardson, *Others* (Lincoln, NE: I Universe, 2004), 1, 577.

5. Hans Louis Trefousse, *Ben Butler* (New York: Twayne Publishers, 1957), 114.

6. Drew Gilpin Faust, *Mothers of Invention* (Chapel Hill: University of North Carolina Press, 1996), 198.

7. Ashkenazi, *Solomon Diary*, 355–356.

8. General Order No. 28, OR, Series 2, Vol. 15, 426.

9. Jewish teenager Clara Solomon wished Butler could have as many ropes around his neck as there were ladies in the city and that each could have a pull (Ashkenazi, *Solomon Diary*, 419).

10. Giselle Roberts, *The Confederate Belle* (University of Missouri Press, 2003), 138.

11. Eli N. Evans, *Judah P. Benjamin* (New York: Free Press, 1988, 167).

12. *Ibid.*, 168.

13. Quoted by Rosen, *Jewish Confederates*, 291.

14. *Ibid.*, 293.

15. After the war, the Phillipses moved back to Washington, where Philips resumed his law career. David T. Morgan, "Eugenia Levy Phillips: The Civil War Experiences of a Southern Jewish Woman," in Samuel Proctor and Louis Schmier (eds.), *Jews of the South* (Macon, GA: Mercer University Press, 1984), 95–106; Rosen, *Jewish Confederates*, 280–304.

16. Trefousse, *Butler*, 286.

17. OR, Series 3, Vol. 2, 690.

18. Rosen, *Jewish Confederates*, 277.

19. *Ibid.*

20. *Ibid.*

21. On wartime reconstruction, see Louis P. Masur, *Lincoln's Last Speech* (New York: Oxford University Press, 2015).

22. Clifford L. Egan, "Friction in New Orleans: General Butler versus the Spanish Consul," *Louisiana History* 9 (Winter 1968), 43–52.

23. *New York Times*, December 20, 1862, 4.

24. Zacharie to Banks, November 16, 1862, Banks Papers, Box 25.

25. Jonas to Lincoln, December 30, 1860, ABL LOC.

26. Zacharie to Seward, November 24, 1862, Seward Papers, University of Rochester, Rush Rhees Library (hereafter RRL).

27. Lincoln to Banks, November 25, 1862, Lincoln Manuscripts, Brown (University) Digital Repository, https://repository.library.brown.edu/studio/item/bdr:72350/

28. *Ibid.*

29. Grant to General Joseph Dana Webster, November 10, 1862, OR, Series 1, Vol. 17, pt. 2, Mississippi to the Tennessee rivers.

30. Quoted in Stephen V. Ash, "Civil War Exodus," in Adam Mendelsohn (ed.), *Jews and the Civil War; A Reader* (New York: New York University Press, 2010), 363–384, 364.

31. *New York Times*, December 25, 1862, 2. On cotton profiteering, see Surdam, "Traders," 302–304; Ludwell H. Johnson, "Northern Profit and Profiteers," *Civil War History* 12 (June 1966), 101–115.

32. Brooks D. Simpson, *Ulysses S. Grant. Triumph over Adversity, 1822–1865* (Boston: Houghton Mifflin Co., 2000), 163.

33. Massachusetts Senator Henry Wilson denounced Benjamin as a member of "that race who stoned the prophets and crucified the redeemer of the world." *New York Times*, March 15, 1862; *Jewish Messenger*, March 21, 1862. Tennessee editor William "Parson" Brownlow called Benjamin the "little Jew of the bogus Confederacy" (*New York Times*, March 28, 1862). As the prejudice deepened, other members of the Confederate cabinet were denounced as Jews. General Butler pointed his finger at "Mr. [Christopher] Memminger [Confederate Treasury Secretary, and] Mr. [Stephen] Mallory [Confederate Secretary of the Navy] is also of the Jewish faith or nationality." Quoted in Simonoff, *Jewish Participants*, 151). Neither was Jewish. Memminger was a German Lutheran; Mallory was Roman Catholic (Simonhoff, *Jewish Participants*, 151).

34. Barbara Straus Reed, "Jewish Press Coverage of an Anti-Semitic Act," in David B. Sachsman, S. Kittrell Rushing, and Debra Reddin van Tuyll (eds.), *The Civil War and the Press* (New Brunswick, NJ: Transaction Publishers), 326.

35. Ulysses S. Grant, *The Papers of Ulysses S. Grant* (hereafter PUSG), John Y. Simon (ed.) (Carbondale: Southern Illinois University Press, 1967), 7, 50.

36. Sherman to Rawlins, OR series 1, Vol. 17, pt. 2, 140–141; M. A. Dewolfe Howe (ed.), *Home Letters of General Sherman* (New York: Charles Scribner's Sons, 1909), 154; Sherman to Chase, August 11, 1862, in William Tecumseh Sherman, *Memoirs of General W. T. Sherman* (New York, Library of America, 1990), 286.

37. *Corinth War Eagle*, a soldier newspaper quoting Grant. PSUG, 7, 52.

38. Or., Ser. 1, Vol. 22, 479; PSUG, 7, 50.
39. Grant to Colonel Joseph Dana Webster, his superintendent of military railroads, November 10, 1862, PSUG, 6, 283.
40. Lincoln to Banks, November 25, 1862, RRL.
41. Grant to Major General Stephen A. Hurlbut, November 26, 1862, OR, Series I, Vol. 17, pt. 2, 330.
42. PSUG, 6, 394.
43. OR, Series I, Vol. 17, pt. 2, 424.
44. The Mack brothers were major suppliers of uniforms for the Union army. On Henry Mack, see Michael W. Rich, "'Henry Mack: An Important Figure in Nineteenth-century Jewish History," *American Jewish Archives* 47 (1995), 266–267, 273–274; *The Israelite*, December 13, 1861, reprinted in "Clothing for the Army of the Union," *American Jewish Archives* 13 (November 1961), 174–175.
45. Caesar Kaskel to Lincoln, December 29, 1862. The letter is reproduced in Zola, *We Called Him Rabbi*, 106.
46. Markens, "Lincoln," 118.
47. Ibid.
48. Halleck to Grant, January 4, 1863, OR Series I, Vol. 17, pt. 2, 530.
49. Kelton to Grant, January 5, 1863; PSUG, 7, 54.
50. Halleck to Grant, January 21, 1863, PSUG, 7, 54n.
51. OR, Series 1, Vol. 17, pt. 2, 544. As soon as word that Lincoln had countermanded Grant's order expelling Jews from his department flashed through Washington, Lincoln's long- time friend and ally, Illinois Congressman Elihu Washburne, dashed off a note to Lincoln, saying he hoped that his order repealing Grant's edict expelling Jews from his district wasn't true. He personally considered it, he said, "the wisest order yet made by a Military Command." Washburne added that from his "own personal observation," it "was necessary." Washburne to Lincoln, January 7, 1863, OR, Series 1, Vol. 18, pt. 1, 544.
52. Julia Grant, *The Personal Memoirs of Julia Dent Grant*, John Y. Simon (ed.) (NY: G. P. Putnam's Sons, 1975), 107.
53. Ulysses S. Grant, *Personal Memoirs of U.S. Grant* (New York: Charles I. Webster & Company, 1885).
54. Markens, "Lincoln," 122.

Chapter 15

1. Lincoln to August Belmont, July 31, 1862, CW, Vol. 5, 350.
2. Banks to Mary Banks, January 15, 1863, Banks Papers, Box 5.
3. George H. Hepworth, *Whip, Hoe, and Sword* (Boston: Walker, Wise & Co., 1864), 90.
4. OR, Series 1, Vol. 15, 311; Vol. 27, 639; James G. Hollandsworth Jr., *Pretense of Glory: The Life of General Nathaniel P. Banks* (Baton Rouge, LA: Louisiana State University Press, 1998), *Pretense of Glory*, 95–96.
5. George H. Hepworth, *Whip, Hoe, and Sword: The Gulf-Department in '63* (Boston: Walker, Wise and Company, 1864), *Whip, Hoe, and Sword*, 27–28.
6. General Orders No. 114, December 21, 1862; OR Series 1, Vol. 15, 615; *New York Herald*, February 15, 1863, 1.
7. R. Banks, *King of Louisiana*, 574.
8. John A. Stevenson to Confederate Secretary of War, George Randolph, November 10, 1862, OR, Series 1, Vol. 15, 862.
9. C. A. Weed and A. J. Butler to Banks, December 27, 1862, Banks Papers, Box 26. The handwritten bribe offer is reproduced in Robert Werlich, *'Beast' Butler* (Washington, D.C.: Quaker Press, 1962), n.p.
10. Chester G. Hearn, *When the Devil Came Down to Dixie* (Baton Rouge, LA: Louisiana State University Press, 1977), 6, 196.
11. Banks to Mary Banks, January 16, 1863, Banks Papers, Box 26.
12. R. Banks, *King of Louisiana*, 870, 1280–1281.
13. Ibid., 8.
14. Ibid.
15. Banks to Mary Banks, August 17, 1846, ibid., Box 5.
16. Mary Banks to Banks, November 9, 1869, Banks Papers, Box 4.
17. Mary Banks to Banks, March 16, 1863, ibid., Box 3.
18. Banks to Mary, January, 1868, http://hcaauctions.com/lot-10720.aspx.
19. General Alpheus Williams, quoted in R. Banks, *King of Louisiana*, 272.
20. William Stevens Robinson, *"Warrington" Pen-Portraits: A Collection of Personal and Political* (Boston: Mrs. W. S. Robinson, 1877), 438.
21. *New York Times*, March 14, 1859, 4.
22. E.g., *Chicago Tribune*, July 23, 1859,

1; *Rock Island* (Illinois) *Argus*, September 9, 1859, 2; (New Orleans) *Times-Picayune*, December 22, 1859, 2.

23. *Ibid.*, 213.
24. Rosen, *Jewish Confederates*, 28.
25. Elliott Ashkenazi, *The Business of Jews* (Tuscaloosa, AL: University of Alabama Press, 1988), 5-11.
26. Banks to Isaac [sic] Zacharie, January 1, 1863, Banks Papers, Box 26. The letter was not in Banks' own handwriting, so the misspelling of Issachar's name as "Isaac" was not necessarily because Banks was not as yet on a first-name basis with Issachar.
27. Kursheedt to Zacharie, January 7, 1863, Banks Papers, Box 26.
28. Dix to Halleck, October 21, 1862, OR Series 1, Vol. 18, 435.
29. Zacharie to Banks, January 11, 1863, Banks Papers, Box 26.
30. Expense account, Zacharie to Banks, February 25, 1863, LOC, Banks Papers, Box 75. See Appendix 3 for this and Issachar's other expenses for February and March 1863.

Chapter 16

1. Zacharie to Banks January 15, 18, 1863, Banks Papers, Box 26.
2. Zacharie to Banks, January 13, 1863, *ibid*.
3. Zacharie to Banks, January 12, 1863, Banks Papers, Box 26.
4. *Ibid.*
5. Zacharie to Banks, January 29, 1863, *ibid*.
6. Zacharie to Banks, January 25, 1863, *ibid*.
7. Zacharie to Banks, January 11, 1863, *ibid*.
8. Zacharie to Banks, January 29, 1863, *ibid*.
9. *Ibid.*
10. *Ibid.*
11. *Ibid.*
12. Korn, *American Jewry*, 87.
13. Zacharie to Banks, January 31,1863, Banks Papers, Box 26.
14. *Ibid.*
15. Quoted in James Marten, "The Making of a Carpetbagger: George S. Denison and the South, 1854-1866," *Louisiana History* 34 (Spring 1993), 136. Denison's salary came from a Supreme Court Case, *U.S. vs. Flanders*, 112 U.S. 188, November 3, 1884.

16. Denison to Salmon P. Chase, February 1, 1863; Edward G. Bourne (ed.), *Diary and Correspondence of Salmon P. Chase* (Washington, D.C.: American Historical Association, 1902), Vol. 2, 353 (hereafter Chase Diary).
17. Denison to Chase, February 12, 1863, Chase Diary, 353-359.
18. Thomas Durant, quoted by Joseph G. Tregle, Jr., "Thomas J. Durant," *Louisiana Journal of Southern History* 45 (November 1979), 495. Denison's corruption is documented in *U.S. vs. Flanders*, 112 U.S. 88, November 3, 1884, and the Smith Brady Commission, *Testimony Received*, Book B, 134-42, I, 164-170, 816-22, II, 673-79, 699-701, 715-721.
19. Denison to Chase, Chase Diary, February 12, 1863, 359-360.
20. Denison to Chase, February 1, February 12, 1863, Chase Diary, Vol. 2, 353.
21. Shepley to Butler, February 20, 1863; Butler and Marshall, *Private and Official Correspondence*, 3, 14; Hollandsworth, *Pretense of Glory*, 155. On Shepley, see Candace Kanes, "George F. Shepley," Maine Memory Network, https://www.mainememory.net/sitebuilder/site/2176/page/3613/display?use_mmn=1, accessed July 2, 2017.
22. Joseph Hill to General Banks, March 3, 1863, U.S. Archives, Record Group 393, Army Continent Commands, 1821-1920, Department of the Gulf Letters Received (Civil), Box 4.
23. Hill to Banks, March 13, 1863, *ibid.*, Box 2.
24. NARA, Department of the Gulf, Register of Letters Received, RG 393, pt. 1, entry 1920, Box 2. The agreement, dated March 7, 1863, along with other letters from Issachar, was later found in 1865 during a search of Betterton's house by General Stephen A. Hurlbut.
25. *Memphis Daily Appeal*, April 17, 1863, 1.
26. OR Series IV, Vol. 1, 500, 503.
27. The (New Orleans) *Crescent*, October 30, 1861, 2.
28. Betterton to Banks, July 22, 1863, NARA, Box 2.
29. Zacharie to Banks, March 7, 1863, quoted by Segal, "Isachar Zacharie," 94.
30. OR. Series 1, Vol. 26, 863; *Congressional Record*, December 12, 1867, 147; R. Banks, *King of Louisiana*, 911; Richard Taylor, *Destruction and Reconstruction*, Rich-

ard B. Harwell (ed.) (New York: Longmans Green & Co., 1955), 20. Banks was a poor money manager. In February 1864, Banks' departmental surgeon, B. F. Stevenson, wrote home, "there seems to be some hitch in the monetary affairs of this department … the military treasury at New Orleans is just now empty." Troops had not been paid in four months. B. F. Stevenson, *Letters from the Army, 1862–1864* (Cincinnati: Robert Clarke, 1886), 306.

31. Zacharie to Banks, January 29, 1863, Banks Papers, Box 26.

32. Expense account, Zacharie to Banks, Banks Papers Box 75.

33. *New York World*, February 18, 1863, 1; Boston Herald, February 19, 1863, 2.

34. Zacharie to Lincoln, February 19, 1863, ABL LOC.

35. *Ibid.*

36. Zacharie to Banks, December 28, 1863, Banks Papers, Box 30.

37. To deal with the financial crisis stemming from the war, in 1861, the Republican-dominated Congress voted to institute a national flat rate income tax of 3 percent on annual income above a personal exemption of $800, equivalent to $15,000 today, and 7.5% on income above $10,000. The government also authorized issuance of a national paper currency, popularly called "greenbacks," increases in tariff rates, and an increase in the national debt through public borrowing. Lincoln signed the measures into law in August 1861. Sheldon D. Pollack, "The First National Income Tax, 1861–1872," *The Lawyer* 67 (2014), 311–312; 311–330). In 1864, the rate was boosted to 5% after a $600 exemption.

38. U.S. IRS Tax Assessment Lists, 1862–1918 (ancestry.com).

39. *Ibid.*

40. Zacharie to Lincoln, February 19, 1863, ABL.

41. Basler, *Collected Works*, Vol. 4, 148.

42. Robinson, "Warrington," 437.

43. Banks to Mary, March 21, 1863, Banks Papers, Box 5; R. Banks, *King of Louisiana*, 765, 863.

44. Zacharie to Banks, January 28, 1863, ibid.

45. Banks to Mary, February 24, 1863, Banks Papers, Box 5.

46. Leonard V. Huber, "The Battle of the Handkerchiefs," *Civil War History* 8 (March 1962), 50.

47. Zacharie to Lincoln, January 14, 1863, ABL LOC.

48. *Ibid.*

49. *New York Herald*, March 28, 1863, 2.

50. (New Orleans) *Times-Picayune*, March 8, 1863, 2.

51. Banks, "To the President," March 6, 1863, Banks Papers, Box 26, original in Seward Papers, RRL.

52. Hollandsworth, *Pretense of Glory*, 95; OR Series 1, Vol. 15, 640; Series 3, Vol. 3, 187–190.

53. Andrew Weintraub, "The Economics of Lincoln's Proposal for Compensated Emancipation," *American Journal of Economics and Sociology* 32 (April 1973), 177.

54. Gabor S. Boritt, *Lincoln and the Economics of the American Dream* (Urbana, IL: University of Illinois Press, 1994), 239.

55. Banks, "To the President," March 6, 1863, Banks Papers, Box 26, original in Seward Papers, RRL.

56. Zacharie to Banks, December 28, 1863, Banks Papers, Box 30.

57. Telegram from Zacharie to Lincoln, March 17, 1863, ABL LOC, Series 1, General Correspondence.

58. Charles Johnson to Betterton, March 20, 1863, Archives RG 393, Letters Received, Box 4, Betterton file.

59. Lincoln to Zacharie, March 25, 1863, Brown Digital Repository, Brown University Library, 72336, https://rcpository.library.brown.edu/studio/item/bdr:72336/.

60. Lincoln to Seward, March 26, 1863, RRL.

61. Zacharie to Lincoln, March 27, 1863, Lincoln Papers, LOC.

62. *Ibid.*

63. Zacharie to Banks, March 27, 1863, NARA, RG 393, Department of the Gulf, Letters Received, Bureau of Civil Affairs, 1863.

64. Seward to Banks, March 26, 1863, Banks Papers, Box 75, original in RRL.

65. *Ibid.*

66. R. Banks, *King of Louisiana*, 761.

67. The Evolution of the U.S. Intelligence Community—An Historical Overview, https://fas.org/irp/offdocs/int022.html.

68. House of Representatives, 38th Congress, 1st Session, *Letter from the Secretary of the Treasury Transmitting Statements Showing Receipts and Expenditures for the Year Ending June 30, 1863*, 154. By comparison,

Major General Rosecrans was only allotted $4,000, and General Shepley, Louisiana's military governor, was only allotted $10,000.
69. R. Banks, *King of Louisiana*, 816, 1280–1281.
70. Mary Banks to Banks, April 1, 1863, Banks Papers, Box 26.
71. Quoted in Surdam, "Traders," 307.
72. *Ibid.*
73. Theodore Calvin Peace and James G. Randal, *The Diary of Orville Hickman Browning* (Springfield, IL: Illinois State Library, 1925), xxiii. Lincoln personally approved permits to trade with the South for friends, including one for Robert Lamon, the brother of Lincoln's long-time friend and self-appointed bodyguard, Ward Hill Lamon, for 50,000 bales of cotton and one for long-time friend Leonard Swett for 150,000 bales of cotton. Surdam, "Traders," 305.
74. Mary to Banks, April 6, 1863, Banks Papers, Box 26.
75. *Ibid.*, May 14, 1863.
76. (New Orleans) *Times-Picayune*, March 7, 1863, 2; *New York Herald*, March 28, 1863, 2.
77. Mary to "My Dear Husband," May 14, 1863, Banks Papers, Box 26.
78. *Ibid.*, April 1, 1863.
79. Harrington, *Fighting Politician*, 6, 129.
80. *Ibid.*, 135.
81. R. Banks, *King of Louisiana*, 816, 1280–1281.

Chapter 17

1. R. Banks, *King of Louisiana*, 762.
2. Banks to Seward, April 17, 1863, Banks Papers, Box 26.
3. Zacharie to Banks, April 18, 1864, Banks Papers, Box 28.
4. *Ibid.*
5. *Ibid.*
6. Zacharie to Seward, April 18, 1863, RRL.
7. Betterton to Banks, July 22, 1863, NARA, Betterton file.
8. Zacharie to Lincoln, April 20, misdated April 25, 1863, NARA, RG 393, Department of the Gulf, Letters Received Bureau of Civil Affairs, 1863, F–L.
9. Zacharie to Banks, April 23, 1863, Bank Papers, Box 28.
10. Halleck to Banks, May 23, 1863, OR 26, pt. 1, 500.
11. *Burlington* (Vermont) *Daily Times*, May 8, 1863, 4; (New Orleans) *Times-Picayune*, May 12, 1863, 2.
12. M. Winer, "Report from America," quoted by Glanz, *Studies*, 67.
13. Zacharie to Lincoln, May 9, 1863, ABL LOC.
14. *Cincinnati Enquirer*, May 21, 1863, 1.
15. *New York Herald*, June 13, 1863, 8.
16. On Gutheim, see Korn, *American Jewry*, 47–51; Scott Langston, "James K. Gutheim as a Southern Reform Rabbi, Community Leader and Symbol," *Southern Jewish History* 5 (2000), 69–102; Max Heller, *Jubilee Souvenir of Temple Sinai 1872-1922* (New Orleans, 1922), 48-51.
17. Zacharie to Banks, May 3, 1863, Banks Papers, Box 27.
18. *Ibid.*
19. Gutheim to Leeser, May 8, 1863, Korn, *American Jewry*, 48; Benjamin, *Three Years in America*, 317.
20. Korn, *American Jewry*, 49.
21. *Ibid.*, 49–50; Langston, "James K. Gutheim," 77–78.
22. Korn, *American Jewry*, 50; *New Orleans Daily Picayune*, May 7, 1904.
23. Zachararie to Banks, May 5, 1863, Banks Papers, Box 27.
24. Zacharie to Lincoln, May 9, 1863, *ibid.*
25. Zacharie to Seward, May 20, 1863, Seward Papers, RRL.
26. Quoted in Rosen, *Jewish Confederates*, 275.
27. Denson to Chase, February 1, February 12, 1863, Chase Diary, 353, 359.
28. Letter Shepley to Butler, Butler and Marshall, *Correspondence*, 14; Hollandsworth, *Pretense of Glory*, 155.
29. Quoted in Korn, *American Jewry*, 163.
30. Tregle, "Durant," 495. On Hahn, see Walter Greaves Cowan and Jack B. McGuire, *Louisiana Governors* (Jackson, MS: University Press of Mississippi, 2008), 90–92.
31. Hahn to Lincoln, May 9, 1863, June 6, 1863, ABL LOC; Tregle, "Durant," 504.
32. Richardson to Banks, June 22, 1863, Banks Papers, Box 27; Richardson to Banks, July 22, 1863, NARA, RG 393, Letters Received Bureau of Civil Affairs, Department of the Gulf, 1863, Q–Z, Box 4.
33. *Baltimore Sun*, May 9, 1863, 1.
34. Betterton to Banks, July 22, 1863, NARA, Betterton file.
35. Tregle, "Durant," 508. On Plumley,

see *Journal of the House of Representatives* 20 (1888), 162–163.
36. Plumley to Banks, September 5, 1863, NARA, Betterton file.
37. Banks to Brigadier General James Bowen, Provost Marshall, September 7, 1863, NARA, Betterton file.
38. Betterton to Butler, *Private and Official Correspondence of Gen. Benjamin F. Butler* (privately published, Jesse Ames Marshal: 1917), Vol. 422.
39. Betterton File.
40. *The Commission on Corrupt Practices in the South* (hereafter Smith-Brady), 4 volumes; RG 94, Records of the Adjutant General's Office, 1780's–1914.
41. Smith-Brady, Vol. 1, 214.
42. Montgomery testimony, Smith Brady.
43. Zacharie to Banks, May 5, 1863, Banks Papers, Box 26.
44. *Ibid.*, Vol. I, 232, Vol. II, 699–701, Vol. III, 254–56, 260–64, 364.
45. R. Banks, *King of Louisiana*, 1200.
46. William F. Smith and James T. Brady, *Commission on Corrupt Practices in the Gulf, Final Report, September 23, 1865*, RG 94, Records of the Adjutant General's Office. No one took any interest.

Chapter 18

1. Zacharie to Seward, May 20, 1863; Seward Papers, RRL.
2. Zacharie to Banks, June 1, 1863, Banks Papers, Box 26.
3. Zacharie to Banks, December 28, 1863, *ibid.*, Box 30.
4. Zacharie to Banks, December 28, 1863, *ibid.*, Box 30.
5. Zacharie to Seward, June 20, 1863, *ibid.*, Box 27.
6. **Ibid**.
7. *Ibid*.
8. Banks to General William Emory, July 2, 1863, Banks Papers, Box 27.
9. Harrington, *Fighting Politician*, 126
10. T. Michael Parish, *Richard Taylor* (Chapel Hill, NC: University of North Carolina Press, 1992), 457. Gordon was married to Taylor's younger sister.
11. Banks to Seward, July 2, 1863, Banks Papers, Box 27.
12. Banks to Holabird, July 2, 1863, *ibid.*, Box 27.
13. $730 for himself, $365 for his secretary, and $342, "for rent of rooms" at the St. Charles Hotel.
14. Zacharie to Banks, July 4, 1863 Banks Papers, Box 27.
15. Zacharie to Banks, July 30, 1863, Banks Papers, Box 28.
16. Wilfred B. Yearns Jr., "The Peace Movement in the Confederate Congress," *Georgia Historical Quarterly* 41 (March 1957), 2.
17. *Ibid.*, 6; *Cleveland Plain Dealer*, July 11, 1863, 3; *Macon (GA) Telegraph*, July 18, 1863, 1.
18. Doris Kearns Goodwin, *Team of Rivals* (New York: Simon & Schuster, 2005).
19. Cleveland *Plain Dealer*, July 11, 1863, 3. Gideon Welles, *Diary of Gideon Wells* (Boston: Houghton Mifflin Company, 1911), 358–363.
20. O.R. Series I, volume 6, 84; Welles, *Diary*, 362.
21. Lehrman Institute, "Abraham Lincoln and Peace," http://www.abrahamlincolnsclassroom.org/abraham-lincoln-in-depth/abraham-lincoln-and-peace/.
22. *Ibid*.
23. Jaques to Lincoln, May 23,1863, quoted in James R. Gilmore, *Personal Recollections of Abraham Lincoln and the Civil War* (London: John Macqueen, 1899), 148–149.
24. Zacharie to Seward, July 16, 1863, RRL.
25. *Ibid*.
26. Banks to Seward, July 2, 1863, Banks Papers, Box 27.
27. *New York Herald*, July 1, 1863, 1.
28. Ibid.
29. Zacharie to Seward, July 18, 1863 and July 20, 1863, Banks Papers, Box 27.
30. Zacharie to Banks, July 30, 1863, Banks Papers, Box 28.
31. *Ibid*.
32. *New York World*, July 20, 1863, 4.
33. *Ibid*.
34. *Ibid*.
35. *Ibid*.
36. Zacharie to Lincoln, July 20, 1863, ABL LOC.
37. Zacharie to Banks, July 30, 1863, Banks Papers, Box 28.
38. *Ibid*. Historian Fred Harrington speculates that based on that remark and other comments, Issachar had Banks' nomination as the Republican candidate in mind when he proposed his mission to Richmond. Fred Herrington, "A Peace Mission," *American Historical Review* 46 (October 1940), 76–86, 80, n13.

39. *Ibid.*
40. *Ibid.*

Chapter 19

1. Zacharie to Banks, September 8, 1863, Banks Papers, Box 28.
2. *Ibid.*
3. *Ibid.*
4. Johnson to Banks, September 24, 1863, Banks Papers, Box 28.
5. Banks to Lincoln, misdated September 11, 1863, ABL LOC.
6. Zacharie to Banks, September 8, 1863, Banks Papers, Box 28.
7. *Ibid.*
8. *Ibid.*
9. Lincoln to Foster, misdated August 28, 1863, Brown Digital Repository, https://repository.library.brown.edu/studio/item/bdr:; Zacharie to Banks, October 9, 1863, Banks Papers, Box 29.
10. Issachar to Lincoln, September 20, 1863.
11. Johnson to Banks, September 24, 1863, Banks Papers, Box 28.
12. Zacharie to Banks, October 9, 1863, Banks Papers, Box 29.
13. Zacharie to Benjamin, September 28, 1863, Domestic correspondence of Confederate Department of State in Zola, *We Called Him Rabbi*, 59.
14. *Ibid.*
15. *Ibid.*
16. Zacharie to Lincoln, September 29, 1863, ABL LOC.
17. Zacharie to Banks, October 9, 1863, Banks Papers, Box 29.
18. *Ibid.*
19. R. Banks, *King of Louisiana*, 765, 863.
20. Zacharie to Banks, October 9, 1863, Banks Papers, Box 29.
21. *New York Herald*, October 8, 1863, 6.
22. *Ibid.*
23. W. H. Watford, "Confederate Western Ambitions," *Southwestern Historical Quarterly* 44 (October 1940), 294.
24. *New York Herald*, October 8, 1863, 6.
25. *Ibid.*, October 9, 1863, 6.
26. *New York Herald*, July 9, 1863, 7.
27. Zacharie to Banks, October 16, 1863, Banks Papers, Box 29.
28. *Ibid.*
29. Zacharie to Seward, October 16, 1863, RRH (the dates are off).
30. Zacharie to Banks, October 24, 1863, Banks Papers, Box 29.
31. *Ibid.*
32. *New York Herald*, October 21, 1863, 6.
33. Greeley had tried to arrange what turned out to be a failed peace initiative between Lincoln and Confederate agents who supposedly were acting on behalf of Jefferson Davis. James M. McPherson, "No Peace without Victory, 1861–1865," *American Historical Review* 109 (February 2004), 1–18.
34. *New York Herald*, October 21, 1863, 6.
35. *Ibid.*
36. Zacharie to Lincoln, October 22, 1863, ABL LOC.
37. Johnson to Banks, October 29, 1863, Banks Papers, Box 29.
38. *New York Herald*, November 17, 1863, 6.
39. *Ibid.*
40. Zacharie to Banks, December 28, 1863, Banks Papers, Box 30.
41. *Ibid.*
42. *Ibid.*
43. *Ibid.*
44. *Ibid.*

Chapter 20

1. Johnson to Banks, January 22, 1864.
2. Rosengarten and Rosengarten, *A Portion of the People*, 127–128.
3. Zacharie to Lincoln, February 13, 1864, ABL LOC.
4. Markens, "Lincoln," 155; *New York Tribune*, February 12, 1864, 190.
5. OR, Series I, Vol. 15, 245.
6. Cohen to Zacharie, March 5, 1864, NARA, RG entry 36, correspondence 1798–1918, Miscellaneous Letters Received, 1801–1884, Doc. No. 291966.
7. *Ibid.*
8. Zacharie to Banks, March 26, 1864, Banks Papers, Box
9. Zacharie to Lincoln May 13, 1864, ABL LOC.
10. *Jewish Messenger*, May 13, 1864, 141. Korn muses that Issachar must have used his influence to intercede for several other Jews in trouble for such a large congratulatory party. Korn, *American Jewry*, 199.
11. *Ibid.*
12. *Ibid.*
13. *New York World*, September 24, 1864. Mordecai became a prominent member of

the Gold Board, which became the New York Stock Exchange, and publisher of *The New Era & Illustrated Southern Weekly* in New Orleans.
  14. Quoted in Korn, *American Jewry*, xxii.
  15. Reports of Committees: 44th Congress, 1st Session, Senate, Vol. 2 (Washington DC: Government Printing Office, 1876), Report No. 370.
  16. Lincoln to Pomeroy, November 8, 1863, ABL LOC.
  17. https://civilwarbookofdays.org/tag/samuel-pomeroy/.
  18. Raphall to Lincoln, March 17, 1864, ABL LOC. As a further token of his appreciation, Raphall sent Lincoln several photographs of himself.
  19. Samuel F. Chalfin to Levy, July 16, 1864, ABL LOC.
  20. Lincoln to Fessenden, August 2, 1864, Brown Digital Repository, https://repository.library.brown.edu/studio/item/bdr:72311/.
  21. Zacharie to Lincoln, undated, RRH.
  22. Lincoln to Zacharie, September 19 1864, ABL LOC.
  23. Zacharie to Lincoln, September 21, 1864 ABL LOC.
  24. *New York Herald*, quoted in *Charleston, Evening Post*, September 19, 1900, 10.
  25. *Ibid.*
  26. *Boston Herald*, September 17, 1900, 10. On Samuel Cutler Ward, see Kathryn A. Jacob, "King of the Lobby," *Smithsonian Magazine* 32 (May 2001), 122–131.
  27. Joseph Barber, *War Letters of a Disbanded Volunteer* (New York: Frederick A. Brady, 1864), 203, 211.
  28. *Ibid.*
  29. *Ibid.*

Chapter 21

  1. *New York World*, July 12, 1864, 2.
  2. *Pittsburgh Daily Post*, July 21, 1864, 2.
  3. Benj. F. Butler, *Autobiography and Personal Reminiscences of Major-General Benj. F. Butler, Butler's Book* (Boston: A.M. Thayer & Co., 1892), 434.
  4. Horace Greely, August 18, 1864, quoted in the *New York Sun*, June 30, 1889, 3.
  5. Thurlow Weed to William H. Seward, August 22, 1864, ABL LOC.
  6. Quoted in *Wisconsin Daily Patriot*, January 9, 1864, 2.
  7. The Constitution mandated that if a President did not sign a bill presented to him less than 10 days before the end of the congressional session, it was void. If presented more than 10 days before the end of the congressional session, a bill automatically became law even if the President did nothing.
  8. The "manifesto" is reprinted in http://www.let.rug.nl/usa/documents/1851-1875/the-wade-davis-manifesto-august-5-1864.php.
  9. Frémont had been the Republican party's nominee in 1856 when it first formed, but he lost to Democrat James Buchannan.
  10. Peace Democrats wore copperhead badges made from copper pennies that bore the likeness of the Goddess of Liberty on them. Wood Gray, *The Hidden Civil War* (New York: Viking Press, 1942), 140–141.
  11. On Jacques and Gilmore and their mission, see Kirkland, *Peacemakers*, 85–96. Gilmore wrote an extensive description of their meeting, "Our Visit to Richmond," for the *Atlantic* (14 [September 1864], 372–373). The article is reprinted online at: https://www.theatlantic.com/magazine/archive/1864/09/our-visit-to-richmond/522843/.
  12. Edward Chase Kirkland, *The Peacemakers of 1864* (New York: Macmillan, 1927), 92. Davis' comments were widely quoted in the newspapers: *Boston Evening Transcript*, July 22, 1864; *New York Times*, July 29, 1864.
  13. Charles Graham Halpine, *The Life and Adventures, Songs, Services, and Speeches of Private Miles O'Reilly* (New York: Carleton Publishers, 1864), 211.
  14. Basler, *Collected Works*, Vol. 7, 514.
  15. On November 11, 1864, after he was reelected, Lincoln tore open the envelop and read them the memorandum. John Hay, *Lincoln and the Civil War* (New York: Dodd Mead & Co., 1939), 237.
  16. *Clearfield* (Pennsylvania) *Republican*, September 14, 1864, 2. Despite complaints about the tax on annual income, the law did not provide any means for enforcement, so in reality, it did not affect so many people that it became an issue in the election.
  17. Lincoln to Zacharie, September 19, 1864, ABL LOC.
  18. Zacharie to Lincoln September 21, 1864, *ibid*.
  19. Zacharie to Seward, September 21, 1864, RRH.

20. Abram J. Dittenhoefer, *How We Elected Lincoln* (New York: Harper Brothers, 1916), 4.

21. Dittenhoefer became friends with Lincoln after the 1864 election and visited him several times at the White House. "I often found him sitting in the business office of the White House having on a black, threadbare, alpaca coat, out at the elbows and in slippers." Markens, "Lincoln," 138. In later life, Dittenhoefer was appointed a justice of the City Court of New York, was a delegate to several Republican national conventions, and was chairman of the Republican Central Committee of New York. Markens, "Lincoln," 139.

22. *New York World*, September 23, 1864, 7.

23. *Philadelphia Press*, May 9, 1864, 2. Chestnut Street was the location of two other Jewish chiropodists, Levi Lindoman at 702 Chestnut and 1342 Chestnut, and Marcus Goldberg, at 1208 Chestnut. Charles E. Krausz to Bertram Korn, March 3, 1955, American Jewish Archives. As noted, medically trained physicians scorned chiropody, enabling Jews to become dominant practitioners in the profession.

24. Issachar was so famous by this time that the incident was reported by several national and foreign newspapers: *New York Times*, September 23, 1864; September 29, 1864; *New York World*, September 23, 1864, 7; (New York) *Courrier des Etats-Unis*, September 24, 1864, 2; (Sheffield and Rotherham) *Independent*, October 12,1864, 4: *Glasgow Herald*, October 14, 1864, 7; *Dublin Freeman's Journal*, October 12, 1864, 3.

25. *The Sun*, September 23, 1864, 4.

26. Historian Charles Segal contacted the New York Police Commissioner's Office about the incident, but the records of the shooting had been destroyed. Segal, "Isachar Zacharie," 117, n135).

27. *New York World*, September 24, 1864, 4. James Tucker, General Banks' secretary, said that when he was in Washington, Issachar was "at the President's house a good deal. I saw him there two or three times." Smith Brady Commission, 256.

28. *Daily* (Columbus) *Ohio Statesman*, September 29, 1864, 2.

29. *Lancet*, October 15, 1864, 444.

Chapter 22

1. John C. Waugh, *Reelecting Lincoln* (New York: Crown Publishers, 1998), 16.

2. *Cincinnati Gazette*, quoted in the *Buffalo Evening Courier and Republic*, October 21, 1863, 2.

3. Jonathan D. Sarna and Benjamin Shapell, *Lincoln and the Jews, A History* (New York: Thomas Dunne Books, 2015), 174.

4. Quoted in Naomi W. Cohen, *Encounter with Emancipation* (Philadelphia: Jewish Publication Society, 1984), 130.

5. *Ibid.*, 130.

6. *Ibid*.

7. *Ibid.*, 131; Korn, *American Jewry*, 13.

8. Korn, *American Jewry*, 13.

9. Washburne to Lincoln, January 7, 1863, OR, Series 1, Vol. 18, pt. 1, 544.

10. *The Israelite*, March 22, 1861, 300; March 29, 1861, 308.

11. *The Israelite*, November 4, 1864, 148.

12. *The Israelite*, November 4, 1864, 148.

13. *Ibid*.

14. The Belmont Stakes, the third leg of horseracing's Triple Crown, is named after Belmont, who inaugurated the race in 1867.

15. *Chicago Tribune*, quoted in *The Israelite*, September 1864.

16. *Philadelphia Illustrated New Age*, November 2, 1864, 2. On the alleged influence of the Rothschilds in American politics, see Glanz's chapter, "The Rothschild Legend in America," in *Studies*, 358–383.

17. Quoted by Kurt F. Stone, *The Jews of Capitol Hill* (Lanham, MD: Scarecrow Press, 2011), 18.

18. *The Israelite*, September 16, 1864, 2.

19. Charles Francis Adams, *An Autobiography* (Boston: Houghton Mifflin Co., 1916), 94–95.

20. Moos to Johnson, September 16, 1864, Graf, *Papers of Andrew Johnson*, 168.

21. *Ibid*.

22. George M. D. Bloss, *Life and Speeches of George H. Pendleton* (Cincinnati: Miami Print and Publishing Co., 1868), 50.

23. Bertram W. Korn, "Congressman Clement L. Vallingham's Championship of the Jewish Chaplaincy in the Civil War," *American Jewish Historical Quarterly* 53 (December 1963), 188–191.

24. Cohen to Lincoln, September 1, 1863, *Jewish Record*, October 24, 1862, 2.

25. "John A. McAllister's Civil War: The Philadelphia Home Front," http://www.librarycompany.org/mcallisterexhibition/section5.htm. This document was discovered by Jonathan Sarna in a collection of 19th-century Jewish-American documents donated to Princeton University. Other than its existence, nothing is known about the organization or its members.
26. Isaacs to Lincoln, October 26, 1864, ABL LOC.
27. *Jewish Messenger*, October 28, 1864, 124.
28. Hay to Isaacs, November 1, 1864, ABL LOC.
29. Samuel A. Lewis to Lincoln, October 26, 1864, *ibid*.
30. Zacharie to Lincoln, November 3, 1864, ABL LOC.
31. The phrase "my good and faithful servant" is unusual for a Jew to say since it is taken from the New Testament (Matthew 25:14–30). Issachar's sending his regards to Mary implies he was also on good terms with her, although Mary never mentioned him in any of her letters or recorded comments.
32. Allen Nevins, *The War for the Union* (New York: Charles Scribners and Sons, 1959), Vol. 7, 138.
33. George Templeton Strong, November 8, 1864, *Diary* (New York: Macmillan, 1952), 510.
34. Howard B. Rock, *Haven of Liberty: New York Jews in the New World, 1654–1865* (New York: New York University Press, 2012), 247.

Chapter 23

1. W. T. Sherman to Abraham Lincoln, December 22, 1864, ABL LOC.
2. Zacharie to Lincoln, December 26, 1864, ABL LOC.
3. *New York Herald*, January 21, 1865, 1.
4. Pass for J. G. Cohen, quoted in Jonathan D. Sarna and Benjamin Shapell, *Lincoln and the Jews, A History* (New York: Thomas Dunne Books, 2015), 182.
5. Lincoln, "pass for Issachar Zacharie," Brown University, https://repository.library.brown.edu/studio/item/bdr:72290/.
6. Lincoln to Sherman, December 27, 1864, Brown University, https://repository.library.brown.edu/studio/item/bdr:72290/.
7. Zacharie to Lincoln, December 1864, ABL LOC.
8. *Springfield* (Massachusetts) *Republican*, December 29, 1864, 2.
9. "Edwin Stanton's Whipping Boy," https://www.historynet.com/edwin-stantons-whipping-boy.htm; Binzel, personal communication.
10. *New York Times*, January 6, 1865, 4.
11. *New York Herald*, January 21, 1865, 1.
12. A few months after Issachar's visit, due to wounds he had earlier suffered in battle, he relinquished his command and was reassigned to another, less demanding command in Florida. After the war, he remained in the army and developed techniques for underwater demolition. John G. Foster biography, http://www.thelatinlibrary.com/chron/civilwarnotes/foster.html, accessed December 13, 2015.
13. *New York Herald*, January 21, 1865, 1.
14. *Ibid*.
15. *Ibid*.
16. *Ibid*.
17. *Sacramento Daily Union*, February 20, 1865, 1; (New Orleans) *Times-Picayune*, February 2, 1865, 7; *Rochester* (New York) *Daily Union and Advertiser*, January 24, 1865, 1.
18. *Detroit Free Press*, January 11, 1865, 2.
19. Segal, "Isachar Zacharie," 118.
20. *Ibid*., 86.
21. John Chipman Gray and John Codman Ropes, *War Letters 1862–1865* (Boston, MA: Houghton Mifflin Co., 1927), 442. On Gray, Ezra R. Thayer, Samuel Williston, and Joseph Beale, "John Chipman Gray," *Harvard Law Review* 28 (April 1915), 539–549.
22. Rosen, *Jewish Confederates*, 55–58. I thank William Binzel for alerting me to this and other instances of Stanton's and Yulee's interactions. Other than John Gray, no one accused Stanton of anti–Semitism, and Stanton's actions on behalf of Yulee and Wolf speak otherwise.
23. Hurlbut was later accused of illicit trading and stealing silver sequestered at the Custom House, and he resigned his commissions to avoid court martial. Jeffery H. Lash, *A Politician Turned General* (Kent, OH: Kent State University Press, 2003), 169–170.
24. Simon Wolf, *The Presidents I Have Known from 1860–1918* (Washington, D.C.: Byron S. Adams, 1918), 10. Wolf's *American Jew as Patriot* documented the service

of Jews in the Civil War in both the Union and the Confederacy.
   25. *New York World*, January 30, 1865, 5.
   26. *Columbia* (Connecticut) *Register*, February 4, 1865, 2.
   27. Lincoln to Stanton, January 25, 1865, Basler, *Collected Works*, Vol. 8, 238.
   28. Stanton to Lincoln, January 25, 1865, ABL LOC.
   29. Lincoln to Stanton, January 25, 1865, Basler, *Collected Works*, Vol. 8, 238.
   30. Stanton to Lincoln, January 25, 1865, ABL LOC.
   31. Bertram W. Korn, "Lincoln and the Jews," *Journal of the Illinois State Historical Society* 48 (Summer 1955), 181–182.
   32. Zacharie to Lincoln, undated, ABL LOC.
   33. *New York Herald*, January 26, 1865, 5.

Chapter 24

   1. *Philadelphia Inquirer*, April 14, 1865; June 9, 1865; March 21, 1867; (New York) *Daily Graphic*, March 14, 1873.
   2. *New York Herald*, July 8, 1869, 10.
   3. *New York Evening Telegraph*, March 20, 1867, 8.
   4. *Phoenix* (AZ) *Weekly Republican*, October 4, 1900, 6.
   5. *Ibid.*, October 15, 1870, Banks Papers, Box 51.
   6. Zacharie to Banks, October 15, 1870, Banks Papers, Box 51.
   7. Zacharie Banks, March 23, 1872, Banks Papers, Box 51.
   8. Ron Chernow, *Grant* (New York: Penguin Press, 2017), 609–611.
   9. Zacharie to Banks, October 21, 1868, Banks Papers, Box 51.
   10. Chernow, *Grant*, 615.
   11. *Richmond Whig*, August 11, 1868, 1.
   12. Brooks D. Simpson, *The Reconstruction Presidents* (Lawrence: University Press of Kansas, 1998), 133.
   13. Jonathan D. Sarna, *When General Grant Expelled the Jews* (New York: Schocken Books, 2012), 66.
   14. Quoted by Chernow, *Grant*, 617.
   15. A detailed analysis of divisions among Jews with respect to Grant in the 1868 election can be found in Sarna, *Grant*, 50–79.
   16. *The Israelite*, February 28, 1868, 4.
   17. Sarna, *Grant*, 60.
   18. *Ibid.*, 77.
   19. *New York Times*, November 30, 1868, 4.
   20. Sarna, *Grant*, 77; Chernow, *Grant*, 623.
   21. Philip Quilbet, "Cheap Notoriety," *The Galaxy* 7 (April 1869), 596.
   22. *New York Herald*, November April 23, 1869, 7.
   23. *Ibid.*, April 24, 1869, 7.
   24. Sarna, *Grant*, 83–84, 87–90.
   25. Mark Twain and Charles Dudley Warner, *The Gilded Age* (Chicago: American Publishing Co., 1873).
   26. Thomas A. Bailey, *Presidential Saints and Sinners* (New York: Free Press, 1981), 101.
   27. *Ibid.*
   28. Zacharie to Banks, May 13, 1872, Banks Papers, Box 51.
   29. Banks to wife, March 9, 30, April 14, May 7, 11, 1869; May 23; July 1, 1870, Banks Papers, Box 5.
   30. R. Banks, *King of Louisiana*, 1435.
   31. Harrington, *Fighting Politician*, 210.
   32. Zacharie to Banks, May 13, 1872, Banks Papers, Box 51.
   33. *New York Evening Post*, July 9, 1872, 3.
   34. *Brooklyn Daily Eagle*, July 16, 1872, 2, 7.
   35. *Chicago Post*, July 18, 1872, 2.
   36. *Boston Traveler*, July 18, 1872, 4.
   37. *Sacramento Daily Union*, July 19, 1872.
   38. Zacharie to Banks, July 23, 1872, Banks Papers, Box 51.
   39. *New York World*, August 2, 1872, 1.
   40. *New York Tribune*, July 7, 1872, 5.
   41. *New York Times*, November 30, 1968, 2.
   42. *Ibid.* 4.
   43. Sarna, *Grant*, 82–103.
   44. *New York Times*, August 17, 1872, 1
   45. *New York Tribune*, October 7, 1861, 6.
   46. *Jewish Messenger*, August 8, 1872, 4.
   47. Zacharie to Banks, August 1, 1872, Banks Papers, Box 51.
   48. *Ibid.* August 3, 1872, Banks Papers, Box 51.
   49. *Ibid.*
   50. *Ibid.*
   51. *Ibid.* August 4, 1872, Banks Papers, Box 51.
   52. *Ibid.* August 3, 1872, Banks Papers, Box 51.
   53. *Ibid.* March 28, 1874.

54. Banks remained in Congress off and on until 1890, when he finally retired. He died in 1894.

55. *New York Herald*, August 5, 1873, 7.

56. A copy of the handwritten note is reproduced in Jonathan D. Sarna and Benjamin Shapell, *Lincoln and the Jews, A History* (New York: Thomas Dunne Books, 2015), 185. When Issachar reprinted Grant's letter in his testimonial book, he changed the text of the letter. In place of the words after "slightest pain," he substituted "and now some time since the operation, I must say that his operations [implying more than one] have been effectual." I. Zacharie (comp.), *Testimonials to I. Zacharie* (London: privately published, 1875), 6.

57. George Alfred Townsend, *Washington, Outside and Inside* (Cincinnati, OH: James Betts & Co., 1874), 112–116.

Chapter 25

1. James Stuart Olson, *Encyclopedia of the Industrial Revolution in America* (Westport, CT: Greenwood Press, 2002), 191.

2. Quoted by Michael A. Bellesiles, *1877: America's Year of Living Violently* (New York: New Press, 2010), 1.

3. Barton A. Myers, *Rebels against the Confederacy* (New York: Cambridge University Press, 2014), 233–235.

4. House of Representatives (HR), 43rd Congress, 2nd Session, 1874–75, Report No. 142. (Washington, D.C.: Government Printing Office, 1875), 130.

5. HR, 43rd Congress, 1st Session, Report No. 817, 124.

6. Lincoln and Seward to Zacharie, September 23, 1862, HR 43rd Congress, 1st Session, Report No. 817, 123.

7. Stanton to Zacharie, September 24, 1862, *ibid*.

8. General Tucker Black to Zacharie, November 21, 1862, *ibid*.

9. Zacharie to Banks, June 1, 1874, Banks Papers, Box 51.

10. Banks to Zacharie, June [?] 1874, in Banks manuscript, copy in Segal, "Isachar Zacharie," 120–121.

11. HR, 43rd Congress, 1st Session, Report 817, 123–126. In fact, Congress did approve payment of $6,719 to Colonel Jacques "for services performed and money expended" visiting Richmond on several occasions "acting under instructions." The payment, Louisiana Congressman Frank Morey, the bill's sponsor, said, had been approved by Lincoln and would have been paid but for the untimely death of the President. Congressional Globe, 42nd Congress, Third Session, 1873, Vol. 46, pt. 2, 1020. Although Lincoln had approved Jacques' mission, he made it clear he was acting on his own, and not, as Jaques claimed, "employed by the late President Lincoln in the secret service of the Government."

12. (Chicago) *Daily Inter Ocean*, February 18, 1874, 3.

13. (New York) *Daily Graphic*, May 15, 1875, 3.

14. *Indiana Herald*, May 27, 1875, 2.

15. *Biloxi* (Mississippi) *Herald*, September 22, 1888, 6. Twenty years later, an editorial in the *New York Times* cited Issachar's claim as one of a number of "Freaks of Legislation. Odd Bills and Reports to Congressional Committees…. There was perhaps no better example of one of these doubtful and musing claims," it chuckled, "than that of Issachor [sic] Zacharie, a gentleman learned in the profession of extracting corns, who plied his trade during the war of the rebellion." To illustrate how "freakish" his claim was, it reproduced much of the War Committee's report verbatim. *New York Times*, January 14, 1896, 10.

16. Reprinted in the *Indiana State Sentinel*, May 20, 1875, 6.

17. *New York Times*, January 14, 1896, 10.

Chapter 26

1. *London Morning Post*, Aug. 30, 1875, 8.

2. *The Business Directory of London* (London; J.S.C. Morris, 1884), 736.

3. *Royal Blue Book: Court and Parliamentary Guide* for May 1897 and January 1900 (London: Kelly's Directories), 1429.

4. *Pall Mall Gazette*, August 6, 1875, 15; *Masonic Standard*, August 7, 1875, 4.

5. Thomas Dent Mutter was one of the most famous surgeons of his day, renowned not only for his skill, but also for performing surgical procedures in front of an audience of other physicians. The Mutter Medical Museum in Philadelphia is named after him.

6. *London Morning Post*, Aug. 30, 1875, 8.

7. *Masonic Standard*, Nov. 3, 1900, 19.

8. Dagnall, "Issachar Zacharie," 231.

9. *Freemasons and Masonic Illustrated*, September 29, 1900, 568.

10. *Washington Evening Star*, March 2, 1880, 4.
11. *Ibid.*
12. *London Medical Press and Circular* 29 (March 10, 1880), 199–200. On Fairbank, *Transactions of the Obstetrical Society of London* 23 (1882), 155.
13. *Our Society Journal*, 13 (August 1890), 14.
14. *London Morning Post*, September 25, 1880, 7; *Lloyd's Weekly Newspaper*, October 3, 1880, 3.
15. Issachar's Masonic activities are summarized in *The Freemason's Chronicle*, October 24, 1896, 196.
16. The order was based on the scriptural story of the enduring Biblical friendship between David and Johnathan. In 1937, to commemorate the order's Jubilee, the order created a pendant to mark the occasion. The pendant had a star of David at its center and "DJ" in the center of the star, standing for the Biblical friendship of David and Jonathan. Beneath the star was the Latin motto *Semper Fidelis* (always faithful). *Semper Fi(delis)* was adopted as the Marine Corps' mottos in 1883.
17. *The Masonic Review* 74 (1890), 152.
18. *Truth*, June 20, 1895, 1552; *Post Office London Directory for 1895*, pt. 2, 76.
19. William Banting, *Letter on Corpulence, Addressed to the Public* (London: Harrison, 1864). Before becoming the best-selling author of his diet book, Banting had been a funeral director to the Royal family, burying such luminaries as Queen Victoria and Kings George III and IV and Edward VII.
20. Invented by P. W. Seymour, the Magneticon was heralded as a cure-all for every and any ailment. P. W. Seymour, *The Magneticon* (Cheltenham: G. F. Poole, n.d.).
21. *London Morning Post*, September 19, 1894, 6. Mumford listed himself as "surgeon-chiropodist, Late Pupil of the Eminent Dr. Zacharie, London." Mumford dedicated his *The Human Foot: Its Ailments Painlessly Treated* "to my esteemed friend and tutor the late Dr. Zacharie."

Chapter 27

1. *New York Herald*, September 17, 1900, 3; March 4, 1906, 1; "Find a Grave, Mary Ann Lawson Zacharie."
2. Dowling Family Genealogy, Roots-Web world, ID: I462961, http://wc.rootsweb.ancestry.com/cgi-bin/igm.cgi?op=GET&db=dowfam3&id=I462961.
3. Amelia and Clara were the only children mentioned in Issachar's estate. England & Wales, *National Probate Calendar (Index of Wills and Administrations)*, 1858–1966, probate date November 1, 1900, ancestry.com 1900 England and Wales Probate.
4. Divorce Court File, 368, Appellant: Joseph Edward Hughes. Respondent: Amelia Lavinia Hughes. Co-respondent: John William Hughes. http://discovery.naitonalarchives.gov.uk/details/r/C7983605, accessed December 14, 2018.
5. Ancestry.com.
6. *Ibid.*
7. *Ibid.*
8. *Boston Globe*, July 22, 1893, 4.
9. *London Standard*, September 30, 1891, 3.
10. *Boston Globe*, July 23, 1893, 4.
11. *Ibid.*
12. *Boston Globe*, November 16, 1889, 5.
13. *Pharmaceutical Journal*, January 17, 1908, 71.
14. Ancestry.com.
15. *Pall Mall Gazette*, January 21, 1881, 5, www.myheritage.com/names/victoria_Zacharie, accessed November 29, 2018.
16. Adolph, born 1882 (died 1930), Mariposa, born 1883, and Edith Constance Blumenthal, born 1891, www.myheritage.com/names/edith_Blumental, accessed June 24, 2018.
17. *Bristol Mercury and Daily Post*, September 12, 1894, 6.
18. *Ibid.*
19. An Act of Parliament of the United Kingdom of Great Britain and Ireland (Ottawa: Samuel Edward Dawson, 1908) 137–138. Their son Beaumont Edward Zacharie Gammell served as a Lieutenant in the Royal Air Force in World War I and died in April 1918, seven months before the war ended.
20. Charles C., Samuel, Florence Mariposa, and Marian.
21. *New York Tribune*, August 7, 1901, 14. Major Charles C. Zacharie served as a physician in the American army during World War I. He died in 1948. Charles' daughter Marian married Samuel Stayton, one of the first families of Milford, Delaware. Her maid of honor was her sister, Florence Mariposa. Charles C. Zacharie was the groom's best

man (*Seneca* Falls) *County Courier-Journal*, October 8, 1903, 1.
22. *Official Gazette of the United States Patent Office*, 37 (December 7, 1886), 1076.
23. England & Wales, *National Probate Calendar (Index of Wills and Administrations)*, 1858–1966, probate date November 1, 1900, ancestry.com1900 England and Wales Probate.
24. *New York Herald*, September 17, 1900, 10.
25. *Baltimore Sun*, September 17, 1900, 2.
26. *Charleston Evening Post*, September 19, 1900, 10.
27. (New Orleans) *Times-Picayune*, September 17, 1900, 10.
28. *New York Herald*, September 17, 1900, 3.
29. *Ibid.*
30. *Freemason and Masonic Illustrated*, 39 (September 29, 1900), 568.
31. *Freemason Chronicle*, September 29, 1900, 147.
32. *Ibid.*
33. *Masonic Standard*, November 3, 1900, 19.
34. *Freemason's Chronicle*, September 29, 1900, 147.
35. *Freemason and Masonic Illustrated*, 39 (September 29, 1900), 569.
36. *Freemason's Chronicle*, September 29, 1900, 147. Issachar is not listed in J. S. Harfield's *Commercial Directory of the Jews of the United Kingdom* (London: Hewlett & Pierce, 1894).
37. *Freemason Chronicle*, October 27, 1900, 194; *Masonic Standard*, November 3, 1900, 19.

Chapter 28

1. *Jewish Messenger*, June 20, 1890, 5.
2. Adams, *Politics*, 6.
3. *Ibid.*, 139.
4. *Jewish Messenger*, June 29, 1877.
5. Simon Wolf, *Selected Addresses and Papers of Simon Wolf* (Cincinnati: Union of Hebrew Congregations, 1926), 105.
6. Isaac Markens, *The Hebrew in America* (New York: privately published, 1888).
7. *Ibid.*, 130–131.
8. Wolf, *American Jew as Patriot*.
9. J. M. Rogers, "Jewish Soldiers in the Union Army," *North American Review* 153 (1891), 761–762.
10. Markens "Lincoln," 109–165.

11. *Ibid.*, 163.
12. *Ibid.*, 164.
13. Isaac Markens, "Jews Close to Lincoln," *The Advocate: America's Jewish Journal* (February 28, 1914), 89.
14. *Ibid.*
15. Louis Sterne, *Seventy Years of an Active Life* (London: privately published, 1912), 72.
16. Sander L. Gilman and Steven I. Katz, *Anti-Semitism in Times of Crisis* (New York: New York University Press, 1993), 10.
17. Leon Spitz, "Reflections on Lincoln," *Wisconsin Jewish Chronicle*, February 9, 1945, 1.
18. *Ibid.*
19. Bertram Jonas, "Exploding a Myth," *The Sentinel*, February 8, 1934, 6. Jonas was rumored to be a pseudonym for Philip Hochstein, editor of the *Newark Star Ledger* and the *New York Jewish Week*. Michael E. Staub, *Torn at the Roots: Jewish Liberalism in Crisis* (Columbia University Press, 2002), 188. Jonas wrote several other articles defending Jews against their enemies (e.g., "If Broadway Went Aryan," *American Jewish World*, January 17, 1936, 5) and continued writing up into the 1970s: "When El Fatah Goes to Shul," *Jewish Week*, September 2, 1971, 1; "Refugees from the Jewish Pulpit," *Canadian Jewish Chronicle*, October 18, 1945, 5, 16; "When Lincoln Fought Bigotry," *Jewish Spectator*, 1938, v, 33–35.
20. *Ibid.*
21. *Ibid.*
22. *Ibid.*
23. Alberta A. Woldman, "Lincoln's Jewish Doctor," B'nai Brith National *Jewish Monthly*, February 1937, 189; 1938, 248; *Fort Myers (Florida) News-Press*, March, 9, 1940, 3; *Detroit Free Press*, March 9, 1940, 4; *Wisconsin Jewish Chronicle*, March 22, 1940, 6; *Cleveland Plain Dealer*, March 9, 1940, 14.
24. *The Sentinel*, March 28, 1940, 35.
25. Quoted by the *Indianapolis Jewish Post*, April 6, 1940, 5. As those more worthy, the *Advocate* cited. among others, Judah Benjamin, "U.S. Senator from Louisiana, and one of the heroes of the Southern Confederacy."
26. Louis Gershenfeld, *The Jew in Science* (Philadelphia: Jewish Publication Society of America, 1934) 182; Solomon R. Kagan, *Jewish Contributions to Pittsburg Post-Gazette Medicine in America from Colonial Times to*

the Present (Boston, MA: Boston Medical Publishing Co., 1939), 274.

27. *Pittsburg Post-Gazette*, March 27, 1941, 2; *Greenfield* (Indiana) *Daily Reporter* July 30, 1941, 8; *Corpus Christi* (Texas) *Caller Times*, March 17, 1941, 3; *Winchester* (Kansas) *Star*, August 22, 1941, 3; *Urbana* (Virginia) *Southside Sentinel*, September 11, 1941, 7; *Aiken* (South Carolina) *Standard*, August 22, 1941, 3.

28. *Pittsburg Post-Gazette*, March 27, 1941, 2.

29. *Wisconsin Jewish Chronicle*, February 8, 1946, 7. The pinochle game was also reported by the *Indianapolis Jewish Post*, February 8, 1946, 17.

30. David Schwartz, "Abe Lincoln and Zion. His Thoughts on a Jewish Home," *The Sentinel* (February 10, 1949), 11.

31. *Wisconsin Jewish Chronicle*, February 6, 1959, 7.

32. *Ibid.*, September 30, 1959, 1.

33. Korn, *American Jewry*, 230–239. An earlier history by Charles Segal, "Isachar Zacharie," had also highlighted Issachar's now forgotten career and relationship with Lincoln, but that biography was mainly read by academic historians.

34. Eugene Friedberg, "Issachar Zacharie," *Journal of the National Association of Chiropodists* 44 (April 1954), 36.

35. *Ibid.*, 38.

36. *Honolulu Star-Bulletin*, April 28, 1950.

37. *Bloomington* (Indiana) *Pantagraph*, May 6, 1950, 7.

38. *Cleveland Plain Dealer*, September 20, 1950, 19; *Seattle Daily Times*, August 16, 1950, 27; *Canton* (Ohio) *Repository*, July 28, 1950, 16; *St. Louis Obispo Telegram-Tribune*, July 27, 1950; *Lexington* (Kentucky) *Leader*, August 1, 1950, 7.

39. Christopher Morley, "Lincoln's Doctor's Dog," *The Saturday Review* 38 (February 12, 1955), 9–10, 40–42.

40. *Petaluma* (California) *Argus-Courier*, July 1, 1960), 2.

41. David Schwartz, "Lincoln's Corn Doctor," *Wisconsin Jewish Chronicle*, February 12, 1960, 7.

42. *Fort Myers* (Florida) *News Press*, April 23, 1961, 5.

43. *Rapid City* (South Dakota) *Journal*, April 23, 1961, 2.

44. *Palm Beach* (Florida) April 23, 1961, 34.

45. *Minneapolis Star Tribune*, April 23, 1861, 13.

46. *Hartford* (Connecticut) *Courant*, April 23, 1961, 4.

47. *Corpus Christi* (Texas) *Caller-Times*, April 23, 1961, 6.

48. *Arizona Republic*, May 1, 1964, 1; March 15, 1967. The Hudson Country Podiatry Society said it had tried unsuccessfully "to revive interest in restoring the office in today's modern army." *Jersey City* (New Jersey) *Journal*, February 11, 1970, 22.

49. *Indianapolis Star*, June 18, 1978, 18.

50. *Wisconsin Jewish Chronicle*, February 10, 1967, 8.

51. Harry Bloch, "Issachar Zacharie (1827–1900): A Chiropodist of the 19th Century," *Journal of the American Podiatry Association* 61 (May 1971), 180–185.

52. *Philadelphia Inquirer*, April 5, 1987, 59.

53. Jonathan D. Sarna and Benjamin Shapell, *Lincoln and the Jews, A History* (New York: Thomas Dunne Books, 2015), 126.

54. https://historynewsnetwork.org/article/150822.

55. Korn, *American Jewry*, 201.

56. Segal, "Isachar Zacharie," 122.

57. *New York World*, September 24, 1864, 4.

58. *New York Herald*, October 3, 1862, 2; Zacharie to Lincoln, February 19, 1863, ABL LOC.

59. *Melbourne Argus*, April 14, 1865, 7. Joe Miller was an English actor in the early 18th century whose name became an eponym ("Millerism") for current and bawdy jokes. John Mottley, *Joe Miller's Complete Jest Book: Being a Collection of the Most Excellent Bon Mots, Brilliant Jests, and Striking Anecdotes in the English Language* (London: H. N. G. Bohn, 1859).

60. Zola, *We Called Him Rabbi*, 45–46.

61. Segal, "Isachar Zacharie," 122.

62. Mitchel Abidor, "Honest Abe and the Children of Abraham. Much Ado About the Inconsequential," *Jewish Currents*, http://jewishcurrents.org/honest-abe-and-the-children-of-abraham-e7756, accessed July 28, 2015).

63. Zola, *We Called Him Rabbi*, 53.

64. The phrase, with a change of tense, is from William Faulkner's *Requiem for a Nun*.

65. Walt Whitman, "Song of Myself," 1.1, https://whitmanarchive.org/published/LG/1891/poems/27.

66. Whitman appended "anonymous" reviews to the end of his 1860 edition of *Leaves of Grass*, praising his own greatness. James Franco, "'Song of Myself' Why Walt Whitman Was the Original Kayne West," https://www.vice.com/en_us/article/8gdne5/walt-whitman-was-the-original-kanye.
67. *Businessinsider.com*, May 7, 2012; *New York Times*, April 26, 2019.
68. Zola, *We Called Him Rabbi*, 53.
69. *Jewish Messenger*, May 13, 1864, 141.
70. *Ibid.* Issachar's name is listed in the 1850s among the new member of Congregation Mikveh Israel in Savannah when he visited his parents (Rubin, *Third to None*, 129), and he kept abreast of national and international events affecting Jews through his subscription to the *Jewish Messenger*. Historian Charles Segal contended that Issachar was a Jew in name only. Segal considered him an "oddity" rather than a figure of importance in American Jewish history (Segal, "Isachar Zacharie," 122).
71. Zola, *We Called Him Rabbi*, 53.

Bibliography

Government and Local Documents

Commission on Corrupt Practices in the South, four volumes; RG 94, Records of the Adjutant General's Office, 1780's–1914.
Congressional Series of the United States Public Documents, Vol. 1627, 43rd Congress, House of Representatives (HR), Committee on War Claims.
House of Representatives (HR), 43rd Congress, 2d Session, 1874-'75, Report No. 142. Washington, D.C.: Government Printing Office, 1875.
House of Representatives (HR), 43rd Congress, 2d Session, 1874-'75, Report No. 743. Washington, D.C.: Government Printing Office, 1875.
House of Representatives (HR) 43rd Congress, 2d Session, 1874-'75, Report No. 787. Washington, D.C.: Government Printing Office, 1875.
Medway Archives and Local Studies Center.
National Archives and Records Administration, Department of the Gulf, Register of Letters Received, RG 393.

Books and Articles

Abel, E. Lawrence. *A Finger in Lincoln's Brain*. Santa Barbara, CA: Praeger, 2015.
Abel, Ernest L. "Maryland-born James Ryder Randall Penned One of the Civil War's Most Stirring Songs in Honor of His State." *America's Civil War* (July 1988), 78–82.
Abidor, Mitchel. "Honest Abe and the Children of Abraham. Much Ado about the Inconsequential." *Jewish Currents*. http://jewishcurrents.org/honest-abe-and-the-children-of-abraham-e7756.
Abrahamsohn, Abraham. *An Interesting Account of the Travels of Abraham Abrahamsohn to America, especially to the Goldmines of California and Australia*, reprinted in Ava F. Kahn (ed.), *Jewish Voices of the California Gold Rush. A Documentary History, 1849–1880*. Detroit: Wayne State University Press, 2002.
Adams, Charles Francis. *An Autobiography*. Boston: Houghton Mifflin Co., 1916.
Adams, Peter. *Politics, Faith and the Making of American Judaism*. Ann Arbor: University of Michigan Press, 2014.
Anbinder, Tyler. *City of Dreams: The 400-Year Epic History of Immigrant New York*. Boston, MA: Houghton Mifflin Harcourt, 2016.
Ash, Stephen V. "Civil War Exodus. The Jews and Grant's General Order No. 11," in Adam Mendelsohn (ed.). *Jews and the Civil War; A Reader*. New York: New York University Press, 2010.
Ashkenazi, Elliott. *The Business of Jews in Louisiana, 1840–1875*. Tuscaloosa: University of Alabama Press, 1988.
Bailey, Thomas A. *Presidential Saints and Sinners*. New York: Free Press, 1981.

Baltzell, E. Digby. *Philadelphia Gentlemen: The Making of a National Upper Class.* New Brunswick: Transaction Publishers, 2011.
Banks, Raymond H. *King of Louisiana, 1862–1865, and Other Government Work. A Biography of Major General Nathaniel Prentice Banks, Speaker of the U.S. House of Representatives.* Las Vegas, NV: R. H. Banks, 200.
Banting, William. *Letter on Corpulence, Addressed to the Public.* London: Harrison, 1864.
Baracca, Angelo, Jungen Renn, and Helge Vendt (eds.). *The History of Physics in Cuba.* New York: Springer, 2014.
Barber, Joseph. *War Letters of a Disbanded Volunteer: Embracing His Experiences as Honest Old Abe's Bosom Friend and Unofficial Adviser.* New York: Frederick A. Brady, 1864.
Barnes, Michael F. "Presentation on the Order." www.orderofthesecretmonitor.co.unk/News_27.html, accessed July 19, 2015.
Basler, Roy, ed. *Collected Works of Abraham Lincoln.* New Brunswick, NJ: Rutgers University Press, 1953.
Bellesiles, Michael A. *1877: America's Year of Living Violently.* New York: New Press, 2010.
Benjamin, I.J. *Three Years in America, 1859–1862.* Philadelphia: Jewish Publication Society of America, 1956.
Bentley, Elizabeth P. *Passenger Arrivals at the Port of New York 1830–1832.* Baltimore: Genealogical Publishing Co., 2000.
Berkowitz, Henry. "Notes on the History of the Earliest German Jewish Congregation in America." *Publications of the American Jewish Historical Society* 9 (1901), 123–127.
Bieder, Alexander. "Sephardim in Eastern Europe." http://www.avotaynu.com/sephardim.htm, accessed September 12, 2015.
Blaisdell, Albert F. *Our Bodies and How We Live: An Elementary Text-Book of Physiology.* Boston: Lee and Shepard, 1891.
Bloch, Harry. "Issachar Zacharie (1827–1900) A Chiropodist of the 19th century." *Journal of the American Podiatry Association* 61 (May 1971), 180–185
Bloss, George, M.D. *Life and Speeches of George H. Pendleton.* Cincinnati: Miami Print and Publishing Co., 1868.
Boritt, Gabor S. *Lincoln and the Economics of the American Dream.* Urbana: University of Illinois Press, 1994.
Bourne, Edward G. (ed.). *Diary and Correspondence of Salmon P. Chase.* Washington, D.C.: American Historical Association, 1902.
Brands, H.W. *The Man Who Saved the Union: Ulysses Grant in War and Peace.* New York: Random House, 2012.
Brooks, David. *The Road to Character.* New York: Random House, 2015.
Brown, Malcolm, and Judith Samuel. "The Jews of Bath." *Jewish Historical Society of England* 29 (1982–1986), 150–168.
Brown University Digital Repository. https://repository.library.brown.edu/studio/item/bdr.
Burrows, Edwin G., and Mike Wallace. *Gotham. A History of New York City to 1898* New York: Oxford University Press, 1999.
Butler, Benjamin F. *Autobiography and Personal Reminiscences of Major-General Benj. F. Butler, Butler's Book.* Boston: A. M. Thayer & Co., 1892.
Butler, Benjamin F., and Jessie Ames Marshall. *Private and Official Correspondence of Gen. F. Butler.* Privately published, 1917.
Cadwaller, Sylvanus. *Three Years with Grant* (Lincoln: University of Nebraska Press, 1996).
Chernow, Ron. *Grant.* New York: Penguin Press, 2017.
Cohen, Marcie Ferris, and Mark I. Greenberg. *Jewish Roots in Southern Soil: A New History.* Waltham, MA: Brandeis University, 2006.
Cohen, Naomi W. *Encounter with Emancipation. The German Jews in the United States 1830–1914.* Philadelphia: Jewish Publication Society, 1984.

Cordell, Eugene F. *The Medical Annals of Baltimore.* Baltimore: Williams & Wilkins, 1903.
Dagnall, J. C. "Isachar Zacharie, an Incompleted Study." *British Journal of Chiropody* 22 (1957), 228–229.
Dagnall, J. Colin. "The English Influence on the Beginnings of American Podiatry," in Lisbeth M. Molloway, *A Fast Pace Forward.* Philadelphia, Pennsylvania College of Podiatric Medicine, 1987, 6–18.
Dagnall, J. Colin. "The History of Chiropodial Literature." *The chiropodist* 20 (July 1965), 173–184.
Dana, Charles A. *Recollections of the Civil War. With the Leaders at Washington and In the Field in the Sixties.* New York: D. Appleton and Co., 1909.
Danziger, Gustav Adolf. "The Jew in San Francisco: The Last Half Century." *Overland Monthly and Out West Magazine* 25 (April 1895), 381–410.
Deutsch, Gotthard Deutsch. "Mortara Case." *Jewish Encyclopedia*, Vol. 9. New York: Funk and Wagnalls, 1905.
Dick, Everett. *The Dixie Frontier: A Social History of the Southern Frontier from the First Transmontane Beginnings to the Civil War.* Norman: University of Oklahoma Press, 1948.
Dickens, Charles. *The Pickwick Papers.* Originally published, 1837. New York: Books, Inc., 1867.
Dickens, Charles. *The Uncommercial Traveler and Additional Christmas Stories.* Boston: Houghton, Good and Co., 1879.
Dietz, Robert Edwin, and Frederick Dietz. *1913: A Leaf from the Past: Then and Now.* New York: R.E. Dietz Company, 1914.
Diner, Hasia R. "Buying and selling 'Jewish': The Historical impact of Commerce on Jewish Communal Life." In Jack Wertheim (ed.), *Imagining the American Jewish Community.* (Waltham, MA: Brandeis University Press, 2007), 28–46.
Dinnenhoefer, Abram J. *How We Elected Lincoln: Personal Recollections of Lincoln and Men of His Time.* New York: Harper Brothers, 1916.
Dinnerstein, Leonard. *Antisemitism in America.* New York: Oxford University Press, 1994.
Dorchester, Daniel. *Latest Drink Sophistries versus Total Abstinence.* Boston: Frank Wood, 1883.
Doyle, Elisabeth J. "Greenbacks, Car Tickets, and the Pot of Gold: The Effects of Wartime Occupation on the Business Life of New Orleans, 1861–1865." *Civil War History*, 5 (December 1959), 347–362.
Durlacher, Lewis. *A Treatise on Corns, Bunions, the Diseases of Nails, and the General Management of the Feet.* Philadelphia: Lea & Blanchard, 1845.
Edel, Leon. *Henry James. The Untried Years.* Philadelphia: J. B. Lippincott, 1953.
Egan, Clifford L. "Friction in New Orleans: General Butler versus the Spanish Consul." *Louisiana History* 9 (Winter 1968), 43–52.
Eisenberg, John. *Surgical and Practical Observations on the Diseases of the Human Foot; with Instructions for Their Treatment. To Which Is Added Advice on the Management of the Hand.* London: John Eisenberg, 1845.
Eleff, Zev. *Who Rules the Synagogue? Religious Authority and the Formation of American Judaism.* New York: Oxford University Press, 2016.
Ellis, Franklin. *History of Cattaraugus Co., New York.* Philadelphia: L. H. Everts, 1879.
Elzas, Barnett A. "Leaves from My Historical Scrap Book." *Charleston Sunday News*, no. 6 (March 2, 1908), 4.
Elzas, Barnett Abraham. *The Jews of South Carolina: From the Earliest Times to the Present Day.* Philadelphia: J. B. Lippincott, 1905.
Engelman, Uriah Z. "The Jewish Population of Charleston: What Stunted Its Growth and Prevented Its Decline?" *Jewish Social Studies* 13 (July 1951), 195–210.
Epstein, Lawrence J. *A Treasury of Jewish Anecdotes.* Northvale, NJ: Jason Aronson, 1989.

Errington, Elizabeth Jane. *Emigrant Worlds and Transatlantic Communities: Migration to Upper Canada.* Montreal, Canada: McGill-Queen's University Press, 2007.

Evans, Eli N. *Judah P. Benjamin. The Jewish Confederate.* New York: The Free Press, 1987.

Evans, Eli N. "The War Between Jewish Brothers in America," in Jonathan D. Sarna and Adam Mendelsohn (eds.). *Jews and the Civil War.* New York: New York University Press, 2010, 27–46.

Faust, Drew Gilpin. *Mothers of Invention. Women of the Slaveholding South in the American Civil War.* Chapel Hill, NC: University of North Carolina Press, 1996.

Federal Trade Commission. "FTC Issues Facts for Business Guide on Avoiding Fake Degrees," February, 2005, www.ftc.gov/opa/2005/02/diplomamills.htm.

Fellman, Michael. *Citizen Sherman. A Life of William Tecumseh Sherman.* New York: Random House, 1995.

Fermer, Douglas. *James Gordon Bennett and the* New York Herald: *A Study of Editorial Opinion in the Civil War Era, 1854–1867.* New York: St. Martin's Press, 1986.

Flower, Frank Abial. *Edwin McMasters Stanton: The Autocrat of Rebellion, Emancipation and Reconstruction.* Akron, OH: Saalfield Publishing Company, 1905.

Foster, George G. *New York in Slices: By an Experienced Carver.* New York: W. F. Burgess, 1849.

Freemon, Frank R. *Gangrene and Glory: Medical Care during the American Civil War.* Urbana: University of Illinois Press, 2001.

Friedberg, Eugene. "Issachar Zacharie." *Journal of the National Association of Chiropodists* 44 (April 1954), 36–38.

Friend, Henry C. "Abraham Lincoln and the Court Martial of Surgeon General William A. Hammond." *Commercial Law Journal* (March 1957), 71–78.

Furgurson, Ernest B. *Freedom Rising: Washington in the Civil War.* New York: Vintage Books, 2004.

Gartner, Lloyd P. "Emancipation, Social Change and Communal Reconstruction in Anglo-Jewry 1789–1881." *Proceedings of the American Academy for Jewish Research* 54 (1987), 73–116.

Gershenfeld, Louis. *The Jew in Science.* Philadelphia: Jewish Publication Society of America, 1934.

Gilman, Sander L., and Steven I. Katz. *Anti-Semitism in Times of Crisis.* New York: New York University Press, 1993.

Gilmore, James R. *Personal Recollections of Abraham Lincoln and the Civil War.* London: John Macqueen, 1899.

Glanz, Rudolf. "German-Jewish Names in America." *Jewish Social Studies* 23 (July 1961), 143–169.

Glanz, Rudolf. "Notes on Early Jewish Peddling in America." *Jewish Social Studies* 7 (April 1945), 119–136.

Glanz, Rudolf. *Studies in Judaic Americana.* New York: Ktav Publishing House, 1970.

Goodman, Robert Justin. *Political Repression in 19th Century Europe.* London: Routledge Taylor & Francis, 2013.

Goodwin, Doris Kearns. *Team of Rivals.* New York: Simon & Schuster, 2005.

Gorton, Gary. "Ante Bellum Transportation Indices." Unpublished article. Wharton School, University of Pennsylvania. August 1989, n.p.

Graf, LeRoy P. (ed.) *The Papers of Andrew Jonson: 1864–1865.* Knoxville: University of Tennessee, 1986.

Grant, Julia Dent. *The Personal Memoirs of Julia Dent Grant: Mrs. Ulysses.* John Y. Simon (ed.). New York: Putnam, 1975.

Grant, Ulysses S. *The Papers of Ulysses S. Grant.* John Y. Simon (ed.). Carbondale: Southern Illinois University Press, 1967.

Gray, John Chipman Gray, and John Codman Ropes. *War Letters 1862–1865*. Boston, MA: Houghton Mifflin Co., 1927.
Gray, Wood. *The Hidden Civil War: The Story of the Copperhead*. New York: Viking Press, 1942.
Greenberg, M.I. "Becoming Southern: the Jews of Savannah, Georgia, 1830–70." *American Jewish History,* 86 (March 1998), 55–75.
H. "The Pathology of Drunkenness or the Physical Effects of Alcoholic Drinks, with Drawings of the Drunkards Stomach." *Botanico-Medical Recorder* 11 (1843), 115.
Hagy, James William. *Directories for the City of Charleston, South Carolina for the Years, 1849, 1852, and 1855*. Baltimore, MD: Genealogical Publishing Co., 1998.
Hagy, James William. *This Happy Land: The Jews of Colonial and Antebellum Charleston*. Tuscaloosa: University of Alabama Press, 1993.
Hair, William I. "Stagecoaches and Public Accommodations in Antebellum Georgia." *Georgia Historical Quarterly* 68 (Fall 1984), 323–333.
Halpine, Charles Graham. *The Life and Adventures, Songs, Services, and Speeches of Private Miles O'Reilly*. New York: Carleton Publishers, 1864.
Hammond, William A. *A Statement of the Causes which Led to the Dismissal of Surgeon-General William A. Hammond from the Army (with a Review of the Evidence Adduced before the Court)*. New York: Hammond, 1864.
Harrington, Fred Harvey. *Fighting Politician. Major General N. P. Banks*. Philadelphia: University of Pennsylvania Press, 1948.
Harrington, Fred Harvey. "A Peace Mission of 1863." 46 (October 1940), 76–86.
Harris, Bogardus, and Labbatt Harris. *San Francisco City Directory: For the Year Commencing October 1856*. San Francisco: Whitton, Towne & Co., 1856.
Harris, William C. "The Hampton Roads Peace Conference: A Final Test of Lincoln's Presidential Leadership." *Journal of the Abraham Lincoln Association* 21 (Winter 2000), 30–61.
Haumann, Heiko. *A History of East European Jews*. New York: Central European University Press, 1990.
Hay, John. *Lincoln and the Civil War in the Diaries and Letters of John Hay*. New York: Dodd Mead & Co., 1939.
Hearn, Chester G. *When the Devil Came down to Dixie: Ben Butler in New Orleans*. Baton Rouge: Louisiana State University Press, 1997.
Heller, Max. *Jubilee Souvenir of Temple Sinai 1872–1922*. New Orleans: Temple Sinai, 1922.
Hepworth, George H. *Whip, Hoe, and Sword: The Gulf-Department in '63*. Boston: Walker, Wise & Co., 1864.
Heritage Auction. *Lattimer Collection of Lincolniana*. Dallas, TX: Heritage, 2008.
Hobbes, R. G. *Reminiscences of 70 Years Life, Travel & Adventure; Military and Civil, Scientific and Literary*. London: Elliot Stock, 1893.
Hobbes, Robert George. *Civil Service in Sheerness and Chatham Dockyards. Home and Foreign Travel*. London: Elliot Stock, 1895.
Hollandsworth, James G., Jr. *Pretense of Glory: The Life of General Nathaniel P. Banks*. Baton Rouge: Louisiana State University Press, 1998.
Holzer, Harold. "Lincoln and the Jews." Jewish Historical Society of Greater Washington. http://www.jhsgw.org/exhibitions/online/lincolns-city/exhibits/show/mr-lincolns-city/essays/holzer.
Holzer, Harold. *Lincoln and the Power of the Press*. New York: Simon & Schuster, 2014.
Holzer, Harold. *The Lincoln-Douglas Debates: The First Complete, Unexpurgated Text*. New York: Fordham University Press, 2004.
House of Representatives, Committee on War Claims. "Issachor [sic] Zacharie." 43rd Congress, 1st Session, Appendix, Report No. 817. Washington, D.C.: Government Printing Office, 1874.

Howe, Daniel W. *What Hath God Wrought, The Transformation of America 1815–1848.* New York: Oxford University Press, 2009.

Howe, M.A. Dewolfe (ed.). *Home Letters of General Sherman.* New York: Charles Scribner's Sons, 1909.

Huber, Leonard V. "The Battle of the Handkerchiefs." Civil War History 8 (March 1962), 48–53.

An Illustrated History of San Joaquin County, California: Containing a History of San Joaquin Country from the Earliest Period of its Occupancy to the Present Time, together with Glimpses of Its Future Prospects; with … Biographical Mention of Many of Its Pioneers and also Prominent Citizens of Today. Chicago: Lewis Pub Co., 1890.

Isaacs, Joakim. "Candidate Grant and the Jews." *American Jewish Archives* (April 1965), 3–16.

Isaacs, Myer S. "A Jewish Army Chaplain." *Publications of the American Jewish Historical Society* 12 (1904), 127–137.

Iser, Alexander. *The California Hebrew and English Almanac for the Year 5612, Corresponding with the Years 1851–1852.* San Francisco: Alexander Iser, 1851.

Jacob, Kathryn A. "King of the Lobby." *Smithsonian Magazine* 32 (May 2001), 122–131.

Jaher, Frederic Cople. *A Scapegoat in the New Wilderness. The Origins and Rise of Anti-Semitism in America.* Cambridge, MA: Harvard University Press, 1994.

Jewish Virtual Library. "Four Founders: Isaac Leeser." http://www.jewishvirtuallibrary.org/jsource/loc/Leeser.html, accessed June 17, 2015.

John A. McAllister's Civil War: The Philadelphia Home Front. http://www.librarycompany.org/mcallisterexhibition/section5.htm.

Johnson, Ludwell H. "Northern Profit and Profiteers: The Cotton Rings of 1864–1865." *Civil War History* 12 (June 1966), 101–115.

Jonas, Bertram. "Exploding a Myth." *The Sentinel,* February 8, 1934, 6.

Jonas, Bertram. "If Broadway Went Aryan." *American Jewish World,* January 17, 1936, 5.

Jonas, Bertram. "Refugees from the Jewish Pulpit." *Canadian Jewish Chronicle,* October 18, 1945, 5, 16.

Jonas, Bertram. "When El Fatah Goes to Shul." *Jewish Week,* September 2, 1971, 1.

Jonas, Bertram. "When Lincoln Fought Bigotry." *Jewish Spectator,* September 1938, 33–35.

Kagan Solomon R. *Jewish Contributions to Pittsburg Post-Gazette Medicine in America from Colonial Times to the Present.* Boston: Boston Medical Publishing Co., 1939.

Kahn, Ava F., and Adam M. Mendelsohn (eds.). *Transnational Traditions: New Perspective on American Jewish History.* Detroit: Wayne State University, 2014.

Kenison, Nehemiah. *The New Revelation; Or Dreams Relating to the Mysteries of the Soul.* St. Louis: Privately published, 1879.

Kimball, Charles Proctor. *The San Francisco City Directory.* San Francisco: Journal of Commerce Press, 1850.

Kippen, Cameron. "A Potted History of Professional Foot Care." http://foottalk.blogspot.com/2008/12/potted-history-of-podiatry.html.

Kirkland, Edward Chase. *The Peacemakers of 1864.* New York: Macmillan Co., 1927.

Knight, Charles. *The British Mechanic's and Labourer's Handbook, and True Guide to the United States: With Ample Notices Respecting Various Trades and Professions.* London: C. Knight, 1840.

Knox, Thomas W. *Camp-Fire and Cotton-Field: Southern Adventure in Time of War.* New York: Blelock and Co., 1865.

Korn, Bertram W. *American Jewry and the Civil War.* Philadelphia: Jewish Publication Society of America, 1951.

Korn, Bertram W. "Lincoln and the Jews." *Journal of the Illinois State Historical Society* 48 (Summer 1955), 181–190.

Korn, Bertram W. "Congressman Clement L. Vallingham's Championship of the Jewish Chaplaincy in the Civil War." *American Jewish Historical Quarterly* 53 (December 1963), 188–191.

Korn, Bertram Wallace. *Jews and Negro Slavery in the Old South, 1789–1865.* PA: Elkins Park, 1961.

Krausz, Charles E. *Issachar Zacharie, 1827–1900, A Fast Pace Forward: Chronicles of American Podiatry.* Philadelphia: Pennsylvania College of Podiatric Medicine, 1987.

Laborde, Peggy Scott, and John Magill. *Canal Street: New Orleans' Great Wide Way.* Gretna, LA: Pelican Publishing Co., 2006.

Lachoff, Irwin, and Catherine C. Kahn. *The Jewish Community of New Orleans.* Charleston, SC: Arcadia, 2005.

Lambert, Richard S. *For the Time Is at Hand. An account of the Prophesies of Henry Wentworth of Ottawa. Friend of the Jews, and Pioneer of World Peace.* London: Andrew Melrose, 1947.

Lash, Jeffery H. *A Politician Turned General: The Civil War Career of Stephen Augustus Hurlbut.* Kent, OH: Kent State University Press, 2003.

Leebo, Alisa. *First Person Jewish.* Minneapolis: University of Minnesota Press, 2008.

Leech Margaret. *Reveille in Washington 1860–1865.* New York: Harper & Brothers, 1941.

Levine, Yitzchok. "Isaac Leeser." http://personal.stevens.edu/~llevine/Isaac%20Leeser_v3.pdf.

Lewi, Maurice J. (ed.). *The Text Book of Chiropody.* New York: School of Chiropody, 1914.

Liebmann, Walter H. "The Correspondence between Solomon Etting and Henry Clay." *Publications of the American Jewish Historical Society* 17 (1909), 81–82.

London, Caroline. "The Marie Antoinette Dress that Ignited the Slave Trade." https://www.racked.com/2018/1/10/16854076/marie-antoinette-dress-slave-trade-chemise-a-la-reine, accessed February 10, 2018.

Lynch, Jack. "A Guide to Eighteenth-Century English Vocabulary." http://andromeda.rutgers.edu/~jlynch/C18Guide.pdf, accessed December 26, 2015.

MacDougall, Phillip. *Chatham Dockyard, 1815–1865. The Industrial Transformation.* Surrey, UK: Ashgate Publishing, 2009.

Mackay, Charles. *Life and Liberty in America.* New York: Harper & Brothers, 1859.

Marcus, Jacob R. (ed.). *Memoirs of American Jews.* Philadelphia: Jewish Publication Society, 1956.

Marcus, Jacob Rader. *United States Jewry 1776–1985.* Detroit: Wayne State University Press, 1989, 1991.

Markens, Isaac. "Jews Close to Lincoln." *The Advocate: America's Jewish Journal* (February 28, 1914), 89.

Markens, Isaac. "Lincoln and the Jews." *Publications of the American Jewish Historical Society* 17 (1909), 109–165.

Marks, Maurice. "Recent History of Chiropody." In James Marten, "The Making of a Carpetbagger: George S. Denison and the South, 1854–1866." *Louisiana History* 34 (Spring 1993), 133–161.

McPherson, James M. "No Peace without Victory, 1861–1865." *American Historical Review* 109 (February 2004), 1–18.

Meade, Robert Douthal. *Judah P. Benjamin: Confederate Statesman.* Baton Rouge: Louisiana State University Press, 1943.

"The Medical Department of the United States Army." *Medical Times and Gazette* 1 (January 1863), 90.

M'Elroy, A. A. *M'Elroy's Philadelphia Directory, for 1839.* Philadelphia: A. M'Elroy, 1839.

M'Elroy, A. A. *M'Elroy's Philadelphia Directory, for 1840.* Philadelphia: A. M'Elroy, 1840.

M'Elroy, A. A. *M'Elroy's Philadelphia City Directory for the Year 1844.* Philadelphia: Edward C. Biddle, 1844.

Meyer, Martin A. *Western Jewry. An Account of the Achievements of the Jews and Judaism in California.* San Francisco, CA: Emanu-el, 1916.
Michael, Robert, and Philip Rosen. *Dictionary of Antisemitism from the Earliest Times to the Present.* Lanham, MD: Scarecrow Press, 2007.
Molloway, Lisbeth M. *A Fast Pace Forward.* Philadelphia: Pennsylvania College of Podiatric Medicine, 1987.
Morais, Henry Samuel. *The Jews of Philadelphia: Their History from the Earliest Settlement to the Present Time.* Philadelphia: Levytype Co., 1894.
Morgan, David T. "Eugenia Levy Phillips: The Civil War Experiences of a Southern Jewish Woman," in Samuel Proctor and Louis Schmier (eds.), *Jews of the South*. Macon, GA: Mercer University Press, 1984.
Morley, Christopher. "Lincoln's Doctor's Dog." *The Saturday Review* 38 (February 12, 1955), 9–10, 40–42.
Mott, Valentine. "The Fractured Penis of Laceration of the Corpus Cavernosum Penis, Commonly Called Fracture of the Penis." *Transactions of the New York Academy of Medicine* 1 (1848), 99.
Mottley, John. *Joe Miller's Complete Jest Book: Being a Collection of the Most Excellent Bon Mots, Brilliant Jests, and Striking Anecdotes in the English Language.* London: H.G. Bohn, 1859.
Muller, Gilbert H. *William Cullen Bryant: Author of America.* Albany: State University of New York Press, 2008.
Myers, Barton A. *Rebels Against the Confederacy.* New York: Cambridge University Press, 2014.
Nashe, Thomas. *The Unfortunate Traveller* (London: T. Scarlet, 1594), in Ronald B. McKerrow (ed.), *The Works of Thomas Nashe.* London: A. H. Bullen, 1904.
Nau, John Frederick Nau. *The German People of New Orleans, 1850–1900.* Leiden: E. J. Brill, 1958.
Nesfield, K. M. "The Jew from a Gentile Standpoint." *Overland Monthly and Out West Magazine* 25 (April 1895), 410–420.
Nevins, Allen. *The War for the Union.* New York: Charles Scribner and Sons, 1959.
O'Connell, JoAnne. *The Life and Songs of Stephen Foster: A Revealing Portrait of the Forgotten.* Lanham, MD: Rowman & Littlefield, 2016.
Officer, Lawrence H., and Samuel H. Williamson. "Five Ways to Compute the Relative Value of a UK Pound Amount, 1270 to Present." https://www.measuringworth.com/ukcompare/relativevalue.php, accessed December 28, 2015.
Olson, James Stuart. *Encyclopedia of the Industrial Revolution in America.* Westport, CT: Greenwood Press, 2002.
Olson, Sherry. "Downwind, Downstream, Downtown: The Environmental Legacy in Baltimore and Maryland." *Environmental History* 12 (October 2007), 845–866.
Oz, Amos Oz, and Fania Oz-Salzberger. *Jews and Words.* New Haven, CT: Yale University Press, 2012.
Parish, T. Michael. *Richard Taylor, Soldier Prince of Dixie.* Chapel Hill: University of North Carolina Press, 1992.
Pearson, John. "A Brief History of Chiropody and Podiatry." https://johnrpearson.wordpress.com/tag/a-brief-history-of-chiropody-and-podiatry/, accessed May 25, 2015.
"The Peerage and Its Corns." *The Spectator* 22 (1849), 299.
Pollack, Sheldon D. "The First National Income Tax, 1861–1872." *The Lawyer* 67 (2014), 311–330.
Post, Alfred Charles. *Eulogy on the Late Valentine Mott.* New York: Balliere Brothers, 1866.
Quilbet, Philip. "Cheap Notoriety." *Galaxy* 7 (April 1869), 594–598.
Rance, Caroline. *The Quack Doctor: Historical Remedies for All Your Ills.* Stoud, UK: History Press, 2013.

Reed, Barbara Straus. "Jewish Press Coverage of an Anti-Semitic Act: Grant's Order N," in David B. Sachsman, S. Kittrell Rushing and Debra Reddin van Tuyll (eds.), *The Civil War and the Press*. New Brunswick, NJ: Transaction Publishers, 1999, 325–348.
Reznikoff, Charles. *The Jews of Charleston*. Philadelphia: Jewish Publication Society of America, 1950.
Rich, Michael W. "'Henry Mack': An Important Figure in Nineteenth-century Jewish History." *American Jewish Archives* 47 (1995), 261–279.
Richardson, Darcy G. *Others: Third Party Politics from the Nation's Founding to the Rise and Fall of the Greenback-Labor Party*. Lincoln, NE: I Universe, 2004.
Rippy, J. Fried. "Mexican Protest of the Confederates." *Southwestern Historical Quarterly* 22 (April 1919), 291–317.
Roberts, Giselle. *The Confederate Belle*. Columbia: University of Missouri Press, 2003.
Robinson, William Stevens. *"Warrington" Pen-Portraits: A Collection of Personal and Political*. Boston: Mrs. W. S. Robinson, 1877.
Rock, Howard B. *Haven of Liberty: New York Jews in the New World, 1654–1865*. New York: New York University Press, 2012.
Rock, Howard B. "Upheaval, Innovation and Transformation: New York City Jews and the Civil War." *American Jewish Archives Journal* 64 (2012), 1–26.
Rogers, J. M. "Jewish Soldiers in the Union Army." *North American Review* 153 (1891), 761–762.
Roseboom, Eugene H. *A History of Presidential Elections: From George Washington to Richard M. Nixon*. New York: Macmillan, 1970.
Rosen, Robert N. *Jewish Confederates*. Columbia: University of South Carolina Press, 2000.
Rosenberg, Charles E. *The Cholera Years. The United States in 1832, 1849, and 1866*. Chicago: University of Chicago Press, 1987.
Rosengarten, Theodore, and Dale Rosengarten. *A Portion of the People. Three Hundred Years of Southern Jewish Life*. Columbia: University of South Carolina Press, 2002.
Rothschild, Alonzo. *Lincoln, Master of Men: A Study in Character*. Boston: Houghton Mifflin Company, 1908.
Rubin, Saul Jacob. *Third to None. The Saga of Savannah Jewry, 1733–1983*. Savannah, GA: Self-published, 2013.
Rutkow, I. M. "Valentine Mott (1785–1865), the Father of American Vascular Surgery; A Historical Perspective." *Surgery* 85 (April 1979), 441–450.
Ryan, Joan. *Women Naval Dockyard Workers in Two 19th Century Dockyard Towns: Chatham and Plymouth*. M. Ph., University of Greenwich, 2011.
Sachar, Howard M. *A History of the Jews in America*. New York: Knopf Doubleday, 1992, 166.
Salzman, Jack, and Cornel West (eds.). *Struggles in the Promised Land: Towards a History of Black-Jewish Relations*. New York: Oxford University Press, 1997.
Sarna, Jonathan D. "The Impact of the American Revolution On American Jews." *Modern Judaism* 1 (September 1981), 149–160.
Sarna, Jonathan D. "Port Jews in the Atlantic: Further Thoughts." *Jewish History* 20 (2006), 214, 213–219.
Sarna, Jonathan D. *When General Grant Expelled the Jews*. New York: Schocken Books, 2012.
Sarna, Jonathan D., and Adam Mendelsohn (eds.). *Jews and the Civil War: A Reader*. New York: New York University Press, 2011.
Sarna, Jonathan D., and Benjamin Shapell. *Lincoln and the Jews: A History*. New York: Thomas Dunne Books, 2015.
Schecter, Frank I. "An Unfamiliar Aspect of Anglo-Jewish History." *American Jewish Historical Quarterly* 25 (1917), 63–74.

Schosteck, Robert. "Dr. Zacharie as a Author, June 1967. American Jewish Archives, document SC-13336.

Schwartz, David. "Abe Lincoln and Zion. His Thoughts on a Jewish Home." *The Sentinel* (February 10, 1949), 11.

Schwartz, David. "Lincoln's Corn Doctor." *Wisconsin Jewish Chronicle,* February 12, 1960, 7.

Schwartz, Mrs. David Bea. "The Oldest Jewish Cemetery in the West, Stockton, California." http://www.wsjhistory.com/oldest_jewish_cemetery.htm, accessed September 10, 2015.

Scroggins, Mark. *Hannibal: The Life of Abraham Lincoln's First Vice President.* Latham, MD: University Press of America, 1994.

Segal, Charles M. "Isachar Zacharie: Lincoln's Chiropodist." *Publications of the American Jewish Historical Society,* 43 (December 1953), 71–126.

Seymour, P.W. *The Magneticon.* Cheltenham: G.F. Poole, n.d.

Shappes, Morris U. *A Documentary History of the Jews in the United States 1654–1875.* New York: Schocken Books, 1971.

Sherman, William T. *Home Letters of General Sherman,* M.A. Dewolfe Howe (ed.). New York: Charles Scribner's Sons, 1909.

Shpall, Leo. "The First Synagogue in Louisiana." *Louisiana Historical Quarterly* 21 (1938), 520–522.

Silverman, Jason H. "The Law of the Land Is the Law" in John Y. Simon "That Obnoxious Order." *Civil War Times Illustrated* 23 (1984), 12–17.

Simonhoff, Harry. *Jewish Participants in the Civil War.* New York: Archo Publishing Co., 1963.

Simpson, Brooks D. *The Reconstruction Presidents.* Lawrence: University Press of Kansas, 1998.

Simpson, Brooks D. *Ulysses S. Grant. Triumph Over Adversity, 1822–1865.* Boston: Houghton Mifflin Co., 2000.

Simpson, Brooks D., and Jean V. Berlin (eds.). *Sherman's Civil War: Selected Correspondence of William T. Sherman, 1860–1865.* Chapel Hill: University of North Carolina Press, 1999.

Smith, J. Russell Smith. "Line Traffic in the United States Coasting Trade." *The Railroad Gazette* 44 (March 1908), 376–378.

Staub, Michael E. *Torn at the Roots: Jewish Liberalism in Crisis.* New York: Columbia University Press, 2002.

Stephen, Sir Leslie, and Sir Sidney Lee (eds.). *Dictionary of National Biography.* London: Oxford University Press, 1921–1922.

Stern, Norton B., and William M. Kramer. "Sephardic Leadership of Early California Jewish Life." *Western States Jewish History* 17 (April 1985), 227.

Sterne, Louis. *Seventy Years of an Active Life.* London: Privately published, 1912.

Stone, Kurt F. *The Jews of Capitol Hill: A Compendium of Jewish Congressional Members.* Lanham, MD: Scarecrow Press, 2011.

Strong, George Templeton. *Diary.* New York: Macmillan, 1952.

Surdam, David G. "Traders or Traitors: Northern Cotton Trading During the Civil War." *Business and Economic History* 28 (Winter 1999), 301–312.

Sussman, Lance J. *Isaac Leeser and the Making of American Judaism.* Detroit, MI: Wayne State University Press, 1995.

Tarshish, Allan. "The Charleston Organ Case." *American Jewish Historical Quarterly* 54 (June 1975), 411–449.

Taylor, Richard. *Destruction and Reconstruction: Personal Experiences of the Civil War,* Richard B. Harwell (ed.). New York: Longmans Green & Co., 1955.

Telushkin, Joseph. *Jewish Humor. What the Best Jewish Jokes Say About the Jews.* New York: Perennial, 2002.

Temkin, Sefton D. "Isaac Mayer Wise and the Civil War," in Sarna and Mendelson, *Jews and the Civil War*, 161–180.
Testimonials to I. Zacharie, Late Chiropodist General, United State Army. London: S. Firth and Ellis, 187–?.
Thayer, Ezra R., Samuel Williston, and Joseph Beale. "John Chipman Gray." *Harvard Law Review* 28 (April 1915), 539–549.
Thomas, Benjamin, and Harold M. Hyman. *Stanton: Life and Times of Lincoln's Secretary of War*. New York: Alfred A. Knopf, 1962.
Thomas, Benjamin P. *Abraham Lincoln: A Biography*. New York: Knopf, 1952.
Tinkham, George H. *History of San Joaquin Country California with Biographical Sketches of the Leading Men and Women of the County Who Have Been Identified with Its Growth and Development from the Early Days to the Present*. Los Angeles, CA: Historic Record Co., 1923.
Townsend, George Alfred. *Washington, Outside and Inside*. Cincinnati, OH: James Betts & Co., 1874.
Treagle, Joseph G., Jr. "Thomas J. Durant, Utopian Socialism, and the Failure of Presidential Reconstruction in Louisiana." *Journal of Southern History* 45 (November 1978), 485–512.
Trefousse, Hans Louis. *Ben Butler: The South Called Him BEAST!* New York: Twayne Publishers, 1957.
Trow, J. F. *Trows's New York City Directory, 1857–1858*. New York: J. F. Trow.
Twain, Mark, and Charles Dudley Warner. *The Gilded Age: A Tale of Today*. Chicago, IL: American Publishing Co., 1873.
Veach, Damon. "N.Y. Ship Lists Transcribed from Originals." (New Orleans) *Times-Picayune*, March 21, 1999. http://www.nola.com/ancestors/archive/1999/la032199.html, accessed May 20, 2015.
Von Bort, Ph. *General Grant and the Jews*. Privately published, 1868.
Von Drehle, David. *Rise to Greatness: Abraham Lincoln and America's Most Perilous Year*. New York: Picador, 2013.
Voorsanger, Jacob. *The Chronicles of Emanu-el: Being an Account of the Rise and Progress of the Congregation Emanu-el Which Was Founded in July 1850 and Will Celebrate Its Fiftieth Anniversary December 23 1900*. San Francisco, CA: Geo. Spaulding Co., 1900.
Watford, H.H. "Confederate Western Ambitions." *Southwestern Historical Quarterly* 44 (October 1940), 161–187.
Waugh, John C. *Reelecting Lincoln: The Battle for the 1864 Presidency*. New York: Crown Publishers, 1998.
Waxman, Jonathan. "Arnold Fischel: Unsung Hero in American Israel." *American Jewish Historical Quarterly* 60 (June 1971) 325–243.
Weekly Gleaner, A Periodical Devoted to Religion, Education, Biblical and Jewish Antiquities, Literature and General News 1 (January–December 1857).
Weintraub, Andrew. "The Economics of Lincoln's Proposal for Compensated Emancipation." *American Journal of Economics and Sociology* 32 (April 1973), 171–177, 177.
Welles, Gideon. *Diary of Gideon Wells*. Boston: Houghton Mifflin Company, 1911.
Whitman, Walt. "Mannahatta." *Leaves of Grass*. Philadelphia: David McKay, c. 1900.
Whittock, Nathaniel. *The Complete Book of Trades*. London: John Bennen, 1837.
Williams, William. *The New York Annual Register*. New York: J. Seymour, 1832.
Willis, Nathaniel P. "Pencilling by the Way." *New York Mirror*, November 19, 1831, 158.
Wilson, Samuel, Jr., and Bernard Lemann. *New Orleans Architecture*. Gretna, LA: Pelican Publishing Co., 1998.
Woldman, Alberta A. "Lincoln's Jewish Doctor." *B'nai Brith National Jewish Monthly*, February 1937, 189; 1938, 248.
Wolf, Edwin, and Maxwell Whiteman. *The History of the Jews of Philadelphia from Colo-*

nial Times until the Age of Jackson. Philadelphia: Jewish Publication Society of America, 1975.

Wolf, Simon. *The American Jew as Patriot, Soldier and Citizen.* New York: Brentanos, 1895.

Wolf, Simon. *The Presidents I Have Known from 1860–1918.* Washington, D.C.: Press of Byron S. Adams, 1918.

Wooster, Ralph Wooster. *The Secession Conventions of the South.* Westport, CT: Greenwood Press, 1976.

Yearns, Wilfred B., Jr. "The Peace movement in the Confederate Congress." *Georgia Historical Quarterly* 41 (March 1957), 1–18.

Yuhl, Stephanie E. "Hidden in Plain Sight: Centering the Domestic Slave Trade in American History." *Journal of Southern History* 79 (August 2013), 593–624.

Zacharie, I. *Corns Operations on the Feet.* Privately published, 1862.

Zacharie, I. *Surgical and Practical Observations on the Disease of the Human Foot, with Instructions for Their Treatment, to Which is Added Advice on the Management of the Hand.* New York: Charles B. Norton, 1860.

Zola, Gary P. *We Called Him Rabbi. Abraham Lincoln and American Jewry, A Documentary History.* Carbondale: Southern Illinois University Press, 2014.

Newspapers

Aiken (South Carolina) *Standard*
Alexandria Gazette
Arizona Republic
The Ark, and Old Fellows' Western Magazine
Baltimore American and Commercial Daily Advertiser
Baltimore Sun
Biloxi (Mississippi) *Herald*
Bloomington (Indiana) *Pantagraph*
Boston Courier
Boston Globe
Boston Traveler
Bristol Mercury and Daily Post
Brooklyn (New York) *Daily Eagle*
Buffalo Evening Courier and Republic
Camden (South Carolina) *Journal*
Canton (Ohio) *Repository*
Charleston Courier
Charleston Magazine
Charleston Southern Patriot
Charleston Sunday News
Chicago Daily Inter Ocean
Chicago Post
Cincinnati Enquirer
Clearfield (Pennsylvania) *Republican*
Cleveland Plain Dealer
Columbia (South Carolina) *Daily Phoenix*
Columbia (Connecticut) *Register*
Corpus Christi Caller Times
Courrier des Etats-Unis
Daily Alta California

Daily (Columbus) *Ohio Statesman*
Daily National Whig (Washington, D.C.)
Daily (Philadelphia) *Pennsylvanian*
Detroit Free Press
Dublin Freeman's Journal
Fort Myers News-Press
The Freemason
Freemasons and Masonic Illustrated
Glasgow Herald
Greenfield (Indiana) *Daily Reporter*
Greenville (Alabama) *Advocate*
Hartford (Connecticut) *Times*
Honolulu Star-Bulletin
Indiana Herald
Indiana State Sentinel
Indianapolis Star
The Israelite
Jewish Messenger
Lexington (Kentucky) *Leader*
Lloyd's Weekly Newspaper
London and Paris Observer
London Medical Press and Circular
London Morning Post
London Standard
Louisville (Kentucky) *Daily Democrat*
Macon Telegraph
Manchester Daily Mirror
Marshall County Republican
The Masonic Review
Masonic Standard
Melbourne Argus
Memphis Daily Appeal

Bibliography

Minneapolis Star Tribune
The Nation
New Hampshire Sentinel
New London (Connecticut) *Daily Chronicle*
New Orleans Daily Delta
(New Orleans) *Times-Picayune*
New Orleans Weekly Delta
New York Atlas
New York Commercial Advertiser
New York Daily Graphic
New York Daily News
New York Evangelist
New York Evening Post
New York Evening Telegraph
New York Herald
New York Journal of Commerce
New York Mirror
New York Times
New York Tribune
New York World
Norwich Mercury
Ottawa (Kansas) *Herald*
Pall Mall Gazette
Petaluma (California) *Argus-Courier*
Philadelphia Dollar Newspaper
Philadelphia Evening Telegraph
Philadelphia Illustrated New Age
Philadelphia Inquirer
Phoenix (Arizona) *Weekly Republican*,
Pittsburgh Daily Post
Pittsburgh Post-Gazette
Public Ledger
Pulaski (Tennessee) *Citizen*
Rapid City (South Dakota) *Journal*
Richmond (Virginia) *Daily Dispatch*
Richmond (Virginia) *Wig*
Rochester (New York) *Daily Union and Advertiser*
Sacramento Daily Union
Sacramento Steamer
St. Louis Obispo Telegram-Tribune
San Francisco Daily Placer Times and Transcript
San Francisco Weekly Pacific News
San Joaquin Republican
South Eastern Gazette
The Spectator
Springfield (Massachusetts) *Republican*
The Standard
Transactions of the Obstetrical Society of London
Truth
Urbana (Virginia) *Southside Sentinel*
Washington (D.C.) *Constitution*
Washington (D.C.) *Daily National Intelligencer*
Washington (D.C.) *Daily Union*
Washington (D.C.) *National Republican*
Washington Evening Star
The Weekly Gleaner as a Voice to Israel
Winchester (Kansas) *Star*
Wisconsin Daily Patriot
Wisconsin Jewish Chronicle
Worcester Daily Spy
Yorkville (South Carolina) *Enquirer*

Index

Abidor, Mitchell 196, 198
abolition 56, 70–71, 130; *see also* Garrison, William Lloyd; Goodell, William
"About Jews" 160
Abraham Lincoln Street (Jerusalem) 76
Abrahmsohn, Abraham 40
Academy of Medicine (Cuba) 46
Adams, Abigail 179
Adams, Pres. John 179
Adler, Rabbi Liebman 56
Albion House 39
Alexandria, Virginia 65
American Israelite see *Israelite*
The American Jew as Patriot, Soldier and Citizen 189
American Jewish Publication Society 203n12
American Jewry and the Civil War (Korn) 193
anaconda plan 80
Anderson, Maj. Robert 54–55, 157; *see also* Fort Sumter
Andrews, Gen. Rufus F. 62
anti-Catholicism 150
anti-Semitism 45, 54, 74–75, 98, 149, 158–159, 169, 189–190, 192, 211n29, 214n33; abolitionists 56; Generals 81–82, 85–86, 99, 114–115, 211; politicians 114, 150–151; *see also* Benjamin, Juda P.; General Orders No. 11
Antietam 160
Antoinette, Queen Marie 14
Army of the Potomac 59
Ashkenazim 6, 50
assimilation 16
Astaire, Fred 91
Astor, John Jacob 44
Atlantic crossing 8–9
Austen, Jane 179
Australia 38, 196; *see also* Simon, Mrs. Hugh

Backer, Abraham 41, 204n39
Baker, Lafayette C. 159
Baltimore, Maryland 27, 30, 92; convention 142; Gay Street 28; Jewish population 166; Lexington St. 28; rabbis 56; riot 58–59; synagogues 56
banishment of Jews 6

Banks, Mary 89, 91, 103; bribe 101; distrusts Zacharie 108–109; hostess 103, 109
Banks, Gen. Nathaniel P. 2, 83, 85, 99, 106, 115, 133, 165, 174, 181, 196; administration 89–90, 112; appearance 91, 103; Catholic support 135; chastised 112, 168; early years 91; ego 103; finances 109; Grant 112; Greeley 168–169, 171; instructions to Zacharie 94; Jewish support 135; love letters 91; marriage 91; military ineptitude 93, 138–139, 197; nicknames 91, 93; personality 103, 109; politics 92; Port Hudson siege 111; praised by Zacharie 97–98, 102, 111–112, 120; praises Zacharie 105, 119, 121; presidential aspirations 92–93, 109, 119, 129, 134, 138, 197; Red River campaign 111, 139, 175; reinstates registered enemies decree 103, 112; replaced by Canby 139; rumored running mate 135; salary 109; secret services fund 91; temperament 91; vanity 91–92; war claims 177
Banks, Raymond 107
Banks Club 126
Banting, William 226, 19
Bar Mitzvah 13
Barber, Joseph see *Disbanded Volunteer*
barber surgeon 19
Barinds, Dr. E. 22, 24–25
Barnes, Surgeon General Joseph 157
Barnet, Dr. Samuel M. 136; partner and student 136; shoots Zacharie 147–148
Baton Rouge 25, 96–98
Battles of the Wilderness 142
Beauregard, Gen. Pierre Gustave Toutant 53
Beckwith, Colonel Amos 116
Bee Gees 179
Belmont, August 150–151
Benjamin, Confederate Secretary of State Judah 2, 119, 122, 126, 132, 144, 189, 193, 197–198 214n33; anti-Semitism against 86, 150–151; New Orleans 25; slave owner 16; Zacharie 128
Benjamin, Rebecca De Mendes 15
Benjamin, Solomon 15
Bennett, James Gordon 71, 103, 123, 130, 132, 158; appearance 70; editor 61; Lincoln

245

Index

70; personality 134; Seward 123; Zacharie 132–133
Benton, Sen. Thomas Hart 34
Beth Elohim (Charleston) synagogue 54
Betterton, William G. 99–101, 105–107–108, 114–116, 159
Billy Wilson's Zouaves 59
Blair, Francis Preston, Jr. 165
"Blue Bloods" 58
Blumberg, Maj. Leopold J. 160–161
B'nai Brith 12, 152, 159; Grant's expulsion order
B'nai Jershurum (Children of Righteousness) 113
Board of Delegates of American Israelites 152
Bonaparte, Prince Louis Napoleon 29
Bonaparte, Napoleon 20–21, 61, 91
Booth, John Wilkes 171
Boston 11, 28, 31, 86
Bowen, Gen. James 133
Bowery 44–45, 208n15
Bowery B'hoys 45
Brady, James Topham 117; *see also* Smith-Brady Commission
Bright, Charlotte 16
Broadway 124; businesses 43; hotels 44; manure 43; omnibus 44; Zacharie home and office 166
Brooks, David 45
Brough, John 151
Brown, Benjamin Gratz 168
Browning, Orville 108, cotton trading 218n73
Brownlow, William "Parson" 214n33
Bryant, William Cullen 64, 67, 72; attitude to Jews 47; Cooper Union introduction 60; editor 46 "indefatigable walker" 46–47; introductory letter to Lincoln for Issachar 60; lunch with Walt Whitman 47; at White House 60; Zacharie 47–48, 60
Buchanan, Pres. James 52, 73, 92
Burnside, Gen. Ambrose E(en}181, 196
Butler, Andrew 90–91, 116
Butler, Maj. Gen. Benjamin 89, 98, 103–104, 114–116, 142, 144, 154, 158, 181; anti–Semitism 82, 214n33; appearance 81; "Beast" 81; corruption 90; disliked by Lincoln 81; finances 91; military command of New Orleans 81; reassigned 89; recalled 83; registered enemies 83; "woman's order" 81, 90; *see* Phillips, Eugenia Levy
"butterfly effect" 14

Calhoun, Sen. John C. 36, 44, 196
California 36, 38; good rush 36; *see also* cemeteries, San Francisco; Stockton; synagogues
California Podiatry College 193
Cameron, Simon 63
Canby, Gen. Edward 139
Carnegie, Andrew 174
Cass, Sen. Lewis 34, 196
Causes and Cures of Diseases of the Feet ('Cleaveland) 33

cemeteries, importance of 38; *see also* Weber, Capt. Charles
Certificate Book *see* Corns
Chalard, J.E. 100
chaplain controversy 77
Charleston Home Guard 54–55
Charleston, South Carolina 13–14, 24–25, 53–55, 97, 128, 136, 149; exports 13–14; Jews 14, 136, 150; King Street 15, 128; Sabbath restrictions 15; slave trade 16; *see also* Fort Sumter; Pember, Phoebe Yates Levy
Chase, Secretary of Treasury Salmon P. 62, 85–86, 92, 101, 119, 139, 144; appoints George Denison customs collector 98; Chief Justice 117; opposes peace mission 129; son-in-law 117; *see also* Denison, George
Chatard, Ferdinand 205n7
Chatard, Pierre 29, 205n7
Chatham England 41; dockyard 4; environs 4; Jewish population 5; occupations of Jews in 5; reputation 4; synagogue 5; Zacharie family home 4; *see also* Cottage Jews' Tabernacle; Dickens, Charles
Chatham Street (NY) 45
Chernow, Ronald 166
Chicago 77, 145, 146; Jewish population 166
chiropody 45; history 19–20; Jews prominent in 21; New York City 45; origin of term 20; snobbery of physicians toward 20, 31, 222n23
chiropody corps 59–60, 62–65, 67, 71, 74, 156, 187, 192
"Chiropody in the Army" 60
cholera 7, 201n23
Cialis(en}32; *see also* fractured penis
Cincinnati, Ohio 44, 56, 113; Jewish population 166; Jewish vote 149; rabbis 44, 56, 113; synagogues 56, 113
City Point, Virginia 120
Clay, Sen. Henry 34–35, 44, 104, 196; *see also* testimonials
Cleveland, C.H. 33
Cleveland, Ohio 143
Code Noir 25
Coffey, Titian J. 126
Cohen, Amelia 6; marries Jonathan 6
Cohen, A.S. 152
Cohen, Eliezer 6, 41
Cohen, Jacob G. 137, 156; arrested 137; asks Zacharie for help 137; flees North 137; released 137; Zacharie nephew 137, 156
Cold Harbor 142
Coleman's Hotel (Washington) 29
Collins, Mr. 102
Columbus, Georgia 113, 204n39
Commission on Corrupt Practices in the South *see* Smith-Brady Commission
Committee on War Claims 174–175
compensated emancipation 105, 127
Confederate States of America 53; debt 118; strategic advantages 59; *see also* Benjamin,

Index 247

Judah; Davis, Jefferson; Stephens, Alexander
Cooper, Dr. Astley Paston 30–31, 45, 180, 197
Cooper Union Address 44, 60
copperheads 143
Corbin, Abel 167
corn collection 172; Grant 172–173; Lincoln 172; McClellan 172; Sheridan 172; Thomas 172; *see also* Banks; Burnside; Clay; Lecompte; Seward
Corns, Operations on the Feet 160, 206
Cottage Jews' Tabernacle 5
cotton 13–14, 80, 102, 138, 218*n*73; corruption 106; dependence on 85, profiteering 85–86, 108, 102, 136; shortages 85, "white gold" 85
crinoline 44
Cuba 2, 46, 83
Curtin, Andrew 149

Dana, Charles 63
Davis, Henry Winter 142
Davis, Confederate Pres. Jefferson 86, 90, 100, 105, 120, 126, 130, 133, 144
Denison, George 98; animosity to Zacharie 98–99; anti-Semitism 98, 114; Butler ally 98; Chase informant 98, 117, 114; *see also* Smith Brady Commission
De Polignac, Prince Camille 182
Depression 7, 174, 179; cause for emigration 7; collapse of banking industry 174
Dessau, Abraham 11, 204*n*39
Dessau, David 184
Dessau, Jacob H. 11, 13, 204*n*39
Dessau, M.H. 11
Dessau, Morland 184–185
Dessau family name 11
Dickens, Charles 4; attitude to Jews 5; childhood 4, 31
Disbanded Volunteer 140–141
Dispersed of Judah (synagogue) 56, 94, 113
Diseases of the Human foot (Zacharie) 197
Dittenhoefer, Abram J. 147, 222*n*21
Dix, Gen. John Adams 73, 81, 94, 138, 154; congratulates Zacharie 138; governor 213*n*22
Dixie 112
Donaldsonville 25
Douglas, Stephen 66, 91, 143
Duke of Wellington 20, 29, 35
Duncan, H.C. 115
Durant, Thomas 98
Durlacher, Lewis 21
Durlacher, Solomon 20

Eckman, Julius 41
Egypt 19
1860 election 53
1864 election 146–155
1868 election 165–166
1872 election 169–170
Einhorn, Rabbi David 56
Eisenberg, John 29, 33, 49

Eisenhower, Gen. Dwight 179
11th New York Infantry 59
Elizabeth, Queen 4
Ellsworth, Col. Elmer 59
Ellsworth's Zouaves(en}59; *see also* Ellsworth, Col. Elmer
Emancipation Proclamation 62, 67, 76, 105, 142, 165
Emery, Gen. William 118
England 5, 7; *see also* Chatham; sea port towns
Erie Canal 4
Erlich, Myer Jacobs M. 55
Eureka Benevolent Society 37

Fairbank, Dr. Thomas 181–182
Farragut, Adm. David G. 80–81, 90
Federal Trade Commission 46
feet(en}18; blackmail concerning 19
Fessenden, Treasury Secretary William P. 140
First Hebrew Congregation (Washington) 69
Fisk, Jubilee Jim 167
Fort Pickens 115
Fort Sumter 53–56, 157; *see also* Anderson, Gen. Robert; Valentine, Isaac
Fortress Monroe(en}69, 73–74, 84, 94, 127, 129, 175; corns of 5000 men removed 175; *see* Dix, Gen. John Adams; Foster, Gen. John Gray
49-Service *see* Yom Kippur
Foster, Gen. John Gray 127–128, 157; corns 128
fractured penis 32
Franklin, Lew 37
Freemasons 41–42, 182, 187; *see also* Order of the Secret Monitor
Frémont, John C. 93, 143–144

garment industry 44
Garrison, William Lloyd 56
Gates of Mercy (Sephardic synagogue) 25
General Orders No. 11 ("Jew Order") 151, 154, 166, 169; explanations for 87; Grant's presidential election issue Lincoln's awareness of 85; omitted in memoir 88; reaction to 87; revocation 88; *see also* Kaskel, Cesar; "obnoxious order"; Paducah, Kentucky; Washburne, Elihu
George IV, King 30
Gettysburg 120, 122, 142, 144
Gibson, Dr. Charles Bell 29, 205*n*7
Gibson, Dr. William 32, 34
gilded age 167
Gilmore, Richard *see* Jaques
gold rush(en}36
Goodell, William 70
Goodwin, Doris Kearns 120
Gordon, Martin, Jr. 118–119, 123, 126
Gore, Albert Arnold 50
Gould, Jay 167
Grant, Frederick 88
Grant, Jesse 87, 215*n*44

Grant, Julia 88; *see also* "obnoxious order"
Grant, Gen. Ulysses S. 93, 110, 117, 142, 144, 181; administration 165; anti–Semitism 86, 94; appoints Jews 169; Black Friday scandal 167; Blair running mate 165; brother-in-law Corbin bribed 167; corns removed by Zacharie 171, 225*n*56; demeanor 165; election of 166, 170; entertained by Banks 110; feet 173; Greeley opponent 167; opposes cotton trading 85–86; political experience 165; Reconstruction policy 167; restricts movements of Jews 85–86, 94; stupidity 167; suppresses Smith-Brady commission report 117; Vicksburg campaign 111, 114, 119; war hero 166; *see also* General Orders No. 11
Grantism 167
Gratz family 12
Gray, Maj. John Chipman 158; anti–Semitism 159
Greeley, Horace 75, 103, 133, 142; anti–Semitism 75, 169; death 170; editor 75; Banks' endorsement 168; presidential bid 167–168
Greenbacks 217*n*37
Grier, Justice R.C. 34
Gurley, Congressman John Addison 88
Gutheim, Rabbi James K. 113

Hahn, Michael 108, 127
Hall, Dr. Marshall 33
Halleck, Gen. Henry W. 88, 138; chastises Banks 112; *see also* General Orders No. 11
Halley, Edmond 4
Halpine, Charles Graham 145
Hamlin, Vice-President Hannibal 92, 103, 144
Hamond, Surgeon Gen. William 60, 62, 65, 74–75, 156
Handel, George Frederic 179
Handy, Dr. W.H. 29, 205*n*7
Harlan, Judge J. 35
Harper, Thomas 114, 116
Harrington, Fred 109
Hay, John 1, 67, 153
Head and Feet of the Nation 71, 189; *see also* Bennett, James Gordon
Hebrew Leader 136
Helbing, August 37
Hendrix, Jimi 179
Henrick Hudson (ship) 9
Highgate Cemetery 184, 187
Hill, Joseph H. 99
Hilton Head 157, 159–160
Hippocrates 19
HireRight.com 48
Holabird, Col. Samuel Beckley 119
Hunter, Stephen 99
Hurlbut, Gen. Stephen A. 159, 223*n*23

immigration 5, 8–9, 188; *see also* Knight, Charles
intermarriage 26, 52
Internal Revenue Service 102

Isaacs, Myers Samuel 56; challenges Jewish vote 152–153, 166, 169–170 ; see also *Jewish Messenger*
Israelite 56

Jackson, Gen. Thomas "Stonewall" 93, 211*n*9
Jaques, James F. 121; peace initiative 144–145
Jay Cooke & Company 174
Jerusalem 76
"Jew Order" *see* General Orders No. 11
Jewish Messenger (Weekly) 52, 56–57, 88, 152–153, 166, 169
Jewish Record of New York (newspaper) 152
Jewish Union Republican Association 152
Jewish Vote 147, 149, 151, 155; bribes for 152–153
Johnson, Pres. Andrew 117, 143; anti–Semitism 151; appoints Grant 165; appoints Lorenzo Thomas Secretary of War 165; impeachment 165; Reconstruction 165; suppresses Smith-Brady Commission report 117; suspends Stanton 165
Johnson, Charles 95, 106, 116, 157; Banks booster 126; concern for Zacharie 134
Jonas, Abraham 76, 84, 189; appearance 76; businesses 77; family 77; Freemason 77; Lincoln friend 84; postmaster 77; strategizing 149
Jonas, Bertram 227*n*19; challenges Jewish influence on American politics 191
Jonas, Charles 213*n*6

Kahler, Dr. 67
Kaskel, Cesar J. 87
Keesing, Barnett 39
Keesing, Mrs. Hanna Solomon 37, 39
Kelston, Colonel John C. 88
Kenison, Nehemiah 21–22
Kennedy, Pres. John F. 166
Kentucky 85
Key, Philp Barton 131
Knight, Charles 9; *see also* Immigration
Know-Nothings 150
Korn, Bertram Wallace 97, 160, 191, 193; *American Jewry and the Civil War* 193
Kursheedt, William 94–95

Ladies Confederate Memorial Association 114
La Grange, Georgia 113
Lane, Jim 142
Lawson, Mary Ann(en}13; parents 26
Lecompte, Sen. Samuel D. 35
Lee, Gen. Robert E. 120
Lee, Adm. Samuel 120
Leeser, Isaac 12, 56, 113, 203*n*12; hazan Mikveh Israel 12; views on slavery 56
Lefferts, Col. Marshall 58
L'Engant, Pierre Charles 4
Levy, Capt. Cheme 139
Levy and Dietes 96

Index

Lewis, Sen. Dixon H. 34
Lewis, Samuel A. 136–137, 153
Lewis, Col. Theodore 100
Liberal Republican party 167
Liberator 56
Life and Adventures of Private Miles O'Reilly see Halpine
Lincoln, Abraham 2, 4, 53–54, 56, 60, 175, 181, 189–192, 194–196, 198; "About Jews" 160; appearance 1, 66–67; appoints Jewish chaplains 150, 154; boots 67; calls for volunteers 58, 142; compensated emancipation 127; Cooper Union 44, 60; countermands Grant's anti–Jewish order 150, 154; electoral vote 147; feet 1, 66–67; humor 72, 102, 137; gait 67; Jewish roots 57; office 66; pardons Jews 137, 153, 191; peace terms 130, 144; pocket veto 143; reconstruction plans 82; relationship with Jews 2, 76; religion 1; Soldier's Home 67; testimonials for Zacharie 1, 67–68; Zionism 2, 76–77; *see also* Bennett, James Gordon; Emancipation Proclamation; Ten Percent Plan
Lincoln, Mary 1, 62, 71, 137
Lincoln, Robert 57
Lincoln and the Jews (Markens) 34–35, 195
Lincoln Street (Jerusalem) 76
Lincoln Union League Club 88
Lincoln's Doctor's Dog 193
Lion, Heyman 20
London 5, 7, 43, 179
Longstreet, Gen. James 121
Louisiana 82–83, 89, 93, 96, 119, 138
Loyal Family 16

Mack brother 87, 215*n*44
Macon, Georgia 128
Magniton 226*n*20
Maguire, Prof. Hugh Holmes 36
Mallory, Confederate Secretary of Navy Stephen R. 128, 214*n*33
Markens, Isaac 188–190
Mason, Jackie 44
Masons *see* Freemasons
McClellan, Maj. Gen. George B. 64, 67, 132, 144–145, 150, 181, 196; anti–Semitism 211*n*29; Catholic vote for 154; corns removed by Zacharie 172; German and Irish vote for 154–155; Jewish vote for 151; *see also* testimonials
McKinzie and Williams 97
McMellon, James 21–22
Meade, Gen. George 149
Memphis 86
Mendelssohn, Moses(en}11
Metairie Cemetery 114
Mexico 130; Confederate invasion of 133
Michelbacher, Rabbi Max 55
Mikveh Israel (Charleston) 12, 203*n*12
Mikveh Israel (Savannah) 41
Miller, Joe 228*n*59

Mobile, Alabama 24, 82, 97, 102
Monk, Henry Wentworth 76
Montefiore, Sir Moses 52
Montgomery, Robert 117; *see also* Smith-Brady Commission
Montgomery, Alabama 24, 100, 113
Moos, Herman 151
Morais, Rabbi Sabato 56
Mordecai, Benjamin 136
Mordecai, Goodman L. 136–137, 153, 191; *see also* Lewis, Samuel L.
Mordecai, Moses Cohen 55
Morley, Christopher 193
Morris, Congressman Isaac 169
Mortara case 52
Mother Goose of Military Corns 72
Mott, Dr. Valentine 32, 35, 45, 49, 197; use of name to promote patent medicine and cleaning products 33–34
Mumford, W. Prince 183
Mumford, William B. 81
Museum of Corns 166, 171–172
Mutter, Dr. Thomas Dent 180, 226*n*5
Myers, Samuel 56

naming 6; traditional Jewish practices among Ashkenazim and Sephardim 50
National Democratic Party 150
National Union Party 143–144
Nevins, Allan 154
New Orleans 2, 24, 26–27, 82, 87–89, 96–98, 100, 102–103, 118, 121, 124, 133, 139; blockaded 80; Canal Street 25, 56; Chartres Street 25; corruption in 106; fifth column 93; fortifications 80; French Quarter 25; Jews barred from 11; Jews in 25, 84, 93, 105, 112; nickname 25; population 25; St. Charles Street 25; starvation 80; surrender 80; synagogues 94, 114; women 55–56, 81, 90, 112–113 ; *see also* Banks, Nathaniel; Butler, Benjamin; Farragut, David G.; Solomon, Clara; women's order
New York City 9–11, 28, 31–32, 54, 56, 58–59, 106–107, 122, 126, 129, 137, 152, 154, 156, 164; Bowery 44, 59; Dead Rabbits 45; distance to Philadelphia 10; Five Points 45; garment industry 44; hotels 44, 84; immigrants 147; Jewish vote 147, 149, 154–155; omnibuses 43–44; regiments 54, 58–59; traffic 44
New Zealand 39; *see also* Keesing, Hanna
Noah, Mordecai Manuel 56

"obnoxious order" 88
Occident and American Jewish Advocate (Journal) 203
"Ode to Dr. Zacharie" 72
Old Capitol Prison 136
Opdyke, George 62, 211*n*18
Opelousas, Louisiana 111–112
Order of the Secret Monitor 42, 182–183, 226*n*16; Zachaire as Supreme Ruler 182–183

250 Index

packet ships 8
Paducah, Kentucky 87
Palmer, William 109
Panama passage 38–39
Papal Decree 19
Parker's Fancy Store (Washington) 29
Peace Democrats see copperheads
pedders 5, 11, 25, 55, 86 88; as spies 94, 97; Broadway 43; Chatham Street 45; hazards of 12; Jewish 12; Sabbath considerations 12, 45
Pember, Phoebe Yates Levy 55
Pemberton, Gen. John 102, 107, 114–115, 118
Pendleton, Congressman Georg H. 144
Peretz, Isaac Leib 6
Philadelphia 10–11, 13, 26, 28, 31, 56, 97, 113, 126, 134, 164, 194; campaigning headquarters 134; Jewish population 166; rabbis 56; Zacharie office 136; *see also* Leeser, Isaac; Mikveh Israel; Rodeph Shalom
Philadelphia Club 1
Phillips, Eugenia Levy 82
Phillips, Philip 82
Plumley Maj. Benjamin Rush 116; corruption of 117; defends Betterton 117
pocket veto 143, 221*n*7
podiatry *see* chiropody
The Poetry of the Foot 48
Poland 5–6
Polk, Pres. James 29, 108
Pomeroy, Samuel 139
Pope, Gen. John 143
Pope Pius IX 52
Port Hudson 111, 114, 118, 133
port towns *see* seaport towns
Poznanski, Rabbi Gustavus 54, 210*n*9
presidential elections 53, 146–155, 165–166, 169–170
Pretts, David 118, 123
Prince of Wales 20

Quimby, Gen. J.T. 86

rabbinical views on slavery 56; support for Confederacy 54–55, 113; *see also* Einhorn, David; Gutheim, James; Lesser, Isaac; Michelbacher, Max; Pozanski, Gustavus; Raphall, Morris
Radical Democracy Party 143
Raphall, Rabbi Morris J. 56; asks Lincoln's help 139; congratulates Zacharie 138
Rawlins, Gen. John 86
Red River campaign 111–112, 175
Regiment of Reserves 55; *see also* Charleston Home Guard
registered enemies 83, 103, 117, 121
Republican party radicals 150; anti–Semitism 150; *see also* Butler, Benjamin; Johnson, Andrew, Wade, Ben; Wilson, Henry
Richardson, Detective John 115, 117; *see also* Smith-Brady Commission

Richmond, Virginia 2, 55 73, 100, 102, 106, 108, 119, 121, 127, 189
Robinson, William 92, 103
Rock, Howard 154
Rodeph Shalom (Pursuit of Peace) 12–13, 203*n*13–14
Rogers, Ginger 91
Roosevelt, Pres. Franklin 190
Rosecrans, Gen. William 121
Rothschilds 150
Russia 6

Sacramento 37
St. Charles Hotel 95–96, 100, 102, 104, 113, 115
St. Thomas Hospital 30
Salieri, Antonio 4
San Francisco 39, 45; Issachar's address 42; Jewish businesses in 36–37; prices 36–37
Sangre Judia (Jewish Blood) 201*n*12
Sarna, Jonathan 34, 76, 166, 195; *see also Lincoln and the Jews*
Savannah, Georgia 128, 156, 161; Mikveh Israel synagogue 41; Zacharie family in 137, 208*n*33
Schwartz, David 192–194
Scott, Gen. Winfield 205*n*7
seaport towns 11; Jewish preference for 5; *see also* peddlers
Second Confiscation Act 82
Secret Services fund 91, 106–107, 109–110
Seddon, Confederate Secretary of War James A. 128, 214*n*33
Segal, Charles M. 35, 196
Segar(en}16
Sephardim 16, 25, 113, 150; differences between Ashkenazim 6; naming traditions 6; origins 6; Poland homeland 6; precept 16; synagogues; *see also* Ashkenazim; synagogues
73 Illinois Regiment 121
Seward, Col. William H. 107, 111
Seward, Secretary of State William H. 44, 83, 92, 101–102, 106, 111, 118, 122, 133, 142, 145, 175, 196; appearance 123; approves Zacharie going to New Orleans 84; Chicago convention 146; corns 68; discourages Zacharie peace initiative 132; fondness for cigars 131; home 131–132; invites Zacharie to dinner 131–132; testimonial to Zacharie 68; unaware of Zacharie peace initiative 129
Seymour, Horatio 165
Shapell, Benjamin 34; *see also Lincoln and the Jews*
Shenandoah Valley 142, 145
Shepley, Gen. George 99, 114, 124
Sheridan, Gen. Philip 172
Sherman, Gen. William T. 139, 142, 145, 156, 158 161; anti–Semitism 86; Atlanta campaign 139, 145
*Sh'ma(*en}55, 210*n*14
Shreveport, Louisiana 25, 56–57, 138; *see also Jewish Messenger*

Sickles, Congressman Dan 131, 211*n*24
Silk Stocking Regiment 58
Singleton, James 108
6th Massachusetts Volunteer Militia 58
6th New York Volunteers 59
slavery 55, 89; opposing rabbinical views 55; outlawed 14; *see also* abolition; Emancipation Proclamation
Simon, Mrs. Hugh 38
slop seller 7
Smith, Dr. Nathan R. 29, 204*n*7
Smith, Gen. William Farrar 117; *see also* Smith-Brady Commission
Smith-Brady Commission 117
Solomon, Clara 56, 81, 214*n*9
Southern Historical Society 113
Spain, expulsion of Jews 6
Spotsylvania 142
Sprague, Sen. William 117
stagecoach transport 24
Stanton, Secretary of War Edwin M. 60, 65, 120, 133, 149, 156, 175, 191, 196; appearance 63; arrests Zacharie 158; asthma 157; defends Dan Sickles 211*n*24; defends David Yulee 159; demeanor 63–64; Freemason 156; issues pass to Zacharie 68–69, 73, 175; meets with Sherman 158–159; office 64; refuses Levy reinstatement 140; suspended by Johnson 165; work ethic 63; Zacharie relationship 63–64, 68, 156
steerage 8
Stephens, Confederate Vice Pres. Alexander 120–123
Sterne, Louis 190
Stevens, Thaddeus 63
Stevenson, Surgeon B.F. 217*n*30
Stockton 37, 43; Hebrew Benevolent Society 40; Issachar business in 39–41; violence in 39–40
Strauss, Johann II 4
Strong, George Templeton 70
Surgical and Practical Observations on the Diseases of the Human Foot 48–49; editions 33; plagiarism 33
Swett, Leonard 218*n*37
synagogues 5, 12, 13, 25, 54–56, 41, 69, 94, 113, 114

taxes 102, 217*n*37, 221*n*16
Taylor, Gen. Richard 118
Temple Sinai 114
Ten Percent Plan 142
testimonials: fake 45; from Cabinet members 68; from Congressmen and Senators 34–35; from Generals 64–65; from physicians 29–34; from presidents 67–68, 171
Texas 112, 138
"Thirteen at Table" 181–182
Thomas, Gen. George H. 172
Thomas, Maj. Gen. Lorenzo 165
Titanic 8

Townsend, George Alfred 171
trains 10, 24
A Treatise on Corns, Bunions, and the Diseases of Nails (Durlacher) 49
Tucker, Gen. John 69, 222*n*27
Turo, Judah 25
Twain, Mark 167

Usher, Secretary of Interior John Palmer 145

Valentine, Lt. Isaac 55; *see also* Fort Sumter
Vallandigham, Clement L. 151
Viagra 32; *see also* fractured penis
Vera Cruz, Mexico 100
Vicksburg 94, 96, 102, 111, 114, 119, 122, 142, 144
Victoria, Queen 21, 30, 181

Wade, Sen. Benjamin F. 143; anti-Semitism 150
Wade-Davis Bill 143
War Letters of a Disbanded Volunteer 140
Ward, Sam 140
Washburne, Congressman Elihu 150; defends Grant's edict 215*n*51
Washington, Gen. George 107
Washington, D.C. 58–59, 84, 104, 128, 136; Coleman's Hotel 29; synagogue 69; wartime 63; weather 53
Washington Light Infantry 136
We Called Him Rabbi 76
Weber, Capt. Charles 40; *see also* cemeteries
Webster, Daniel 44
Weed, Thurlow 103, 142
Weekly Gleaner 41
Welles, Gideon 92, 120
Whitman, Walt 47, 197–198
Whitney, Eli 4, 14
Whitridge, Dr. John 205*n*7
Wilde, Oscar 179
Willard Hotel 69, 121
Wilson, Sen. Henry 150; anti-Semitism 150, 214*n*33; vice-president 150, 169
Winder, Confederate Provost Marshall Gen. John H. 128
Wise, Isaac Meyer 44; chastises John Brough 151; opinion of Lincoln 57; opinion of New York 44; opinion on slavery 56; reacts to Henry Wilson Jewish slurs 150
Wolf, Simon 12, 188, 223*n*22; *American Jews as Patriot, Soldier and Citizen* 189; arrested 159; B'nai Brith 159
Woman's Order 81, 90
women 55; loyalty to South 56, 81; *see also* Moses, Catherine; Pember, Phoebe; Phillips, Eugenia; Solomon, Clara

Yom Kippur 37, 39, 69
Yulee, David Levy 151, 223*n*22

Zacharie, Amelia (daughter) 40; adultery 184; divorce 184; leaves for England 164; marries 164, 184

Zacharie, Amelia (mother) 6–7; borrows money from Dessaus 12; death 41; household 16; millinery store in Philadelphia 12; residence 16; shop in Charleston 14–15; slaves 16

Zacharie, Amelia Lavinia (sister) 6; marriage 11, 204*n*39

Zacharie, Charles Lawson (son) 27; children 227*n*21; marriage 164, 185; medical degree 185

Zacharie, Clara Louise (daughter) 41, 179; children 184; divorce 184; Morland Dessau scandal 184; sues pharmacist 185

Zacharie, Eliazer (brother) 6, 12, 54, 137; California 38; death 184; joins local militia 54–55; marriage 184; perfumer 43

Zacharie, Fanny (sister) 6; marriage 11

Zacharie, Issachar: accusations against 99, 101, 105, 123; advertisements 18, 22–23, 25–26, 28, 64; ambition 2, 50, 125–127, 133, 197–198; appearance 1, 66–67, 134, 189; arrest and acquittal 26–27; arrival in America 9; Baltimore 27–28; Betterton sting 99–102; British citizenship 1, 84, 176; campaigns for Banks 126; campaigns for Lincoln 146, 149; certificate book 206; character 2; children 27, 40; Chiropodist-Gen. of the United States Army 179, 181, 194; Chiropodist-in-chief 148; corns collection 172; criticizes Lincoln 130; dentistry 28; departs America 179; diamonds 164; dinner parties 109, 124, 138, 140, 164, 181–183, 186; "Doctor" 23, 46; early career 18, 22, 138, 197; education 197; envoy 2; expense account 95, 102, 119; failed diplomacy 132; Freemason 41, 156, 195; funeral 187; Goodman Mordecai 136, 154; Grant reelection 168; grocery 43; Greeley 168, 170; Hammond 62; honored 137; illness 106; influence on profession 193; *Jewish Messenger* 52; Judah Benjamin 129–131; lampooned 145; London home and office 179; Magniton 226*n*20; mansion 140; marriage 13, 26, 164, 185; member of Mikveh Israel (Savannah) 41; *mohel* 39–40; *Mother Goose of Military Corns* 72; monument to 177, 192; Mrs. Banks misgivings about 108; museum of corns 166, 171; name change 50; obituaries 186–187; "observations about the city" 97; "Ode to Dr. Zacharie" 72; Order of the Secret Monitor 41–42; parents 5–6, 13, 15; peacemaker 101, 105–107, 118, 122, 124, 127, 136, 189; personal secretary 95; personality 2, 46, 48, 73–74, 84, 97–98 101, 104–105, 112, 122, 124, 126 130, 132, 138, 146, 154, 170, 179, 181, 195–197; plagiarism 2, 197; profiteering 102; promises Jewish vote 135, 147; relationship with Banks 97–98, 102–104, 168, 170; religiosity 52; robbed 42; St. Charles Hotel residence 95–96, 115; Savannah family 157, 161; scholarship in name of 193; Secret Service fund 106, 181; sends Lincoln fruit boxes 137, 140, 154, 157; servants 51; shot 136, 147–149; siblings 6–7, 11–12; spy 2, 95, 97, 115, 124, 127; Stanton 62, 64; Stockton 40- 41; students 136, 183; taxes 102; treats Lincoln's feet 66; war claims 175–178, 225*n*11, 225*n*15; wealth 43, 102, 124, 164, 186; see also Chiropody corps; *Corns, Operations on the Feet*; testimonials, Generals

Zacharie, Jane (sister) 6, 41, 204*n*39

Zacharie, Jonathan (father) 5, 7, 9; bankruptcy; 12; birth 5, 9; emigration to America 7–8; emigration to Chatham 5; militia 54–55; name change 6; peddling 5, 12; Poland 5; respectability 7; salesman 5; Savannah residence 208; Sephardic heritage 6; synagogue membership 12

Zacharie, Mariposa (daughter) 185; death 185; marriage 185

Zacharie, Martha (sister) 6

Zacharie, Mary Ann (wife) 13, 26 137, 164

Zacharie, Rebecca (sister) 6; marriage 137, 204*n*39

Zacharie, Samuel Purdy (son) 36, 185; children 186; medical degree 185; patent rights from father 186

Zacharie, Victoria Mariposa (daughter) 51

Zacharie-Bully, Edith (granddaughter) 185

Zacharie Scholarships in Podiatry 193–194

Ziegler 96

Zionism 76, 213*n*2

Zola, Gary 76, 196, 198; estimation of Zacharie 196–198